Picture Inclusion!
Snapshots of
Successful Diverse Classrooms

Picture Inclusion!
Snapshots of
Successful Diverse Classrooms

by

Whitney H. Rapp, Ph.D.

Katrina L. Arndt, Ph.D.

Susan M. Hildenbrand, Ed.D.

St. John Fisher College
Rochester, New York

·P·A·U·L·H·
BROOKES
PUBLISHING Cº.®

Baltimore • London • Sydney

Paul H. Brookes Publishing Co.
Post Office Box 10624
Baltimore, Maryland 21285-0624
USA

www.brookespublishing.com

Copyright © 2019 by Paul H. Brookes Publishing Co., Inc.
All rights reserved.

"Paul H. Brookes Publishing Co." is a registered trademark of
Paul H. Brookes Publishing Co., Inc.

Typeset by Progressive Publishing Services, York, Pennsylvania.
Manufactured in the United States of America by
Versa Press, Peoria, Illinois.

The individuals described in this book are composites or real people whose situations are masked and are based on the authors' experiences. In all instances, names and identifying details have been changed to protect confidentiality.

Purchasers of *Picture Inclusion! Snapshots of Successful Diverse Classrooms* are granted permission to download, print, and photocopy the handouts and forms in the text for educational purposes. These materials may not be reproduced to generate revenue for any program or individual. Photocopies may only be made from an original book. *Unauthorized use beyond this privilege may be prosecutable under federal law.* You will see the copyright protection notice at the bottom of each photocopiable page.

Library of Congress Cataloging-in-Publication Data

Names: Rapp, Whitney H., author. | Arndt, Katrina L., author. | Hildenbrand, Susan M., author.
Title: Picture inclusion! : snapshots of successful diverse classrooms / by Whitney H. Rapp, Katrina L. Arndt and Susan M. Hildenbrand.
Description: Baltimore, Maryland : Paul H. Brookes Publishing Co., 2019. | Includes bibliographical references and index.
Identifiers: LCCN 2018044686 (print) | LCCN 2018060918 (ebook) | ISBN 9781681252957 (epub) | ISBN 9781681252940 (pdf) | ISBN 9781681252933 (pbk.)
Subjects: LCSH: Inclusive education—United States. | Learning disabled children—Education (Elementary)—United States. | Children with social disabilities—Education (Elementary)—United States. | Education, Elementary—Curricula—United States. | Curriculum planning—United States.
Classification: LCC LC1201 (ebook) | LCC LC1201 .R36 2019 (print) | DDC 371.9/046—dc23
LC record available at https://lccn.loc.gov/2018044686

British Library Cataloguing in Publication data are available from the British Library.

2023   2022   2021   2020   2019

10   9   8   7   6   5   4   3   2   1

Contents

About the Downloads

Purchasers of this book may download, print, and/or photocopy the list of inclusive supports and list of resources, provided in Appendices A and B, for educational use. These materials are included with the print book and are also available at https://downloads.brookespublishing.com/picture-inclusion for both print and e-book buyers.

About the Authors

Whitney H. Rapp, Ph.D., St. John Fisher College, Rochester, New York 14618

Dr. Rapp is Associate Professor of Inclusive Education at St. John Fisher College, where she teaches courses on inclusive education pedagogy, assessment, and classroom management. Dr. Rapp holds a bachelor's degree in elementary education and psychology from the State University of New York at Potsdam and master's and doctoral degrees in special education from Michigan State University.

Dr. Rapp's current research interests include universal design for learning (UDL) throughout the school years and college, as well as strategies for executive functioning. She is the author of the textbook *Universal Design for Learning: 100 Ways to Teach All Learners* (Paul H. Brookes Publishing Co., 2014) and coauthor of the textbook *Teaching Everyone: An Introduction to Inclusive Education* (with K. L. Arndt; Paul H. Brookes Publishing Co., 2012).

Dr. Rapp presents at local, state, national, and international conferences on UDL and inclusive education pedagogy.

Katrina L. Arndt, Ph.D., St. John Fisher College, Rochester, New York 14618

Dr. Arndt is Professor of Inclusive Education at St. John Fisher College, where she teaches courses on educational technology, inclusive education pedagogy, assessment, and upper elementary literacy. Dr. Arndt earned her bachelor's degree in philosophy from Grinnell College and master's degree in educational psychology from the University of Minnesota. She completed a Certificate of Advanced Study (C.A.S.) in disability studies and a doctoral degree in special education at Syracuse University.

Dr. Arndt's research interests include qualitative research, participatory action research, and the least restrictive environment (LRE). She is the coeditor of the collections *Foundations of Disability Studies* and *Emerging Perspectives on Disability Studies* (with M. Wappett, Palgrave Publishing, 2013) and coauthor of *Teaching Everyone: An Introduction to Inclusive Education* (with W.H. Rapp; Paul H. Brookes Publishing Co., 2012).

Dr. Arndt has served as an expert for school districts and the U.S. Attorney's office on issues related to the LRE, and she presents locally and nationally on issues related to inclusive education.

Susan M. Hildenbrand, Ed.D., St. John Fisher College, Rochester, New York 14618

Dr. Hildenbrand is Associate Professor of Inclusive Education and Associate Dean of the Ralph C. Wilson, Jr., School of Education at St. John Fisher College. She teaches courses on inclusive education pedagogy, assessment, and classroom management. Dr. Hildenbrand earned her bachelor's degree in elementary education from the University of Michigan and her master's degree in reading and learning disabilities from DePaul University. She received her doctoral degree in teaching and curriculum from the University of Rochester.

Dr. Hildenbrand's research interests include positive classroom management, student teaching, and service learning, and she presents local and nationally on these topics. She has also created and delivered professional development training sessions on trauma-sensitive pedagogy and instructional strategies for more than 100 in-service teachers and administrators in the region.

For the Reader

Student profiles and lesson plans may include mentions of specific products or web sites used for support. The authors include these as resources they and the teachers with whom they work have found helpful in their experience as educators, but this does not constitute a product or web site endorsement from Brookes Publishing. Note also that all web links were functional at the time the manuscript was being prepared for publication but are subject to change. If a reader finds a given link no longer works because the location of that resource has changed, then the reader can try searching the name of that resource or name of the associated organization.

Foreword

On a crisp autumn day in 1990, I tuned into a radio interview with the authors of a just-released book titled *50 Simple Things You Can Do to Save the Earth*. A group of scientists cowrote this book to promote a very clear message for people everywhere—you don't have to be a scientist in order to make a positive impact on the environment. Instead, you could take small steps that would make a significant difference.

In the 1990s, recycling wasn't really a "thing" yet, and most people had never heard the term "global warming." There were a few environmental groups that you could join, but they seemed more focused on protecting the whales or protesting nuclear power plants. The average stay-at-home mom or corporate ladder climber had to be enthusiastically committed to seeking out ways to become involved, something many didn't have the time for. And then along came this little book filled with truly simple things anyone could do to make a difference. Immediately a bestseller, it went on to spawn several variations in dozens of languages.

This message resonated very deeply with me in regard to inclusion. At the time, I was a special education teacher with a strong belief in inclusive practices. I owned several thick textbooks on the topic and had attended lectures by university professors who were considered experts. In my enthusiasm, I tried to engage other teachers in discussions about inclusion. Their response was always the same: "I don't have time for one more thing." Teachers, then and now, are loaded down with work, overwhelmed by too many district initiatives, and hassled by legal mandates. They care enormously for the students in their classes and must judiciously select how to spend their precious minutes of professional development time. So the idea of "50 simple things" hit me like a lightning bolt. This is what was needed for the inclusion movement—a book of simple strategies that any teacher could do to be more inclusive in their classroom. I began writing it that very night.

Ideas for Inclusion: The Classroom Teacher's Guide was just the first of several books I wrote for educators but set the tone for all of them—simple things anyone can do to make a difference. Published in 1994, my first book filled a need teachers expressed then and still express today—"I don't need all the research and history. Just tell me how to do it."

Luckily, Whitney H. Rapp, Katrina L. Arndt, and Susan M. Hildebrand are ready to meet that same need twenty-five years later. *Picture Inclusion! Snapshots of Successful Diverse Classrooms* provides us with concrete examples of how, with the right mindset and strategies, we can engineer successful learning experiences for all students.

In Chapter 1, the authors provide us with a reminder of essential foundational elements, from having high expectations to structuring valuable participation opportunities. As they explain, "Presuming competence is an attitude—one that shapes actions in the classrooms and includes a default assumption that the student is capable until we have clear evidence otherwise." Low expectations have devastating consequences, as the authors point out in several vignettes. Students who experience high expectations and high supports in general education classrooms will be the most successful.

How is it done? Clearly drawn pictures show us how. We learn about Bridget's favorite movement breaks, Greg's need for space, and Taylor's sense of humor. We then get to explore how teachers address these and other students' needs in a variety of different lessons. The authors share ideas for technology integration, regulation scales, differentiation of graphic organizers, a Move and Learn area, and a Calming Corner. While the examples are presented in the context of first-, third-, or fifth-grade lessons, creative teachers will easily be able to adapt them to other grade levels.

Looking for more? Each chapter presents new, innovative strategies that are simple to implement. Learn how puzzles are used to support Antoine, desk maps are used to improve Justice's organization of materials, and a beautifully wrapped gift box can grab everyone's attention. Explore excellent examples of how to adapt for students on alternate standards, use eye-tracking tools for students with attention issues, and develop cooperative learning jigsaw activities. The strategies are practical and teacher friendly.

As I read each chapter, different students of mine popped to mind. I kept thinking, "That sounds just like Hector," or "I wish I had thought of that for Tamika." In-depth descriptions of all the children in each class ensure that readers will be able to relate the lessons to many of their current students, no matter what their unique strengths and needs.

While this book is rich in a wide range of simple teaching strategies, I also appreciate the emphasis on small group instruction. Small group work, whether readiness-based or mixed-readiness, allows students increased opportunities to respond and provides teachers with the chance to effectively assess how students are learning. Each of the lesson examples describes the type of small grouping practices that might occur, so that the reader can visualize a variety of structures. As you read through each of the lessons, consider mapping out the small group structures so that you will have a variety of images in mind the next time you plan a lesson.

Collaborative planning, or coplanning, is a foundational element of a successful inclusive classroom. The authors share examples of collaboration with related professionals, paraeducators, and a variety of other specialists. Each of these team members brings unique talent and experience to the inclusive classroom and must be fully utilized. As the authors state, "It is hard to overstate the importance" of these team members.

So much has happened in the environmental field since the 1990s. Most of us would not have imagined that recycling and composting would become everyday occurrences, classrooms and offices would be going paperless, and electric cars would be common. This dramatic change occurred because early visionaries imagined a better way. What might happen if we could imagine fully inclusive schools where every student is successful? Luckily, we don't have to just imagine it. *Picture Inclusion!* shows us classrooms where it is happening, today, so that it can happen for you and your students tomorrow.

Anne M. Beninghof

Acknowledgments

Many individuals contributed their expertise and insights as we prepared this book. First, we wish to acknowledge and express our sincere appreciation to the many educators who shared their insights, lesson ideas, strategies, and art with us. We especially thank Lisa Jordan, from Brighton Central School District; Vivian Rapp from Brighton High School; Dr. Tracy Nelson from South Dakota State University; and the teachers and administrators at East Rochester Elementary School, particularly Sue Liquori, Mark Denecke, Sarah Sigmon, Matt Lafontaine, Brian Touranjoe, Jennifer Iacucci, Jessica Vacchetto, Katie Rubert, Mykel Sapienza, Kathy Vosburgh, Ina Vento, Laurie Davis, Jennifer Perna, Lori Chans, Julie Warner, Christina Rucci, Denise Alfieri, Hannah Cicero, Jason Brownell, Alyse Palumbo, Erin Hagreen, Larry Hohl, Christina Kowal, Dereen Hopiavuori, David Thering, Marisa Philip, Casey VanHarssel, Mary Gullace, and Mark Linton.

We extend our gratitude to Tess Hoffman, Jolynn Gower, Stephanie Henderson, and Jackie Mahler of Brookes Publishing for guiding and encouraging us throughout the construction of this book and for their consistent support, which ultimately brought this book to completion.

FROM WHITNEY

I would like to acknowledge the many innovative colleagues, families, students, and future teachers I have the tremendous fortune to work with every day. Their dedication to hard work and problem solving to make a difference in schools has greatly influenced this book. I owe great thanks to my family for their endless encouragement and for listening to me tirelessly when I need to think out loud. Steve, your feedback is brilliant and thought provoking. You are handy to have around.

FROM KATRINA

I would like to acknowledge the many students who shaped my understanding of inclusion, community, and how to create classroom environments that support all students. My first class at Southwest High School in Minneapolis, Minnesota, taught me more than I will ever be able to express, and I particularly thank Stephanie, Dan, Paul, Tony, Dennis, Wally, Juanita, and Sarah.

I also want to thank my immediate and extended family for their support and understanding during the long process of developing this project. Lauren is the best listener and support anyone could ever ask for!

FROM SUSIE

I would like to acknowledge all of the teacher candidates who I have worked with over the past 12 years who continuously help me to see inclusion from different, fresh perspectives as they begin their careers as the inclusive educators of tomorrow. Deepest gratitude to Bruce, Jack, and Megan for their never-ending support and encouragement.

Introduction

This book is intended as a resource for teachers and schools determined to include all students, regardless of diverse need, in lessons based on general education curriculum. Our purpose is to demonstrate how lessons in any content or special area can be planned so that all students' individual needs are met, directly or indirectly.

More teachers are being prepared as inclusive educators through inclusive education or dual certification programs. Academic and social benefits of inclusive educational settings have been demonstrated for all students (Cole, Waldron, & Majd, 2004; Cosier, Causton-Theoharis, & Theoharis, 2013; Dessemontet, Bless, & Morin, 2012; Helmstetter, Curry, Brennan, & Sampson-Saul, 1998; Hunt & Farron-Davis, 1992; Hunt, Farron-Davis, Beckstead, & Goetz, 1994; McDonnell, Thorson, & McQuivey, 2000; McGregor & Vogelsberg, 1998; Wagner, Newman, Cameto, & Levine, 2006; Waldron, Cole, & Majd, 2001).

There is no doubt that all teachers must be prepared to teach diverse learners in a variety of settings. It is important to ground all educators in the theory of inclusive practice and provide them with specific practices to enact that theory in real-life classrooms.

There are texts on the market that address the need for theory to practice. There are texts that offer general ideas for differentiation and UDL, that offer specific strategies but are disability specific or categorical in nature, or that offer specific noncategorical strategies by content area but do not include lesson plan formats or structures. There are texts that offer specific lesson plan structures or formats but focus only on including one or two students with significant cognitive disabilities.

The purpose of this book is to pull all of this together. All teachers face classes with very diverse needs. Yes, they may have one or two students with significant cognitive disabilities, but they will almost certainly also have students with individualized education programs (IEPs) for other needs, students with 504 plans, students with diverse cultural and linguistic needs, and students who have experienced stressors and trauma. Teachers need theory-to-practice strategies and lesson plan examples that show how lessons can be planned to include all of these students while maintaining high expectations, building community, managing the classroom, and meeting standards and IEP/504 goals.

This text focuses on grades K–5 and all academic content and special areas (English language arts [ELA], math, science, social studies, art, music, physical education, and technology). This introductory section summarizes each chapter in the book, explains the reasons we chose various learning standards on which to focus, and provides an overview of alternate assessment for students with complex learning needs and our perspective on the topic.

HOW THIS BOOK IS ORGANIZED

Chapter 1 consists of two parts—theoretical foundations and practical applications of inclusive education. Foundational theories include the models of disability, least dangerous assumption (Jorgensen, 2005) and presumed competence, and full citizenship in the classroom (Kliewer, 1998). Practical applications include differentiation, universal design for learning (UDL), multi-tiered systems of support, response to intervention (RTI), embedded instruction, clustering, and addressing the whole child.

Chapters 2, 3, and 4 are the grade-level chapters. They present three classrooms, Grades 1, 3, and 5, respectively. Each classroom includes 20 students with a substantial range of diverse cognitive, social, emotional, behavioral, physical, linguistic, and cultural characteristics and learning needs. Each chapter includes 20 individual "snapshot" student profiles, supplemented with IEPs and Section 504 plans for 3–5 students; a weekly chart of services provided by related services professionals; and 8 detailed lesson plans. The student snapshots provide a summary of all essential information the teacher needs to know in order to meet each student's unique needs:

- Name, age, grade, disability classification if applicable, and family information

- Interests, strengths, and needs

- Ways to support engagement, input, and output in the classroom

- Professionals who work to support the student

- Learning goals

- Inclusive practices that facilitate mastery of these goals

We have also built flexible instructional time (FIT) into the day. Every student takes part in FIT at the same time, but they are engaged in different activities depending on their individual needs. Some services, based on best practice in the field, need to occur through one-to-one interaction or in small groups outside of the classroom. For example, best practice in English as a new language (ENL) instruction indicates focused, small-group instruction for entering ENL students (New York State Education Department, 2014). To align with these research-based practices while maintaining the integrity of a fully inclusive learning environment, these pull-out lessons occur during FIT, so no one misses new content instruction or social opportunities that are happening in the general education environment without them. FIT supports include occupational therapy, physical therapy, speech-language therapy, ENL instruction, math or reading support, acceleration instruction, counseling, and psychological support. This is an excellent time to provide Tier 2 RTI supports to students who need them. Students who do not need any of these supports regularly can use FIT to review work with the classroom teacher, make up missed work, go to support instruction in any area, or take part in yoga or mindfulness exercises in the sensory room. FIT is intended to support every student in what they need most at a given time.

Students who are classified with disabilities or conditions that affect their daily functioning are afforded IEPs or 504 plans that detail their educational goals, supports, and services. Our belief is that having goals, supports, and services specifically outlined is an effective practice for all students. All students in the classroom are better supported when attention is paid to the goals and needs of all students and inclusive practices are outlined for each one. Each inclusive practice implemented supports multiple students in the classroom—if not all of them—directly or indirectly via ripple effect. For example, providing a variety of pencil grips may be an important support for a student who has dysgraphia, but this support also helps many typically developing elementary students manage writing tasks without becoming fatigued.

The weekly chart of services provided by related services professionals for each grade level shows how multiple professionals need to work together in the context of the general education classroom to meet all needs. The shaded sections of the charts indicate times when related services professionals co-teach in the classroom to provide direct services to students as well as times when they consult with the classroom teacher to provide indirect services.

The eight lesson plans in each chapter are written for ELA, math, science, social studies, art, music, physical education, and technology. Each plan is based on understanding by design (UBD) lesson planning—first, identifying the standard or goal being taught; second, identifying the performance tasks needed to assess mastery toward the goals; and third, designing the lesson activities. Each of these lesson plan sections includes a list of inclusive practices to use during that part of the lesson to support all students.

The inclusive practices that appear in the student snapshots and lessons address a dozen different areas of support, with the specific area indicated by the abbreviation at the beginning of the practice. For example, two frequently used practices are as follows:

1. CR1. Provide culturally responsive curricular materials, materials that reflect student interests, and resources other than textbooks.

2. SR4. Ensure that all students are familiar with regulation scales, and many have them at their desks for self-checks. Some are for voice volume and emotional escalation; some for effective use of work time; and some for interest or independence level for an activity.

In these examples, CR stands for "cultural responsiveness;" SR stands for "self-regulation." A key to these supports is provided with Chapters 2–4, along with a classroom map showing how to design the physical space to support all students' needs.

Chapter 5 follows the grade-level chapters and reviews theoretical foundations represented in the book, directs the reader toward future practical application, and raises questions for future exploration. The two Appendices are the Inclusive Practices Bank (Appendix A) and the Resources for Inclusion list (Appendix B). The Inclusive Practices Bank provides all the inclusive practices listed on student snapshots and applied in lesson plans, along with others that may be helpful for future planning. The intent is that this is just a starting point for the teacher to develop an even more comprehensive bank of practices that emerge as a result of supporting many individual students in many lessons, often across the grade levels. The Resources for Inclusion list contains readings, web sites, product suppliers, blogs, and centers that are available to teachers who are determined to include all students, regardless of diverse needs, in lessons based on general education curriculum.

LEARNING STANDARDS

If we had not known it already from our experience teaching, our work on this book made clear to us that the only thing all states have in common regarding learning standards is that they all subscribe to a set of standards. Beyond that, they are widely different. Many use the Common Core State Standards (CCSS) for ELA and math, but not all. Some use the Next Generation Science Standards (NGSS), but not all. Some use the National Education of the Arts standards, but not all. Some use the Society of Health and Physical Educators (SHAPE) standards, but—you guessed it—not all. We use different standards for different lessons and content areas in an effort to create a resource that is relevant to all teachers, regardless of state standards. We accomplish two things by doing this. First, we can connect to as many different areas of the country as possible without having to include 50 sets of lesson plans. Second, we can show that a lesson can be planned in any content area that supports every student toward a goal, regardless of the standard or goal being taught.

Table I.1 shows the body of standards used for each lesson. The most widely used standards are used more often.

Table I.1. Content standards used for each lesson in Grades 1, 3, and 5

Content area	First grade	Third grade	Fifth grade
English language arts (ELA)	Next Generation Learning Standards (NGLS)—Print Concepts, Writing	NGLS—Reading Informational Text and Reading Literary Text; lesson also addresses a related Common Core ELA standard for Reading Informational Text	NGLS—Literary and Informational Text
Math	Common Core State Standards (CCSS)—Measurement and Data	CCSS—Operations and Algebraic Thinking	CCSS—Geometry
Science	Next Generation Science Standards (NGSS)—From Molecules to Organisms: Structures and Processes	NGSS—Motion and Stability: Forces and Interactions	NGSS—Matter and Its Interactions
Social studies	Ohio State Social Studies Standards Strand: History Theme: Families Now and Long Ago, Near and Far Topic: Heritage	Ohio State Social Studies Standards Strand: Economics Theme: Communities: Past and Present, Near and Far Topic: Scarcity	Ohio State Social Studies Standards Strand: Government Theme: Regions and People of the Western Hemisphere Topic: Roles and Systems of Government
Art	National Core Art Standards for Visual Arts (NCAS-VA)—Creating	New York State Learning Standards for the Arts: Visual Arts Standards	NCAS-VA—Creating
Music	National Association for Music Education (NAFME)—General Music: Creating	NAFME—General Music: Creating	NAFME—General Music: Creating
Physical education	Society of Health and Physical Educators (SHAPE)—Motor skills and movement patterns	SHAPE—Health-enhancing physical fitness	SHAPE—Value of physical activity
Technology	International Society for Technology in Education (ISTE)—Innovative Designer	ISTE—Knowledge Constructor	ISTE—Innovative Designer

ALTERNATE ASSESSMENT

This section defines *alternate assessment* and discusses three types before presenting our perspective on the use of alternate assessment.

What Is Alternate Assessment?

Alternate assessments are used in place of state standardized assessments to evaluate the performance of students who are unable to participate in the state assessments, even with accommodations in place. Alternate assessments provide students with significant intellectual disabilities and students who need alternate ways to gain access to assessments inclusion in the educational accountability system (National Center on Educational Outcomes [NCEO], 2017). By including students in the accountability system, we can see how a school, district, or state is doing in terms of overall student progress. The Individuals with Disabilities Education Act Amendments (IDEA) of 1997 (PL 105-17) first mandated that states report how students with disabilities will participate in general education curriculum and how their progress will be measured (Kleinert & Kearns, 2001). The Individuals with Disabilities Education Improvement Act (IDEA) of 2004 (PL 108-446) contains new language about individual appropriate accommodations on state and district testing and new requirements for alternate assessments. The child's IEP must include a statement of any individual appropriate accommodations that are necessary to measure the academic achievement and functional performance of the child on state and districtwide assessments. If the student takes an alternate assessment on a particular state or districtwide assessment, then an explanation must be provided as to why the student cannot participate in the regular assessment and how the particular alternate assessment selected is appropriate for the child (Section 614 [d][1][A][VI]).

Three types of alternate assessments have been in place: 1) alternate assessment based on alternate achievement standards, 2) alternate assessment based on grade-level standards, and 3) alternate assessment based on modified achievement standards.

Alternate Assessments Based on Alternate Achievement Standards   These assessments are based on grade-level content but are reduced in depth, breadth, and complexity for students with the most significant intellectual disabilities. There is a difference in what the student must know and do in order to be considered proficient in the content assessed, but the students are learning academic content that is clearly linked to the same grade-level content as their peers (NCEO, 2016a). Done right, these alternate assessments and alternate achievement standards still address the essential academic core of the content standards. Although more than 1% of a district's student population might take this type of alternate assessment, a cap of 1% has been placed on the use of the scores in accountability to avoid placing an inappropriate proportion of students in a lower achievement bracket. This essentially means only students with the most significant disabilities should be assessed on alternate achievement standards.

Alternate Assessments Based on Grade-Level Achievement Standards   These assessments are based on grade-level content and are not reduced in depth, breadth, or complexity. There is no difference in what the students must know to be considered proficient in the content assessed, but they are unable to gain access to or perform on the grade-level assessment the way it is, even with accommodations. So, the students are provided a different format or context for the assessment.

Alternate Assessments Based on Modified Achievement Standards   In the past, some states have created assessments based on modified academic achievement standards. These are for students who received instruction on grade-level content but were unlikely to achieve proficiency, so the achievement standards are modified, essentially lowering the bar rather than addressing the essential academic core of the content standards. This type of alternate assessment has been phased out by most states (NCEO, 2016c).

Different states have approached alternate assessment in different ways. Every state has determined alternate assessments based on alternate achievement standards. The best way to stay up to date on each state's policies, procedures, and reporting is to visit the Department of Education web site for the particular state.

Perspectives on Alternate Assessment/Alternate Standards

Some educators feel that alternate assessment based on alternate standards lowers standards or expectations. We feel that while this can be the case, this is not necessarily always the case. There is language in the literature surrounding alternate assessment with which we agree.

Jorgensen, McSheehan, Schuh, and Sonnenmeier (2012) identified four indicators of effective ongoing assessment and evaluation of learning for students with disabilities:

1. Documentation of students' academic learning represents the full depth, breadth, and complexity of state-adopted general education academic standards.

2. Assessment reports reflect students' abilities and needs rather than deficits.

3. If students have difficulty communicating, then assessment tools and strategies are chosen accordingly and assessment results are qualified accordingly.

4. Teachers and related services providers use ongoing dynamic assessments, and findings from discrete, one-time assessment tools are used with caution.

In a statement supporting alternate assessment, TASH (2014) mentioned the reauthorization of the Elementary and Secondary Education Act in 2002 (PL) mandating that schools be accountable for the progress of all students, including those from subgroups vulnerable to poor educational outcomes, through standardized assessments and alternate assessments. The importance of providing an alternate assessment for students with cognitive disabilities is that they are provided with a way to gain access to an assessment that accurately indicates their performance levels. Once their performance levels are revealed, that data can be used as part of a system to improve instruction to improve the performance of all students. TASH noted that "while teaching and assessing students with significant cognitive disabilities may be challenging, these students have repeatedly demonstrated they can and do learn academic content when they are provided effective instruction and meaningful, individualized support" (2014, p. 1).

Kleinert and Kearns (2001) identified principles of alternate assessments. They must be integrally tied to effective instruction, be based on authentic instruction of real-life skills, allow the student to apply knowledge and skills, not be a single snapshot of performance, reflect performance from optimal student supports, be integrally tied to individualized curricular focus and general education curriculum, be developed to reflect knowledge and skills needed in meaningful contexts with rich social opportunities, and improve instruction and results for students who take them.

Assessments and end goals should be a match for individual students and their own challenge levels, allowing them to experience academic content in a general education context in their zone of proximal development. Opposing alternate standards for students with complex learning needs because you feel that these standards lower or water down expectations runs the risk of an all or nothing mentality and practice in which students must master the same standards and performance tasks across the board, without differentiation. If you set up an all or nothing situation, then we believe it will end up being nothing, which runs the risk of leaving students with disabilities out (If you cannot do 100%, then you get 0%, because there is no alternative). We are concerned that opposing alternate assessment standards for a small subset of students with disabilities is a setup for excluding those children with disabilities because they are not able to meet grade-level standards. If no alternate standards are in place for these students, then some people may conclude that they do not need access to general education because they are not expected to meet standards.

Although we applaud and strive for high expectations for all students, we do not agree with doing the exact same thing for all students. Better alternate assessment than failure to meet all standards. We do not believe that alternate is lower. We believe alternate is differentiation, scaffolding, and support in the zone of proximal development. Providing alternate (differentiated) standards and performance tasks provides students with access, experience, engagement, and meaningful interaction with all general education curriculum in an inclusive setting. Providing alternate assessment based on alternate achievement standards presumes competence of content for all students, although some may have different productivity. Alternate assessment does not equal lower or lesser standards. Alternate assessment equals alternate standards that are still high-quality, albeit differentiated, standards! Alternate assessment is a meaningful way to assess whether students have grasped the big idea of the standard.

Think about what the standards should reflect. Rather than expecting all students to "compare the early civilizations of the Indus River Valley and the Huang-He of China," we should be asking all students, "How does where you live affect how you live?" All students can walk away with the same big idea, the essential understanding, even though the assessment product or process looks different. A student with a cognitive disability may not independently read articles or write essays about early civilizations, but he or she can listen to stories and talk about people. He or she can understand that where you live affects how you live. Including students with complex learning needs helps the teacher identify the key understandings *all* students should have. Teaching all students makes teachers teach better.

A note about this book: It began in a meeting one of the authors attended in support of a student with significant executive functioning needs. The parents, school administrators, and teachers present were brainstorming ways to support the student who was finding it difficult to manage the many layers of homework due each day as well as the many materials required for each class. One of the attendees suggested the student be excused from some of the work to lessen the load. The response by the parents was a resounding, "No! Don't dumb it down." The student was entirely capable of the work and the workload. This particular situation did not require less work or excusal from responsibilities. This particular situation required supports such as an extra set of materials at home and in each classroom, a customized planner, materials posted online so they could be retrieved if lost, and concept maps of the steps and parts of each assignment, proportionate in size to the amount of work required for each part.

Individual students need different interventions that support them in doing their best work to the highest expectations possible. That means do not leave them out. Do not give them something else entirely. Do not keep them from the general education curriculum because they cannot demonstrate mastery in the same way as others. Do not make them take too big a step. Do not make them take too small a step at a time.

Do scaffold. Do instruct in the zone of proximal development (Vygotsky, 1978). Do design to individual needs. Do provide multitiered instruction in meaningful contexts with diverse peers. This book shows how that can be done in even the most diverse classrooms.

For my parents, Carol and George, with love, gratitude, and admiration
—W.H.R.

For my parents, Jennifer and David Arndt, my first and best teachers
—K.L.A.

For my Mom and Dad, who taught me to fight for those who need it most
—S.M.H.

Inclusion

From Theory to Practice

This chapter introduces ideas and theories that are the foundation for this book. We have found that although many teachers support our ideas about inclusion, they do not always have a clear idea of what those ideas look like in practice. This book is designed to explain how to enact inclusive practices for all students, supporting students with and without individualized education programs (IEPs) or 504 plans or English as a new language (ENL) learners, in the same classroom. You may be thinking, "That's nice, but that's pie-in-the-sky dreaming, and it's not possible."

We think our ideas are more than pie in the sky. We think inclusion is possible for all students, regardless of the range in diversity in the classroom. We also believe all students can meet high academic standards through the praxis of inclusive teaching, the unity between the theory and practice of inclusive teaching. This means the practice—what teachers say and do in the classroom and how they plan, instruct, assess, and structure their classrooms—is grounded on research-based education theories of inclusive teaching, as well as what they believe about inclusion. This practice continually evolves through critical reflections on their experiences in a diverse classroom. Teachers will continue to learn and develop as they get to know individual students and research what is needed to support their learning and development.

If informed practice, critical reflection on experiences, and an unwavering belief in the ability of all students to learn together without "dumbing down" the content are present, then inclusive teaching is possible so that all students can meet high standards, regardless of the range of diversity.

In this book, we discuss theoretical foundations, the impact of each foundation on successful inclusion in diverse classrooms, and how these translate into specific practices for supporting all students, even in vastly diverse classroom settings, without dumbing down the curriculum. Inclusion is sometimes code for segregation—when "inclusion classroom" is used to describe one class in a grade level, what does that mean about the other classes in that grade level? Do they not include students with disability labels? Are those rooms actually segregated? That is not what inclusion means to us.

In this chapter, we address the misconception that we hear people (e.g., educators, teacher education students, families, opponents to inclusion) voice on occasion: "[12:1:1] classes are necessary because some students need them. Some students are more successful in [12:1:1] classes." Different people might substitute various other conditions for the ones noted in the brackets. It is important to analyze what is working in the special class that seems successful—smaller class size, fewer transitions during the day, highly/specially trained professionals, presence of paraprofessional(s), and family collaboration. Let's examine each of these classroom conditions.

Smaller class sizes. Class sizes for segregated special education classes are often smaller because only students with IEPs are in them, which is problematic on many levels.

Students with disabilities who do not have regular contact with typically developing peers lack access to peer models of typical speech and social interaction or a group of peers with whom to engage. Consider the case of a young girl with intellectual disabilities and autism spectrum disorder (ASD). The child was placed in a segregated classroom with peers who also had intellectual disabilities and ASD, and the result was a classroom of six children, none of whom used speech. At first glance, the small class—only six students with a teacher and two teaching assistants—seemed responsive to her needs. But the classroom provided no typically developing peers to model typical speech and social interactions. Students' access to academics was limited, and the room was loud and chaotic. Several students used challenging behavior (a teacher code phrase that can include tantrums) to communicate, and the result for all children was an environment that felt like the farthest thing from a learning environment. Having access to general education would have served all the children much better, and the special education classroom could have been used as a safe space to relax, regroup, and be calm. In that scenario, after using a quiet space to regroup, students return to the general education classroom—where routines, academic curricula, and social interactions continue.

Fewer transitions. Fewer transitions during the day can support learning. Students in elementary school typically make transitions from the classroom to specials, such as art, physical education, and music, and to lunch and recess. Those transitions can be reduced or adapted by allowing a student to make a transition before or after the rest of the class, travel with an adult or peer buddy, or eliminate one or more transitions and allow the student to remain in the general education setting with appropriate supervision and tasks that mirror what the rest of the class is doing. The number of transitions is typically very high for high school students (and some middle school students)—transitions between multiple classes, sometimes as many as nine in a day, plus a lunch period and perhaps a home base or homeroom. Add in the stress of physically traveling throughout a high school complex, and some students are not able to make a transition as often as most. Some high schools use a schedule of four periods a day on alternating day cycles, which reduces the number of transitions, but it can be confusing. Checking in every morning with the same teacher—often a special education teacher in a resource or support setting—can help some students. It can also help to include one or even two classes that provide instruction in a content area (coordinated with the content area teacher), provide instruction in study skills or test-taking skills, or provide time to take a test with extended time or work on homework with support.

Highly/specially trained professionals. Highly trained professionals do not need to be kept in separate classrooms; special education teachers can do a great deal in the general education setting. In fact, we believe that special education teachers are best utilized in settings with children with and without disabilities; supporting all students is best done in a classroom that includes all students. The result can be powerful for the classroom when a special education teacher is available to a general education teacher or co-teaches with a general education teacher. This is a shift in thinking about how services are provided—from placements to organizing the structure of classrooms. Sailor and McCart supported this shift and noted:

> One present day argument, which applies to all students identified for services under IDEA but particularly those with the most significant disabilities, is that educators should support a reauthorization that redirects the focus of policy away from *placements* of individual children and instead toward the *structural elements* of a system necessary to ensure that effective instruction and high-quality interventions are readily available for all students, regardless of learning style, disability, or risk factors. . . . The desired result of these systemic changes would be improved services for all students with disabilities, including those students who typically need a greater level of support. (2014, p. 57)

The authors noted that such a shift, which would result in more inclusive practices, is more than ideology with little evidence to support it. They continued:

> Evidence supports inclusive education (Fisher & Meyer, 2002; Foreman, Arthur-Kelly, Pascoe, & King, 2004; Logan & Keefe, 1997; Peetsma, Vergeer, Roeleveld, & Karsten, 2001; Wehmeyer, Lattin, Lapp-Rincker, & Agran, 2003) and indicates improved academic and social outcomes. There is additional evidence indicating a direct benefit to general education students when exposed to practices supporting students with more extensive needs (Lenz, Deshler, & Kissam, 2004; Luiselli, Putnam, Handler, & Feinberg, 2005; Manset & Semmel, 1997). (2014, pp. 57–58)

Clearly, the idea that students with disabilities, including those with extensive support needs, need to be isolated to be taught is not accurate. It is a misconception.

Paraprofessionals. Paraeducators, sometimes called *teaching assistants* or *paraprofessionals,* are integral to inclusive practice. The National Education Association (NEA; 2015) addressed the importance of paraprofessionals, reminding us of the role they play:

> "The range and flexibility of paraprofessional positions make it difficult for most folks to understand exactly where our role begins and ends," says Sandie Blankenship, a special education paraeducator in North Kingstown, Rhode Island. "But I feel like we're the mortar that fits where it needs to fit to keep the whole structure together." Across America, paraeducators are indeed "keeping it together" by supporting and strengthening the curriculum taught by teachers, assisting with school instructional programs, and enabling teachers to spend more individualized time with students. (para. 5–6)

Paraeducators are absolutely key to strong inclusive practice. The paraeducator is often the key to how inclusive a student's education is—by how he or she supports social interactions, makes academic content accessible, and supports the comfort needs of the student in ways that make it acceptable and appropriate that everyone gets what they need in the classroom. It is hard to overstate the importance of the paraeducator for inclusive practice. A wonderful resource for schools is *The Paraprofessional's Handbook for Effective Support in Inclusive Classrooms* (Causton-Theoharis, 2009).

Family collaboration. Family collaboration plays a large role in the success of students. Jorgensen et al. (2012) identified the following indicators for meaningful, effective family–school partnerships: family priorities are reflected on IEPs, families and educators recognize each other's efforts in positive ways, families have the resources and information needed to advocate for their children's education, families attend meetings on a regular basis at mutually convenient times, and families have access to community-based services that support healthy family functioning. All of this can happen in any setting.

Each of the previous conditions, which are associated with special education, could lead to students' success. Having a disability or IEP is not necessary for success, however. Rather, these supports can benefit any student. If they are implemented in diverse, inclusive classrooms, then their benefit could be increased and even more students could experience success. With this in mind, we now examine the theoretical foundations underlying inclusion and their practical application.

THEORETICAL FOUNDATIONS OF INCLUSIVE PRACTICE

This section presents the theoretical grounding for the praxis, or practice, chapters that make up the heart of the book. We begin by reviewing three theoretical foundations of inclusive practice—the way models of disability affect how educators think about teaching, the least dangerous assumption (Jorgensen, 2005), and the idea of full citizenship (Kliewer, 1998).

Models of Disability

Rapp and Arndt reviewed three models of disability in their book, *Teaching Everyone* (2012)—the social model, the pity/charity model, and the medical model—that shape how educators think about disability and children with disability labels. New ways of talking about disability and children with disabilities come up, but these three models remain a clear way of separating differences in how educators think about disability at a very foundational level. The models of disability are reviewed below.

Three Models of Disability

The Medical Model

The medical model **perceives disability as abnormal and sick, as an illness that needs treatment by the medical profession.** The field of medicine has been important in diagnosing disorders, finding cures for diseases, educating people about health, and advancing science to support long, healthy lives for people. Immunizations, a healthy diet, getting exercise are a part of our lives because of the field of medicine. At the same time, some professionals in the field of medicine extend the authority of their profession too far. This problem is apparent when doctors try to predict what the life of a person with a disability might be like and tell families that there is no hope, or a child with cerebral palsy will never walk or talk or learn, or a child with Down syndrome cannot live at home. This is not something that can be predicted. If families make decisions about their child's care based on a doctor's overly pessimistic predictions, then that doctor has exerted too much control over that child's future, even if he or she was well intentioned. Historically, this situation has been all too common given society's deference to the medical profession. In addition, when a child with a disability is viewed solely with the medical model, he or she will never be considered a competent, progressing student until the disability is cured and eliminated, making it a constant unrealistic struggle to obtain society's definition of normalcy. The rationale of the medical model is that the medical profession is the best-equipped field to understand and support people with disabilities. But this can be damaging to people with disabilities.

Linton noted, "The disability studies' and disability rights movement's position is critical of the domination of the medical definition and views it as a major stumbling block to the reinterpretation of *disability* as a political category and to the social changes that could follow such a shift" (1998, p. 11). The field of medicine has said that disability is a medical issue—and the general public should not be involved in deciding how people with disabilities should be treated because they are not equipped to decide what is best.

The medical model is intertwined with ideology that the norm is something for which to strive. Davis (1995) explored the way that the norm was constructed and the average became desirable. Once the norm was established, people with disabilities were seen as undesirable and rejected. The medical profession, with the development of genetics and eugenics, took on people with disabilities as a population on which to experiment, which was a relief to the majority population; they could marginalize and ignore people with disabilities, trusting medicine to deal with them. The medical profession was influenced by industrialization and the scientific ideal of the norm and shaped their practice toward eliminating any experience that fell outside a mythical normal part of the bell curve.

The Pity/Charity Model

The pity/charity model is a second model for thinking about disability. Jerry Lewis epitomizes the pity model. His telethon to raise funds for the Muscular Dystrophy Association includes using terms such as *cripple* and referring to a wheelchair as "that steel imprisonment" (Bennetts, 1993, p. 9). The pity/charity model **constructs people with disabilities as pitiful because they are sick** (Charlton, 1998, pp. 10, 34). It allows people without disabilities to patronize people with disabilities, feeling good about their support and goodwill charity. In fact, many professionals in rehabilitation and special education are motivated by this pity/charity instinct, which makes relationships between people with disabilities and the professionals who work with (and sometimes for) them uneasy. The result is a minimum of accessible housing, transportation, employment, and education. The disability rights movement sees these benefits of membership in society not as gifts, but as rights that need to be afforded to every member of society as a matter of course. Reframing the pity/charity model includes educating society that every person has the right to clean, safe, affordable housing, transportation, employment, and education.

The Social Model

As a precursor to the social model, Bogdan and Biklen identified *handicapism* as "a set of assumptions and practices that promote the differential and unequal treatment of people because of apparent or assumed physical, mental, or behavioral differences" (1977, p. 14). Addressing the socially constructed nature of how people with disabilities are treated, they analyze how handicapist attitudes reinforce oppressive practices of labeling and segregation.

The social model is designed to replace the medical and pity/charity models by thinking about disability in a completely new way. Earlier conceptions of disability tended toward an individual, medical, or "personal tragedy" model (Barnes, Oliver, & Barton, 2002, p. 4). A personal tragedy treats disability as an individual issue, one to be managed alone or within the family. The idea that people with disabilities are members of the larger society that has a responsibility to respond to disability or support them was not yet present. The social model of disability **proposes the idea that "'disability' is not a product of personal failings, but is socially created** . . . rather than identifying disability as an individual limitation, the social model identifies society as the problem, and looks to fundamental political and cultural changes to generate solutions" (Barnes et al., 2002, p. 5). Winter (2003) proposed that the two premises of the social model are that "people with impairments are disabled by society's blatant failure to accommodate to their needs" (in Barnes et al., 1999, p. 2) and "people with impairments can and should take control of their own lives as much as possible" (p. 8).

(From Rapp, W. H., & Arndt, K. L. [2012]. *Teaching everyone: An introduction to inclusive education* [pp. 8–10]. Baltimore, MD: Paul H. Brookes Publishing Co.)

The next two sections review two important concepts—the least dangerous assumption (Jorgensen, 2005) and presuming competence. The chapter then discusses what it means for students to have full citizenship in the classroom.

The Least Dangerous Assumption

Handicapism: "A set of assumptions and practices that promote the differential and unequal treatment of people because of apparent or assumed physical, mental, or behavioral differences" (Bogdan & Biklen, 1977, p. 14).

Least dangerous assumption: A standard of practice that "asserts that in the absence of conclusive data educational decisions should be based on assumptions which, if incorrect, will have the least dangerous effect on the student" (Donnellan, 1984, p. 142).

The least dangerous assumption is a way of thinking about students—particularly students with disabilities, although making the least dangerous assumption has broad application—that fundamentally shapes how educators think about teaching. Specifically, the least dangerous assumption "asserts that in the absence of conclusive data educational decisions should be based on assumptions which, if incorrect, will have the least dangerous effect on the student" (Donnellan, 1984, p. 142).

To review the least dangerous assumption, Jorgensen (2005) explained how a prevailing paradigm—a current way of thinking, a shared world view—affects our thinking, particularly about students with disabilities. Students with disabilities are often considered incapable, fragile, and in need of protection from typically developing peers. The results to inclusive practice are devastating when students with disabilities are perceived in this way.

Common Assumptions About Intellectual Ability   Jorgensen (2005) noted four main prevailing ideas about intelligence and competence. First, intelligence can be reliably measured. Second, intellectual disability means low levels of intelligence. Third, students who have "mental retardation" (the term *intellectual and developmental disabilities* is now used) cannot learn much in general education, so there are limited benefits to attending general education. Fourth, when educators cannot be sure that a student knows, understands, can learn, or has something to say, they presume that the student does not, in fact, know, understand, learn, or communicate.

Prevailing paradigm:
A shared world view
that is strong and
institutionalized
(Jorgensen, 2015).

The Impact of Assumptions: Jack's Story   The impact of different assumptions—
more dangerous versus less dangerous—can be profound. Nottingham and Dearde (2013)
used the least dangerous assumption to change how teachers and aides interacted with
Jack, a student with ASD. The researchers found that over a 20-month period, as adult
expectations, exposure to language, and literacy tasks increased,

> Jack demonstrated his ability to respond to more complex questions. Therefore by increas-
> ing his opportunities and reasons to communicate, the under-estimation of his cognitive
> abilities and literacy skill became evident. We contest that he had the means (ability to
> point) and cognitive ability to follow instructions prior to our intervention but was not
> being given the opportunity to demonstrate these as he was dependent on adult choice of
> activity. (2013, p. 242)

The educational staff who worked with Jack were initially skeptical about the study. They
believed that Jack's responses were random, even when he correctly selected words from
a printed list and was repeatedly correct. It is hard to challenge a prevailing paradigm,
and these school staff were faced with the uncomfortable truth that they had been deny-
ing Jack access to academics not out of any ill will but because they were underestimating
what he could understand.

The consequences of underestimating Jack are devastating in terms of the lost time he
can never get back. Nottingham and Dearde noted that

> once he was consistently identifying the correct word from a choice of six, staff began to
> recognize that Jack could read. The fact that Jack had not been seen by the speech and
> language therapists working in his school presumably indicates that his language was
> thought to be at the same level as his cognitive abilities. As Jack was 12 years old by the
> end of this intervention this mis-apprehension could have deprived him of many years of
> more appropriate education. (2013, p. 243)

The Importance of Presuming Competence

The moral of Jack's story is that educators must always presume competence. Educators
must assume that if they are unable to tell if a student is able to understand, then the
disconnect is on their end—not a lack of capacity on the part of the student. Presuming
competence is an attitude—one that shapes actions in the classrooms and includes a default
assumption that the student is capable until educators have clear evidence otherwise.

For many years, that clear evidence has been observation that a student may not seem
to be paying attention, but educators now know that there are many ways a student might
look when paying attention. Clear evidence has been a lack of production—the student is
taking in information but is unable to report what he or she is learning in consistent or
traditional ways.

The risks of deprivation of opportunity skyrocket when competence is not presumed.
Ido Kedar eloquently speaks to the risk. Kedar has autism, and he published a book of
essays titled *Ido in Autismland: Climbing Out of Autism's Silent Prison* (2012) when he was a
teenager. He noted in a blog post:

> My childhood was not easy because I had no means to communicate at all, despite my
> 40 hours a week of intensive ABA therapy. I pointed to flashcards and I touched my nose,
> but I had no means to convey that I thought deeply, understood everything, but was locked
> internally. Meticulously collected data showed my incorrect answers to flashcard drills,
> but the limitations of theory are in the interpretations.
>
> My mistakes were proof to my instructors of my lack of comprehension or intelli-
> gence, so we did the same boring, baby lessons year after boring year. How I dreamed of
> being able to communicate the truth then to my instructors and my family too, but I had
> no way to express my ideas. All they gave me was the ability to request foods and basic
> needs.

Here is what I would have told them if I could have when I was small. My body isn't under my mind's complete control. I know the right answer to these thrilling flashcards, unfortunately my hand isn't fully under my control either. My body is often ignoring my thoughts. I look at my flashcards. You ask me to touch 'tree,' for example, and though I can clearly differentiate among tree, house, boy and whatever cards you have arrayed, my hand doesn't consistently obey me. My mind is screaming, "Don't touch house!" It goes to house. Your notes say, "Ido is frustrated in session today." Yes, frustration often occurs when you can't show your intelligence and neurological forces impede communication between mind and body and experts then conclude that you are not cognitively processing human speech.

In my childhood I feared I would remain stuck forever in this horrible trap, but I was truly fortunate to be freed when I was 7 when my mother realized my mind was intact, and both my parents searched to find a way to help me communicate without tactile support.

Thousands of autistic people like me live life in isolation and loneliness, denied education, condemned to baby talk and high fives, and never able to express a thought. The price of assuming that nonverbal people with autism have impaired thinking is a high one to families and to people who live in solitary confinement within their own bodies. It is high time professionals rethought their theories. (Kedar, 2014)

Sue Rubin narrates the story of her life in the documentary *Autism Is a World* (Wurzburg & Rubin, 2005). She shares how her family, teachers, and other professionals worked to help her express what she was learning, thinking, and feeling. Over time, and with the use of facilitated communication, Sue learned to type words to express herself.

Prior to age 13, Sue did not communicate with speech; she hurt herself; she did not seem to be understanding anything happening around her. She is a classic example of the kind of child often deemed too disabled to benefit from inclusive education. Sue's family and teachers used the least dangerous assumption with her. They continually provided Sue with access to academic and social opportunities that were age appropriate, even though she was not responding in ways that would demonstrate her cognitive understanding or social engagement, which illustrated her family and support team's willingness to presume competence without evidence. Even if their assumptions had been incorrect, the effect was much less dangerous than depriving her of these opportunities. Sue explains on her web site how her life changed when she started typing to communicate:

> In 1991, at age 13, I started typing to communicate, and my entire life changed. I had been labeled as a typical, low-functioning person with autism, and I participated in Special Day classes starting with Infant Stimulation when I was eighteen months old. Living in Whittier, California, I always spent a part of the day in regular classes so I was exposed to regular-education curriculum, but no one knew I was learning, including me. I was so autistic that words floated over my head and made no sense until I started typing to communicate. I then listened with understanding and was able to participate in regular-education classes. (Rubin, 2014, para. 2)

There are many blogs and books by and about people who appear to be severely disabled and incapable of learning at first or second glance. Emma Zurcher-Long (n.d.) is a young woman in New York City whose blog includes a resource of other blogs and posts "Written by Non-Speaking Autistics." A list of blogs by people with ASD is included in the Resources for Inclusion appendix of this book.

Full Citizenship

Kliewer (1998) conducted qualitative research about schooling and children with Down syndrome, and a model for thinking about how typical children see students with disabilities in the inclusive classroom emerged from that research. He found that full citizenship

Full citizenship:
Being a member of the community, including four facets: a belief that one can think, that one is an individual, that reciprocal relationship is possible, and a shared place to be with others (Kliewer, 1998).

in the classroom—belonging to the class community, being a member of the class—encompasses four facets:

1. A belief in one's ability to think

2. A belief in one's individuality

3. A belief in reciprocity of the relationship

4. A shared location.

This section reviews the facets of citizenship and the importance of each in inclusive settings. First, believing that someone can think seems so fundamental. However, some people may have an underlying skepticism about the capacity students with disabilities have to understand information, learn new information, and retain information. Just as girls are often underestimated in math and science in the United States (Shapiro & Williams, 2012), students with disabilities are often underestimated in all academic areas. The evidence of underestimating students with disabilities is undeniable. New York State's report (Figure 1.1) on the status of students with disabilities is a clear case in point. It is not our intention to single out New York State alone; we believe that similar data, if reported in a similar way, would be exactly the same across the country.

Students with disabilities lacked access to coursework and testing in math in New York State. The percentage of students with disabilities who took the state exam in math gradually rose over a 10-year period. At the same time, the number of students passing the exam also rose. The graph in Figure 1.1 does not show a lack of ability in the earliest reporting years. Rather, it shows a lack of access to academic content and assessment.

Second, everyone is an individual. Yet, students with disabilities are sometimes seen as a label. Statements such as, "All children with Down syndrome are happy" or "Those ADD kids are always wild" are inaccurate, rude, and limit the ability to see each student as a rich, complex, nuanced person with strengths, quirks, weaknesses, and preferences. The ease of stereotyping is strong, and a lack of familiarity with students with disabilities may lead some people to make generalizations where there really should not be generalizations. Inclusive classroom education is essential to decrease the lack of familiarity school personnel have with a range of diverse abilities.

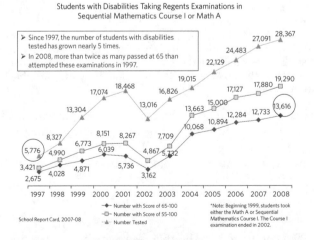

Figure 1.1. Increase in access and performance: Students with disabilities in New York State taking a math exam in high school. (From Cort, R. H. [2009]. *The State of Special Education 2009*. Retrieved from http://www.p12.nysed.gov/specialed/techassist/Statewide-Oct09/Oct09statewide.ppt)

Third, reciprocity of the relationship means that students with and without disabilities benefit from knowing each other. Sometimes we hear comments about students without disabilities such as, "He is so kind to that kid in his class" or "She really loves helping him out when he needs help with reading." There is nothing wrong with such statements if those same students without disabilities also recognize the strengths the student with disabilities has and sees him or her as an individual with likes, dislikes, personality, and interests. Reciprocity means that both parties benefit. The prevailing paradigm about students with disabilities in inclusive classrooms is that they benefit from exposure to typically developing peers. What is missing from this paradigm is that students without disabilities also benefit (Grant & Jones-Goods, 2016; Hunt, Hirose-Hatae, Doering, Karasoff, & Goetz, 2000; Murawski & Dieker, 2008; Peck, Staub, Gallucci, & Schwartz 2004). Without this second piece, the risk is that students with disabilities are only the recipients of help; never offering it, never contributing to the community, except to receive support and, by receiving support, make others feel good. This is dangerous for citizenship.

Finally, a shared location means literally that: a place to be together where all meaningfully contribute, are valued for what they bring to the class community, and are missed when they are absent. For some, this means a classroom setting. We hope that is what it means for all children.

CLASSROOM APPLICATION OF INCLUSIVE PRACTICE

The first half of this chapter introduced ideas that many readers may be familiar with—models of disability, the least dangerous assumption and importance of presuming competence, and citizenship. This section reviews the application of inclusive practices. We defined *praxis* as having two parts: a strong theoretical knowledge base and a strong ability to put theory into practice in the classroom. The second part is where theories are tested and where we get to explore what working from a social model of disability, making the least dangerous assumption, presuming competence, and affirming full citizenship look like in actual practice. Where students hang their coats, where they sit for instruction, who they learn from, and which peers they work with can be a praxis of exclusion or a praxis of inclusion. We advocate for a praxis that celebrates the contributions and abilities of all children. This section reviews four ideas that are highly relevant to a praxis of inclusion: universal design for learning (UDL); response to intervention (RTI) or providing multiple tiers of supports; embedded instruction; and clustering. It also discusses how to address the whole student and all of his or her needs and how to serve all students, including those with different needs.

The discussion about students with disabilities and models of inclusion within the field of education has often been driven almost entirely by special education (Sailor, Doolittle, Bradley, & Danielson, 2009). The conversation has shifted in recent years from special education alone to a shared conversation between special education and general education. Sailor and McCart argued that

> it is time for a different approach: a *schoolwide* approach to inclusive education, driven by MTSS [multi-tiered system of support], guided by design teams of both general and special educators, utilizing universal design for learning (UDL) principles, and implemented in a manner resulting in demonstrable gains for *all students*. (2014, p. 59)

Evidence that this kind of approach is possible is easy to see (we hope the same is true for you). For example, a fifth-grade general education teacher we know attended a professional development workshop on how to write IEPs for students with disabilities. He was pleased with the practical skills he learned and commented that the professional development training for IEPs was among the most useful he had ever attended. A general education teacher commenting about the usefulness of IEPs is a great indicator that the shift toward inclusive practice has happened; this teacher probably was not writing IEPs 15 or 10 or perhaps even 5 years ago. He is now co-teaching and knows how to think about IEP goals and objectives for the few students in his classroom who benefit from having an IEP. We are hopeful that this example is more typical than not as all schools work to support all students.

We review the current demographics of students served through special education, including low- and high-incidence disabilities and the range of challenges teachers face, in the "Intersection of Expectations and Supports" section. For example, teachers developing inclusive practices for students with needs related to learning disabilities may face different challenges than teachers of students with significant disabilities. Complying with testing requirements or ensuring test accommodations may be different challenges than building portfolios or designing and using test modifications.

For every child who learns in a segregated setting for a particular reason, there is a similar child with similar needs in an inclusive setting. This idea that there is a developmental twin for every child who is segregated is one that helps educators quickly move past all the reasons inclusion is not working in one setting to thinking about how and why it is working in another. That mindset helps educators see possibilities instead of barriers and conceptualize inclusive practice as a systemwide issue instead of an issue specific to one particular student.

Academic Intervention Services (AIS) are available in New York State and can be assigned to any student based on low test scores. This practice is inclusive as all students may get needed support because eligibility for special education is not a requirement.

Universal Design for Learning

UDL is a term increasingly present in educational settings. This section lays out the foundations of UDL and why it is essential when planning inclusive practices. This review of UDL is excerpted with permission from *Universal Design for Learning in Action: 100 Ways to Teach All Learners* (Rapp, 2014, p. 2):

> The National Center on Universal Design for Learning (2011) defined UDL as a set of principles to follow when developing a curriculum so that the curriculum meets the needs of every student, giving all students equal opportunities to learn.
>
> As outlined in the Higher Education Opportunity Act of 2008 (PL 110-315), UDL provides flexibility in the ways information is presented, the ways in which students respond or demonstrate knowledge and skills, and the ways in which students are engaged. UDL reduces barriers in instruction and provides appropriate accommodations, supports, and challenges. It also maintains high achievement expectations for all students, including students with disabilities and students with limited English proficiency.
>
> *Why Universal Design for Learning?* The purpose of UDL is to meet the needs of all students in an inclusive classroom. Students are vastly diverse—in what they learn (what they perceive), how they learn (how they process), and why they learn (what interests and motivates them). If a curriculum is designed with an average student in mind, then it will exclude more students than it includes because students learn in different ways. No two students are alike in their thought processes, learning styles, abilities, and interests.
>
> The National Center on Universal Design for Learning (2011) described traditional curricula as having "curricular disabilities" because they are designed only for "average" students and thus fail to meet the needs of real classrooms in which not every student is "average." These curricula present the content in one or two ways that are accessible to certain students, but they offer limited instructional options. Limited options might mean lecture is the only format or all material is from a textbook. A UDL curriculum identifies all the different ways a curriculum needs to be planned so that it can be accessed by all students. Addressing what, how, and why students learn and understanding what each student would report about what he or she learns empowers educators to create classrooms in which all students are full citizens. It also empowers educators to advocate for students so that their needs are met in all settings.

Input: All the different ways students access or take in new information (or, multiple means of representation).

Output: All the different ways students demonstrate their learning (or, multiple means of action and expression).

An important distinction must be made here. UDL is not the same as retrofitting (making after-the-fact adaptations) a traditional curriculum. Rather, UDL is a process by which a curriculum is purposefully and intentionally designed right from the start to address diverse needs (National Center on Universal Design for Learning, 2011). This is a philosophical distinction as well as a technical one. The practice of retrofitting means that some students (typically students) were thought of first, and other students (those who need adaptations) were thought of later. It sends the message that the classroom is made for only some, and others need to be worked in. UDL sends the message that the classroom is made for all.

Finally, UDL is valuable because it fosters the development of expert learners. Expert learners understand how they learn best, and thus they do not just receive content but create ways to gain access to content according to their unique needs. These students show that they are resourceful and knowledgeable by activating their own background knowledge to lend it to the learning situation; identifying and using tools and resources for gaining access to new learning; and transforming unfamiliar knowledge into meaningful, useful knowledge. These students show that they are strategic and goal-directed by making plans for learning, organizing effective resources and strategies to be used, and recognizing their own strengths and weaknesses. These students show that they are purposeful and motivated by setting their own challenges, sustaining the effort and persistence needed to achieve the goals, and monitoring their own interest levels and progress toward goals.

Principles of Universal Design for Learning

There are three primary principles of UDL as originally outlined: 1) provide multiple means of engagement, 2) provide multiple means of representation, and 3) provide multiple means of expression (National Center on Universal Design for Learning, 2011; Rose & Meyer, 2002).

Provide Multiple Means of Engagement   The first principle for designing a curriculum based on UDL is to use many different ways to engage students in learning. Everyone becomes engaged by different types of tasks and learning situations. Some students prefer working alone, whereas others prefer group work. Some prefer open-ended, highly subjective tasks, whereas others prefer structured, objective tasks. Each student is unique in his or her learning preferences and abilities and in the ways he or she engages in various learning opportunities and accesses information to be learned. To increase engagement, teachers need to catch students' interest, help them sustain effort and persist toward a goal, and help them self-regulate their learning behaviors.

Provide Multiple Means of Representation   The second principle to follow when designing a curriculum based on UDL is to provide multiple ways of representing the content to be learned. Rapp and Arndt (2012) described this as *input*. If you provide the content in just one way, then only the students who can gain access to it that way are going to benefit. For example, if a teacher lectures to the class, then students who learn easily by listening will have an easy time learning that content. Students who benefit from visuals such as a looking at a PowerPoint slideshow or pictures or showing text on a display will not do as well. Adding visuals to the lecture supports more students. If you present information in multiple ways, then three things happen: 1) more students are going to have access to the new learning, 2) the new information will be reinforced in multiple ways, and 3) students will be more likely to be expert learners because they will be familiar with multiple ways to receive information and thus will know what works best for them so that they can explore a range of ways to learn new information.

Provide Multiple Means of Action Expression   The third principle to follow when designing a curriculum based on UDL is to provide multiple ways for expression. Rapp and Arndt (2012) described these ways for students to show what they know as *output*. The two most common traditional outputs are writing (e.g., tests, worksheets, essays) and oral responses to teacher-posed questions in class. Although these methods should be continued for the students who are able to demonstrate their learning in these ways, many more options need to be offered as well. To meet the output needs of all learners, options for physical expression, communication, and executive functions (i.e., different ways for organizing, planning, and executing tasks) are essential. Included in this principle is *multiple means of assessment*. It is important to highlight this aspect. Ways in which teachers

Culturally responsive teaching: Teaching by using the cultural knowledge, prior experiences, and performance styles of diverse students to make learning more appropriate and effective for them.

evaluate students must vary along with the ways in which students are engaged in learning, materials are represented, and students represent what they know. Areas explored under multiple means of assessment include formal and informal assessment, formative and summative assessment, and alternative assessments.

UDL is inherently culturally responsive teaching. Culturally responsive teaching is using the cultural knowledge, prior experiences, and performance styles of diverse students to make learning more appropriate and effective. It is teaching to and through the strengths of diverse students (Gay, 2000). It is much more than teaching to a particular race, ethnicity, religion, or other cultural group. It is about connecting with students' cultural learning styles and tools, leveraging the brain's memory and information processing structures, and creating environments that match students' natural ways of learning as well as their lives and backgrounds (Hammond, 2014). Providing multiple means of engagement means connecting with a student's natural way of learning, which comes from his or her cultural background, which is everything about him or her. It is about the groups he or she identifies with, but much more so their individuality within that group. A student's culture includes (and this is not an exhaustive list) his or her race, ethnicity, language, gender identity, sexual orientation, religion or spirituality, age, ability, and neurodiversity.

Multi-Tiered Systems of Support and Response to Intervention

Now that we have reviewed the fundamentals of UDL, we turn to multi-tiered systems of support (MTSS) and RTI. Our focus is on what needs to be done for all students at all times while acknowledging that some students may need more intensive supports. MTSS and RTI describe how teachers and schools build systems of instructional and behavioral support for all students. Students are supported with increasing intensity as needed within systems of support.

MTSS tiers include three levels: high-quality instruction, evidence-based interventions that are moderate in intensity, and individual intervention that is more intensive than earlier interventions. Having fidelity in implementation and considering the linguistic and cultural needs of all students is key for all three levels (Center on Response to Intervention at American Institutes for Research, n.d.b). Data must be collected, reviewed, and used at each level when making decisions about instruction and movement between levels. The Center on Response to Intervention at American Institutes for Research (n.d.a) proposed that MTSS is something of an umbrella that integrates supports for academic and behavioral concerns. Under that umbrella, RTI is used to support students' academic needs. The RTI Action Network described RTI this way:

> Response to Intervention (RTI) is a multi-tier approach to the early identification and support of students with learning and behavior needs. The RTI process begins with high-quality instruction and universal screening of all children in the general education classroom. Struggling learners are provided with interventions at increasing levels of intensity to accelerate their rate of learning. These services may be provided by a variety of personnel, including general education teachers, special educators, and specialists. Progress is closely monitored to assess both the learning rate and level of performance of individual students. Educational decisions about the intensity and duration of interventions are based on individual student response to instruction. RTI is designed for use when making decisions in both general education and special education, creating a well-integrated system of instruction and intervention guided by child outcome data. (n.d., para 1).

RTI shares fundamental principles with the positive behavior interventions and supports (PBIS) model. Both are assessment-based, preventative, multitiered support models that are used to solve problems proactively based on individualized student needs (PBIS,

Multilevel curriculum:
Learning opportunities in which diverse students are participating in a shared activity and have individually appropriate learning outcomes (perhaps at different grade levels) in the same curricular area.

Curriculum overlapping:
Learning opportunities in which diverse students are participating in a shared activity and have individually appropriate learning outcomes from different curricular areas.

2017). Similarities across three tiers of intervention include high-quality academic and behavioral instruction and intervention; preventative, proactive strategies and supports; data-based decision making; monitoring of student progress; and team decision making (Sandomierski, Kincaid, & Algozzine, 2007).

The third level of interventions are sometimes described as *special education.* We resist this ideologically but respect the need for more resources as student needs intensify. The process of referral for special education services is the way schools can get more services and supports, so we understand the realities of using the special education referral process to provide what students need. The caveat is stressing that *special education* is defined as a set of services and supports, not a location.

The fundamental pieces of both frameworks are that general education teachers are more responsible for monitoring students' progress and changing their teaching regularly if students are not showing gains, general and special education teachers work much more closely together than in the past, and the lines between general and special education are blurred because all teachers work to support all students, and the interventions are not location specific and can benefit a wide variety of learners, regardless of their label.

Embedded Instruction

Embedding instruction is a teaching strategy in which students who need supports for full participation in inclusive classrooms are given opportunities to practice individual goals and objectives within an activity or event, during whole-class or small-group instruction, in a manner that expands, modifies, or adapts the activity/event while remaining meaningful and interesting (Horn, Lieber, Li, Sandall, & Schwartz, 2000). Embedded instruction offers an alternative to the viewpoint that IEP goals should be separate and unrelated to the goals and objectives for all learners in a classroom and addressed in separate, special education settings that focus on IEP goals and objectives in isolation and often individually. Instead, IEP goals should be developed to meet the needs and interests of the learner (or groups of learners with similar needs and interests) in a way that is immediately meaningful and functional in the variety of everyday school contexts.

There are several ways to implement embedding, including arranging the classroom environment to be receptive to diverse learner needs, adapting materials, adding new components to existing activities, providing performance cues, and providing special assistance or support. Using the mindset of embedded instruction supports the belief that "implementation of the IEP goals should neither supplant the classroom curriculum nor restrict the child's participation in classroom activities. Implementation should occur within the context of the existing classroom activities and routines" (Horn et al., 2000, p. 208).

Giangreco (2017) described multilevel curriculum and curriculum overlapping. *Multilevel curriculum* means all students' learning outcomes are in the same curricular area. *Curriculum overlapping* means the students' learning outcomes might be in different areas. In both cases, a heterogeneous group of students, with a proportionate number of students with disabilities, is working together interdependently on a shared activity in order to reach appropriate learning outcomes (Rose & Meyer, 2002).

Clustering

Clustering is a key focus for this text. We focus on the concept of clustering student needs to better meet individual student needs as we address differentiation in instructional planning. Teachers who use clustering continuously reflect on key student patterns of learning and plan instruction to address the patterns of learning, as opposed to focusing merely on individual needs, which can be overwhelming and unattainable for a teacher in daily planning. Flexible patterns of grouping may include grouping by skill level, interest, or preferred method of response. Focusing on the patterns of student interests and strengths will benefit many students for a variety of reasons (Tomlinson & McTighe, 2006).

Teachers in cluster classrooms were naturally driven to implement differentiation strategies, breaking the flawed practice of teaching to the middle, which often leaves patterns of student learning need unaddressed (Pierce et al., 2011). Clustering provides for an educational context that not only supports, but also implicitly mandates, differentiated instruction for all learners and promotes gains for all students. Effective clustering allows all students to engage in moderately challenging curriculum that is modified to allow for learning differences among the students in the classroom.

ADDRESSING THE WHOLE STUDENT: ACADEMIC, SOCIAL, AND COMFORT NEEDS

Addressing the whole student means considering all purposes of inclusive supports—academic supports, social supports, and comfort supports. Academic supports focus on academic progress, such as providing a calculator, extended time to take tests, a copy of notes, or a second set of textbooks to keep at home. Social supports attend to the relational piece of schooling, perhaps providing opportunities for partner work, a social skills class, or access to after-school clubs and activities with support. Comfort supports are those that help the student do his or her best work and are unique to the student. Sue Rubin is clear that she benefits from holding plastic spoons in one hand at times. Although it may not seem necessary to report this support on an IEP, it might support her success if everyone is clear that spoons are comforting and are not to be thrown away or taken away from her. A second example Sue talks about in *Autism Is a World* (Wurtzburg & Rubin, 2005) was having a helmet available to her when the urge to hit her head was strong. She could ask for it or put it on herself until the urge lessened. Treating Sue as competent included identifying and honoring her comfort needs and supporting her in deciding when and where to use them (Wurtzburg & Rubin, 2005).

Sometimes academic supports may be stressful on a student (e.g., a student having extra transitions in and out of the classroom because the team is working to get him or her to all the places they think he or she needs to be). Figure 1.2 shows how all three areas need to be supported together for most effective inclusion. A student who is able to do his or her best work in a safe space is in the intersection of all three supports. It is this intersection that needs to be provided for all students.

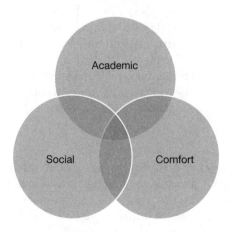

Figure 1.2.   Academic, social, and comfort needs.

INTERSECTION OF EXPECTATIONS AND SUPPORTS

Expectations and supports for students are essential if all students are going to be challenged and included. Expectations and the levels of support provided can range from low to high. Varying combinations of low and high expectations and support are seen in Figure 1.3.

Exclusion from general education classrooms and even neighborhood schools altogether results when there are low expectations and low levels of support for students (lower left quadrant). The assumption is that students with disabilities, particularly those with very complex learning needs, are unable to learn, so they have no place in schools with typically developing children. People come to believe that students with disabilities are scary or bad because they do not see and know students with disabilities. Teachers who do not teach students with disabilities may have a similar sense—students with disabilities are scary or not worth spending time teaching. They are essentially treated as aliens instead of peers (Kliewer, 1998). The idea of being alien is that the students with disabilities may be viewed as so different from other students that they are not even regarded as fully human—they are seen as something altogether different; the result is a sense that they do not need challenging activities or meaningful social relationships. Students stagnate in these settings and show little to no progress because they are neither expected nor supported to do so.

The result is still not positive for students who experience low expectations and high support (lower right quadrant). In these cases, students with disabilities might be enrolled in neighborhood schools, but they are likely placed in separate special education classrooms. Even if students with disabilities are placed in the general education classroom for part of the school day, they are still often segregated from peers working on different activities or curriculum because there are few expectations for academic or social success. Students with disabilities are often segregated from peers in academic classes; we have heard about students being prohibited from enrolling in academic classes. We believe that this happens because the assumption that students cannot meet high expectations is powerful. Statistics about educational placements clearly show a lack of inclusive placement for students with the most complex support needs. In 2008, the U.S. Department of Education noted "that children with multiple disabilities have minimal exposure to the general education classroom with nearly 70% of those spending less than 39% of their time in general education classroom, 25% of whom are in completely segregated settings" (Sailor & McCart, 2014, p. 58). By 2015, those percentages improved for many students, but not all. The National Center for Education Statistics reported that in 2017,

High expectations/low support	High expectations/high support
Mainstreaming	Full inclusion
Squatters	Citizenship and reciprocity
Medical model	Social model
Some students have to prove they can learn	All students can learn
Disability = general inability (so they are out)	Disability = challenge, opportunity, difference
Low expectations/low support	**Low expectations/high support**
Exclusion	Segregation
Aliens	Squatters
Some students can learn	Pity/charity model
Disability = bad, scary	Some students can learn
	Disability = general inability (so typically developing peers must help)

Figure 1.3. Expectations and supports for students.

About 95 percent of students ages 6–21 served under IDEA in fall 2015 were enrolled in regular schools. . . . In fall 2015, the percentage of students served under IDEA who spent most of the school day in general classes was highest for students with speech or language impairments (87 percent). Approximately two-thirds of students with specific learning disabilities (70 percent), visual impairments (67 percent), other health impairments (65 percent), and developmental delays (64 percent) spent most of the school day in general classes. In contrast, 16 percent of students with intellectual disabilities and 13 percent of students with multiple disabilities spent most of the school day in general classes. (National Center for Education Statistics, 2018, p. 7)

The pity/charity model is often at play here, and the underlying belief is that disability is general inability. The result is that students without disabilities are often asked and encouraged to be helpers for the students with disabilities, who are typically visitors to general education. The ideology is that students with disabilities need support, and others do things for them instead of providing supports. Kliewer (1998) talked about this way of thinking. He found that students who were in classrooms with this mindset in place were not aliens—they were known, but they were not citizens. They inhabited a place on the fringe, squatting on the sidelines—squatters, not participants. Students with disabilities in this quadrant notice they are not held to the same expectations as their typically developing peers and may feel that they are so different and damaged that they are not worth the teacher's effort. Many segregated special education classrooms are founded on the beliefs in this quadrant—there is a great deal of support in time, energy, and funding. What is missing is the belief that students with disabilities are capable and should be held to high expectations and supported to be as independent as possible, should be engaged with the general education curriculum, and should be working with peers to learn.

Students who experience high expectations and low support (upper left quadrant) are also squatters. In this context, students are placed (or dumped) in general education settings with very few supports or accommodations in place to help them be successful. Based on the medical model of disability, the belief is that students with disabilities are sick or broken and must be fixed to fit the environment. They must prove that they can learn or they will be segregated again, but they are left to their own devices to prove this. Jorgensen, McSheehan, and Sonnenmeier (2010) pointed out that this undermines the concept of Maslow's hierarchy of needs. Maslow proposed that there are five motivational needs: physiological, safety, belonging and love, esteem, and self-actualization. Needs are hierarchical; lower needs must be addressed before higher needs are influential (Neukrug, Brace-Thompson, Maurer, & Harman, 2015). Basic survival needs are at the bottom, and full self-actualization and realization of one's potential are at the top. The hierarchy establishes that a sense of belonging is needed in order to achieve. Yet, students with disabilities are often expected to achieve before they may belong (Jorgensen et al., 2010), which is evident in the context of high expectations and low support. When left unsupported, students unsurprisingly fail or act out, and the conclusion is drawn that inclusion does not work.

The combination of high expectations with high supports (upper right quadrant) is potent—students are expected to learn, full inclusion is enacted, and disability is seen as a challenge, an opportunity, and a difference. It is this combination that we hope to support with this book by providing practical ways to enact inclusive practices and teach all students. The theoretical grounding for this book is based on the social model of disability and full citizenship in the classroom. Throughout the book, we stand by our unwavering belief that all students can learn and disability means challenge, opportunity, and difference. We have high expectations and presume competence of all students. Supports are provided through the practices of UDL, RTI, embedded instruction, and clustering in order to accommodate the whole child.

Portraits
of Inclusion   Three Diverse Classrooms

Chapters 2, 3, and 4 present three fictional classes: first, third, and fifth grade. The student profiles (snapshots) in this section provide background and information about each of the 20 students in each fictional class. Some students have formal disability labels with an individualized education program (IEP), some have learning needs that are not formally labeled, and some students are English as a new language (ENL) learners. All are unique and have their own stories—family lives, preferences, personalities, strengths, and needs.

We use terms related to English and ENL learners, including the five stages of language development. The designated performance levels in New York State are entering, emerging, transitioning, expanding, and commanding. Each level has clear descriptions for listening, reading, speaking, and writing (EngageNY, n.d.).

We use content-specific language in lesson planning as well. We talk about reading and instructional or independent levels in the English language arts (ELA) lessons; each is determined through regular assessment of reading. Independent level reading is just that—reading that can be done by the student alone. Instruction level material is more challenging, and the student needs support and guidance from the teacher to master it. We considered strategies such as giving end-of-unit assessments as a preassessment for students who are gifted and talented, so students who already know the content can move on to the next unit instead of reviewing material that is already mastered. A second strategy is compacting the material—providing new content at a faster pace with less repetition. Both can be valuable tools in the classroom. Each lesson plan is comprehensive in scope. Figure I.1 outlines the content and structure of each plan.

We use a range of materials and formats in the lessons that we think will be familiar. For example, we use rubrics with "I can" statements, and learning activities in the lesson plans include an anticipatory set, modeling, guided practice, independent practice, and closure. Other examples include varied ways of providing input (e.g., picture books, grade-level texts, slideshows) and multiple options for student output (written or verbal responses, self-assessments, drawing, puzzles).

LESSON NAME

Time allotted:
Standards used:

Context

Each lesson plan includes an introduction that situates the day's lesson in the larger context of what students are learning in a particular content area throughout the school year.

Lesson Objectives

Describes the purpose and goals of the lesson.

Before This Lesson

Provides guidelines for required advance preparation, connecting with team members, and relevant inclusive practices.

Inclusive Practices

A list of inclusive practices (found in the Inclusive Practices Bank in Appendix A) that directly support particular individuals and may indirectly support other students.

Connections With Other Team Members

Provides a list of the team members who the teacher should connect with and why.

Desired Results/"I Can" Statements

Includes the identified lesson/goal standard, related "I Can" statements, and a reminder that all students work toward the same learning goal regardless of which specific inclusive supports they receive.

Assessment Evidence

Summarizes the specific evidence used to assess whether the student has achieved the learning goal.

Classroom Arrangement and Materials

Describe the classroom environment and materials used throughout the lesson to support all students.

Learning Activities

Describes the specific activities the teacher uses to open, conduct, and conclude the lesson, including the allotted time and specific inclusive practices, and, in some instances, sample scripted text with the teacher is supplied in italics and sample worksheets are provided. It also includes an anticipatory set, modeling, guided practice, independent practice, and closure.

Figure I.1.   Structure and content of lesson plans.

KEY TO INCLUSIVE PRACTICES

Specific inclusive practices that directly support particular individuals and may indirectly support other students are included in the student snapshots and the lessons. Following is a key to the abbreviations used to refer to different areas of inclusive practice. (A full Inclusive Practices Bank, organized by area of support, is provided in Appendix A of this book.)

CR: Cultural responsiveness

ES: Environmental supports

LAE: Language–expressive supports

LAR: Language–receptive supports

MS: Math supports

MD: Motor development supports

OS: Organizational supports

R: Reading supports

SR: Self-regulation supports

SS: Social skills supports

TM: Testing modification supports

WS: Writing supports

PREVIEW OF INCLUSIVE SUPPORTS

You will see certain tools and techniques used frequently throughout the lessons as supports for inclusion. Some of these may be familiar; others less so. The following list provides brief descriptions of different tools, techniques, and terms to familiarize yourself with that will help you create more inclusive learning environments.

Calming corner: Area equipped with soft seating, carpet, sensory tools, and so forth where students may go as needed to regroup. The area may be partially secluded with a low bookcase or other furniture arrangement, or it might include a tent or another way to be separate. Some schools allow children to be out of sight (as in a tent), whereas others do not.

Chair bands: These fit between the front legs of a student's chair to allow for resting one's feet or wiggling around.

Choice time: Time during which each student does an activity of his or her own choosing.

Coded classroom: Classroom in which all items and storage units are labeled in students' first languages and braille, with photos.

Color-wheel cuing system: A wheel with red, yellow, and green areas and a spinner to show how a student, group, or whole class is doing with clear parameters for each color. Visit this link at Intervention Central for more information: https://www.interventioncentral.org/classroom_management_color_wheel

Dictation technology: Technology that supports students dictating instead of writing when necessary.

Emotion chart: Chart with pictures representing different emotions; a student can point to a picture to indicate what he or she is feeling.

First-then (executive function): A way to present tasks in order. For example, first math, then recess. This method allows the adult to present what is happening without making a judgment such as, "If you don't do your math, you cannot go to recess."

FM systems: FM systems are used to support people with hearing impairments with a microphone of some kind and a receiver of some kind. Systems are often wireless and include the teacher wearing a microphone and the child having a hearing aid or small speaker that receives input from the microphone.

"I" statements: Conflict-resolution technique based on verbalizing one's own response to a situation.

Mandala: A circular geometric design. We use them as coloring sheets for students who benefit from coloring while listening.

Mindfulness: Teaching children to be aware of their breathing, senses, and surroundings.

Reminder band: Elastic band worn around the wrist as a reminder.

Self-checks: A way for students to individually evaluate their emotions, effort, or performance.

Self-regulation or response scales: A tool for students to self-check and communicate their levels of emotion, effort, performance, or need for assistance.

Standing desks: Desks made for use while standing.

Vidget chairs: Flexible chairs that allow for bouncing and wiggling around. Vidgets are a specific product designed to incorporate children's natural movement and provide multiple seating options. See the Viggi Kids web site for more information: https://www .viggikids.com

CLASSROOM LANDSCAPE

This classroom arrangement (Figure I.2) applies to all grade levels and is universally designed to support all students' needs in the following ways:

- Mobility around the classroom is preserved with ample space around the perimeter of the room and wide aisles around desks and tables.

- The layout of student desks is conducive to working in pairs, small groups, or individually as desks can be easily moved to various configurations while preserving the mobility space around the perimeter.

- There are two tall tables near desks to provide alternative, standing work areas.

- The square rug represents the movement center—it is away from instructional areas and walkways.

- The circle rug represents the "calming corner"—it is near instruction and away from movement or noise.

- The teacher's desk is not in a prominent area—it is private for conversations with individual students.

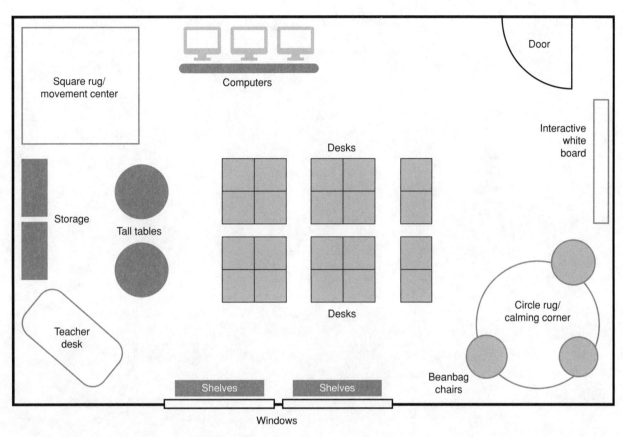

Figure I.2. Universally designed classroom landscape.

- Storage areas are labeled in braille and all first languages and contain fidgets, writing utensils, papers, pencil grips, manipulatives, timers, self-amplifiers, and other assistive technology and materials.

- Computers are loaded with apps and programs to support students' academic needs.

As you read Chapters 2–4, think about how the supports described might be used with, or adapted for, the students you know and the content you teach. Picture full inclusion in your classroom!

Ms. Jackson's First-Grade Class

Ms. Jackson's classroom has 20 students and is culturally and linguistically diverse. For example, Leela has a strong connection to Indian culture and Hindu customs, whereas Oscar speaks both Spanish and English fluently. Two students have 504 plans addressing their needs related to hearing impairment (Charlie) and dysgraphia (Taylor). Two others have IEPs addressing their needs related to speech-language impairment (Bridget) and emotional-behavioral disorder (Steven). Charlie has a hearing impairment, and the teacher of the deaf (ToD) provides support for the classroom teacher. The ToD joins the class three mornings each week to touch base and monitor Charlie's access to communication and self-awareness about his environment and what supports his hearing. The ToD supports Charlie each day during flexible instructional time (FIT). On a day-to-day basis, the teacher knows how to think about background noise, choosing the best seating placement for Charlie based on the acoustics in the room, using the amplifier, and monitoring Charlie during group work. In addition, Bridget receives speech-language therapy during FIT, and Taylor receives occupational therapy 3 days a week. Steven has FIT options such as extended reading, attending a social skill group, working with the teacher, doing yoga, or spending time in a sensory room; these options are also available to Bridget, Charlie, and Taylor in addition to the specific supports they receive pertaining to speech, hearing, and motor skills.

STUDENT PROFILES AND
SUMMARY OF INCLUSIVE SUPPORTS

lives with her mom, Susan, and her dad, Tom. Both are physicians at the local hospital, and they take turns being home by the time Avery gets home from school. Avery loves princesses, dressing up, swimming, and water ballet. She is boisterous and loud and sometimes struggles to share adult attention with others.

Age: 7;0 years/Grade 1

Fountas & Pinnell Reading Level: F (middle of first-grade level)

Math Level: At grade level; good spatial awareness in math

Disability Classification: None

Intervention/Notes: She will benefit from peer support for sharing.

Ways to Support Avery

Engagement	**Environment/Group Work** Assign small groups regularly, mixing groups weekly to support all students getting to know each other.	**Social Skills/Communication** Talking explicitly about when to ask for adult help or attention and when to work independently will support Avery's sharing adult attention. Teach strategies for independent work and asking for help from peers.
Input	**Instructional Methods and Materials** None at this time	**Technology** None at this time
Output	**Self-Management/Executive Functions** Post schedule daily with times. Give 5- and 1-minute warnings at the end of each period to allow time for cleanup and transition.	**Test Accommodations** None at this time

Support Schedule and Flexible Instructional Time (FIT) for Avery

	Monday	**Tuesday**	**Wednesday**	**Thursday**	**Friday**
1:30–2:30 FIT choices	Social skill group Work with teacher Math support Sensory room Yoga	Social skill group Work with teacher Math support Sensory room Yoga	Social skill group Work with teacher Math support Sensory room Yoga	Social skill group Work with teacher Math support Sensory room Yoga	Social skill group Work with teacher Math support Sensory room Yoga

Rapp, Arndt, and Hildenbrand

Goals and Practices

Avery's Goals	Inclusive Practices
Avery will increase her circle of friends and peers for group interactions.	SS9. Allow cooperative work to happen during all content areas with flexible grouping. SS10. Build in time each day for small-group work with peers, assigning individual roles within the group, to scaffold the interactions. SS11. Provide choices in working in pairs or small groups.
Avery will develop increased awareness of appropriate frequency and duration for seeking adult attention.	SR4. Ensure that all students are familiar with regulation scales, and many have them at their desks for self-checks. To support Avery's sharing adult attention, create a list of times that she can request adult attention and a list of things to do during wait time.
Avery will develop increased self-awareness and mindfulness.	SR6. Teach yoga/mindfulness exercises to the whole class.
Avery will improve grade-level math skills.	MS5. Provide multiple sets of counters, plastic linking cubes, and fraction circles; have abacuses available so that all students can choose to use them. MS8. Provide a calculator for operations.

Bridget

lives with her mom, Julia, her grandfather, Frank (Julia's father), her older sister, Bianca (age 10), and her older brother, Brian (age 8). All three children attend the same elementary school. Grandpa Frank is a retired minister, and he came to live with the family when his wife passed away last year. He helps the children after school with homework while Julia is at her job as a store manager. Bridget is quiet and reserved, and she is slow to warm up to people. She loves her family and loves that her grandpa lives with them. They often bake together or work in their garden after school.

Age: 6;4 years/Grade 1

Fountas & Pinnell Reading Level: E (beginning to middle of first-grade level)

Math Level: At grade level

Disability Classification: IEP, Speech-language impairment

Intervention/Notes: Bridget is meticulous and careful in all her work. She benefits from regular breaks for movement and loved participating in the Go Noodle movement program last year. Bridget has a speech-language impairment and has had an IEP since kindergarten.

Ways to Support Bridget

Engagement	Environment/Group Work	Social Skills/Communication
	Provide opportunities to talk in small groups with supportive and friendly peers, which will support her speech goals. Provide frequent movement breaks.	Provide opportunities for Bridget to improve in fluency by collaborating with the speech-language pathologist about inclusive strategies.

(continued)

Bridget's Snapshot *(continued)*

Ways to Support Bridget *(continued)*

Input	**Instructional Methods and Materials** No needs at this time	**Technology** No needs at this time
Output	**Self-Management/Executive Functions** No needs at this time	**Test Accommodations** No needs at this time

Support Schedule and Flexible Instructional Time (FIT) for Bridget

	Monday	Tuesday	Wednesday	Thursday	Friday
1:30–2:30 FIT choices	Speech-language therapy (30 minutes) Then: SLP Extended reading Social skill group Work with teacher Sensory room Yoga	Speech-language therapy (30 minutes) Then: SLP Extended reading Social skill group Work with teacher Sensory room Yoga	Speech-language therapy (30 minutes) Then: SLP Extended reading Social skill group Work with teacher Sensory room Yoga	Speech-language therapy (30 minutes) Then: SLP Extended reading Social skill group Work with teacher Sensory room Yoga	Speech-language therapy (30 minutes) Then: SLP Extended reading Social skill group Work with teacher Sensory room Yoga

Goals and Practices

Bridget's Goals	Inclusive Practices
Bridget will use movement breaks to support her focus.	ES12. Provide a "move and learn" area of the room for all students where they can walk back and forth, jump, or jump rope.
Bridget will demonstrate increased control of fluency throughout the academic day. Bridget will demonstrate increased awareness and control of rate of speech and intelligibility throughout the day.	LAE1. Before group time, give target student a question that can be answered with a new or familiar icon or vocabulary word. LAE5. Use prompts and sentence starters. LAR4. Allow students to work with a partner to take turns retelling details. LAR6. Provide visual cues, signs, rhymes, word play, and vocabulary lists to help word finding.

Rapp, Arndt, and Hildenbrand

Charlie lives with his dads, Eric and Steven, and his younger brother, Spencer (age 4). Eric is a horticulturist, and Steven is a high school teacher in another district. Spencer's adoption was finalized in October, and the whole class was invited to his adoption party. Charlie is sunny and outgoing; he makes friends with everyone. He loves active sports, including soccer.

Age: 6;8 years/Grade 1

Fountas & Pinnell Reading Level: E (beginning to middle of first-grade level)

Math Level: At grade level

Disability Classification: 504 plan, hearing impairment

Intervention/Notes: Charlie has a hearing impairment and wears two hearing aids. He often misses information from peers when they are not facing him, and he will touch peers on the shoulders and ask them to repeat what they said. See Figure 2.1 in the section titled "Supplemental Documentation" for details on his 504 plan.

Ways to Support Charlie

Engagement	**Environment/Group Work** Consider seating Charlie with his back to the wall and away from any air conditioning units or vents.	**Social Skills/Communication** Incorporate recommendations of teacher of the deaf (ToD) to make the classroom socially accessible for Charlie.
Input	**Instructional Methods and Materials** Pair visual and auditory information to support Charlie's access to information. Use visual cues to support Charlie's access to information if he misses a verbal cue. Incorporate additional recommendations of ToD to make instruction accessible for Charlie.	**Technology** Use the technology provided by the ToD to support Charlie's hearing.
Output	**Self-Management/Executive Functions** Support Charlie's self-advocacy skills.	**Test Accommodations** No needs at this time

Support Schedule and Flexible Instructional Time (FIT) for Charlie

	Monday	**Tuesday**	**Wednesday**	**Thursday**	**Friday**
8:00–8:30 Arrival/morning meeting	Teacher of the Deaf (ToD) in classroom		ToD in classroom		ToD in classroom
1:30–2:30 FIT choices	ToD Extended reading Social skill group Work with teacher Yoga	ToD Extended reading Social skill group Work with teacher Yoga	ToD Extended reading Social skill group Work with teacher Yoga	ToD Extended reading Social skill group Work with teacher Yoga	ToD Extended reading Social skill group Work with teacher Yoga

Goals and Practices

Charlie's Goals	Inclusive Practices
Charlie will consistently access information in the classroom.	ES4. For all information that the teacher reviews orally, write the information clearly for all students and/or post on the class web site—announcements, homework assignments, notes, agenda. ES6. Check that the school bell, telephone, and alarms are loud enough for student to hear unaided.
Charlie will meet grade-level expectations in literacy.	R10. Provide the speech-language pathologist with lists of reading and vocabulary words each week.
Charlie will develop self-advocacy skills. He will ask peers and adults to repeat as needed, ask for help when he needs it, and ask others to use the FM or other system to support his access to information.	ES1. All teachers wear the amplifier during any direct instruction or giving of directions. ES2. Substitute teachers, special teachers, and guest speakers are directed to receive instruction on use of the amplification technology. ES3. During small-group activities, give amplifier to student to position in the group's discussion space.

Devin

lives with her mom, Carol, and younger brother, Declan. Carol is a store manager and works during the day. Her sister-in-law (Devin's Aunt Sue) lives next door and works the night shift. The two adults co-parent Devin, Declan, and their two cousins. Devin is serious and calm.

Age: 6;5 years/Grade 1

Fountas & Pinnell Reading Level: J (early second-grade level)

Math Level: At grade level

Disability Classification: None

Intervention/Notes: Devin is a strong reader and loves reading. She benefits from support for socializing with her peers. She does not always know how to start a conversation or make a friend.

Ways to Support Devin

Engagement	**Environment/Group Work** Assign small groups and mixing groups, which will help Devin work with peers in structured ways.	**Social Skills/Communication** Model conversational skills, such as staying on topic and taking turns in conversation.
Input	**Instructional Methods and Materials** No needs at this time	**Technology** No needs at this time
Output	**Self-Management/Executive Functions** No needs at this time	**Test Accommodations** No needs at this time

Rapp, Arndt, and Hildenbrand

Support Schedule and Flexible Instructional Time (FIT) for Devin

	Monday	Tuesday	Wednesday	Thursday	Friday
1:30–2:30 FIT choices	Accelerated instruction	Extended reading Social skill group	Accelerated instruction	Extended reading Social skill group	Accelerated instruction

Goals and Practices

Devin's Goals	Inclusive Practices
Devin will practice conversational skills.	SS1. Use peer groups to practice conversations about topics that are centered around the curriculum.
Devin will increase her circle of friends and peers for group interactions.	SS9. Allow cooperative work to happen during all content areas with flexible grouping. SS10. Build in time each day for small-group work with peers, assigning individual roles within the group, to scaffold the interactions.

Evan

lives with his mom and stepdad, Diane and Tyquan. He sees his dad, Michael, regularly, and his parents would like all information sent to both addresses. His sister, Haley, is a third-grader in the building, and his little brother, Micah, attends the preschool.

Evan is funny, loud, and eager to help. He likes having a class job and enjoys being able to come in a few minutes early to take the chairs off the desks in the morning. He loves taking care of his fish—he has a tank at each house and plans to be a biologist.

Age: 6;9 years/Grade 1

Fountas & Pinnell Reading Level: E (beginning to middle of first-grade level)

Math Level: Below grade, particularly with grouping numbers

Disability Classification: None

Intervention/Notes: Evan goes to the math intervention teacher twice each week for small-group support because his math is below grade level.

Ways to Support Evan

Engagement	Environment/Group Work	Social Skills/Communication
	No needs at this time	No needs at this time
Input	**Instructional Methods and Materials** Provide manipulatives to support his math skills.	**Technology** No needs at this time
Output	**Self-Management/Executive Functions** No needs at this time	**Test Accommodations** No needs at this time

Support Schedule and Flexible Instructional Time (FIT) for Evan

	Monday	Tuesday	Wednesday	Thursday	Friday
11:30–12:15 Math		Math specialist in classroom		Math specialist in classroom	
1:30–2:30 FIT choices	Extended reading Social skill group Work with teacher Math support	Extended reading Social skill group Work with teacher Math support	Extended reading Social skill group Work with teacher Math support	Extended reading Social skill group Work with teacher Math support	Extended reading Social skill group Work with teacher Math support

Goals and Practices

Evan's Goals	Inclusive Practices
Evan will develop his counting skills.	MS1. Incorporate counting into daily routines for the whole class, using small groups for review of basic counting principles with scaffolding.
Evan will develop his grouping skills.	MS5. Provide multiple sets of counters, plastic linking cubes, and fraction circles; have abacuses available so that all students can choose to use them.

Francis lives in two households; his parents, Sara and Paul, divorced and have both remarried, and he and his siblings alternate weeks with each family. His sister, Ariana, is 12, and his brother, Will, is 10. Francis and Will ride the bus together to school. When Francis and his siblings are with their mom and stepdad (David), they also live with Sara and David's infant, Sophie (6 months old). Francis's dad and stepmom, Darlene, have no other children. His parents ask that all information is sent to both parents at the two addresses.

Francis is thoughtful and tender hearted. He loves Sophie and misses his baby sister the weeks he is not with her. He likes to read books about space and plans to be an astronaut.

Age: 6;7 years/Grade 1

Fountas & Pinnell Reading Level: E (beginning to middle of first-grade level)

Math Level: Above grade

Disability Classification: None

Intervention/Notes: Francis has a hard time identifying and sharing feelings; when he is upset, he sometimes says he is sick instead of communicating his feelings.

Ways to Support Francis

Engagement	Environment/Group Work No needs at this time	Social Skills/Communication No needs at this time
Input	Instructional Methods and Materials No needs at this time	Technology No needs at this time

(continued)

Francis's Snapshot *(continued)*

Ways to Support Francis *(continued)*

Output	Self-Management/Executive Functions	Test Accommodations
	Provide Francis support for identifying and acknowledging feelings.	No needs at this time

Support Schedule and Flexible Instructional Time (FIT) for Francis

	Monday	Tuesday	Wednesday	Thursday	Friday
1:30–2:30 FIT choices	Extended reading Social skill group Work with teacher Sensory room Yoga	Extended reading Social skill group Work with teacher Sensory room Yoga	Extended reading Social skill group Work with teacher Sensory room Yoga	Extended reading Social skill group Work with teacher Sensory room Yoga	Extended reading Social skill group Work with teacher Sensory room Yoga

Goals and Practices

Francis's Goals	Inclusive Practices
Francis will increase self-awareness about his feelings.	SR16. Support self-awareness of feelings using poster with 20–30 of the most common feelings.

Greg

lives with his mom, Joanna, and his dad, Jake. Joanna is pregnant and due in 4 months. Joanna is a nurse, and Jake is a graduate student. Greg is active and always moving—except when he is playing video games. His strengths are his knowledge of the television show *Doctor Who,* kids' video games, and his tablet. Sometimes Greg can roughhouse too much; peers are sometimes overwhelmed by him.

Age: 7;3 years/Grade 1

Fountas & Pinnell Reading Level: C (early first-grade level)

Math Level: At grade level

Disability Classification: None

Intervention/Notes: Greg goes to leveled literacy intervention (LLI) during the literacy block for small-group support because his reading is below grade level.

Ways to Support Greg

Engagement	**Environment/Group Work** Provide a variety of seating options that allow Greg to move without disturbing others.	**Social Skills/Communication** Help Greg ask peers and monitor their verbal and nonverbal responses before/during roughhousing at recess or at other times.
Input	**Instructional Methods and Materials** Coordinate supports for reading with the reading intervention specialist.	**Technology** No needs at this time
Output	**Self-Management/Executive Functions** No needs at this time	**Test Accommodations** No needs at this time

Support Schedule and Flexible Instructional Time (FIT) for Greg

	Monday	Tuesday	Wednesday	Thursday	Friday
8:30–9:00 During English language arts (ELA)	Literacy specialist (leveled literacy intervention [LLI]) in classroom	Literacy specialist (LLI) in classroom	Literacy specialist (LLI) in classroom	Literacy specialist (LLI) in classroom	Literacy specialist (LLI) in classroom
1:30–2:30 FIT choices	Extended reading Social skill group Work with teacher Reading support Sensory room	Extended reading Social skill group Work with teacher Reading support Sensory room	Extended reading Social skill group Work with teacher Reading support Sensory room	Extended reading Social skill group Work with teacher Reading support Sensory room	Extended reading Social skill group Work with teacher Reading support Sensory room

Goals and Practices

Greg's Goals	Inclusive Practices
Greg will move as needed to focus on his work.	ES13. Provide choices for seating and workstations (e.g., Vidget chairs, yoga balls, chair bands, standing desks, bean bags). SR2. Allow all students short walks down the hall. SR3. Allow all students breaks in or out of the classroom.
Greg will develop his reading skills to meet first-grade standards.	R2. Have students use picture cue cards, individually or with a partner. This skill can be worked on in small groups, with the question difficulty varied according to student need. R11. Create a variety of word study activities for whole-class use at different levels of understanding (e.g., portable word walls, guess the covered word, speed sorting, add an ending).
Greg will develop his ability to interpret peer cues about roughhousing.	SS6. Encourage active listening by routinely asking students to restate or summarize what has been said by peers.

Haley

lives with her parents, Leah and John, three sisters, and two brothers. Leah is a stay-at-home mom, and John has a construction company. Her sisters are twins Hope and Holly (age 2) and Hannah (age 4); her brothers are Henry (age 9) and Harlan (age 11). Haley's sister Hannah has mild cerebral palsy and uses a walker. Early intervention services are provided in the home several days a week, and Haley likes knowing how to help Hannah. Haley's family is involved in her church, and she sings in the children's choir. She likes acting in plays and telling stories, and she has been described by her parents as "wild and spontaneous." She has many friends in class and gets along with others readily.

Age: 7;1 years/Grade 1

Fountas & Pinnell Reading Level: E (beginning to middle of first-grade level)

Math Level: Below grade

Disability Classification: None

Intervention/Notes: Haley goes to the math intervention teacher twice each week for small-group support because her math is below grade level.

Ways to Support Haley

Engagement	**Environment/Group Work** No needs at this time	**Social Skills/Communication** No needs at this time
Input	**Instructional Methods and Materials** Collaborate with the math intervention specialist about supporting Haley's math skills.	**Technology** No needs at this time
Output	**Self-Management/Executive Functions** No needs at this time	**Test Accommodations** No needs at this time

Support Schedule and Flexible Instructional Time (FIT) for Haley

	Monday	**Tuesday**	**Wednesday**	**Thursday**	**Friday**
11:30–12:15 Math		Math specialist in classroom		Math specialist in classroom	
1:30–2:30 FIT choices	Work with teacher Math support Sensory room Yoga	Work with teacher Math support Sensory room Yoga	Work with teacher Math support Sensory room Yoga	Work with teacher Math support Sensory room Yoga	Work with teacher Math support Sensory room Yoga

Goals and Practices

Haley's Goals	Inclusive Practices
Haley will improve her math skills.	MS2. Offer multiple ways for all students to practice counting, facts, and so forth: sand tray for copying numbers, number magnets on cookie sheets, number line on the floor on which to step. MS5. Provide multiple sets of counters, plastic linking cubes, and fraction circles; have abacuses available so that all students can choose to use them.

Isaiah

lives with his parents, Janice and Colby, and his younger sister, Chloe (age 4). His dad is a pipefitter, and his mom stays home with Chloe. Isaiah likes football and cooking. He loves to cook with both parents and has taken a children's cooking class; he loves cooking shows.

Isaiah is mellow and happy and helps others readily. His calm temperament makes him a good buddy for peers who are anxious or easily stressed. He gravitates toward children who benefit from his calm demeanor.

Age: 6;8 years/Grade 1

Fountas & Pinnell Reading Level: E (beginning to middle of first-grade level)

Math Level: Slightly below grade

Disability Classification: None

Intervention/Notes: Isaiah does not need any particular supports at this time.

Ways to Support Isaiah

Engagement	**Environment/Group Work** Give Isaiah choices about groups often.	**Social Skills/Communication** No needs at this time
Input	**Instructional Methods and Materials** Provide support in math to assist Isaiah in reaching grade-level goals.	**Technology** No needs at this time
Output	**Self-Management/Executive Functions** No needs at this time	**Test Accommodations** No needs at this time

Support Schedule and Flexible Instructional Time (FIT) for Isaiah

	Monday	**Tuesday**	**Wednesday**	**Thursday**	**Friday**
10:00–10:30 During specials	Math specialist in classroom for consultation				
1:30–2:30 FIT choices	Work with teacher Math support Sensory room Yoga	Work with teacher Math support Sensory room Yoga	Work with teacher Math support Sensory room Yoga	Work with teacher Math support Sensory room Yoga	Work with teacher Math support Sensory room Yoga

Goals and Practices

Isaiah's Goals	Inclusive Practices
Isaiah will perform at grade level in math.	MS1. Incorporate counting into daily routines for the whole class, using small groups for review of basic counting principles with scaffolding. MS4. Offer graphic organizers and templates to all students. Stock them in common areas of the classroom, stored neatly in bins with the name and a piece glued to the front, and save them on the computers that students use for work.

Jack lives with his mom, Sarah, his dad, Chris, and his older brother, Jamie (a fourth-grader in this school). Jack is contemplative and has been described as a dreamer. He loves to draw cartoon figures and has a comic book collection. He can get lost in his drawings and sometimes ignores his work to draw cartoons. His conceptual ability is strong, especially for science concepts.

Age: 6;10 years/Grade 1

Fountas & Pinnell Reading Level: E (beginning to middle of first-grade level)

Math Level: At or slightly above grade

Disability Classification: None

Intervention/Notes: Jack benefits from structures that help him refocus on tasks during independent work times.

Ways to Support Jack

Engagement	Environment/Group Work	Social Skills/Communication
	No needs at this time	No needs at this time
Input	**Instructional Methods and Materials**	**Technology**
	No needs at this time	No needs at this time
Output	**Self-Management/Executive Functions**	**Test Accommodations**
	Practicing strategies such as first-then, using a small timer, or using a reminder band will help Jack complete his work during independent work times.	No needs at this time

Support Schedule and Flexible Instructional Time (FIT) for Jack

	Monday	Tuesday	Wednesday	Thursday	Friday
1:30–2:30 FIT choices	Extended reading	Extended reading	Extended reading	Extended reading	Extended reading
	Social skill group	Social skill group	Social skill group	Social skill group	Social skill group
	Work with teacher	Work with teacher	Work with teacher	Work with teacher	Work with teacher
	Reading support	Reading support	Reading support	Reading support	Reading support
	Math support	Math support	Math support	Math support	Math support
	Sensory room	Sensory room	Sensory room	Sensory room	Sensory room
	Yoga	Yoga	Yoga	Yoga	Yoga

Goals and Practices

Jack's Goals	Inclusive Practices
Jack will complete his work during the school day.	OS9. Provide a small 1-hour countdown timer for student's personal use.
	SR12. Provide vibrating wrist alarm to remind student to return to task. (See Resources for Inclusion list in Appendix B.)

Kody

lives with his parents, Linda and Paul, and his 8-year-old sister. Kody's mom is a nurse at a private medical practice, and Kody's father is an army officer who is currently deployed overseas.

Kody is quiet, serious, and introverted. He spends a lot of time by himself on the computer. He loves video games and computer technology. He helped his mom set up a Skype account to videochat with his father when possible.

Age: 6;5 years/Grade 1

Fountas & Pinnell Reading Level: F

Math Level: Above grade

Disability Classification: None

Intervention/Notes: Kody needs support connecting with peers and adults. He rarely speaks to others, even in small work groups with familiar friends.

Ways to Support Kody

Engagement	**Environment/Group Work**	**Social Skills/Communication**
	Have Kody work with a partner first, then build up to working with a group of three. Consider Rebecca or Natalie for a partner.	Ask Kody to help another student with math. Have Kody attend counseling group during lunch.
Input	**Instructional Methods and Materials**	**Technology**
	Provide instructional math games that require two students.	Provide instructional video games that require two students.
Output	**Self-Management/Executive Functions**	**Test Accommodations**
	Encourage Kody to choose at least one partner activity a day.	No needs at this time

Support Schedule and Flexible Instructional Time (FIT) for Kody

	Monday	Tuesday	Wednesday	Thursday	Friday
11:00–11:30 During lunch	Counselor in cafeteria		Counselor in cafeteria		Counselor in cafeteria
1:30–2:30 FIT choices	Extended reading Social skill group Work with teacher Yoga	Extended reading Social skill group Work with teacher Yoga	Extended reading Social skill group Work with teacher Yoga	Extended reading Social skill group Work with teacher Yoga	Extended reading Social skill group Work with teacher Yoga

Goals and Practices

Kody's Goals	Inclusive Practices
Kody will initiate conversations and activities with peers and adults.	SS3. Facilitate a peer lunch group. During lunch, there is one table for students to gather and play games that entails conversation and turn-taking. Some students have reserved spots. Any additional students may sign up to reserve remaining seats each day. SS11. Provide choices in working in pairs or small groups. SS14. Provide opportunities for students to help/tutor others in their areas of strength. SS15. Provide instructional games (e.g., board, card, video) that require at least two students.

Leela

lives with her parents, Abha and Kumar, her older brother, age 10, and her younger brother, age 2. Leela's mother is a chemist, and her father is a general surgeon. The family moved from India when Leela was an infant. Leela often shares details about their Hindu customs in class.

Leela is kind, friendly, and almost always smiling. She loves nature and the outdoors. She often chooses to watch out the class window with her binoculars during choice time. Her conceptual ability is strong, especially for science concepts.

Age: 6;5 years/Grade 1

Fountas & Pinnell Reading Level: C

Math Level: At grade level

Disability Classification: None

Intervention/Notes: Leela goes to LLI during the literacy block for small-group support because her reading is below grade level. She benefits from supports in phonics and decoding.

Ways to Support Leela

Engagement	**Environment/Group Work**	**Social Skills/Communication**
	No needs at this time	No needs at this time
Input	**Instructional Methods and Materials**	**Technology**
	Provide leveled reading books (C–F), especially about animals and zoos.	Provide online reading software programs.
Output	**Self-Management/Executive Functions**	**Test Accommodations**
	No needs at this time	Provide all tests at instructional reading level (C–F).

Support Schedule and Flexible Instructional Time (FIT) for Leela

	Monday	Tuesday	Wednesday	Thursday	Friday
8:30–9:00 During English language arts (ELA)	Literacy specialist (leveled literacy intervention [LLI]) in classroom	Literacy specialist (LLI) in classroom	Literacy specialist (LLI) in classroom	Literacy specialist (LLI) in classroom	Literacy specialist (LLI) in classroom
1:30–2:30 FIT choices	Extended reading Social skill group Work with teacher Reading support Sensory room	Extended reading Social skill group Work with teacher Reading support Sensory room	Extended reading Social skill group Work with teacher Reading support Sensory room	Extended reading Social skill group Work with teacher Reading support Sensory room	Extended reading Social skill group Work with teacher Reading support Sensory room

Goals and Practices

Leela's Goals	Inclusive Practices
Leela will increase reading level to D by October, E by March, and F by June.	R3. Have as many books as possible available on CD. Record yourself reading them if necessary. R6. Build peer reading buddies into daily literacy lesson activities. R9. Incorporate sight word work into station work, with individual lists of sight words available for all learners. R11. Create a variety of word study activities for whole-class use at different levels of understanding (e.g., portable word walls, guess the covered word, speed sorting, add an ending). R13. Ensure that abcmouse.com and Brainzy online reading games are among the apps and software programs installed on all computers and tablets in the classroom. TM5. For all assessments, ensure that the reading level matches student's independent reading level.

Megan

lives with her mother and father, her 9-year-old sister, and her 4-year-old brother. The family has two dogs and a cat. Megan's mother is a teacher, and her father is a chef at a local hotel.

Megan is very happy and giggly. She loves Harry Potter, magic, and riddles. She often brings sandwich bags of little items (e.g., buttons, marbles, pebbles) to school for her "potions" at the water table.

Age: 6;2 years/Grade 1

Fountas & Pinnell Reading Level: F

Math Level: Above grade

Disability Classification: None

Intervention/Notes: Megan often has difficulty keeping track of her belongings and following the morning and dismissal routines.

Ways to Support Megan

Engagement	Environment/Group Work No needs at this time	Social Skills/Communication No needs at this time
Input	Instructional Methods and Materials Provide leveled reading books about magic. Provide math puzzles.	Technology No needs at this time
Output	Self-Management/Executive Functions Provide luggage tags on backpack and cubby. Provide a desk map of items to be used for each lesson. Teach Megan a morning song and a dismissal song to sing to be sure she does each step—make it a "potion" of ingredients to match her interests.	Test Accommodations No needs at this time

Rapp, Arndt, and Hildenbrand

Support Schedule and Flexible Instructional Time (FIT) for Megan

	Monday	Tuesday	Wednesday	Thursday	Friday
1:30–2:30 FIT choices	Extended reading	Extended reading	Extended reading	Extended reading	Extended reading
	Social skill group	Social skill group	Social skill group	Social skill group	Social skill group
	Work with teacher	Work with teacher	Work with teacher	Work with teacher	Work with teacher
	Reading support	Reading support	Reading support	Reading support	Reading support
	Math support	Math support	Math support	Math support	Math support
	Sensory room	Sensory room	Sensory room	Sensory room	Sensory room
	Yoga	Yoga	Yoga	Yoga	Yoga

Goals and Practices

Megan's Goals	Inclusive Practices
Megan will engage in challenging literature and extended studies in math.	CR1. Provide culturally responsive curricular materials, materials that reflect student interests, and resources other than textbooks.
Megan will identify and utilize strategies to keep track of belongings.	OS2. Many students, including the target student, have luggage tags on their backpacks listing items to go home/come back to school. OS7. Tape a small drawing of the inside of the desk to the top of the desk, showing where books, notebooks, writing utensils, or other materials are stored. OS10. Create a coded classroom. Have all items and storage units in classroom labeled in first languages and braille, with photos.
Megan will identify and utilize strategies to follow morning and dismissal routines.	SR14. Teach a song to sing that lists all steps in a routine—customize it to student's interest.

Natalie

lives with her parents, Gloria and Anthony, her older brothers, ages 10 and 9, and her younger sister, age 3. Natalie's mother is a hairdresser, and her father is a recreation therapist at a nursing home.

Natalie is quiet and very inquisitive. She loves building sets and related toys such as LEGOs and K'nex. She is always willing to try new things, and she asks insightful questions.

Age: 6;11 years/Grade 1

Fountas & Pinnell Reading Level: F

Math Level: At grade level

Disability Classification: None

Intervention/Notes: Natalie does not need any particular supports at this time.

Ways to Support Natalie

Engagement	Environment/Group Work	Social Skills/Communication
	Provide opportunities to work in small groups. Natalie will often choose to work alone. She does not mind working in groups, but she will not seek it out.	No needs at this time
Input	**Instructional Methods and Materials** Provide hands-on materials and lessons. Provide leveled reading books about architecture and construction.	**Technology** No needs at this time
Output	**Self-Management/Executive Functions** Offer the choice to work with building sets, make collages, or construct models.	**Test Accommodations** No needs at this time

Support Schedule and Flexible Instructional Time (FIT) for Natalie

	Monday	Tuesday	Wednesday	Thursday	Friday
1:30–2:30 FIT choices	Extended reading Social skill group Work with teacher Sensory room Yoga	Extended reading Social skill group Work with teacher Sensory room Yoga	Extended reading Social skill group Work with teacher Sensory room Yoga	Extended reading Social skill group Work with teacher Sensory room Yoga	Extended reading Social skill group Work with teacher Sensory room Yoga

Goals and Practices

Natalie's Goals	Inclusive Practices
Natalie will initiate working in small groups.	SS9. Allow cooperative work to happen during all content areas with flexible grouping.

Oscar

lives with his mom, Gloria, his brothers, ages 9 and 7, and his sister, age 8. His mother is an insurance agent. The family speaks Spanish and English.

Oscar is very sweet and help-ful. He loves video games and watching television. He likes to play and talk about Transformers. He has a strong memory for details.

Age: 6;7 years/Grade 1

Fountas & Pinnell Reading Level: D

Math Level: At grade level

Disability Classification: None

Intervention/Notes: Oscar is considered an advanced or expanding ENL learner. Oscar benefits from supports in reading and building his independence from adults. He often clings to the teacher or follows close, especially in less structured choice time.

Rapp, Arndt, and Hildenbrand

Ways to Support Oscar

Engagement	**Environment/Group Work**	**Social Skills/Communication**
	Pair Oscar with a peer, then build up to a group of three. Assign roles for group work so Oscar has a clear part.	Provide sentence starters for approaching a peer to play, work together, and so forth.
	Provide a planner for choice time so a predictable structure/schedule for this independent time is available for everyone, particularly Oscar.	
	Provide culturally responsive materials.	
Input	**Instructional Methods and Materials**	**Technology**
	Provide leveled reading books.	Provide reading software and games.
	Provide opportunities for buddy reading.	Provide math software and games.
	Provide graphic organizers for writing and math.	
	Provide manipulatives.	
	Think aloud during instruction.	
	Teach academic language explicitly.	
Output	**Self-Management/Executive Functions**	**Test Accommodations**
	Provide choice time planning sheet.	Provide all tests at instructional reading level (D–E).

Support Schedule and Flexible Instructional Time (FIT) for Oscar

	Monday	Tuesday	Wednesday	Thursday	Friday
1:30–2:30 FIT choices	English as a new language (ENL)	ENL	ENL	ENL	ENL

Goals and Practices

Oscar's Goals	Inclusive Practices
Oscar will increase independence from teacher/adults.	SR13. Provide planning sheet for choice time—student writes name or number or places sticker on planning sheet to indicate which activities to do during choice time.
	SS7. Provide sentence starters for students to use when approaching teachers. Most students have key rings or bookmarks with reminders on them. Some students list advocacy sentence starters (e.g., "I need. . ." "I do better when. . .")
	SS10. Build in time each day for small-group work with peers, assigning individual roles within the group, to scaffold the interactions.
Oscar will increase reading level to E by October, F by March, and G by June.	R3. Have as many books as possible available on CD. Record yourself reading if necessary.
	R6. Build peer reading buddies into daily literacy lesson activities.
	R9. Incorporate sight word work into station work, with individual lists of sight words available for all learners.
	R11. Create a variety of word study activities for whole-class use at different levels of understanding (e.g., portable word walls, guess the covered word, speed sorting, add an ending).
	R13. Ensure that abcmouse.com and Brainzy online reading games are among the apps and software programs installed on all computers and tablets in the classroom.
	TM5. For all assessments, ensure that the reading level matches student's independent reading level.

(continued)

Goals and Practices *(continued)*

Oscar's Goals	Inclusive Practices
Oscar will continue to improve English as a new language (ENL) skills to proficient/commanding level.	CR1. Provide culturally responsive curricular materials, materials that reflect student interests, and resources other than textbooks.
	CR3. Allow for flexible grouping, to move in and out of cooperative learning.
	CR8. Incorporate meaningful sharing of background experiences and perspectives into lessons.
	ES7. Think aloud when writing, spelling, or punctuating on the board/during lessons.
	ES8. Provide all written materials in first languages.
	R8. Provide labels in classroom. Everything in the classroom is labeled with its name in multiple languages. Student's belongings have his/her photo on them.
	MS4. Offer graphic organizers and templates to all students. Stock them in common areas of the classroom, stored neatly in bins with the student's name and a piece of the template glued to the front, and save them on the computers that students use for work.
	MS5. Provide multiple sets of counters, plastic linking cubes, and fraction circles; have abacuses available so that all students can choose to use them.
	MS6. Provide computer/tablet time to use math software and apps (for example, Arthur's math games, Reader Rabbit math, Math Blaster, Kids Academy - 123 Tracing, Number Monster, Wee Kids Math, etc.).
	WS13. Use graphic organizers with the whole class, allowing for student choice. Scaffold the organizers to meet diverse learning needs (e.g., fewer items to fill in, some text provided, use of a word or sentence bank). Stock them in common areas of the classroom and save them on the computers that students use for work.

Padma

lives with her parents, Evelyn and Jay. Padma's mom stays at home, and her dad is a civil engineer.

Padma is outgoing and talkative. She loves everything spooky—witches, bats, mummies, and monsters. She often sneaks up on others and yells, "Boo!" She loves to tell scary stories, which sometimes upset her peers.

Age: 6;8 years/Grade 1

Fountas & Pinnell Reading Level: J

Math Level: Above grade

Disability Classification: None

Intervention/Notes: Padma is performing above grade level in all areas. She benefits from supports in understanding social cues and respecting others' personal space and preferences.

Rapp, Arndt, and Hildenbrand

Ways to Support Padma

Engagement	**Environment/Group Work** Assign roles for group work. Provide morning meeting time to share interests.	**Social Skills/Communication** Provide reminders/cues about personal space and others' interests. Have Padma attend lunch group with the counselor.
Input	**Instructional Methods and Materials** Provide reading materials at instructional/challenging level (J–L). Provide leveled reading books about scary things (e.g., the *Goosebumps* book series) Provide enriched math, science, and English language arts (ELA) instruction.	**Technology** No needs at this time
Output	**Self-Management/Executive Functions** Develop response scales for reading others' reactions to stories and invasion of personal space.	**Test Accommodations** Provide test materials at appropriate reading level (J–K).

Support Schedule and Flexible Instructional Time (FIT) for Padma

	Monday	**Tuesday**	**Wednesday**	**Thursday**	**Friday**
11:00–11:30 During lunch	Counselor in cafeteria		Counselor in cafeteria		Counselor in cafeteria
1:30–2:30 FIT choices	Accelerated instruction	Extended reading Social skill group Work with teacher Yoga	Accelerated instruction	Extended reading Social skill group Work with teacher Yoga	Accelerated instruction

Goals and Practices

Padma's Goals	Inclusive Practices
Padma will recognize others' reactions to conversation topic/personal space and adjust accordingly.	SR4. Ensure that all students are familiar with regulation scales, and many have them at their desks for self-checks. Padma's will support respect of others' personal space and interests during group discussions. SS3. Facilitate a peer lunch group. During lunch, there is one table for students to gather and play games that entails conversation and turn-taking. Some students have reserved spots. Any additional students may sign up to reserve remaining seats each day. SS10. Build in time each day for small-group work with peers, assigning individual roles within the group, to scaffold the interactions. SS13. Use verbal or nonverbal cues to cue the student to use response scale or adjust behavior.
Padma will engage in extended studies/enrichment in English language arts (ELA), math, and science.	CR1. Provide culturally responsive curricular materials, materials that reflect student interests, and resources other than textbooks.

Quinn

lives with his parents, Jacqueline and Carrie. Jacqueline is a high school principal, and Carrie is an ultrasound technician. The family fosters rescue cats and kittens and takes care of them until they have new homes.

Quinn is gentle, friendly, kind, and helpful. He loves dinosaurs and knows a lot about them and about archaeology.

Age: 6;7 years/Grade 1

Fountas & Pinnell Reading Level: E (beginning to middle of first-grade level)

Math Level: At grade level

Disability Classification: None

Intervention/Notes: Quinn is performing at grade level in all areas. He does not have any particular needs at this time.

Ways to Support Quinn

Engagement	Environment/Group Work	Social Skills/Communication
	Consider pairing Quinn with Steven sometimes. They are friends, and Quinn is very patient, which is a support for Steven.	No needs at this time
Input	Instructional Methods and Materials	Technology
	Provide leveled reading books about dinosaurs.	No needs at this time
Output	Self-Management/Executive Functions	Test Accommodations
	Provide a choice to draw for assignments and during choice time. Provide different art supplies.	No needs at this time

Support Schedule and Flexible Instructional Time (FIT) for Quinn

	Monday	Tuesday	Wednesday	Thursday	Friday
1:30–2:30 FIT choices	Extended reading Social skill group Work with teacher Sensory room Yoga	Extended reading Social skill group Work with teacher Sensory room Yoga	Extended reading Social skill group Work with teacher Sensory room Yoga	Extended reading Social skill group Work with teacher Sensory room Yoga	Extended reading Social skill group Work with teacher Sensory room Yoga

Goals and Practices

Quinn's Goals	Inclusive Practices
Quinn will continue to improve on grade level.	No additional needs at this time

Rapp, Arndt, and Hildenbrand

Rebecca

lives with her parents, Rhonda and Claude, and her older sister, age 8. Her mother is a police officer, and her father is a bank manager.

Rebecca is quiet, patient, and neat. She loves art and spends all of her choice time drawing, coloring, or painting.

Age: 6;10 years/Grade 1

Fountas & Pinnell Reading Level: H

Math Level: At grade level

Disability Classification: None

Intervention/Notes: Rebecca is performing at grade level in all areas. She does not have particular needs at this time.

Ways to Support Rebecca

Engagement	**Environment/Group Work** Consider pairing Rebecca with Steven sometimes. They are friends, and she is very patient, which will be a support for Steven.	**Social Skills/Communication** No needs at this time
Input	**Instructional Methods and Materials** No needs at this time	**Technology** No needs at this time
Output	**Self-Management/Executive Functions** Provide a choice to draw for assignments and during choice time. Provide different art supplies.	**Test Accommodations** No needs at this time

Support Schedule and Flexible Instructional Time (FIT) for Rebecca

	Monday	**Tuesday**	**Wednesday**	**Thursday**	**Friday**
1:30–2:30 FIT choices	Accelerated instruction	Extended reading Social skill group Work with teacher Sensory room Yoga	Accelerated instruction	Extended reading Social skill group Work with teacher Sensory room Yoga	Accelerated instruction

Goals and Practices

Rebecca's Goals	**Inclusive Practices**
Rebecca will continue to improve at grade level.	No additional supports needed

Steven

lives with his father, Darren, and his younger brother, age 3. Darren's father owns and operates a small sporting goods store. Steven's mother was diagnosed with cancer while pregnant with his younger brother. She was very ill while undergoing treatment for more than 2 years, then passed away 6 months ago. Steven's dad spends long hours at the store, so Steven and his brother spend a lot of time at both sets of grandparents' homes.

Steven is bouncy and loud, with unpredictable outbursts. He is a very talented artist and loves to draw, paint, and work with clay or anything else he can mold.

Age: 6;9 years/Grade 1

Fountas & Pinnell Reading Level: E (beginning to middle of first-grade level)

Math Level: At grade level

Disability Classification: IEP—emotional-behavioral disorder

Intervention/Notes: Steven does not always engage in academic activities in the classroom, doodling on the back of his papers instead. Steven needs support for his emotional awareness and regulation. He comes on very strong with peers; any frustration quickly escalates to verbal outbursts. He has thrown objects (not at anyone) on a couple of occasions, then curled up and cried.

Ways to Support Steven

Engagement	**Environment/Group Work** Provide opportunities to work in pairs, rather than small groups, at first. Consider Leela, Quinn, or Rebecca. Provide a "calming corner." Provide fidgets, clay, and playdough. Provide opportunities to draw. Conduct regular yoga/mindfulness exercises.	**Social Skills/Communication** Teach all students "I statements" and conflict resolution strategies.
Input	**Instructional Methods and Materials** No needs at this time	**Technology** No needs at this time
Output	**Self-Management/Executive Functions:** Provide response scale. Provide emotion charts. Provide color wheel cuing system. (See resources available on the Intervention Central web site at http://www.interventioncentral.org/classroom_management_color_wheel) Allow breaks and walk in the hall. Provide choice in response—drawing.	**Test Accommodations** No needs at this time

Support Schedule and Flexible Instructional Time (FIT) for Steven

	Monday	Tuesday	Wednesday	Thursday	Friday
10:00–10:30 During specials					Art therapist in art room
11:00–11:30 During lunch	Counselor in cafeteria		Counselor in cafeteria		Counselor in cafeteria

(continued)

Support Schedule and Flexible Instructional Time (FIT) for Steven (continued)

	Monday	Tuesday	Wednesday	Thursday	Friday
1:30–2:30 FIT choices	Primary project	Extended reading Social skill group Work with teacher Sensory room Yoga	Primary project	Extended reading Social skill group Work with teacher Sensory room Yoga	Primary project

Goals and Practices

Steven's Goals	Inclusive Practices
Steven will iden- tify emotions and events/situations that trigger them.	SR4. Ensure that all students are familiar with regulation scales, and many have them at their desks for self-checks. Steven's will support his emotional awareness and regulation.
Steven will identify and utilize strategies that deescalate frus- tration (e.g., fidgets, drawing, calming corner, soft seating, breaks, walks).	SR1. Allow all students to draw or doodle during lessons. SR2. Allow all students short walks down the hall. SR3. Allow all students breaks in or out of the classroom. SR5. Provide all students a choice of seating in the classroom. SR6. Teach yoga/mindfulness exercises to the whole class. SR7. Provide a "calming corner" for all students, equipped with soft seating, carpet, sen- sory tools, and so forth. Students may go to the corner as needed. SR8. Provide fidgets and mandalas to all students.

Taylor

lives with her parents, April and Leslie, and her twin sisters, age 2. April stays at home, and Leslie owns a contractor company.

Taylor is very funny and outgoing. She has a silly sense of humor, is very popular, and is always in the middle of a group of peers. She loves animals and zoos. She has a strong conceptual knowledge, particularly for science concepts.

Age: 7;1 years/Grade 1

Fountas & Pinnell Reading Level: D

Math Level: At grade level

Disability Classification: 504 plan (dysgraphia)

Intervention/Notes: Taylor goes to LLI during the literacy block for small-group support because she is reading below grade level. She needs support in reading and has significant difficulty using writing implements to form letters and numbers.

Ways to Support Taylor

Engagement	**Environment/Group Work** No needs at this time	**Social Skills/Communication** No needs at this time
Input	**Instructional Methods and Materials** Provide leveled reading books (D–G), especially about animals and zoos.	**Technology** Provide pencil grips. Use digital recorder for dictation. Provide dictation software and grammar-checking software. Provide online reading software programs.
Output	**Self-Management/Executive Functions** Provide access to handwriting options and materials. Offer large-format maze puzzles. Provide pencil grips and writing paper with large rule and raised lines.	**Test Accommodations** Provide scribe or dictation technology. Allow access to computer or keyboard, or point to answers. Provide all tests at independent reading level (D–E).

Support Schedule and Flexible Instructional Time (FIT) for Taylor

	Monday	Tuesday	Wednesday	Thursday	Friday
8:30–9:00 During English language arts (ELA)	Literacy specialist (leveled literacy intervention [LLI]) in classroom	Literacy specialist (LLI) in classroom	Literacy specialist (LLI) in classroom	Literacy specialist (LLI) in classroom	Literacy specialist (LLI) in classroom
1:30–2:30 FIT choices	Occupational therapy	Extended reading Social skill group Work with teacher Reading support Math support Sensory room Yoga	Occupational therapy	Extended reading Social skill group Work with teacher Reading support Math support Sensory room Yoga	Occupational therapy

Goals and Practices

Taylor's Goals	Inclusive Practices
Taylor will improve pencil grip and fine motor control used for handwriting.	WS1. Ensure that all students have access to computers and instructional technology for all writing tasks. WS2. Allow for use of paper with raised or wide lines or unlined paper. Stock supplies of each in common areas in the classroom. WS3. Allow for use of pencil grips; provide many choices in a basket in the classroom. WS4. Stock preheaded papers, with templates saved on computers. WS6. Allow for a choice of many different writing implements (e.g., pencils, pens, markers, chalk, gel pens). WS7. Provide access to tracing apps (Kids Academy—123 Tracing).

(continued)

Rapp, Arndt, and Hildenbrand

Taylor's Snapshot *(continued)*

Goals and Practices *(continued)*

Taylor's Goals	Inclusive Practices
Taylor will increase reading level to E by October, F by March, and G by June.	R3. Have as many books as possible available on CD. Record yourself reading if necessary. R6. Build peer reading buddies into daily literacy lesson activities. R9. Incorporate sight word work into station work, with individual lists of sight words available for all learners. R11. Create a variety of word study activities for whole-class use at different levels of understanding (e.g., portable word walls, guess the covered word, speed sorting, add an ending). R13. Ensure that abcmouse.com and Brainzy online reading games are among the apps and software programs installed on all computers and tablets in the classroom. TM5. For all assessments, ensure that the reading level matches student's independent reading level.

SUPPLEMENTAL DOCUMENTATION

As previously noted, four students in this class—Bridget, Charlie, Steven, and Taylor—have documented disabilities necessitating education plans. Charlie's 504 plan addressing his hearing impairment is provided in Figure 2.1 as an example. Take a few minutes to review this documentation to get a deeper sense of his strengths and challenges and the supports that help him succeed.

FIRST-GRADE READING LEVELS

Table 2.1 shows the typical Fountas & Pinnell reading levels for students entering first grade, the levels they typically reach as the school year progresses quarter by quarter, and the Lexile ranges for texts that are appropriate for students reading at that level.

Table 2.1. Reading-level goals for the year

Fountas & Pinnell	Lexile
Beginning of year: D/E	D: 80–450
	E: 80–450
First interval of year: F	F: 80–450
Second interval of year: H	H: 80–450
End of year: J	J: 451–500

Table 2.2 shows each student's Fountas & Pinnell reading level in the fall, along with the corresponding Lexile range for appropriate texts. For some lesson activities involving reading, Ms. Jackson uses this information to group her students and select or create related texts, differentiated by Lexile, that correspond to the reading level of students in each group.

Table 2.2. First-grade reading levels: Fall

Student	Fountas & Pinnell reading level – Fall of first grade	Lexile that aligns with the reading level
Avery	F	80–450
Bridget	E	80–450
Charlie	E	80–450
Devin	J	451–500
Evan	E	80–450
Francis	E	80–450
Greg	C	BR*–70
Haley	E	80–450
Isaiah	E	80–450
Jack	E	80–450
Kody	F	80–450
Leela	C	BR–70
Megan	F	80–450
Natalie	F	80–450
Oscar	D	80–450
Padma	J	451–500
Quinn	E	80–450
Rebecca	H	80–450
Steven	E	80–450
Taylor	D	80–450

*Beginning reader

Panorama Valley Central School District

SECTION 504 ACCOMMODATION PLAN

STUDENT INFORMATION

Student: Charlie Date of birth: February 21 Gender: Male Age: 6;8 years Grade: 1	Contacts: Eric, Father Steven, Father Native language: English Interpreter required: No	Review date: May of next year Plan start: September Plan end: June	Home school: Panorama Valley Recommended school: Panorama Valley Special alerts: Wears hearing aids in both ears (must stay dry)

MEETING INFORMATION

Meeting date: April of this year
Reason: Annual review
Participants: Kindergarten teacher, parents, teacher of the deaf (ToD), school psychologist
Comments: Charlie has a moderate to severe bilateral sensorineural hearing loss and wears hearing aids in both ears. He uses a digital amplifier that is evaluated, programmed, and maintained by the ToD. Kindergarten teacher reports that Charlie is sunny and outgoing. His speech, receptive language, and expressive language are typical for late kindergarten. His reading level is early to mid-kindergarten level (Fountas & Pinnell level E). He is performing on grade level in math. He initiates interactions with peers and knows to tap them on the shoulder to repeat themselves if he misses what they said while not facing him. He actively engages in all academic and free time activities. He enjoys sports, especially soccer.

INITIAL OR MOST RECENT EVALUATIONS/REPORTS

Date March of this year	Evaluation/report Audiological evaluation (see below)

STATE AND DISTRICTWIDE ASSESSMENTS

None

DETERMINATION

It has been determined that the student has a physical or mental impairment that substantially limits a major life activity.

Identify the physical or mental impairment:
Bilateral moderate to severe sensorineural hearing loss

Identify the major life activity affected by this physical or mental impairment:
Hearing

Describe how this impairment substantially limits a major life activity:
Charlie's hearing loss limits access to spoken instruction and incidental opportunities. He is at risk for missing/mishearing auditory information, particularly in noise and at increasing distances from the desired speaker.

PROGRAM ACCOMMODATIONS, MODIFICATIONS, AND SUPPORTS

	Description	Frequency	Duration	Location	Start date
Related services					
Audiological evaluation	Individual Annual audiological evaluation to assess unaided and aided hearing	Once a year	1 hour	Special location	September

1

(continued)

Figure 2.1. Charlie's 504 plan addressing his hearing impairment.

Figure 2.1.   *(continued)*

ToD	Individual/small group Integrated co-teaching with classroom teacher	Daily	30 minutes	Classroom	September
Supplementary aids and services/programs modifications/accommodations					
Preferential seating	Flexible seating near the teacher and away from sources of noise and distraction	Ongoing/daily	Throughout the school day	Classroom	September
Pair visual information with auditory information	Use visual reinforcements for everything in content work	Ongoing/daily	Throughout the school day	Classroom	September
Checks for understanding	Repeat peer comments and questions as needed	Ongoing/as needed	Ongoing as needed	Classroom	September
Assistive technology devices or services					
Hearing aids—provided by the parent	For use in all settings to assist with spoken language	Daily	Throughout the school day	School	September
Digital amplifier	For use by teachers and peers in all settings to assist with spoken language	Daily	Throughout the school day	School	September
Supports for school personnel on behalf of the student					
Audiology consultation	An audiological in-service needs to be held for teachers at the start of the year regarding Charlie's hearing loss and listening needs.	Once a year	1 hour	School	September

TESTING ACCOMMODATIONS

Individual testing accommodations in the administration of districtwide assessments of student achievement and, in accordance with department policy, state assessments of student achievement.

Testing accommodation	Conditions*	Implementation recommendations**
Location with minimal distractions	For all tests	Flexible setting with minimal distractions; may be in the classroom

*Conditions—test characteristics: Describe the type, length, and purpose of the test on which the use of testing accommodations is conditioned, if applicable.
**Implementation recommendations: Identify the amount of extended time, type of setting, and so forth specific to the testing accommodations, if applicable.

SAFETY NET ELIGIBILITY

The student is eligible for the 55–64 Passing Score Safety New and the Compensatory Option of the Safety Net.

2

FIRST-GRADE WEEKLY SCHEDULE

Figure 2.2 provides details about the daily and weekly first-grade class schedule for core subjects and specials as well as FIT. Noted in this schedule are days and times when some students see educational professionals who provide additional services they need (e.g., extra math assistance, counseling, LLI). Review students' individual profiles for additional details about how this schedule meets students' support needs.

Weekly schedule: First-grade related services professionals					
	Monday	Tuesday	Wednesday	Thursday	Friday
8:00–8:30 Arrival/morning meeting	Teacher of Deaf (ToD) (Charlie)		ToD (Charlie)		ToD (Charlie)
8:30–9:30 English language arts (ELA)	Leveled literacy intervention (LLI) (Greg, Leela, Taylor)	LLI (Greg, Leela, Taylor)	LLI (Greg, Leela, Taylor)	LLI (Greg, Leela, Taylor)	LLI (Greg, Leela, Taylor)
9:30–10:00 Social studies					
10:00–10:30 Special	Art Indirect math support with teacher (Isaiah)	Music	Art	Music	Art/art therapy (Steven)
10:30–11:00 Recess					
11:00–11:30 Lunch	Counselor (Kody, Padma, Steven)		Counselor (Kody, Padma, Steven)		Counselor (Kody, Padma, Steven)
11:30–12:15 Math		Math specialist (Evan, Haley, Isaiah)		Math specialist (Evan, Haley, Isaiah)	
12:15–1:00 Science					
1:00–1:30 Special	Physical education	Technology	Physical education	Technology	Physical education
1:30–2:30 Flexible instructional time (FIT)	See student profiles for individualized FIT support choices	See student profiles for individualized FIT support choices	See student profiles for individualized FIT support choices	See student profiles for individualized FIT support choices	See student profiles for individualized FIT support choices
2:30–3:00 Dismissal					

Figure 2.2. Weekly schedule: First-grade related services professionals.

LESSON PLANS

Ms. Jackson has been teaching for 21 years and teaching first grade for the last 7 years. She has certification in early childhood education with an annotation in emergent literacy. Ms. Jackson's professional development goals are to learn more about supporting students with neurologically based disabilities. This year, she has attended two workshops on the topic and has subscribed to an education blog. She has also been working closely with several specialists and related services providers to be sure all of her students are supported.

Following are eight lessons that Ms. Jackson and the specials teachers have chosen to highlight. The ELA lesson expands on the students' knowledge of opinion writing by having them write their opinion about a topic and support it with reasons. The math lesson introduces students to telling time to the hour on both analog and digital clocks. The science lesson introduces students to the way that people have mimicked nature, *biomimicry,* to create solutions to problems. The social studies lesson focuses on the classroom as a community where everyone can contribute to the community's needs, which provides a foundation for students to understand the roles of citizens in government. The art lesson ties into this by having students create individual works of art that contribute to a collective work. The physical education lesson reinforces students' movement and pattern skills by having them role play being cars in the gym, moving safely in certain ways (e.g., hopping, skipping). Students are using ta and ti-ti in music class to count quarter and half notes in their heads, on their bodies, and with clapping. Finally, the technology lesson focuses on using technology to complete an activity on active citizenship.

FIRST-GRADE LESSON: English Language Arts

Time allotted: **40 minutes**

Standards used: New York State Next Generation English Language Arts Learning Standards (New York State Education Department, 2015–2018) were used in this lesson.

Context: Students have worked on their reading and writing skills in ELA throughout the year. They have written narratives, poetry, and informative text. They write two to four sentences at a time and practice basic sentence conventions, such as using a beginning capital letter, including punctuation, and writing complete sentences that include a subject ("who") and a predicate ("what"). They practice checking their own work and peers' work to make sure it follows basic sentence conventions by using rubrics—typically checklists—to evaluate work. For example, the rubric might state "I can . . ." and then provide a list of specific items such as, "use a capital letter at the start of each sentence" or "put spaces between words." Students have recently been reading and discussing examples of opinion writing. Today, they will write their opinion about a topic and support it with reasons.

(Note: We talk about reading levels in ELA using Fountas & Pinnell, a reading system that many districts have adopted and use throughout the elementary grades. Fountas & Pinnell developed Guided Reading and a reading intervention program called LLI. Other districts use Scott Foresman's Reading Street and the same publisher's Reading Recovery, or they use the Developmental Reading Assessment or DRA (Pearson). It is not our intent to endorse a particular reading program in this book; we used Fountas & Pinnell because it is the program in use in the districts we visit often.)

Lesson Objectives

1. Write an opinion on a topic or personal experience; give two or more reasons to support that opinion. (1W1)

2. Recognize the distinguishing features of a sentence (e.g., first word, capitalization, ending punctuation). (1RF1a) (New York State Education Department, 2015–2018)

Before This Lesson

Advance Preparation

1. Share lesson vocabulary list: *opinion, reason.*

2. Prepare model text: *Our mascot is a tiger. I think that is a good mascot. I think tigers are beautiful and strong.*

3. Prepare multiple ways for students to draw and write. Several writing supports from the Inclusive Practices Bank are listed here (see more ideas in Appendix A). All students can gain access to any of these supports; Taylor and Oscar, in particular, will benefit from many of them.

4. Create and copy the What I Think graphic organizer worksheet shown in Figure 2.3. (See also the differentiated version in Figure 2.4.)

5. Create and copy the Writing Rubric shown in Figure 2.5.

INCLUSIVE PRACTICES

WS2. Allow for use of paper with raised or wide lines or unlined paper. Stock supplies of each in common areas in the classroom. This supports Taylor.

WS3. Allow for use of pencil grips—provide many choices in a basket in the classroom. This supports Taylor.

WS4. Stock preheaded papers, with templates saved on computers. This supports Taylor.

WS6. Allow for a choice of different writing implements (e.g., pencils, pens, markers, chalk, gel pens). This supports Taylor.

WS7. Provide access to tracing apps. This supports Taylor. (See the Resources for Inclusion list in Appendix B.)

WS13. Use graphic organizers with the whole class, allowing for student choice. Scaffold the organizers to meet diverse learning needs (e.g., fewer items to fill in, some text provided, use of a word or sentence bank). Stock them in common areas of the classroom and save them on the computers that students use for work. This supports Oscar.

ES8. Provide all written materials in first languages.

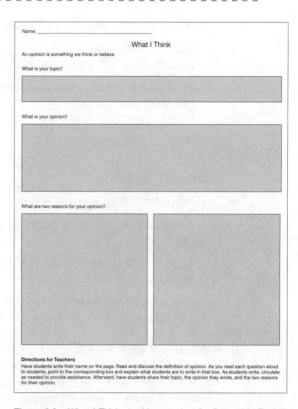

Figure 2.3. What I Think graphic organizer for first-grade English language arts (ELA) lesson.

Figure 2.4. Alternate What I Think graphic organizer for first-grade English language arts (ELA) lesson.

LESSON PLANS

Connections With Other Team Members

- Connect with speech-language pathologist (SLP); provide vocabulary and model text.

- Provide the SLP with lists of reading and vocabulary words each week.

- Connect with ENL teacher for translation into Spanish (to support Oscar).

Desired Results

"I Can" Statements

- I can state an opinion and two reasons for my opinion.

- I can write an opinion and two reasons for my opinion.

- I can use a capital letter for the first word, and I can use punctuation at the end of a sentence.

INCLUSIVE PRACTICES

These apply to all students and should not be differentiated. Regardless of the supports individual students receive, they are all working toward these goals and understandings.

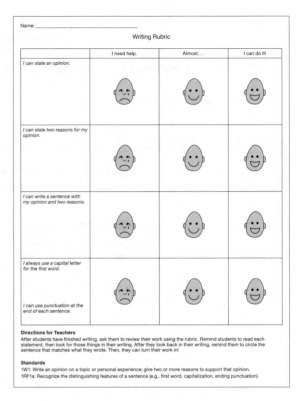

Figure 2.5. Writing Rubric for first-grade English language arts (ELA) lesson.

Assessment Evidence

Assessment evidence will consist of performance tasks, self-assessments, and other evidence that the students are mastering the identified goals and understandings. The following evidence will be used for this lesson:

- Student states opinion and two reasons in class discussion.

- Student completes writing sample using What I Think graphic organizer worksheet (differentiated)

- Student completes the Writing Rubric and shares it orally with a peer.

Classroom Arrangement

- Students will sit on the floor in the front of the room with the teacher for the first part of the lesson.

- Students will choose where to write for the independent writing task: at their desks, on a spot on the floor with a clipboard, at a standing desk, or at a computer station to type instead of handwrite.

- Students will return to the front of the room for the closure to share their writing with others.

INCLUSIVE PRACTICES

ES12. Provide a "move and learn" area of the room for all students where they can walk back and forth, jump, or jump rope. This supports Bridget.

ES13. Provide choices for seating and workstations (e.g., Vidget chairs, yoga balls, chair bands, standing desks, bean bags). This supports Greg.

SR5. Provide all students a choice of seating in the classroom. This supports Steven.

SR7. Provide a "calming corner" for all students equipped with soft seating, carpet, sensory tools, and so forth. Students may go to corner as needed. This supports Steven.

Materials

- What I Think graphic organizer worksheets (differentiated; see note in WS13 and the examples in Figures 2.3 and 2.4)

- Chart paper to model writing

- Whiteboards and markers

- Handwriting paper with rules in two widths

- Writing utensils—pencils, pencil grips

INCLUSIVE PRACTICES

WS13. Use graphic organizers with the whole class, allowing for student choice. Scaffold the organizers to meet diverse learning needs (e.g., fewer items to fill in, some text provided, use of a word or sentence bank). Stock them in common areas of the classroom and save them on the computers that students use for work. This supports Oscar.

    One option for this lesson is to use the top half of the page for opinion and the bottom half for two reasons. A second option is paper with prompts for "What I Think" followed by several lines for writing, followed by "My Reasons" with two to three numbered lines for writing. Other ideas for general graphic organizers are previously listed.

ES1. All teachers wear the amplifier during any direct instruction or giving of directions. This supports Charlie.

SR3. Ensure that all students are familiar with regulation scales, and many have them at their desks for self-checks. Some are for voice volume and emotional escalation; some for effective use of work time; some for interest or independence level for an activity. This supports Avery, Padma, and Steven.

SR8. Provide fidgets and mandalas to all students. This supports Steven.

Learning Activities

Allow for breaks, walks, and use of the "calming corner" during the lesson.

Anticipatory Set

Time: 5 minutes

1. Say: *An opinion is something we think or believe. We might have the same or different opinions. For example, I really like chocolate chip ice cream. Does anyone else like that too?* Ask for a show of hands. *Does anyone really not like that?* Ask for a show of hands.

2. Explain: *When we have opinions, we also have reasons why. For example, I really like chocolate chip ice cream because I like the chunks of candy and I like vanilla.*

INCLUSIVE PRACTICES

SR7. Provide a "calming corner" for all students equipped with soft seating, carpet, sensory tools, and so forth. Students may go to corner as needed.

Modeling

Time: 5 minutes
Model writing an opinion and two reasons with chart paper or on a projection screen or interactive board. For example, say and show the following writing:

Our mascot is a tiger. I think tigers are a good mascot because they are beautiful and strong.

 INCLUSIVE PRACTICES

ES4. Pair visual information with auditory information. Clearly write all the information that the teacher reviews orally or post it on the class web site—announcements, homework assignments, notes, and agenda. This supports Charlie.

Guided Practice

Time: 5 minutes

1. Say: *First, we are going to make a list of things we have opinions about. Then, when we have seven to eight topics, you are going to choose a topic and write your opinion and two reasons for your opinion. We will meet back here when we are done and hear some of our opinions and reasons.*

2. Generate a list (e.g., favorite foods, favorite sports, whether recess should be inside when it is cold, preferences for school mascot). Include perspectives about local events from all cultural backgrounds. For example, when reviewing current events, be sure to review media from mainstream news sources as well as minority group newsletters or newspapers. Ask students what events they attend with their families; support discussion and review of family events in general.

3. Ask students to raise their hand if they know what topic they would like to write about and want to share. Remind them they can choose a topic from the class list or another topic they have a strong opinion about.

4. Some students may want to share their opinion with the group; allow them to do so if time permits. Tell students that if they are having a hard time coming up with a topic, then they should raise their hand during writing time and you will come around to help them.

Independent Practice

Time: 15 minutes

1. Say: *Now it is time for you to write your opinion and reasons. As you do this, choose a place to do your best work. Choose the way you want to write. Here are your choices.* Provide students with differentiated graphic organizer choices as shown in Figures 2.3 and 2.4.

2. Provide multiple ways for students to think about their ideas and write their opinion and two reasons. For example:

   • Provide some students with organizers that include sentence starters inside the boxes, such as "I think. . ." and "I think this because. . ." Read the sentence starters aloud to students and help them orally generate ideas to complete the sentences. Then have students write or type their responses.

- Use questioning to prompt oral responses if students have difficulty formulating an opinion and supporting reasons. For example, ask a question such as *What is your favorite place to visit with your family?* to help the student generate an opinion. Ask a question such as *What do you like best about it?* to help the student generate supporting reasons. As needed, tailor questions to help students identify concrete details (e.g., *Are there special treats you make for your trips?*). Have students respond orally. Then have students write or type their responses.

INCLUSIVE PRACTICES

WS1–WS5. Taylor benefits from WS1–WS5 supports for writing (and others may choose these options):

- WS1. Ensure that all students have access to computers and instructional technology for all writing tasks.
- WS2. Allow for use of paper with raised or wide lines or unlined paper. Stock supplies of each in common areas in the classroom.
- WS3. Allow for use of pencil grips—provide many choices in a basket in the classroom.
- WS4. Stock preheaded papers with templates saved on computers.
- WS6. Allow for a choice of different writing implements (e.g., pencils, pens, markers, chalk, gel pens).

WS13. Use graphic organizers with the whole class, allowing for student choice. Scaffold the organizers to meet diverse learning needs (e.g., fewer items to fill in, some text provided, use of a word or sentence bank). Stock them in common areas of the classroom and save them on the computers that students use for work. This supports Oscar.

ES12. Provide a "move and learn" area of the room for all students where they can walk back and forth, jump, or jump rope. This supports Bridget.

LAE5. Use prompts and sentence starters. This supports Bridget.

SR12. Provide vibrating wrist alarm to remind student to return to task. This supports Jack. (See Resources for Inclusion list in Appendix B.)

Closure

Time: 10 minutes

1. Return to the carpet area. Spend 1–2 minutes reviewing opinions and reasons.

2. Say: *Now that you have had some time to write an opinion and two reasons, we will hear from. . . .* Call on individuals; choose how many (probably four to five) depending on time available.

3. After the first student shares his or her opinion and reasons, ask another student to restate what he or she heard. Ask Greg to restate at least once.

4. Say: *To end our time in writing, here is the Writing Rubric* [see Figure 2.5] *for today. Please fill it out, and then share your opinion with your elbow buddy.*

INCLUSIVE PRACTICES

SS6. Encourage active listening by routinely asking students to restate or summarize what has been said by peers. This supports Greg.

FIRST-GRADE LESSON: Mathematics

Time allotted: 45 minutes

Standards used: The CCSS for Mathematics were used for this lesson.

Context: This year, the students have completed units on adding and subtracting within 20, understanding place value, and learning to apply the concepts "greater than" and "less than" with two-digit numerals. They have recently begun a unit on using clocks to tell time. Today, they will learn how to tell and write time to the hour using analog and digital clocks.

Lesson Objective

Tell and write time in hours and half-hours using analog and digital clocks (Common Core State Standards Initiative, n.d.). (CCSS.Math.Content.1.MD.B.3)

Before This Lesson

Advance Preparation

1. Create analog and digital clock templates. Laminate one for each student. (See Figure 2.6 for an example of the analog template.)

2. Create hours and minute hands (one each per student). Label in English and Spanish. Laminate. (See Figure 2.6.)

3. Create puzzle pieces (one set per pair of students; see Figure 2.7). Label in English and Spanish and laminate.

4. Create icons and sight words for all vocabulary (e.g., analog, digital, time, clock, hour, minute).

Connections With Other Team Members

Consult with ENL teacher for accurate translation.

Figure 2.6. Analog clock template for first-grade math lesson.

Figure 2.7. Sample puzzle pieces for first-grade math lesson.

Desired Results

"I Can" Statements for Objective

- I can recognize that analog and digital clocks are objects that measure time.

- I can identify the hour hand and minute hand and distinguish between the two.

- I can identify analog and digital clocks.

- I can determine where the minute hand must be when the time is to the hour (o'clock).

- I can tell time to the hour using analog and digital clocks.

- I can write time to the hour using analog and digital clocks.

- I can correctly show time to the hour using an analog clock.

INCLUSIVE PRACTICES

These apply to all students and should not be differentiated. Regardless of the supports individual students receive, they are all working toward these goals and understandings.

Assessment Evidence

Assessment evidence will consist of performance tasks, self-assessments, and other evidence that the students are mastering the identified goals and understandings. The following evidence will be used for this lesson:

- Students will write numerical time from an analog clock.

- Students will draw hands on an analog clock to depict the time.

- Students will read digital and analog clocks.

- Students will match numerical (digital) and visual (analog) forms of times.

- Students will respond to exit ticket questions: Why do you need to tell time? Which clock do you like better (state an opinion and two reasons)?

- Students will work with a partner and collaborate to accurately represent a given time on an analog clock. (Teacher will observe this work and collaboration.)

Classroom Arrangement

- Desks are arranged in groups of three or four, facing the board.

- Students may work at desks, at a table, or on the floor.

- A "calming corner" and a "move and learn" area are provided to support students as needed.

 INCLUSIVE PRACTICES

ES12. Provide a "move and learn" area of the room for all students where they can walk back and forth, jump, or jump rope. This supports Bridget.

ES13. Provide choices for seating and workstations (e.g., Vidget chairs, yoga balls, chair bands, standing desks, bean bags). This supports Greg.

SR5. Provide all students a choice of seating in the classroom. This supports Steven.

SR7. Provide a "calming corner" for all students equipped with soft seating, carpet, sensory tools, and so forth. Students may go to the corner as needed. This supports Steven.

CR3. Allow for flexible grouping to move in and out of cooperative learning. This supports Oscar.

Materials

- Laminated analog (see Figure 2.6) and digital clock templates for each student

- Hour hands and minute hands, labeled and in different colors (see Figure 2.6)

- Matching puzzle pieces (one set per pair of students) (see Figure 2.7)

- Demonstration clocks

- Whiteboard/interactive whiteboard

- Whiteboard markers and erasers

- Amplifier

- Regulation scales

- Fidgets

 INCLUSIVE PRACTICES

MS4. Offer graphic organizers and templates to all students. Stock them in common areas of the classroom, stored neatly in bins with the student's name and a piece of the template glued to the front, and save them on the computers that students use for work. This supports Isaiah and Oscar.

ES1. All teachers wear the amplifier during any direct instruction or giving of directions. This supports Charlie.

ES3. During small-group activities, give amplifier to student to position in the group's discussion space. This supports Charlie.

SR3. Ensure that all students are familiar with regulation scales, and many have them at their desks for self-checks. Some are for voice volume and emotional escalation; some for effective use of work time; some for interest or independence level for an activity. This supports Avery, Padma, and Steven.

SR8. Provide fidgets and mandalas to all students. This supports Steven.

Learning Activities

Allow for breaks, walks, and use of the "calming corner" during the lesson.

Anticipatory Set

Time: 5 minutes

1. Ask: *Why do we need to be able to tell time? What are things we need to do at certain times? What happens when we can't tell time?*

2. Show visuals of a lot of different clocks. Ask: *What do you notice about these clocks? What if you could read this kind* [point to a digital clock] *but not this kind* [point to an analog clock]?

3. Provide icons with the sight words for each kind of clock.

INCLUSIVE PRACTICES

SR2. Allow all students short walks down the hall. This supports Greg and Steven.

SR7. Provide a "calming corner" for all students equipped with soft seating, carpet, sensory tools, and so forth. Students may go to the corner as needed. This supports Steven.

LAE1. Before group time, give the target student a question that can be answered with a new or familiar icon or vocabulary word. This supports Bridget.

R8. Provide labels in classroom. Everything in the classroom is labeled with its name in multiple languages. Student's belongings have his or her photo on them. This supports Oscar.

Modeling

Time: 10 minutes

1. Hold up a model of an analog clock. Review the names of the two hands on the clock, pointing and moving the hands as you talk.

2. Say: *Each has its own job. The hour hand keeps track of each hour that has passed, and the minute hand keeps track of the minutes that have passed until the next hour. The hour hand is shorter and slower. The minute hand is longer and faster. Why do you think that is?* Allow time for students to respond.

3. Explain: *Every time the minute hand goes all the way around, it counts 60 minutes, then 1 hour has passed, and the hour hand moves to the next number. For example, this clock shows four o'clock* [point]. *If I move the minute hand all the way around* [demonstrate], *the hour hand goes to the next number because 60 minutes have passed, so now it's five o'clock.*

4. Say: *Now suppose I move the minute hand all the way around again* [demonstrate]. *What number is the hour hand on now?* [Student response: Six.] *Where is the minute hand?* [Student response: It's on the number 12; it's at the top of the circle again; it's pointing straight up.] *What time is it?* [Student response: Six o'clock.] *That's right! How many minutes passed in between five o'clock and six o'clock?* [Student response: 60.]

5. Hold up a model of a digital clock. Say: *On a digital clock, the hour is first* [point], *then the minutes* [point]. *So, when it is four o'clock, what number would show for the hour?* [Student response: Four.] *Does anyone know what number would show for the minutes when it is* exactly *four o'clock?* [Some students may respond with the correct answer; explain as needed.] *When it is exactly four o'clock, the minutes show as two zeroes: 0-0. Then after 1 minute passes, it changes to 0-1, then 0-2 after another minute passes, and so forth.*

6. Ask: *How high do you think the minutes have to count up to before the hour changes?* [Students may respond 59; some may guess 60. Clarify as needed.] *Some of you said "60." Why?* [Student response: Because there are 60 minutes in an hour; because 60 minutes have to pass before the number for the hour changes.]

7. Say: *Your thinking makes sense, but the way the clock works is that the minute part goes all the way up to 59* [demonstrate]. *Then, after one more minute passes, it changes back to 0-0* [demonstrate]. *The hour changes too* [demonstrate] *because it's the start of a new hour.*

8. Ask who has a bedtime of 8:00. Show 8:00 on both clocks, writing and drawing it both ways on the board. Do the same for a bedtime of 9.00.

INCLUSIVE PRACTICES

ES7. Think aloud when writing, spelling, or punctuating on board/during lessons. This supports Oscar.

MS1. Incorporate counting into daily routines for the whole class, using small groups for review of basic counting principles with scaffolding. This supports Isaiah.

ES4. For all information that the teacher reviews orally, write the information clearly for all students or post it on the class web site (e.g., announcements, homework assignments, notes, agenda). This supports Charlie.

Guided Practice

Time: 10 minutes

1. Have students move into small groups.

2. Distribute laminated clocks (analog and digital), markers, minute hands, and hour hands.

3. Say: *I eat dinner at 6:00. Let's show 6:00 on the clock.*

4. Demonstrate on your display analog clock while students draw or place the hour and minute hands on their analog clocks.

5. Demonstrate showing the time on your display digital clock while students write the time on their digital clocks.

6. Do one more example together.

INCLUSIVE PRACTICES

SS9. Allow cooperative work to happen during all content areas with flexible grouping. This supports Avery, Devin, and Natalie.

MS4. Offer graphic organizers and templates to all students. Stock them in common areas of the classroom, stored neatly in bins with the student's name and a piece of the template glued to the front, and save them on the computers that students use for work. This supports Isaiah and Oscar.

ES4. For all information that the teacher reviews orally, write the information clearly for all students or post it on the class web site (e.g., announcements, homework assignments, notes, agenda). This supports Charlie.

Independent Practice

Time: 15 minutes

1. Use real-life examples from the class to give the students several more examples to try on their own. Check to be sure all are accurate.

   - Rebecca has art class at 4:00.

   - Taylor went to a movie at 6:00.

   - Oscar plays video games at 7:00.

   - Padma walks her dog at 8:00.

2. Once you have a chance to ensure everyone is mastering the skill, have students form pairs. Distribute puzzle pieces. There should be a set for each time to the hour.

3. Reinforce students' understanding of times by having pairs work to match puzzle pieces.

 INCLUSIVE PRACTICES

CR1. Provide culturally responsive curricular materials, materials that reflect student interests, and resources other than textbooks. This supports Megan, Oscar, and Padma.

CR8. Incorporate meaningful sharing of background experiences and perspectives into lessons. This supports Oscar.

LAR4. Allow students to work with a partner to take turns retelling details. This supports Bridget.

SS15. Provide instructional games (e.g., board, card, video) that require at least two students. This supports Kody.

Closure

Time: 5 minutes

1. Each student tells what time he or she eats dinner, goes to bed, and so forth and shows it on his or her clock.

2. When asked about their daily routines, some students may respond with times that are not on the hour, such as 7:30. They may or may not know how to show these times on their clocks.

3. Explain: *A time such as 7:30 is tricky because it is after seven o'clock but before eight o'clock. Next time we have math class, we will talk about how clocks show those in-between times. For now, show me where seven o'clock is on your clock.*

FIRST-GRADE LESSON: Science

Time allotted: 45 minutes

Standards used: NGSS[1] were used for this lesson.

Science lessons are often developed using the 5-E model, so terms from this model are added to this plan. The terms *engage, explore, explain, elaborate,* and *evaluate* are incorporated to show how the 5-E format could be adapted for this lesson format.

---

[1]NGSS Lead States. (2013). *Next Generation Science Standards: For states, by states.* Washington, DC: National Academies Press.

NGSS is a registered trademark of Achieve. Neither Achieve nor the lead states and partners that developed the NGSS were involved in the production of this product and do not endorse it.

Context: This 45-minute lesson is part of a unit on biomimicry. This unit can take five to eight lessons, and students are introduced to the way that people have mimicked nature—biomimicry—to create solutions to human problems. This unit meets NGSS 1-LS1-1.

This is the first lesson in the unit. In future lessons, students will explore other examples of ideas from nature and inventions for people; be introduced to vocabulary, including the words *mimic* and *biomimicry;* and use inspiration from nature to create their own invention.

Lesson Objective

From Molecules to Organisms: Structures and Processes. Use materials to design a solution to a human problem by mimicking how plants or animals use their external parts to help them survive, grow, and meet their needs (NGSS, 2013). (1-LS1-1)

CCSS connections: ELA/literacy

With prompting and support, read informational texts appropriately complex for grade. (1-LS1-2; RI.1.10)

CCSS connections: Mathematics

Use appropriate tools strategically. (1-LS3-1; MP.5)

(Note: NGSS are aligned to CCSS in the DCI [Disciplinary Core Idea] Arrangements of the NGSS document in November 2013, and those alignments to ELA-literacy and mathematics are previously shown.)

Before This Lesson

Advance Preparation

1. Gather images of various trees with canopies and various umbrellas. Create a slideshow of 8–10 images.

2. Review the resources available at https://biomimicry.org/biomimicry-examples or other examples of biomimicry available online. Identify any additional examples of biomimicry you would like to share with your class.

3. Prepare copies of the Ideas From Nature graphic organizer shown in Figure 2.8 (one for each student). Prepare copies of the exit ticket (I Can self-assessment) shown in Figure 2.9 (one for each student).

Connections With Other Team Members

No special connections with other team members are needed.

Desired Results

"I Can" Statements

- I can show a picture of a plant or animal that made me think of a way to solve a problem.

- I can explain an invention that solves a problem for people.

- I can explain how the invention is like the plant or animal.

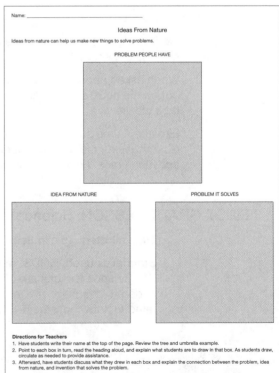

Figure 2.8. Ideas From Nature graphic organizer for first-grade science lesson.

LESSON PLANS

INCLUSIVE PRACTICES

These apply to all students and should not be differentiated. Regardless of the supports individual students receive, they are all working toward these goals and understandings.

Assessment Evidence

Assessment evidence will consist of performance tasks, self-assessments, and other evidence that the students are mastering the identified goals and understandings. The following evidence will be used for this lesson:

- Students work alone or with a partner first and then work in groups of three. Teacher observes the work session.

- Student draws an invention.

- Student provides a verbal explanation of the invention that includes an idea from nature and a product for people.

- Student completes the I Can self-assessment for biomimicry as an exit ticket.

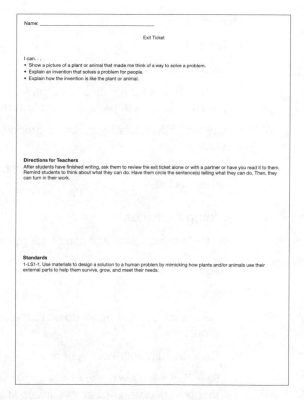

Figure 2.9. Exit ticket (I Can self-assessment) for first-grade science lesson.

Classroom Arrangement

- Students will sit in on the floor in the front of the room with the teacher for the first part of the lesson.

- Students will choose where to think, draw, and write for the guided practice: at their desks, on a spot on the floor with a clipboard, at a standing desk, or at a computer station to type instead of handwrite.

- Students will return to the front of the room for the closure to share their inventions with others.

- A "calming corner" and a "move and learn" area are provided throughout the lesson to support students as needed, and students have their choice of seating.

INCLUSIVE PRACTICES

ES12. Provide a "move and learn" area of the room for all students where they can walk back and forth, jump, or jump rope. This supports Bridget.

ES13. Provide choices for seating and workstations (e.g., Vidget chairs, yoga balls, chair bands, standing desks, bean bags). This supports Greg.

SR5. Provide all students a choice of seating in the classroom. This supports Steven.

SR7. Provide a "calming corner" for all students equipped with soft seating, carpet, sensory tools, and so forth. Students may go to corner as needed. This supports Steven.

LESSON PLANS

Materials

- Umbrella

- Slideshow of pictures (see following)

- Picture books from natural settings (e.g., jungle, fields, forests); have enough available for students to work in pairs with two to three books per pair

- Copies of the Ideas From Nature graphic organizer shown in Figure 2.8 (one for each student)

- Copies of the I Can self-assessment shown in Figure 2.9 (one for each student to use as an exit ticket)

Learning Activities

Allow for breaks, walks, and use of the "calming corner" during the lesson.

Engage

Time: 5 minutes

1. Have each student either come to the central area on the carpet or sit in a chair with the group.

2. Open the umbrella over your head.

3. Say: *Today we are going to talk about how things in nature can help us make inventions that help people. Look at this umbrella and think about the world outside and nature. What does this umbrella remind you of?* Record responses.

4. Say: *It reminds me of a tree—the branches protect the ground underneath from getting wet when it rains. When I hold the umbrella up, the handle of the umbrella is like a tree trunk, and the umbrella is like the branches and leaves of a tree. Standing under a tree with many leaves can keep us dry when it is raining. Why is that?* [Student response: Because the leaves stop the rain from coming down to the ground.] Explain: *Someone looked up at the tree branches and leaves when it was raining and had an idea! What if they created a way to stay dry in the rain and walk around? That is how the umbrella was made!*

5. Say: *Let's look at the umbrella again. Do you see how the top of the umbrella is like the branches and leaves of a tree?* Discuss. If necessary, draw students' attention to the similarity in shape. Ask: *Would we get wet or stay dry if it was raining and we stood under the umbrella?* [Student response: Stay dry.]

INCLUSIVE PRACTICES

SR2. Allow all students short walks down the hall. This supports Greg and Steven.

SR7. Provide a "calming corner" for all students equipped with soft seating, carpet, sensory tools, and so forth. Students may go to corner as needed. This supports Steven.

LAE1. Give target student a question before group time that can be answered with a new or familiar icon or vocabulary word. This supports Bridget.

Explore

Time: 20 minutes

1. Display the slideshow with images of trees and umbrellas that you created. Have students point out what the different trees and umbrellas have in common. [Student response: Each has a canopy overhead.]

2. Say: *Your task is to use these picture books and think about something in nature that might lead to a way to help people. You will draw or create two pictures and explain your drawing. You may work alone or with a friend.*

3. Explain: *The assessment we use for this lesson is self-assessment.* Display the self-assessment and review the statements with students: *I can . . .*

- Show a picture of a plant or animal that made me think of a way to solve a problem.
- Explain an invention that solves a problem for people.
- Explain how the invention is like the plant or animal.

INCLUSIVE PRACTICES

SS9. Allow cooperative work to happen during all content areas with flexible grouping. This supports Avery, Devin, and Natalie.

LAR4. Allow students to work with a partner to take turns retelling details. This supports Bridget.

MS4. Offer graphic organizers and templates to all students. Stock them in common areas of the classroom, stored neatly in bins with the student's name and a piece of the template glued to the front, and save them on the computers that students use for work. This supports Isaiah and Oscar.

Explain

Time: 5 minutes

1. Ask students to return to group space and share pictures. Offer opportunity for several students to show the picture they chose.

2. Ask peers who are listening to restate explanations.

INCLUSIVE PRACTICES

SS6. Encourage active listening by routinely asking students to restate or summarize what has been said by peers. This supports Greg.

Elaborate

Time: 10 minutes

1. Say: *Now that we have seen these inventions, let's add more details.*

2. Divide the class into small groups of three. Say: *For each group, one person will write the group's ideas, and two people will draw pictures.*

INCLUSIVE PRACTICES

SS10. Build in time each day for small-group work with peers, assigning individual roles within the group, to scaffold the interactions. This supports Avery, Devin, Oscar, and Padma.

Evaluate

Time: 5 minutes

1. Give groups of students the I Can self-assessment as an exit ticket.

2. Circulate as they complete the self-assessment. Review the criteria with them, as needed. Say: *Now that science is almost over, it is time for you to think about what you*

can do. Look at your exit ticket. You can read it to yourself, with a partner, or I will read it to you. Think about the following questions for each "I can" sentence: Can you do it when someone helps? Can you do it sometimes? Can you do it every time? You decide, and show which sentence fits what you can do by circling or marking the sentence that matches what you can do.

INCLUSIVE PRACTICES

SS9. Build in time each day for small group work with peers, assigning individual roles within the group, to scaffold the interactions. This supports Avery, Devin, Oscar, and Padma.

FIRST-GRADE LESSON: Social Studies

Time allotted: 40 minutes

Standards used: The Ohio State Social Studies Standards were used for this lesson.

Context: The standards are organized using the components of strands, themes, topics, and content statements. This lesson focuses on the history strand. The theme is Families Now and Long Ago, Near and Far. As noted in the Ohio standards,

> The first-grade year builds on the concepts developed in kindergarten by focusing on the individual as a member of a family. Students begin to understand how families lived long ago and how they live in other cultures. They develop concepts about how the world is organized spatially through beginning map skills. They build the foundation for understanding principles of government and their roles as citizens. (Ohio Department of Education, 2010, p. 9)

The topic of this lesson is heritage and addresses human needs. This topic could typically be covered by discussing families and the different ways that family members contribute to meet the family's needs. To be culturally responsive to the needs of students affected by trauma due to unstable, unpredictable family structures, we focus on the classroom community as a family that all of the students have in common, building a sense of belonging and self-efficacy.

Lesson Objective

Students will understand the following topic and content standard.

Theme: Families Now and Long Ago

Strand: History

Topic: Heritage

Content statement: 3. The way basic human needs are met has changed over time (Ohio Department of Education, 2010, p. 13).

Before This Lesson

Advance Preparation

1. Create bulletin boards and titles in English and Spanish.

2. Create templates for drawing and captioning classroom needs and contributions (see Figures 2.10a and 2.10b). Label chart paper lists in English and Spanish.

Connections With Other Team Members

Consult with the ENL teacher.

Desired Results

"I Can" Statements

- I can describe my classroom community.

- I can name something that students in a class-room need.

- I can name something I do to help the classroom community.

INCLUSIVE PRACTICES

These apply to all students and should not be differen-tiated. Regardless of the supports individual students receive, they are all working toward these goals and understandings.

Assessment Evidence

Assessment evidence will consist of performance tasks, self-assessments, and other evidence that the students are mastering the identified goals and understandings. The following evidence will be used for this lesson:

- Students will list examples of classroom commu-nity needs.

- Students will draw and caption a picture of a classroom need.

- Students will draw and caption a picture of them-selves helping in the classroom.

- Students will share their work and respond to these two prompts:

   1. What is a community?

   2. How can you help your community?

- The teacher will observe students' work as they write, draw, and share.

Classroom Arrangement

- Desks are arranged in groups of three or four.

- Students may choose to work at tables or on the floor.

Figure 2.10a. "I Can Help!" drawing template for first-grade social studies lesson.

Figure 2.10b. "I Can Help!" drawing template for first-grade social studies lesson, Spanish version.

- A bulletin board prepared with the main heading, "Our Community" and the subheadings, "What Our Community Needs" and "Ways I Help Our Community."

- A "calming corner" and a "move and learn" area are provided throughout the lesson to support students as needed, and students have their choice of seating.

 INCLUSIVE PRACTICES

ES12. Provide a "move and learn" area of the room for all students where they can walk back and forth, jump, or jump rope. This supports Bridget.

ES13. Provide choices for seating and workstations (e.g., Vidget chairs, yoga balls, chair bands, standing desks, bean bags). This supports Greg.

SR5. Provide all students a choice of seating in the classroom.

SR7. Provide a "calming corner" for all students equipped with soft seating, carpet, sensory tools, and so forth. Students may go to the corner as needed. This supports Steven.

CR3. Allow for flexible grouping to move in and out of cooperative learning. This supports Oscar.

Materials

- Writing paper (lined and raised line)
- Drawing paper (unlined)
- Templates for pictures and captions
- Markers, crayons, colored pencils
- Pencil grips
- Chart paper and markers
- Amplifier
- Timers
- Regulation scales
- Fidgets

 INCLUSIVE PRACTICES

ES1. All teachers wear the amplifier during any direct instruction or giving of directions.

ES3. During small-group activities, give amplifier to student to position in the group's discussion space. These support Charlie.

WS2. Allow for use of paper with raised or wide lines or unlined paper. Stock supplies of each in common areas in the classroom.

WS3. Allow for use of pencil grips—provide many choices in a basket in the classroom.

WS6. Allow for a choice of different writing implements (e.g., pencils, pens, markers, chalk, gel pens). These support Taylor.

SR4. Ensure that all students are familiar with regulation scales, and many have them at their desks for self-checks. Some are for voice volume and emotional escalation; some for effective use of work time; some for interest or independence level for an activity. This supports Avery, Padma, and Steven.

SR8. Provide fidgets and mandalas to all students. This supports Steven.

CR1. Provide culturally responsive curricular materials, materials that reflect student interest, and resources other than textbooks. This supports Megan, Oscar, and Padma.

CR8. Incorporate meaningful sharing of background experiences and perspectives into lessons. This supports Oscar.

Learning Activities

Allow for breaks, walks, and use of the "calming corner" during the lesson.

Anticipatory Set

Time: 5 minutes

1. Say: *Take a minute to look around at all your classmates. What is something you all have in common, something that is the same about all of you?* [Students' responses will vary. Emphasize the responses about being in first grade, going to the same school, and learning and playing together.]

2. Explain: *All of these things that we have in common make us a community.* Point to and read the bulletin board heading, "Our Community."

3. Say: *Today, I am going to need your help to fill up this bulletin board with special things about our community.*

INCLUSIVE PRACTICES

SR2. Allow all students short walks down the hall. This supports Greg and Steven.

Modeling/Guided Practice

Time: 15 minutes

1. Label a sheet of chart paper on the easel with the heading "What we like about our community."

2. Say: *We are going to make a list of what our classroom community needs to be a place where we feel safe and can learn. I am going to start with "good friends." What else should we list here?*

3. Student responses will vary. If no one mentions academics, then model with another example such as, "lots of books to read."

4. Once there are several suggestions on the list, say: *These are all things our classroom community needs.*

5. Start a new sheet of chart paper with the heading, "What I can do to help our community." Say: *Let's think of things each of us can do to help our community to make sure we have these things.*

6. Read through the first list and ask guiding questions to create a list of ways to help the community. For example:

   • We can take good care of the books or put them back when we are done to make sure there are a lot of nice books to read.

   • We can clean up after ourselves to make sure our classroom is neat and safe.

   • We can use kind words to make sure we are good friends.

INCLUSIVE PRACTICES

CR1. Provide culturally responsive curricular materials, materials that reflect student interest, and resources other than textbooks. This supports Megan, Oscar, and Padma.

SR1. Allow all students to draw or doodle during lessons. This supports Steven.

CR8. Incorporate meaningful sharing of background experiences and perspectives into lessons. This supports Oscar.

R8. Provide labels in classroom. Everything in the classroom is labeled with its name in multiple languages. Student's belongings have his or her photo on them. This supports Oscar.

ES8. Provide all written materials in first languages. This supports Oscar.

Independent Practice

Time: 15 minutes

1. Say: *Now it's time to fill up our bulletin board with our ideas and drawings. Each of us is going to make two drawings. One drawing will show something our classroom community needs, and the second drawing will show us helping our community.* Show own drawing.

2. Explain: *I drew a picture of lots of books in their bins in the class library. I wrote, "I can help our community by taking care of the books in the classroom" at the bottom.*

3. Review all of the materials available for creating drawings and captions (e.g., templates, lined and unlined papers, writing tools).

4. As students work, refer to lists on chart paper if they need ideas.

 INCLUSIVE PRACTICES

OS9. Provide a small 1-hour countdown timer for student's personal use. This supports Jack.

LAE5. Use prompts and sentence starters. This supports Bridget.

Closure

Time: 10 minutes

1. After students complete drawings and captions, have them share their work, prompting them with two questions:

    -   What is a community?

    -   What can you do to help our community?

2. Post each student's work on the bulletin board.

FIRST-GRADE LESSON: Art

Time allotted: 30 minutes

Standards used: The National Core Arts Standards for Visual Arts (NCAS-VA) from the National Coalition for Core Arts Standards (NCCAS) were used to identify standards, essential questions, and enduring understandings for this lesson.

Context: The arts curriculum covers five areas: creating; performing, presenting, and producing; responding; and connecting. Students in prekindergarten (pre-K) through sixth grade build their knowledge and skills in these areas over several years as they learn new techniques, present their original work in different ways, and delve deeper into the historical and cultural facets of art. In this lesson, students are creating original works of art while they investigate the concepts of symmetry and contributing to a collective art project.

Lesson Objectives

1. Generate and conceptualize artistic ideas and work. (NCAS-VA Anchor Standard 1)

2. Engage collaboratively in exploration and imaginative play with materials. (Cr.1.1.1a)

Before This Lesson

Advance Preparation

1. Prepare several different flower templates (see Figure 2.11). Cut out several copies of each so students can choose which one they like.

2. Create multiple projects at various stages for modeling (see Figures 2.12 and 2.13).

Connections With Other Team Members

Check in with the art teacher a day or two before the scheduled art lesson to discuss what supports students might need for specific activities. For this lesson, the art teacher will wear the digital amplifier for Charlie. Taylor and others will need pencil grips and a choice of drawing implements so they can easily color in the flower template. Steven's table will be covered with butcher paper so he can doodle as needed.

As with other specials, art is taught by a specialist; in this case, a certified art teacher.

Figure 2.11. Flower template for first-grade art lesson. Choosing a template is the first stage of creating the individual flower.

Figure 2.12. Individual flower, second stage, first-grade art lesson.

Figure 2.13. Individual flower, third stage, first-grade art lesson.

Figure 2.14. Collective art made up of individual flowers for first-grade art lesson.

Desired Results

"I Can" Statements

- I can create my own artwork.

- I can tell you that each person's artwork can be part of a collective art project.

INCLUSIVE PRACTICES

These apply to all students and should not be differentiated. Regardless of the supports individual students receive, they are all working toward these goals and understandings.

Assessment Evidence

Assessment evidence will consist of performance tasks, self-assessments, and other evidence that the students are mastering the identified goals and understandings. The following evidence will be used for this lesson:

- Students will create a paper flower (e.g., cut, color, paint, glue) using a template of their choosing, a wooden dowel, glue, and a foam block.

- Students will discuss the value of multiple artists contributing to a collective work.

- Students will contribute to a background mural.

- As students work individually and collaboratively, the teacher will observe their work. The teacher will ask questions about their choices in artwork.

- Students will contribute to the closing discussion by answering questions about material and design choice.

Classroom Arrangement

- Students work in groups of two to three at art tables, with choice of seat.

- Kits of art supplies are provided at each art table.

- Flower garden display is set up on side table. Foam blocks in varied sizes are provided on the table. Space for creating a background mural is available on the wall behind the table.

INCLUSIVE PRACTICES

CR3. Allow for flexible grouping to move in and out of cooperative learning. This supports Oscar.

SR5. All students have choice of seating in the classroom. This supports Steven.

Materials

- Clear sheets of paper (one per student)

- Three to four different flower templates (enough so each student has choice of design). See an example in Figure 2.11.

- Kits of supplies; each kit includes the following items: scissors; markers, crayons, colored pencils, and paints; pencil grips; paintbrushes; paper squares; glue/tape; thin wooden dowels/skewers

- Foam blocks

- Butcher paper

- Amplifier

- Regulation scales

- Fidgets

INCLUSIVE PRACTICES

ES1. All teachers wear the amplifier during any direct instruction or giving of directions. This supports Charlie.

ES3. During small-group activities, give amplifier to student to position in the group's discussion space. This supports Charlie.

WS3. Allow for use of pencil grips—provide many choices in a basket in the classroom. This supports Taylor.

WS6. Allow for a choice of different writing implements (e.g., pencils, pens, markers, chalk, gel pens). This supports Taylor.

SR3. Allow all students breaks in or out of the classroom. This supports Avery, Padma, and Steven.

SR8. Provide fidgets and mandalas to all students. This supports Steven.

Learning Activities

Allow for breaks, walks, and use of the "calming corner" during the lesson.

Anticipatory Set

Time: 10 minutes

1. Show your own created flower, an individual work of art (see Figure 2.13). Then show it as part of a collective work (see Figure 2.14).

2. Say: *First we looked at my flower, then we looked at my flower together with a bunch of other flowers that other people made.*

3. Ask: *What did you think of my flower all by itself?* [Students' responses will vary.] Then ask: *What did you think of how all the different flowers looked together?* [Students' responses will vary. Students may respond: "Yours looked different when it was with all the other ones," "It was neat seeing so many different kinds of flowers together," "I wanted to look at them together and then one by one."]

4. Explain: *I made one flower. That was my own individual art project. But I didn't make all of the flowers. Everyone made a flower and then we put them together.*

5. Say: *An art project in which everyone does one little part is called a collective art project. Our class is going to make a collective project today. Everyone will make an individual flower, and then we will put them together to make a collective flower garden.*

Modeling

Time: 5 minutes

1. Explain each step you took in making your flower, thinking aloud as you show the product at each stage.

    *   Select a flower template.

    *   Go over all the different materials available for designing the flower—markers, colored pencils, tissue paper for collage, and so forth.

    *   Explain how you chose to color the middle with marker, paint three petals (see Figure 2.12) and collage three petals, alternately but all in purple, to depict a purple daisy with varying texture (see Figure 2.13).

    *   Attach skewer with glue or tape.

2. Ask students for other ideas so each flower is unique.

INCLUSIVE PRACTICES

ES7. Think aloud when writing, spelling, or punctuating on board/during lessons. This supports Oscar.

SR7. Provide a "calming corner" for all students equipped with soft seating, carpet, sensory tools, and so forth. Students may go to the corner as needed.

Guided to Independent Practice

Time: 10 minutes

1. Circulate to help and ask questions about material/design choices while students create their own flowers.

2. Have students place finished products in foam.

3. Ask: *What does our garden need? A background!*

Independent Practice

Time: 5 minutes

1. Lay out long sheets of butcher paper for mural.

2. Have students collaboratively draw grass, bugs, trees, and so forth all over the butcher paper.

3. Post the mural behind the displayed flowers.

 INCLUSIVE PRACTICES

SS9. Allow cooperative work to happen during all content areas with flexible grouping. This supports Avery, Devin, and Natalie.

CR3. Allow for flexible grouping to move in and out of cooperative learning. This supports Oscar.

Closure

Time: 5 minutes

1. Critique collective work. Ask students:

   • *What are your comments on the individual flowers?*

   • *What do they say about each artist?*

   • *What are your comments on the collective work?*

   • *What does it say about us as a group?*

Student responses will vary. Ask questions to encourage students to comment on specific details of the individual flowers: *What colors did Padma use? Yes, she used lots of different shades of orange and even a little black.* Guide them to think about what the details say about each artist: *Oscar says those colors make him think of Halloween. Did they remind anyone else of Halloween? Padma's flower tells us she loves Halloween and spooky things.* Provide similar guidance in eliciting comments about the collective work.

2. Ask students: *What is good about working together to create a work of art?*

FIRST-GRADE LESSON: Physical Education

Time allotted: 30 minutes

Standards used: The SHAPE America's National Standards & Grade-Level Outcomes for K–12 physical education were used for this lesson.
    This lesson was adapted from Tracy Nelson's (n.d.) Locomotor License lesson.

Context: The physical education curriculum focuses on the areas of motor skills; knowledge of movement and performance in various games and sports; maintaining physical fitness; and safety, responsibility, self-expressions, and social aspects of physical fitness. In kindergarten through sixth grade, students build on their knowledge and skills across all areas. Today, the students are playing a game to practice different locomotive skills, nonlocomotive skills, and following movement patterns modeled by the physical education teacher. In the game, the students will role-play being cars and driving around the gym. Each skill or movement pattern mimics a different part of driving a car (e.g., walking mimics driving slowly, jumping jacks mimics windshield wipers).

As with other specials, physical education is taught by a specialist; in this case, a certified physical education teacher.

Lesson Objectives

1. The physically literate individual demonstrates competency in a variety of motor skills and movement patterns. (SHAPE Standard 1)

2. [The physically literate individual] hops, gallops, jogs, and slides using a mature pattern (S1.E1.1) (SHAPE America, 2013, p. 2).

Before This Lesson

Advance Preparation

1. Create a large name label with a photo for each student (to be placed at each "parking spot").

Connections With Other Team Members

Check in with the physical education teacher a day or two before the scheduled lesson to discuss what supports students might need for specific activities. The teacher will wear the digital amplifier for Charlie for this lesson.

Desired Results

"I Can" Statements

*   I can hop, gallop, jog, and slide in a pattern.

*   I can follow my teacher's pattern of movements around the room and in place.

*   I can move around the room and in place safely.

*   I can tell you why exercise and play are important and healthy.

INCLUSIVE PRACTICES

These apply to all students and should not be differentiated. Regardless of the supports individual students receive, they are all working toward these goals and understandings.

Assessment Evidence

Assessment evidence will consist of performance tasks, self-assessments, and other evidence that the students are mastering the identified goals and understandings. The following evidence will be used for this lesson:

*   Students will perform locomotor skills in general space (e.g., run, walk, gallop, slide).

*   Students will perform nonlocomotor skills in personal space (e.g., run in place, hop, do jumping jacks).

*   Students will name all the body parts exercised.

*   Students will complete a "fist to five" self-assessment. Students will hold up a range of fingers to rate their response to the question, "How much did you like each movement?" A fist represents 0 or the least, and five fingers represents the most.

*   Students will follow class safety rules as the teacher observes.

Learning Plan

Classroom Arrangement

- This lesson should be conducted in a large, open gym space with "parking spots" marked along the walls.

Materials

- Hula hoop for each student
- Music
- Amplifier

INCLUSIVE PRACTICES

ES1. All teachers wear the amplifier during any direct instruction or giving of directions. This supports Charlie.

Learning Activities

Allow for breaks and walks during the lesson.

Anticipatory Set

Time: 5 minutes

1. Assign each student a labeled spot on the floor. Explain that this is their personal space; no one else is allowed to be on their "parking spot."

2. Have students move their arms around to be sure they are spaced safely away from others so they do not bump into each other.

3. Have them look around to remember their "parking spot" and who is next to them.

INCLUSIVE PRACTICES

SR2. Allow all students short walks down the hall.

SR3. Allow all students breaks in or out of the class. These support Greg and Steven.

Modeling/Guided Practice

Time: 5 minutes

1. Say: *We're going to practice leaving our spots to move around. We'll be ready to move like a car in traffic once we know how to move around without bumping into anyone.*

2. Walk around the gym in the general space, demonstrating how to keep personal space even when moving around.

3. Have students move around for 1–2 minutes, being careful to keep personal space.

4. Briefly review each movement.

Independent Practice

Time: 15 minutes

1. Say: *Now we are ready for your cars!*

2. Give each student a hula hoop, explaining that it is their car. Explain that it is important that they do not crash into other cars when driving their car around the general space.

3. Tell students that you are the traffic cop looking for safe drivers. Your job is to direct traffic by showing them which movement to do in their cars.

4. Say: *While the music plays, do what I do to drive your car. Go back to your parking space when the music stops.*

5. Direct students to move through the room in different ways with their cars. For example:

   • Driving on a slow road = walking

   • Driving on the highway = running

   • Driving on a bumpy road = skipping

6. Play the game for about 10 minutes. Then direct students to return to their "parking spots."

7. Review nonlocomotor skills in "parking spots:"

   • Windshield wipers = jumping jacks

   • Run in place = rev the engine

   • Hop on one foot = flat tire

Closure

Time: 5 minutes

1. Ask: *What are all the body parts we exercised today?* [Students' responses will vary.] Guide students as needed to identify the parts of the body they used.

2. Say: *We also worked our hearts and lungs. Why is that important?* [Students' responses will vary.] As needed, remind students that moving around makes your heart and lungs work a little harder while you move, which helps those parts do their jobs better.

3. Say: *We also improved our balance and our coordination—meaning our ability to make our body move the way we plan. Why is that important?* [Students' responses will vary.] As needed, remind them that balance and coordination can help make you better at all kinds of physical activities, such as dancing and playing sports.

4. Have students complete a "fist to five" self-assessment. Ask: *How much did you like each movement?* [Responses will vary.]

5. Ask: *How do you like this game as a way to get exercise?* [Responses will vary.]

FIRST-GRADE LESSON: Music

Time allotted: 30 minutes (30 minutes allotted for specials)

Standards used: National Association for Music Education (NAFME) 2014 General Music standards.

Context: First graders were learning about auxiliary instruments—maracas, triangles, and percussion—prior to this lesson. They were learning songs, practicing echoing, and recognizing and creating patterns. Students are using quarter and eighth notes (ta and ti-ti in first-grade language) in the current unit.

As with other specials, music is taught by a specialist; in this case, a certified music teacher.

Note: This lesson was created in collaboration with Katie Rubert and Mykel Sapienza, music teachers at East Rochester Elementary School in Rochester, New York.

Lesson Objectives

1. Generate musical ideas for various purposes and contexts. (Anchor Standard 1)

2. Generate musical ideas (such as rhythms and melodies) within a given tonality and/or meter. (MU:Cr1.1.3 b.)

Before This Lesson

Advance Preparation

1. Prepare cards for small groups—8 sets of 3 cards (see Figures 2.15 and 2.16).

2. Prepare exit tickets on half sheets of paper (see Figure 2.17).

3. Get vocabulary to other team members: *snowflake, going sledding, gingerbread, quarter note, eighth note.*

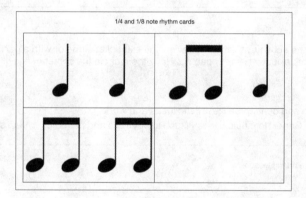

Figure 2.15. Rhythm card (unlabeled) for first-grade music lesson.

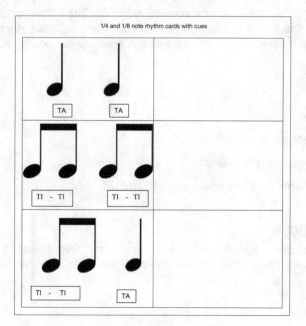

Figure 2.16. Rhythm card (labeled) for first-grade music lesson.

Name: _____

Exit Ticket

	I need help.	I can do it sometimes.	I can do it!
I can say the beat for ta and ti-ti.	I need help to say the beat for ta and ti-ti.	I can say the beat for ta and ti-ti sometimes.	I can say the beat for ta and ti-ti.
I can clap the beat for ta and ti-ti.	I need help to clap the beat for ta and ti-ti.	I can clap the beat for ta and ti-ti sometimes.	I can clap the beat for ta and ti-ti.
I can make a rhythm with two beats using ta and ti-ti.	I can make a rhythm with two beats using ta and ti-ti.	I can make a rhythm with two beats using ta and ti-ti sometimes.	I can make a rhythm with two beats using ta and ti-ti.

Directions for Teachers

After students have finished the activity, ask them to review the exit ticket alone or with a partner or have you read it to them. Remind students to think about what they can do. Have them circle the sentence(s) telling what they can do. Then, they can turn in their work.

Standards

Anchor Standard 1. Generate and conceptualize artistic ideas and work.
General Music MU:Cr1.1.3 b. Generate musical ideas (such as rhythms and melodies) within a given tonality and/or meter.

Figure 2.17. Exit ticket for first-grade music lesson.

Connections With Other Team Members

Check in with the music teacher a day or two before the scheduled music lesson to discuss what supports students might need for specific activities. The music teacher will wear the digital amplifier for Charlie for this lesson. Taylor and others will need pencil grips so they can complete the exit ticket easily. Steven will have scrap paper nearby so he can doodle as needed.

Desired Results

"I Can" Statements

- I can say the beat for ta and ti-ti.
- I can clap the beat for ta and ti-ti.
- I can make a rhythm with two beats using ta and ti-ti.

 INCLUSIVE PRACTICES

These apply to all students and should not be differentiated. Regardless of the supports individual students receive, they are all working toward these goals and understandings.

Assessment Evidence

Assessment evidence will consist of performance tasks, self-assessments, and other evidence that the students are mastering the identified goals and understandings. The following evidence will be used for this lesson:

- The teacher will observe students during group work and small-group work.

- Students will circle the exit ticket statements:

  - I can say the beat for ta and ti-ti.

  - I can clap the beat for ta and ti-ti.

  - I can make a rhythm with two beats using ta and ti-ti.

Classroom Arrangement

- Class is in the music room. Chairs are lined up in rows. Students know which seat is theirs at this point in the year and are comfortable with their assigned row.

- Students may take breaks or walks; there is a "move and learn" area at the back of the room.

INCLUSIVE PRACTICES

ES12. Provide a "move and learn" area of the room for all students where they can walk back and forth, jump, or jump rope. This supports Bridget.

SR5. Provide all students a choice of seating in the classroom. This supports Steven.

Materials

- Microphone amplifier worn by teacher during whole-group instruction and given to Charlie to place in his small group so others' voices are amplified.

- 20 packets of 1/4 and 1/8 note cards (as shown in Figures 2.15 and 2.16): 3 laminated cards per packet

- 20 copies of the exit ticket (see Figure 2.17)

For students who benefit from seeing ta and ti-ti under the appropriate note, use the cards with labeled notes shown in Figure 2.16. For others, give cards with just the notes, as shown in Figure 2.15.

INCLUSIVE PRACTICES

ES1. All teachers wear the amplifier during any direct instruction or giving of directions. This supports Charlie.

ES3. During small-group activities, give amplifier to student to position in the group's discussion space. This supports Charlie.

Learning Activities

Allow for breaks and walks during the lesson.

LESSON PLANS

Anticipatory Set

Time: 5 minutes

1. Have students sit in the seats they are assigned to as they enter the room. Remind everyone that they may take breaks as needed.

2. Open class with a short hello song.

3. Say: *Today we are going to review ta and ti-ti.* Draw a quarter note on the board. *What is this note?* [Student response: quarter note.] *What do we say with this note?* [Student response: ta.]

4. Draw two eighth notes on the board. Say: *What are these notes?* [Student response: eighth notes.] *What do we say with these notes?* [Student response: ti-ti]

5. Say: *First, let's practice those notes. First, say the note in your head when I point to it.* Point to each note in turn.

6. Say: *Now, say the note when I point to it.* Point to each note in turn.

7. Say: *Next, tap the note on your body when I point to it.* Point to each note in turn.

8. Say: *Last, clap the note when I point to it.* Point to each note in turn.

 INCLUSIVE PRACTICES

SR2. Allow all students short walks down the hall. This supports Greg and Steven.

SR3. Allow all students breaks in or out of the classroom. This supports Avery, Padma, and Steven.

Guided Practice

Time: 5 minutes

1. Say: *Now, let's add winter words to our beats.* Snowflake, going sledding, *and* gingerbread *are the words we will use.*

2. Tell students: *The rhythm ta-ta matches the word snow-flake. Say it in your head.* Wait for students to do this. *Then, say it out loud: snow-flake.* Wait for students to do this. *Next, say it out loud and tap it on your legs or body.* Wait for students to do this. *Now, clap it with me.* Clap the rhythm while saying "snow-flake."

3. Explain: *The rhythm ti-ti, ti-ti matches the words go-ing sledd-ing. Say it in your head. Then, say it out loud: go-ing sledd-ing.* Wait for students to do this. *Next, say it out loud and tap it on your legs or body.* Wait for students to do this. *Now, clap it with me.* Clap the rhythm while saying "go-ing sledd-ing."

4. Say: *The rhythm ti-ti ta matches the word gin-ger bread. Say it in your head.* Wait for students to do this. *Then, say it out loud: gin-ger bread.* Wait for students to do this. *Next, say it out loud and tap it on your legs or body.* Wait for students to do this. *Now, clap it with me.* Clap the rhythm while saying "gin-ger bread."

Independent Practice

Time: 10 minutes

1. Say: *Now that we have practiced, you are going to arrange a rhythm. I will give you three cards, one for each beat and word. You will practice each word and put the cards in a line, making a rhythm.*

2. Pass out 1/4 and 1/8 note rhythm cards. For students who benefit from seeing ta and ti-ti under the appropriate note, use those cards. For others, give cards with just the notes.

3. Say: *If you want to work in a group instead of by yourself, then tell me, and we will find a group for you.*

4. Break students into small groups or let them work independently and spread out around the room. Circulate to students and provide support. Get students' attention after 5 minutes of independent practice.

5. Say: *Now that you have practiced making a rhythm with your cards, it is time to get into groups. Each group will choose one rhythm and practice it so that everyone in the group can do it. After you have practiced, we will hear all the groups say and clap their rhythm.*

6. Break students into four groups of five students each. Support groups choosing the way to organize the three cards in a rhythm and practice it.

 INCLUSIVE PRACTICES

SS9. Allow cooperative work to happen during all content areas with flexible grouping. This supports Avery, Devin, and Natalie.

CR3. Allow for flexible grouping to move in and out of cooperative learning. This supports Oscar.

SS11. Provide choices in working in pairs or small groups. This supports Avery.

Performance

Time: 7 minutes

1. Say: *It's time to hear what each group chose! We will take turns clapping and saying the words and listening.* Point to the first group. *Group 1—share your rhythm!* Group 1 claps and says rhythm.

2. Repeat for groups 2, 3, and 4.

Closure (Exit ticket)

Time: 3 minutes

1. Say: *Now that music is almost over, it is time for you to think about what you can do. Look at your exit ticket. You can read it to yourself, with a partner, or I will read it to you. Think about the following questions for each I can sentence: Can you do it when someone helps? Can you do it sometimes? Can you do it every time? You decide, and show which sentence fits what you can do by circling or marking the sentence that matches what you can do.*
   When you are done, put your exit tickets on the desk and your pencils in the bucket, and line up to go back to class!

2. Pass out exit tickets (see Figure 2.17) and pencils. Circulate to assist students as they complete the exit tickets.

FIRST-GRADE LESSON: Technology

Time allotted: 30 minutes (30 minutes allotted for specials)
Adapted with permission of Teaching Tolerance, a project of the Southern Poverty Law Center. The lesson is adapted from "Digital Tools as a Mechanism for Active Citizenship."

Standards used: International Society for Technology in Education—Standards for students (ISTE-S).

Note: Technology lessons can be connected to any content area. In this lesson, technology skills are connected to a three-part lesson on active citizenship.

Context: Students are learning about the concept of active citizenship, and they are familiar with (or will be learning more about) the concepts of web pages and social networks.

As is typical in many school districts, technology is taught by a specialist; in this case, a certified school media specialist.

Lesson Objective

Students use a variety of technologies within a design process to identify and solve problems by creating new, useful, or imaginative solutions. (ISTE 4: Innovative Designer; ISTE, 2017)

Before This Lesson

Advance Preparation

No special preparation is needed apart from connecting with other team members as described next.

Connections With Other Team Members

Consult with the ENL teacher for accurate translation. Check in with the media specialist a day or two before the scheduled technology lesson to discuss what supports students might need for specific activities. The media specialist will wear the digital amplifier for Charlie for this lesson. Taylor and others will need pencil grips so they can easily list ideas. Steven will have scrap paper nearby so he can doodle as needed.

Desired Results

"I Can" Statements

- I can talk about ways people make the community better.

- I can think of ways to make our school better.

- I can help plan ideas to post on our blog.

These statements relate to the essential question: What role does digital technology play in active citizenship?

INCLUSIVE PRACTICES

These apply to all students and should not be differentiated. Regardless of the supports individual students receive, they are all working toward these goals and understandings.

Assessment Evidence

Assessment evidence will consist of performance tasks, self-assessments, and other evidence that the students are mastering the identified goals and understandings. The following evidence will be used for this lesson:

- Students work in small groups as teachers observe.

- Students list ideas in their small groups. The teacher will review the lists of ideas from the small groups.

(Note: There is no independent work in this first lesson; the class is divided into groups for continued work on this project in the next lesson.)

Classroom Arrangement

- Arrange desks in groups of three to four, facing the board.
- Students may work at desks, at tables, or on the floor.
- Provide a "calming corner and a "move and learn" area.

INCLUSIVE PRACTICES

ES12. Provide a "move and learn" area of the room for all students where they can walk back and forth, jump, or jump rope. This supports Bridget.

ES13. Provide choices for seating and workstations (e.g., Vidget chairs, yoga balls, chair bands, standing desks, bean bags). This supports Greg.

SR5. Provide all students a choice of seating in the classroom. This supports Steven.

SR7. Provide a "calming corner" for all students equipped with soft seating, carpet, sensory tools, and so forth. Students may go to the corner as needed. This supports Steven.

CR3. Allow for flexible grouping to move in and out of cooperative learning. This supports Oscar.

Materials

- Pencils
- Lined writing paper

INCLUSIVE PRACTICES

MS4. Offer graphic organizers and templates to all students. Stock them in common areas of the classroom, stored neatly in bins with the student's name and a piece of the template glued to the front, and save them on the computers that students use for work. This supports Isaiah and Oscar.

ES1. All teachers wear the amplifier during any direct instruction or giving of directions. This supports Charlie.

ES3. During small-group activities, give amplifier to student to position in the group's discussion space. This supports Charlie.

SR3. Ensure that all students are familiar with regulation scales, and many have them at their desks for self-checks. Some are for voice volume and emotional escalation; some for effective use of work time; some for interest or independence level for an activity. This supports Avery, Padma, and Steven.

SR8. Provide fidgets and mandalas to all students. This supports Steven.

Learning Activities

Allow for breaks, walks, and use of the "calming corner" during the lesson.

Anticipatory Set

Time: 5 minutes

1. Tell students: *People have used technology over the past decade to be activists. An activist is someone who wants to make things better.*

2. Show an example of advocacy or helping others from the local news. Explain how the individual or group worked as activists. Encourage students to talk about how what the person/people did helped to make things better.

3. Explain: *When we talk about being activists, we get to decide what needs to get better at our school and make a plan for making things better. Today, we are going to think of things that we want to make better. We'll talk about ways to do that. Then, we will talk about sharing ways to make things better using our web site and blog.*

4. Say: *In the second lesson, we will write the sentences we want to use on the web site and blog. If people see our ideas, then they might try to do those things! Finally, we will put a survey on our web site in a few weeks to see if what we did changed how people think or act.*

 INCLUSIVE PRACTICES

SR2. Allow all students short walks down the hall. This supports Greg and Steven.

SR7. Provide a "calming corner" for all students equipped with soft seating, carpet, sensory tools, and so forth. Students may go to the corner as needed. This supports Steven.

LAE1. Before group time, give target student a question that can be answered with a new or familiar icon or vocabulary word. This supports Bridget.

R8. Provide labels in classroom. Everything in the classroom is labeled with its name in multiple languages. Student's belongings have his or her photo on them. This supports Oscar.

Modeling/Guided Practice

Time: 5 minutes

1. Say: *In our school, our motto is.* [List motto for school.] *That makes me think about ways to make our school better.* List examples of citizenship: keeping our school yard tidy, being kind to others in the lunchroom, and being an ally when we see someone being bullied.

2. Ask: *Can anyone think of more ways to make our school better?* [Responses will vary.] Elicit two to three additional examples of citizenship and add them to the list.

3. Say: *Now, in your small groups you are going to make a list of things you would like to make better in our classroom or our school.*

 INCLUSIVE PRACTICES

ES7. Think aloud when writing, spelling, or punctuating on board/during lessons. This supports Oscar.

Independent Practice

Time: 10 minutes

1. Divide the class into small groups of three to four students. Remind students that the group will work together to come up with more ideas about how to make the classroom or school a better place. Have each group choose a scribe to list ideas.

2. Circulate among the groups as they work. Answer questions and assist students in recording ideas, as needed.

3. Each group's scribe writes a list of ideas.

INCLUSIVE PRACTICES

SS9. Allow cooperative work to happen during all content areas with flexible grouping. This supports Avery, Devin, and Natalie.

MS4. Offer graphic organizers and templates to all students. Stock them in common areas of the classroom, stored neatly in bins with the student's name and a piece of the template glued to the front, and save them on the computers that students use for work. This supports Isaiah and Oscar.

ES4. For all information that the teacher reviews orally, write the information clearly for all students or post it on the class web site (e.g., announcements, homework assignments, notes, agenda). This supports Charlie.

Whole-Group Instruction

Time: 5 minutes

1. Give each group a few moments to review their list.

2. Then, call on each group to share its list with the class. As the whole class reviews all the ideas generated, list them on the board. In this process, condense similar ideas.

3. Work with the class to choose three ideas to share in the next tech lesson. Keep other ideas for future use.

INCLUSIVE PRACTICES

CR1. Provide culturally responsive curricular materials, materials that reflect student interests, and resources other than textbooks. This supports Megan, Oscar, and Padma.

CR8. Incorporate meaningful sharing of background experiences and perspectives into lessons. This supports Oscar.

Closure

Time: 5 minutes
Close with a review of the ideas the class chose to talk about next time that will make the class or school better.

Mr. Albert's Third-Grade Class

Mr. Albert's classroom has 20 students and is culturally and linguistically diverse. For example, one student, Nathaniel, has recently moved to the United States from Ukraine, whereas another, Victoria, speaks Mandarin at home. Students' interests, needs, families at home, and strengths are also diverse. One student, Ethan, has a 504 plan addressing needs for attention-deficit/hyperactivity disorder (ADHD), and three others have IEPs addressing their needs related to visual impairment, autism spectrum disorder, and the specific learning disability (SLD) dyscalculia. Kacey has a visual impairment, and a certified orientation and mobility specialist (COMS) provides support for Kacey and Mr. Albert. The COMS, teacher of visually impaired (TVI), or occupational therapist works with Kacey during flexible instructional time (FIT) to gain independent skills in and around the classroom and school building. Mr. Albert knows how to think about physical arrangement, seating, and predictable organization of materials on a day-to-day basis. Another student, Sebastian, has autism spectrum disorder and works with the SLP daily. He also enjoys the sensory room and yoga. Finally, Odette has dyscalculia and works with the math specialist three times a week during FIT. The math specialist also supports Mr. Albert in the classroom during math time. Read the student profiles for information about each child in the class before reviewing these third-grade lesson plans.

STUDENT PROFILES AND
SUMMARY OF INCLUSIVE SUPPORTS

lives with his parents, Aria and Peg, and his two pet ferrets. Aria is a lawyer, and Peg is a paralegal in the same law firm.

Antoine is quiet and thoughtful. He is very small for his age. He is on grade level in all subject areas and follows directions well. His reading level with Fountas & Pinnell is M. Antoine is eager to please the teacher and likes to be called on to help. Antoine loves jigsaw puzzles, handheld puzzles (e.g., Rubik's cube, number slide puzzles), brainteasers, and books.

Age: 8;4 years/Grade 3

Fountas & Pinnell Reading Level: M

Math Level: At grade level

Disability Classification: None

Intervention/Notes: Antoine is on grade level in all subjects. He is anxious and easily startled by loud noises or sudden movements. He does not like to be touched unexpectedly. He is on a low dose of Zoloft for his anxiety; it is showing minimal impact, but his parents are very reluctant to increase the dosage.

Ways to Support Antoine		
Engagement	**Environment/Group Work** Pair with preferred peer who is calm and quiet in nature; building up to larger groups and outgoing peers. Use a predictable schedule; provide Antoine advance notice of alarms/drills. Use noise-reducing headphones during drills. Use "calming corner" in classroom whenever needed. Provide fidget (number slide puzzle) whenever needed.	**Social Skills/Communication** No needs at this time
Input	**Instructional Methods and Materials** No needs at this time	**Technology** No needs at this time
Output	**Self-Management/Executive Functions** Use "calming corner" whenever needed. Encourage Antoine to keep a number slide puzzle in pocket. Provide response scale—help Antoine identify triggers that escalate anxiety; scaffold Antoine in recognizing higher levels of anxiety.	**Test Accommodations** No needs at this time

Support Schedule and Flexible Instructional Time (FIT) for Antoine

	Monday	Tuesday	Wednesday	Thursday	Friday
10:00–11:00 FIT choices	Extended reading Social skill group Work with teacher Sensory room Yoga	Extended reading Social skill group Work with teacher Sensory room Yoga	Extended reading Social skill group Work with teacher Sensory room Yoga	Extended reading Social skill group Work with teacher Sensory room Yoga	Extended reading Social skill group Work with teacher Sensory room Yoga

Goals and Practices

Antoine's Goals	Inclusive Practices
Antoine will increase tolerance for group interactions.	SS3. Facilitate a peer lunch group. During lunch, there is one table for students to gather and play games that entails conversation and turn-taking. Some students have reserved spots. Any additional students may sign up to reserve remaining seats each day. SS9. Allow the cooperative work to happen during all content areas with flexible grouping. SR3. Allow all students breaks in or out of the classroom.
Antoine will recognize escalating anxiety and utilize coping strategies to self-calm.	SR4. Ensure that all students are familiar with regulation scales, and many have them at their desks for self-checks. Antoine's will support his awareness of anxiety and need for calming strategies. SR6. Teach yoga/mindfulness exercises to the whole class. SR7. Provide a "calming corner" for all students, equipped with soft seating, carpet, sensory tools, and so forth. Students may go to the corner as needed.

Bobby lives with his mother, Patricia, his father, Roberto, and his older brother (age 10). The family speaks both Spanish and English at home. Patricia is an ENL teacher, and Roberto is a contractor. All members of the family are bilingual in Spanish and English.

Bobby is friendly and outgoing. He has many friends in the classroom. Bobby loves magic and card tricks. He always has a deck of cards in his backpack for free time and recess. He loves to share his newest trick with friends and teach them the secret.

Age: 8;7 years/Grade 3

Fountas & Pinnell Reading Level: M

Math Level: At grade level

Disability Classification: None

Intervention/Notes: Bobby is on grade level in all subjects. It takes him longer to complete math problems because he is not fluent with multiplication facts. For many facts, he still adds the numbers up on his fingers or draws groups on paper. He can work through grade-level problems independently, but this slows him down. Bobby also benefits from supports in material management. He often misplaces items and puts things away in the wrong place, and he has a messy desk and cubby.

Ways to Support Bobby

Engagement	**Environment/Group Work** No needs at this time	**Social Skills/Communication** No needs at this time
Input	**Instructional Methods and Materials** Encourage use of fingers, scratch paper, and manipulatives for math facts. Provide a multiplication chart.	**Technology** Provide math software and apps.
Output	**Self-Management/Executive Functions** Provide questions as reminders to keep shoes tied, chair in, and backpack in cubby.	**Test Accommodations** Do not time his math fact practice sheets.

Support Schedule and Flexible Instructional Time (FIT) for Bobby

	Monday	**Tuesday**	**Wednesday**	**Thursday**	**Friday**
10:00–11:00 FIT choices	Work with teacher Math support Sensory room Yoga	Math support	Work with teacher Math support Sensory room Yoga	Math support	Work with teacher Math support Sensory room Yoga

Goals and Practices

Bobby's Goals	**Inclusive Practices**
Bobby will increase math fact fluency and multistep problem solving to third-grade level.	MS5. Provide multiple sets of counters, plastic linking cubes, and fraction circles; have abacuses available so that all students can choose to use them. MS6. Provide computer/tablet time to use math software and apps (e.g., Arthur's math games, Reader Rabbit math, Math Blaster, Kids Academy–123 Tracing, Number Monster, Wee Kids Math).
Bobby will improve on cleaning up after himself, keeping area neat, and keeping aisles clear.	OS8. Post reminder questions in key locations, prompting students to self-check materials, work, and so forth.

Chelsea

lives with her mom, Danielle, older brother (age 12), and older sister (age 11). The family rents a room in their home to local college students who help care for the children while Danielle attends classes, so Chelsea often shares stories about her babysitters.

Chelsea is friendly and polite. She is very neat and organized and likes to straighten things up around the classroom. She wears glasses and cleans them several times a day.

She likes playing board games, assembling jigsaw puzzles, coloring mandalas, and playing with dolls. Chelsea is mature for her age and prefers to converse with adults or play by herself.

Age: 8;8 years/Grade 3

Fountas & Pinnell Reading Level: R

Math Level: At grade level

Disability Classification: None

Intervention/Notes: Chelsea is at a fourth-grade level in ELA. She likes things to be very orderly around the classroom and sometimes gets upset if things are left out or not put away in the right place.

Ways to Support Chelsea

Engagement	**Environment/Group Work** Provide a lens cleaning cloth at her desk so she does not need to get up to clean her glasses or throw tissues away.	**Social Skills/Communication** Pair Chelsea with peers to help around the room. Lunch group with counselor once per week.
Input	**Instructional Methods and Materials** No needs at this time	**Technology** No needs at this time
Output	**Self-Management/Executive Functions** Provide a response scale; help Chelsea identify triggers that escalate annoyance with disarray/disorder in the classroom.	**Test Accommodations** No needs at this time

Support Schedule and Flexible Instructional Time (FIT) for Chelsea

	Monday	Tuesday	Wednesday	Thursday	Friday
10:00–11:00 FIT choices	Extended reading Social skill group Work with teacher Sensory room Yoga	Extended reading Social skill group Work with teacher Sensory room Yoga	Extended reading Social skill group Work with teacher Sensory room Yoga	Extended reading Social skill group Work with teacher Sensory room Yoga	Extended reading Social skill group Work with teacher Sensory room Yoga

Goals and Practices

Chelsea's Goals	Inclusive Practices
Chelsea will recognize her need for order and recognize when she is getting upset about disorder.	SR4. Ensure that students are familiar with regulation scales, and many have them at their desks for self-checks. Chelsea's will support her awareness of anxiety over disorder and use of calming strategies.
Chelsea will identify and utilize coping strategies to self-calm.	SR4. (See above.)

Mr. Albert's Third-Grade Class

Deirdre

lives with her dad, John, her younger brother who is in first grade, and their two big dogs. John writes a column for a magazine and works from home.

Deirdre is very talkative and outgoing. She has many friends in the classroom. Deirdre loves horses and riding. She often talks about her horse and the stables where she takes lessons. Deirdre and her family are vegan.

Age: 8;8 years/Grade 3

Fountas & Pinnell Reading Level: K

Math Level: At grade level

Disability Classification: None

Intervention/Notes: Deirdre benefits from support in reading comprehension and writing. She has difficulty retelling stories in chronological order and often misses details in her retellings. She rarely chooses to read on her own, and her father reports she resists silent reading at home, although she loves to be read to.

Ways to Support Deirdre

Engagement	**Environment/Group Work** No needs at this time	**Social Skills/Communication** No needs at this time
Input	**Instructional Methods and Materials** Offer books about horses and riding. Provide opportunities for buddy reading. Use Leveled Literacy Intervention.	**Technology** Provide computer software and apps to improve reading comprehension. Provide books on CD to listen and read at the same time.
Output	**Self-Management/Executive Functions** No needs at this time	**Test Accommodations** No needs at this time

Support Schedule and Flexible Instructional Time (FIT) for Deirdre

	Monday	Tuesday	Wednesday	Thursday	Friday
9:00–9:30 During English language arts (ELA)	Literacy specialist (leveled literacy intervention [LLI]) in classroom	Literacy specialist (LLI) in classroom	Literacy specialist (LLI) in classroom	Literacy specialist (LLI) in classroom	Literacy specialist (LLI) in classroom
10:00–11:00 FIT choices	Extended reading Social skill group Work with teacher Reading support	Extended reading Social skill group Work with teacher Reading support	Extended reading Social skill group Work with teacher Reading support	Extended reading Social skill group Work with teacher Reading support	Extended reading Social skill group Work with teacher Reading support

Goals and Practices

Deirdre's Goals	Inclusive Practices
Deirdre will increase reading time to improve fluency and comprehension.	R3. Have as many books as possible available on CD. Record yourself reading them if necessary. R6. Build peer reading buddies into daily literacy lesson activities. R13. Ensure that abcmouse.com and Brainzy online reading games are among the apps and software programs installed on all computers and tablets in the classroom.

Ethan

lives with his mother, Andrea, his father, Paul, and two sisters (ages 2 and 3). His dad is a plumber, and his mother is a registered nurse but currently stays at home full time.

Ethan is an energetic, delightful boy who finds joy in everything he does. He has many friends and is often a leader in the classroom. Ethan's interests include LEGOs, K'nex, and other building sets; playing outside; and bugs and insects.

Age: 8;5 years/Grade 3

Fountas & Pinnell Reading Level: M

Math Level: At grade level

Disability Classification: 504 plan, ADHD

Intervention/Notes: Although Ethan is capable of grade-level work in all academic areas, he has difficulty completing assignments, activities, and tests in a timely manner and correctly, due to his lack of focus. He requires extra time for tests and a quiet location free of distractions. Ethan takes prescription medication at home before school every day to support his ADHD. He often prefers interacting with his peers to working on assignments, and he can distract his peers from completing their work as well. Organization of materials and time is a challenge for Ethan, and he frequently has missing assignments. See Figure 3.1 in the section titled "Supplemental Documentation" for details about Ethan's 504 plan for managing his ADHD.

Ways to Support Ethan

Engagement	Environment/Group Work	Social Skills and Communication
	Offer varied seating, such as stability balls, beanbag chairs, or cafe tables to stand while working. Provide a basket of fidgets for the whole class to help students focus. Provide a few offices within the classroom for Ethan to choose to work at when he is having difficulty focusing. Build in movement breaks throughout the day, such as Brain Gym or GoNoodle. (See Resources for Inclusion in Appendix B for more about these resources.) Have class materials such as pencils, paper, and calculators available.	Provide verbal prompts indicating when it is appropriate to talk with classmates and when it is time to work independently. Provide several opportunities for small-group work to allow Ethan to socialize throughout the day.

(continued)

Ethan's Snapshot *(continued)*

Ways to Support Ethan *(continued)*

Input	**Instructional Methods and Materials**	**Technology**
	Present information in chunks.	Use tablet technology and apps to help Ethan keep track of assignments and homework.
	Use frequent checks for comprehension (e.g., ask for restatement, retelling).	
Output	**Self-Management/Executive Functions**	**Test Accommodations**
	Use tablet technology and apps to help Ethan keep track of assignments and homework.	Provide extended time.
		Provide alternative setting.
	Color-code according to classes, folders, notebooks, and assignments.	Provide alternative seating.

Support Schedule and Flexible Instructional Time (FIT) for Ethan

	Monday	Tuesday	Wednesday	Thursday	Friday
9:30–10:00 During specials				Technology specialist in classroom with teacher for consultation	
10:00–11:00 FIT choices	Extended reading Social skill group Work with teacher Sensory room Yoga	Extended reading Social skill group Work with teacher Sensory room Yoga	Extended reading Social skill group Work with teacher Sensory room Yoga	Extended reading Social skill group Work with teacher Sensory room Yoga	Extended reading Social skill group Work with teacher Sensory room Yoga

Goals and Practices

Ethan's Goals	Inclusive Practices
Ethan will select seating, as needed, to be part of a group or have a quiet, individual work space.	SR5. Provide all students a choice of seating in the classroom.
Ethan will successfully complete a test in a location that helps him focus.	TM1. Plan for a variety of types of tests, timed and untimed, to allow success for all students.
Ethan will utilize electronic ways to stay organized and color-code class materials.	OS1. Support the use of a planner of each student's design/choosing customized for his or her subject areas and materials.
Ethan will recognize the need for, and utilize, movement breaks and options for engaging multiple senses.	SR3. Allow all students breaks in or out of the classroom. SR8. Provide fidgets and mandalas to all students. SR9. Provide chunked or coded materials to all students. SS9. Allow the cooperative work to happen during all content areas with flexible grouping.

Rapp, Arndt, and Hildenbrand

Fabian

lives with his mother, Riga, and his father, Aman. He has an older sister in fifth grade and a younger sister in second grade. His parents own a small grocery store and work from open to close (8 a.m.–8 p.m.). The children all get off the bus at the store and help out or do homework in the break room until closing time.

Fabian laughs a lot and has a great sense of humor. He is very friendly and supportive of his peers. He is often heard saying, "Way to go!" Fabian loves to play soccer and tag, and he is proud of being old enough to help out in the store.

Fabian is Muslim and eats a vegetarian diet. Students on the bus and in the class-room have repeated a few things they have heard in the media about Muslims and deportation. Fabian does not appear to be affected right now.

Age: 8;10 years/Grade 3

Fountas & Pinnell Reading Level: N

Math Level: At grade level

Disability Classification: None

Intervention/Notes: Fabian is progressing well in all academic areas and receives positive reports from specials teachers.

Ways to Support Fabian

Engagement	**Environment/Group Work** Encourage conversations about diverse beliefs and backgrounds. Encourage conversations about similarities and differences.	**Social Skills/Communication** No needs at this time
Input	**Instructional Methods and Materials** No needs at this time	**Technology** No needs at this time
Output	**Self-Management/Executive Functions** No needs at this time	**Test Accommodations** No needs at this time

Support Schedule and Flexible Instructional Time (FIT) for Fabian

	Monday	**Tuesday**	**Wednesday**	**Thursday**	**Friday**
10:00–11:00 FIT choices	Extended reading Social skill group Work with teacher Yoga	Extended reading Social skill group Work with teacher Yoga	Extended reading Social skill group Work with teacher Yoga	Extended reading Social skill group Work with teacher Yoga	Extended reading Social skill group Work with teacher Yoga

Goals and Practices

Fabian's Goals	**Inclusive Practices**
Fabian will continue to progress in all areas.	CR1. Provide culturally responsive curricular materials, materials that reflect student interests, and resources other than textbooks. CR2. Provide opportunities (e.g., morning meetings) for discussions about perspectives, events, diversity, culture, and interests and opportunities to problem-solve with students.

Gabrielle

lives with her mother, Anne, her father, Peter, and her two younger brothers (ages 7 and 6). Gabrielle's mother is a computer technician, and her father is a business executive who travels often.

Gabrielle is very athletic and loves sports and outdoor games. She takes karate and plays club lacrosse. Gabrielle benefits from movement and hands-on activities.

She often leaves her seat during independent work time to ask questions, then skips or dances back to her seat.

Age: 8;9 years/Grade 3

Fountas & Pinnell Reading Level: P

Math Level: At grade level

Disability Classification: None

Intervention/Notes: Gabrielle is performing well in all subject areas and is reading above grade level.

Ways to Support Gabrielle

Engagement	**Environment/Group Work** Provide a seat cushion or exercise ball that encourages movement while seated. Encourage use of fidgets. Allow choice of seating/standing while working.	**Social Skills/Communication** No needs at this time
Input	**Instructional Methods and Materials** Encourage movement in lessons as much as possible. Allow for walks up and down the hallway. Utilize physical games in lessons (e.g., Twister math).	**Technology** No needs at this time
Output	**Self-Management/Executive Functions** No needs at this time	**Test Accommodations** No needs at this time

Support Schedule and Flexible Instructional Time (FIT) for Gabrielle

	Monday	**Tuesday**	**Wednesday**	**Thursday**	**Friday**
10:00–11:00 FIT choices	Social skill group Sensory room Yoga	Social skill group Sensory room Yoga	Social skill group Sensory room Yoga	Social skill group Sensory room Yoga	Social skill group Sensory room Yoga

Goals and Practices

Gabrielle's Goals	**Inclusive Practices**
Gabrielle will recognize her need to move and utilize options while working.	SR2. Allow all students short walks down the hall. SR5. Provide all students a choice of seating in the classroom. SR6. Teach yoga/mindfulness exercises to the whole class.

Heaven

lives with her mother, Janice, her brother (age 9), and twin sisters (age 5). Heaven's mother owns her own hair salon, and they live above the salon.

Heaven is outgoing and boisterous. She wears bright clothes, beads in her hair, and many wrist bangles, and she often wears a part of a dress-up costume to school (e.g., crown, tiara, fluffy boa). She loves costumes and theater. She is in a drama club and has performed in a few community productions. She writes her stage name, Heaven-La-Heaven, on her papers.

Sometimes peers describe Heaven as "pushy" or "bossy." She often takes the lead during free time (not usually with others' approval) and directs everyone in roles in her play. She likes to be with a lot of classmates, but they often avoid her due to her assertive and dominant behavior.

Age: 8;9 years/Grade 3

Fountas & Pinnell Reading Level: O

Math Level: At grade level

Disability Classification: None

Intervention/Notes: Heaven is a strong reader (above grade level) and on grade level in writing and math. She has an above grade-level vocabulary. Heaven benefits from social skill supports.

Ways to Support Heaven

Engagement	**Environment/Group Work** Assign roles during group work with very specific directions for each role.	**Social Skills/Communication** Use cue words and signals (colors on the regulation scale) to indicate when she is becoming aggressive. Have Heaven work with a counselor on leadership skills and recognizing when others feel too pushed.
Input	**Instructional Methods and Materials** No needs at this time	**Technology** No needs at this time
Output	**Self-Management/Executive Functions** Encourage use of skills (e.g., sentence starters, "pausers") when cued by teacher that she is at higher levels on the rating scale. Heaven should eventually recognize this herself and use her skills.	**Test Accommodations** No needs at this time

Support Schedule and Flexible Instructional Time (FIT) for Heaven

	Monday	Tuesday	Wednesday	Thursday	Friday
10:00–11:00 FIT choices	Social skill group Work with teacher Yoga	Social skill group	Social skill group Work with teacher Yoga	Social skill group	Social skill group Work with teacher Yoga
11:30–12:00 During lunch	Counselor in cafeteria		Counselor in cafeteria		Counselor in cafeteria

Goals and Practices

Heaven's Goals	Inclusive Practices
Heaven will recognize when peers are becoming uncomfortable or avoiding her company because she is being too aggressive, and she will utilize social skills to better collaborate with peers during play time.	SS3. Facilitate a peer lunch group. During lunch, there is one table for students to gather and play games that entails conversation and turn-taking. Some students have reserved spots. Any additional students may sign up to reserve remaining seats each day. SS5. Ensure that all students have an opportunity to contribute to or consult the Social Skill Manual for advice. SS6. Encourage active listening by routinely asking students to restate or summarize what has been said by peers. SS10. Build in time each day for small-group work with peers, assigning roles within the group, to scaffold the interactions. SR4. Ensure that all students are familiar with regulation scales, and many have them at their desks for self-checks. Heaven uses hers to rate her level of assertiveness/aggressiveness with peers. SR10. Teach strategy of self-monitoring: identify behavior, design self-monitoring strategy, and teach strategy (Menzies, Lane, & Lee, 2009). PEER—Pause, Evaluate peer's response, Empathize with their point of view or interests, Respond—is Heaven's strategy.

Ian

lives with his parents, Greig and Richard, and his older sister (age 10). Greig is an advertising executive, and Richard is a large-animal vet. They live on a small farm on the outer edge of the district with several house pets and barn animals.

Ian is quiet, very pleasant, and polite. He is kind to others and helpful whenever needed. Ian loves animals, nature, the outdoors, drawing, and painting. He reports that he would like to be a small-animal vet when he grows up.

Ian is quite shy and rarely initiates conversation with peers or adults. He often watches others on the playground or in the art center and seems eager to join, but he will not approach unless asked. Ian does not raise his hand to contribute voluntarily during class but always answers when called on by the teacher.

Age: 8;11 years/Grade 3

Fountas & Pinnell Reading Level: N

Math Level: At grade level

Disability Classification: None

Intervention/Notes: Ian is on grade level in all subjects. He has good work habits, is able to focus well on tasks until they are finished, and hands in very neat work. He is shy and benefits from supports to help him socialize.

Ways to Support Ian

Engagement	**Environment/Group Work**	**Social Skills/Communication**
	Assign roles during group work with very specific directions for each role.	Provide sentence starters to use when approaching someone for a conversation. Provide prequestions during lessons so Ian knows the questions he will be asked ahead of time and can build up to volunteering the answer. Have Ian work with a counselor to increase initiation of conversations.
Input	**Instructional Methods and Materials** No needs at this time	**Technology** No needs at this time
Output	**Self-Management/Executive Functions** No needs at this time	**Test Accommodations** No needs at this time

Support Schedule and Flexible Instructional Time (FIT) for Ian

	Monday	Tuesday	Wednesday	Thursday	Friday
10:00–11:00 FIT choices	Extended reading Social skill group Work with teacher	Social skill group	Extended reading Social skill group Work with teacher	Social skill group	Extended reading Social skill group Work with teacher
11:30–12:00 During lunch	Counselor in cafeteria		Counselor in cafeteria		Counselor in cafeteria

Goals and Practices

Ian's Goals	Inclusive Practices
Ian will initiate conversation with peers, contribute to group discussions, and approach others for help or interaction.	SS1. Use peer groups to practice conversations about topics that are centered around the curriculum. SS3. Facilitate a peer lunch group. During lunch, there is one table for students to gather and play games that entail conversation and turn-taking. Some students have reserved spots. Any additional students may sign up to reserve remaining seats each day. SS7. Provide sentence starters for students to use when approaching teachers. Most students have key rings or bookmarks with reminders on them. Some students list advocacy sentence starters (e.g., "I need. . ." "I do better when. . .") SS10. Build in time each day for small-group work with peers, assigning individual roles within the group, to scaffold the interactions. SS12. Strategically use pre-questions before discussions. Provide two to three questions on index cards that will be asked during discussion so student can formulate answers in advance and be encouraged to volunteer during discussion.

Justice

lives his mother, Sharice, his father, Terrell, and his two younger brothers (ages 6 and 4). Justice's mother is a fourth-grade teacher at the elementary school he attends, and his father is a history professor at a local college.

Justice is very easy going and works well with everyone. He has many friends, and his friends see him as a leader. Justice enjoys reading and loves space, planets, and NASA. He often chooses to search the computer for images and articles about space during free time.

Age: 8;8 years/Grade 3

Fountas & Pinnell Reading Level: S

Math Level: At grade level

Disability Classification: None

Intervention/Notes: Justice is on grade level in all subjects except reading. He reads far above grade level. He benefits from supports in material management and task completion. Justice often misplaces items or finds them on the floor, at the bottom of his backpack, and so forth. The teacher often finds him lost in thought during independent seat work and needs to redirect him to his task. He returns to the task immediately and amiably but loses focus again after 3–4 minutes.

Ways to Support Justice

Engagement	**Environment/Group Work** Use labeled bins for school work, bell work, notes home, and so forth.	**Social Skills/Communication** No needs at this time
Input	**Instructional Methods and Materials** No needs at this time	**Technology** Provide a wrist vibrator set at 5 minutes to remind Justice to return to work.
Output	**Self-Management/Executive Functions** Provide self-check questions reminding Justice to check that papers and supplies are in the right place at the end of each lesson. Provide extra pencils and have paper available in the classroom. Provide an extra set of books at home.	**Test Accommodations** No needs at this time

Support Schedule and Flexible Instructional Time (FIT) for Justice

	Monday	Tuesday	Wednesday	Thursday	Friday
10:00–11:00 FIT choices	Extended reading Work with teacher Sensory room Yoga	Extended reading Work with teacher Sensory room Yoga	Extended reading Work with teacher Sensory room Yoga	Extended reading Work with teacher Sensory room Yoga	Extended reading Work with teacher Sensory room Yoga

Goals and Practices

Justice's Goals	Inclusive Practices
Justice will use strategies to keep track of important materials.	OS2. Many students have luggage tags on their backpacks listing items to go home/come back to school. OS7. Tape a small drawing of the inside of the desk to the top of the desk, showing where books, notebooks, writing utensils, or other materials are stored. OS8. Post reminder questions in key locations, prompting students to self-check materials, work, and so forth. OS10. Create a coded classroom. Have all items and storage units in classroom labeled in first languages and braille, with photos.
Justice will independently return to work and sustain task (with use of wrist vibrator if needed).	SR12. Provide vibrating wrist alarm to remind student to return to task. (Justice's wrist alarm is set to vibrate at 5-minute intervals.)

Kacey

lives with her mom, Bridget, her dad, Jerry, her pet fish, and her dog. Her older brother is in the service and deployed. Bridget is a medical transcriber and works from home, and Jerry is a physical therapist at a sports medicine clinic.

Kacey is thoughtful and quiet. She is confident and is willing to try new things with support. Kacey loves swimming and playing with her dolls representing girls from different eras of American history.

Age: 8;3 years/Grade 3

Fountas & Pinnell Reading Level: I

Math Level: At grade level

Disability Classification: IEP, visual impairment

Intervention/Notes: Kacey benefits from help organizing her desk and personal items. She struggled in reading in first and second grades. In addition, Kacey is legally blind from glaucoma. She has some remaining vision, which is limited to peripheral vision in one eye and seems to be changing. A TVI will work with her regularly, and her parents have a brief presentation they can do for the class about glaucoma and Kacey's vision if requested.

Ways to Support Kacey

Engagement	Environment/Group Work	Social Skills/Communication
	Be consistent with room arrangement. Always push in chairs and fully close doors and drawers. Do not use floor easels with splayed legs. Use tabletop easels. Make a yellow taped path that is always clear of obstacles from the door to • Kacey's desk • The small-group work station • The teacher's desk Include braille labels on all student desks and cubbies with student names.	Include braille labels on all student desks and cubbies with student names. Use names when calling on all students. Model and expect that everyone in the room will say his or her name when speaking. Plan time for teacher of visually impaired (TVI) and certified orientation and mobility specialist (COMS) to meet the class and explain services.

(continued)

Kacey's Snapshot (continued)

Ways to Support Kacey (continued)

Input	**Instructional Methods and Materials** Use verbal description of all visuals, motions, text, and illustrations (use descriptors in addition to color). Use think-alouds as you move about the room, organize and distribute materials, prepare an activity, and pace a lesson. Provide hands-on materials—manipulatives, sticky-wikki, puff paint. Provide braille labels on all books at Kacey's reading level.	**Technology** Request talking clock, talking calculator, and other talking devices. Use brailler, braille labeler, and other braille access provided by TVI. Provide tactile dice.
Output	**Self-Management/Executive Functions** Use braille labels on desk contents. Offer information instead of help. Keep time aloud. Fold poster board into folders to store large braille pages.	**Test Accommodations** Provide tests in braille or read them aloud.

Support Schedule and Flexible Instructional Time (FIT) for Kacey

	Monday	Tuesday	Wednesday	Thursday	Friday
10:00–11:00 FIT choices	Speech-language therapy	Occupational therapy	Speech-language therapy	Certified orientation and mobility specialist (COMS) in classroom, in school, and on grounds	Speech-language therapy
1:00–1:30 During specials	Adaptive physical education teacher in physical education				
1:30–2:00 During math	Teacher of visually impaired (TVI) in classroom	TVI in classroom	TVI in classroom	TVI in classroom	TVI in classroom
2:30–3:00 During dismissal	COMS in classroom	COMS in classroom	COMS in classroom	COMS in classroom	COMS in classroom
Counselor	Available as needed				
Social worker	Available as needed				

Rapp, Arndt, and Hildenbrand

Goals and Practices

Kacey's Goals	Inclusive Practices
Kacey will recognize, and understand the use of • Alphabet • Punctuation • Composition signs • Single-letter whole-word contractions • Lower cell whole-word signs • Whole- and part-word one-cell contractions	ES7. Think aloud when writing, spelling, or punctuating on board/during lessons. ES8. Provide all written materials in braille.
Kacey will increase braille reading speed, fluency, and competency.	ES8. Provide all written materials in braille. Teacher of visually impaired and certified orientation and mobility specialist push in to general education classroom so Kacey can work with peers.
Kacey will efficiently utilize reference sections of her textbooks and additional classroom resources on teacher request by • Gaining access to table of contents • Gaining access to chapter headings • Scanning text for headings	ES9. Provide tabs marking sections of reference books (with braille labels).
Kacey will demonstrate an improvement in the functional use of left and right for travel and orientation.	ES10. Think aloud when walking in the hallways, making turns, staying to the right, making the transition through doorways, and so forth.
Kacey will demonstrate an improvement in the understanding of comparative sizes for functional use in orientation and mobility.	ES11. Model and teach the class about identifying self and locations in the room ("It's under the window on the top shelf" versus "It's over there by Paige.").
Kacey will demonstrate an improvement in recognizing and using landmarks and clues for orientation purposes.	ES11. Model and teach the class about identifying self and locations in the room ("It's under the window on the top shelf" versus "It's over there by Paige.") MS2. Offer multiple ways for all students to practice counting, facts, and so forth: sand tray for copying numbers, number magnets on cookie sheets, number line on the floor on which to step. Provide sand, magnets, rice, and so forth for Kacey. MS5. Provide multiple sets of counters, plastic linking cubes, and fraction circles; have abacuses available so that all students can choose to use them. MS7. Provide digital/talking clocks, talking calculators, and so forth. ES17. Provide materials for target student to explore with hands when objects are described.

Latoya

lives with her mother, Juanita, her stepfather, Lavar, her sister (age 10), and her step-brother (age 12). Latoya's mother remarried last month, and the family moved into Latoya's stepfather's home, so Latoya and her sister are new to the school and district. Latoya's mother is a dental assistant and has recently gone back to work, and Latoya's stepfather is a contractor. Latoya is friendly and kind to others. She is just getting to know her classmates, but she seems to be getting along with them well. Latoya likes video games and talks about having two different kinds of popular gaming consoles since her mother and stepfather joined households.

Age: 8;5 years/Grade 3

Fountas & Pinnell Reading Level: L

Math Level: At grade level

Disability Classification: None

Intervention/Notes: Latoya is on or near grade level in all areas but needs reteaching of some concepts due to gaps from what was covered in her previous school. Latoya is easily frustrated when working on a new task and cries easily when upset. In speaking with Latoya's mother, the teacher has realized that a few of the stories that Latoya has shared with her peers are untrue.

Ways to Support Latoya

Engagement	**Environment/Group Work** Allow for breaks to color or use computer. Conduct regular yoga/mindfulness exercises. Provide a "calming corner."	**Social Skills/Communication** Group Latoya with students whose strengths are making friends and encouraging peers—Deirdre, Fabian, Justice.
Input	**Instructional Methods and Materials** Provide review sessions with the teacher during lunch to talk and go over missed concepts outside of class time.	**Technology** No needs at this time
Output	**Self-Management/Executive Functions** Use ratings scale for stressors; utilize coping skills when frustrated.	**Test Accommodations** No needs at this time

Support Schedule and Flexible Instructional Time (FIT) for Latoya

	Monday	Tuesday	Wednesday	Thursday	Friday
10:00–11:00 FIT choices	Counseling	Review sessions with teacher in classroom	Extended reading Social skill group Work with teacher	Extended reading Social skill group Work with teacher	Extended reading Social skill group Work with teacher
11:30–12:00 During lunch		Counselor in cafeteria		Counselor in cafeteria	

Goals and Practices

Latoya's Goals	Inclusive Practices
Latoya will utilize rating scale to indicate level of frustration, anxiety, or feeling overwhelmed.	SR4. Ensure that all students are familiar with regulation scales, and many have them at their desks for self-checks. Latoya's will support her awareness of increasing anxiety.
Latoya will utilize strategies to de-escalate independently (e.g., take a break; draw, color, or use computer; write a note to mom in journal).	SR3. Allow all students breaks in or out of classroom. SR6. Teach yoga/mindfulness exercises to the whole class. SR7. Provide a "calming corner" for all students, equipped with soft seating, carpet, sensory tools, and so forth. Students may go to the corner as needed. SR8. Provide fidgets and mandalas to all students. (Latoya will benefit from having mandalas to color.)
Latoya will increase positive interactions with peers.	SS3. Facilitate a peer lunch group. During lunch, there is one table for students to gather and play games that entail conversation and turn-taking. Some students have reserved spots. Any additional students may sign up to reserve remaining seats each day.

Maddox

lives with his mother, Zenith, and his younger sister (age 3). Maddox's mom is a store manager at the mall during the day and attends business school at night.

Maddox is outgoing and very talkative. He loves movies, especially science fiction, and knows all the details about *Star Wars* and *Star Trek*.

Age: 8;10 years/Grade 3

Fountas & Pinnell Reading Level: L

Math Level: At grade level

Disability Classification: None

Intervention/Notes: Maddox is on grade level in most subjects, but his reading fluency and comprehension are slightly below grade level. He would benefit from regular independent reading. Maddox also benefits from support in listening to peers' interests and recognizing when he is dominating the conversation.

Ways to Support Maddox

Engagement	**Environment/Group Work** Provide opportunities for buddy reading.	**Social Skills/Communication** Support peer interactions, turn-taking, and listening to others' interests.
Input	**Instructional Methods and Materials** Provide graphic novels on science fiction topics at third-grade reading level to encourage Maddox to read more often.	**Technology** Provide reading apps, such as abcmouse.com and Brainzy. Provide books on CD.
Output	**Self-Management/Executive Functions** No needs at this time	**Test Accommodations** No needs at this time

Support Schedule and Flexible Instructional Time (FIT) for Maddox

	Monday	Tuesday	Wednesday	Thursday	Friday
10:00–11:00 FIT choices	Reading support	Extended reading Social skill group Work with teacher Reading support	Reading support	Extended reading Social skill group Work with teacher Reading support	Reading support
11:30–12:00 during lunch		Counselor in cafeteria		Counselor in cafeteria	

Goals and Practices

Maddox's Goals	Inclusive Practices
Maddox will improve reading fluency and comprehension to third-grade level by the end of the school year.	R3. Have as many books as possible available on CD. Record yourself reading them if necessary. R6. Build peer reading buddies into daily literacy lesson activities. R13. Ensure that abcmouse.com and Brainzy online reading games are among the apps and software programs installed on all computers and tablets in the classroom.
Maddox will increase independent reading time and the variety of books he reads.	CR1. Provide culturally responsive curricular materials, materials that reflect student interests, and resources other than textbooks. This will include culturally responsive reading material for Maddox.
Maddox will improve turn-taking in conversations with peers.	SS3. Facilitate peer lunch group. During lunch, there is one table for students to gather and play games that entail conversation and turn-taking. Some students have reserved spots. Any additional students may sign up to reserve remaining seats each day.

Rapp, Arndt, and Hildenbrand

Nathaniel lives with his mother, Carole, his father, Henry, and his twin brother, who is in a different third-grade classroom. Nathaniel's mother is a pediatric surgeon, and his father is an oncologist. They are from Ukraine. Nathaniel's parents are working in the United States for 2 years as visiting surgical fellows. All family members speak Ukrainian and Russian and are learning ENL. Nathaniel is solemn and quiet. He is very interested in space, planets, and NASA, so he spends a lot of time with Justice during free time, searching for images and articles online. Justice is very talkative, which helps Nathaniel learn new vocabulary.

Age: 8;9 years/Grade 3

Fountas & Pinnell Reading Level: L

Math Level: Above grade level

Disability Classification: None

Intervention/Notes: According to the ENL teacher, Nathaniel is considered a beginning or entering ENL learner. Nathaniel is quickly learning English but is reluctant to speak in English. He is happy to tell his peers the words for classroom objects in Russian. He is making the transition from the silent/receptive stage to the early production stage of ENL, with approximately 800 receptive and active words used in one- to two-word phrases.

Ways to Support Nathaniel

Engagement	**Environment/Group Work** Label classroom in braille, Ukrainian, Russian, Spanish, and English. Place Nathaniel in groups with Justice while he gets to know others. Create predictable, comfortable, and culturally responsive environment through the following choices: comprehensive input context clues, increased verbal interaction, active participation in all activities, predictable routines, consistent formats for work, and purposeful seating.	**Social Skills/Communication** Utilize think-write-pair-share.
Input	**Instructional Methods and Materials** Pair all information with visuals. Provide materials in Ukrainian. Co-plan and co-teach with English as a new language (ENL) teacher Explicitly teach/translate academic language, new concepts, and symbol systems (e.g., comma vs. decimal) through the following means: drawn time lines, charts, highlighting, Venn diagrams, think-alouds, and learning logs. Write legibly. Give purposeful step-by-step directions.	**Technology** Translator Manipulatives
Output	**Self-Management/Executive Functions** No needs at this time	**Test Accommodations** Provide extended time when translation is needed. Provide authentic performance tasks.

Support Schedule and Flexible Instructional Time (FIT) for Nathaniel

	Monday	Tuesday	Wednesday	Thursday	Friday
8:00–9:00 During morning meeting and English language arts (ELA)	English as a new language (ENL) teacher in classroom	ENL teacher in classroom	ENL teacher in classroom	ENL teacher in classroom	ENL teacher in classroom
10:00–11:00 FIT choices	ENL	ENL	ENL	ENL	ENL

Goals and Practices

Nathaniel's Goals	Inclusive Practices
Nathaniel will increase fluency in spoken and written English.	CR1. Provide culturally responsive curricular materials, materials that reflect student interest, and resources other than textbooks.
	ES4. For all information that the teacher reviews orally, write the information clearly for all students and/or post it on the class web site—announcements, homework assignments, notes, agenda.
	ES7. Think aloud when writing, spelling, or punctuating on the board/during lessons.
	LAE1. Before group time, give target student a question that can be answered with a new or familiar icon or vocabulary word.
	LAR2. Embed one-step directions into whole-class morning routines, such as handing in homework, completing and handing in bell work, and following attendance procedures.
	LAR4. Allow students to work with a partner to take turns retelling details.
	R1. Provide charts of academic language and symbols.
	R6. Build peer reading buddies into daily literacy lesson activities.
	R8. Provide labels in classroom. Everything in the classroom is labeled with its name in multiple languages. Student's belongings have his or her photo on them.
	R9. Incorporate sight word work into station work, with individual lists of sight words available for all learners.
	R11. Create a variety of word study activities for whole-class use at different levels of understanding (e.g., portable word walls, guess the covered word, speed sorting, add an ending).
	R12. Create word wall in braille and first languages at child height for all to touch and read. Add braille words and words in multiple languages to all printed words throughout the classroom.
	MS2. Offer multiple ways for all students to practice counting, number facts, and so forth: sand tray for copying numbers, number magnets on cookie sheets, number line on the floor on which to step.
	MS4. Offer graphic organizers and templates to all students. Stock them in common areas of the classroom, stored neatly in bins with the student's name and a piece of the template glued to the front, and save them on the computers that students use for work.
	OS4. Provide seating options for the whole class.
	TM1. Plan for a variety of types of tests, timed and untimed, to allow success for all students.
	TM5. For all assessments, ensure that the reading level matches student's independent reading level.
	WS13. Use graphic organizers with the whole class, allowing for student choice. Scaffold the organizers to meet diverse learning needs (e.g., fewer items to fill in, some text provided, use of a word or sentence bank). Stock them in common areas of the classroom and save them on the computers that students use for work.

(continued)

Goals and Practices *(continued)*

Nathaniel's Goals	Inclusive Practices
Nathaniel will increase verbal interaction with peers.	CR2. Provide opportunities (e.g., morning meetings) for discussions about perspectives, events, diversity, culture, and interests and opportunities to problem-solve with students. SS1. Use peer groups to practice conversations about topics that are centered around the curriculum.

Odette

lives with her grandmother, Roseanna, and her cousin. Her cousin is in first grade at the same school. Roseanna is at home with the children.

Odette has a silly sense of humor and a vivid imagination. She likes to make up stories that entertain her many friends. She is very sociable and liked by her peers. Odette loves cooking, baking, and watching chef shows with her grandmother.

Age: 8;11 years/Grade 3

Fountas & Pinnell Reading Level: O

Math Level: Below grade

Disability Classification: IEP, SLD, dyscalculia

Intervention/Notes: Odette made good progress in reading in first and second grades, and she now reads above grade level. She benefits from supports in math instruction. Odette demonstrates difficulty keeping track of time, following multistep directions, sequencing events, recalling names, and keeping track of where materials are stored. Odette performs below grade level in math facts, problem solving, telling time, and money skills.

Ways to Support Odette

Engagement	Environment/Group Work	Social Skills/Communication
	Use heterogeneous grouping with students who effectively use manipulatives for modeling.	Use names when calling on all students. Model and expect that everyone in the room will say his or her name when speaking.
Input	**Instructional Methods and Materials** Encourage use of fingers, scratch paper, and manipulatives for math facts; use a multisensory approach (concrete to representational to abstract). Incorporate diagrams and draw out math concepts during lessons. Provide graph paper. Use colored pencils to differentiate problems. Use mnemonic devices for math concepts. Teach rhythms and songs for remembering math facts. Use think-alouds as you move about the room, organize and distribute materials, prepare an activity, and pace a lesson.	**Technology** Provide computer software and apps for math fact drill and practice.

(continued)

Odette's Snapshot *(continued)*

Ways to Support Odette *(continued)*

Output	Self-Management/Executive Functions	Test Accommodations
	Provide timers. Provide a visual schedule (with icons). Keep time aloud.	Provide extra time on math tests. Allow use of manipulatives on tests.

Support Schedule and Flexible Instructional Time (FIT) for Odette

	Monday	Tuesday	Wednesday	Thursday	Friday
10:00–11:00 FIT choices	Social skill group Work with teacher Math support Yoga	Math support	Social skill group Work with teacher Math support Yoga	Math support	Social skill group Work with teacher Math support Yoga
1:30–2:00 During math	Math specialist in classroom		Math specialist in classroom		Math specialist in classroom

Goals and Practices

Odette's Goals	Inclusive Practices
Odette will count the value of mixed coins up to $1 and mixed bills up to $20. Odette will count out change from purchases up to $10.	ES7. Think aloud when writing, spelling, or punctuating on the board/during lessons. MS5. Provide multiple sets of counters, plastic linking cubes, and fraction circles; have abacuses available so that all students can choose to use them.
Odette will tell time on an analog clock to the nearest minute. Odette will read a calendar to identify the current date, including the day, month, year, and day of the week.	ES7. Think aloud when writing, spelling, or punctuating on the board/during lessons. MS5. Provide multiple sets of counters, plastic linking cubes, and fraction circles; have abacuses available so that all students can choose to use them. MS7. Provide digital/talking clocks, talking calculators, and so forth.
Odette will apply the concept of addition to combine sets and find the total amount. Odette will apply the concept of subtraction to find the difference in numeric value between two sets. Odette will identify and apply symbols (+, -) to accurately complete number sentences.	ES7. Think aloud when writing, spelling, or punctuating on the board/during lessons. MS5. Provide multiple sets of counters, plastic linking cubes, and fraction circles; have abacuses available so that all students can choose to use them.
Odette will demonstrate an improvement in the functional use of left and right for travel and orientation.	ES10. Think aloud when walking in the hallways, making turns, staying to the right, making the transition through doorways, and so forth.

Paige

lives with her Aunt Meg and her Uncle Jim. They breed and show dogs.

Paige is very small for her age. She is sweet, patient, and kind. She has one or two close friends in the class and seems very happy to spend her time with them. Paige loves fairies, unicorns, and mythical creatures. She has a vivid imagination and often makes storybooks about fairies.

Age: 8;9 years/Grade 3

Fountas & Pinnell Reading Level: O

Math Level: Above grade level

Disability Classification: None

Intervention/Notes: Paige is on or above grade level in all subjects. There are no concerns about her academic progress at this time.

Ways to Support Paige

Engagement	**Environment/Group Work** Be sure to call on Paige during discussions. She likes to listen but does not always raise her hand.	**Social Skills/Communication** No needs at this time
Input	**Instructional Methods and Materials** Provide books and create instructional materials about fairies and mythical creatures.	**Technology** No needs at this time
Output	**Self-Management/Executive Functions** No needs at this time	**Test Accommodations** No needs at this time

Support Schedule and Flexible Instructional Time (FIT) for Paige

	Monday	**Tuesday**	**Wednesday**	**Thursday**	**Friday**
10:00–11:00 FIT choices	Extended reading Social skill group Work with teacher Yoga	Extended reading Social skill group Work with teacher Yoga	Extended reading Social skill group Work with teacher Yoga	Extended reading Social skill group Work with teacher Yoga	Extended reading Social skill group Work with teacher Yoga

Goals and Practices

Paige's Goals	**Inclusive Practices**
Paige will continue to progress in all areas.	CR1. Provide culturally responsive curricular materials, materials that reflect student interests, and resources other than textbooks. CR2. Provide opportunities (e.g., morning meetings) for discussions about perspectives, events, diversity, culture, and interests and opportunities to problem-solve with students.

Randolph

lives with his mother, Diane, his father, John, and his three brothers (ages 11, 10, and 5). Randolph's mother is a home health aide, and his father is a real estate agent.

Randolph is very active and athletic. He loves sports and outdoor games of all kinds, especially baseball. He is extremely competitive and turns most activities/lessons into a race or contest. A couple of his peers enjoy this and join in; others do not like it and tell him to stop.

Age: 9;1 years/Grade 3

Fountas & Pinnell Reading Level: P

Math Level: Above grade level

Disability Classification: None

Intervention/Notes: Randolph is performing on or above grade level in all subjects. He benefits from supports for cooperative learning (rather than competing with others all the time).

Ways to Support Randolph

Engagement	**Environment/Group Work** Assign roles in group work. Use morning meeting activities that require cooperation.	**Social Skills/Communication** Provide opportunities for all students to reflect on their self-awareness of competitiveness and secondary motivators. Build cooperative interaction skills.
Input	**Instructional Methods and Materials** Provide choice of competitive (against self or clock) and cooperative activities for lessons, homework, and so forth. Encourage students to choose one of each.	**Technology** No needs at this time
Output	**Self-Management/Executive Functions** No needs at this time	**Test Accommodations** No needs at this time

Support Schedule and Flexible Instructional Time (FIT) for Randolph

	Monday	**Tuesday**	**Wednesday**	**Thursday**	**Friday**
10:00–11:00 FIT choices	Extended reading Social skill group Work with teacher Yoga	Extended reading Social skill group Work with teacher Yoga	Extended reading Social skill group Work with teacher Yoga	Extended reading Social skill group Work with teacher Yoga	Extended reading Social skill group Work with teacher Yoga
11:00–11:30 During recess	Psychologist on playground		Psychologist on playground		Psychologist on playground

Goals and Practices

Randolph's Goals	Inclusive Practices
Randolph will increase awareness of his competitive nature/motivation and regulate it when interacting with peers during cooperative activities.	SS4. Strategically use games at recess. The psychologist goes to recess every day with the fourth and fifth grades and organizes a few playground games to facilitate friendly competition skills.
	SS10. Build in time each day for small-group work with peers, assigning roles within the group, to scaffold the interactions.
	SR4. Ensure that all students are familiar with regulation scales, and many have them at their desks.
	Randolph uses his to regulate his level of competitiveness.
	SR10. Teach strategy of self-monitoring: identify behavior, design self-monitoring strategy, teach strategy (Menzies et al., 2009).

Sebastian

lives with his parents, Louise and Jennifer, his two brothers in high school, and one sister who is in kindergarten. Both of Sebastian's parents work at the hospital; Louise works the first shift as a social worker, and Jennifer works the overnight shift as an ER nurse.

Sebastian is very interested in computers and gaming. He plays video games daily. His parents are conscious of the amount of time he spends playing, and they do impose limits, though less so for Sebastian than for his siblings because video games can be a support to calm Sebastian when he is agitated or overwhelmed. He loves to look through gaming catalogs and visit the video game store. Sebastian knows a lot about computers and rarely needs support using them.

Sebastian is able to connect with other children his age through Internet gaming, but he has difficulty initiating interactions with his fellow students in the classroom.

Sebastian is able to create a three-paragraph essay with support, and he is able to develop more advanced writing pieces when he can choose the topic of the essay. He is gifted in math.

Age: 9;2 years/Grade 3

Fountas & Pinnell Reading Level: P

Math Level: Above grade level, especially with computational skills

Disability Classification: IEP, autism

Intervention/Notes: Sebastian is nonverbal, uses a text-to-speech device, and has a full-time one-to-one aide. He has difficulty with reading comprehension when reading colloquial terms, slang, or idiomatic phrases. Sebastian is mildly sensitive to bright light, loud noise, and crowded spaces. He will avoid these or withdraw if he is able. He does not react externally. Sebastian prefers a predictable schedule. He benefits from seeing a visual display of the schedule, especially if there is a change.

Ways to Support Sebastian

Engagement	**Environment/Group Work**	**Social Skills/Communication**
	Use a variety of lighting, including floor lamps instead of overhead lighting, to diminish the overall brightness in the classroom.	Train Sebastian's classmates to use the text-to-speech device so they can support Sebastian in small-group work.
	Offer varied seating, such as stability balls, beanbag chairs, and pub tables to stand at while working.	Place Sebastian in a variety of small groups to increase his circle of friends.
	To ease Sebastian's anxiety about possible changes in his schedule, post a daily schedule on Sebastian's desk with icons he can manipulate as the day progresses.	Create a lunch group for a more natural setting to encourage and improve communication skills, particularly response phrases Sebastian can use when approached by others.
Input	**Instructional Methods and Materials**	**Technology**
	Provide materials for one-to-one aide to preview.	Provide a text-to-speech device.
		Continue to explore communication possibilities with a tablet, encouraging interaction with classmates also using tablets.
Output	**Self-Management/Executive Functions**	**Test Accommodations**
	To ease Sebastian's anxiety about possible changes in his schedule, post a daily schedule on Sebastian's desk with icons he can manipulate as the day progresses.	Provide extended time (x 1.5).
		Allow use of keyboard.
		Provide location with minimal distractions.

Support Schedule and Flexible Instructional Time (FIT) for Sebastian

	Monday	Tuesday	Wednesday	Thursday	Friday
10:00–11:00 FIT choices	Speech-language therapy for 30 minutes. Then: Sensory room Yoga	Speech-language therapy for 30 minutes. Then: Sensory room Yoga	Speech-language therapy for 30 minutes. Then: Sensory room Yoga	Speech-language therapy for 30 minutes. Then: Sensory room Yoga	Speech-language therapy for 30 minutes. Then: Sensory room Yoga
11:30–12:00 During lunch	Counselor in cafeteria		Counselor in cafeteria		Counselor in cafeteria
Occupational therapist	Consult available to teacher as needed				

Rapp, Arndt, and Hildenbrand

Goals and Practices

Sebastian's Goals	Inclusive Practices
Sebastian will initiate interaction with peers in small-group settings in 4 out of 5 opportunities.	SS1. Use peer groups to practice conversations about topics that are centered around the curriculum. Support one-to-one aide working with various other students and knowing all students.
Sebastian will appropriately acknowledge an interaction initiated by others by giving an appropriate response, either verbal or nonverbal.	SS9. Allow cooperative work to happen during all content areas with flexible grouping.
Sebastian will identify what happened first, in the middle, and last regarding a previously read story, past event, or situation.	WS13. Use graphic organizers with the whole class, allowing for student choice. Scaffold the organizers to meet diverse learning needs (e.g., fewer items to fill in, some text provided, use of a word or sentence bank). Stock them in common areas of the classroom and save them on the computers that students use for work.
When given commonly used sight words, Sebastian will accurately read with 98% accuracy in 3 out of 4 trials.	R7. Use partner activities or games to increase a student's understanding of long and short vowel sounds. R13. Ensure that abcmouse.com and Brainzy online reading games are among the apps and software programs installed on all computers and tablets in the classroom.
While reading a passage, Sebastian will use knowledge of consonants, consonant blends, and common vowel patterns to decode unfamiliar words with 80% accuracy in 3 trials.	R11. Create a variety of word study activities for whole-class use at different levels of understanding (e.g., portable word walls, guess the covered word, speed sorting, add an ending).

Tabitha

lives with her mother, Joy, and her four sisters (ages 10, 6, 4, and 2). Joy runs a child care in their home.

Tabitha is fun loving and happy, often laughing, humming, or skipping. She enjoys jewelry making and often brings in bracelets to give to friends and teachers.

She likes to talk and play with others, but she prefers to work alone when it comes to work because she needs to think through things in her own time and space. Tabitha is aware of this need.

Age: 8;6 years/Grade 3

Fountas & Pinnell Reading Level: N

Math Level: At grade level

Disability Classification: None

Intervention/Notes: Tabitha is performing on or slightly above grade level in all subjects, but she takes a while to process, especially if there is a lot of reading and writing required for a task. She prefers to work alone.

STUDENT SNAPSHOTS

Ways to Support Tabitha

Engagement	**Environment/Group Work** Assign group roles; scaffold cooperative learning by allowing for group discussion, then break off into individual work time.	**Social Skills/Communication** No needs at this time
Input	**Instructional Methods and Materials** Code assignments to support processing time. Chunk assignments to work a little at a time and rest in between.	**Technology** Provide KNFB reader app, which converts text to speech or braille.
Output	**Self-Management/Executive Functions** No needs at this time	**Test Accommodations** Provide extra time for teacher-made tests. Provide choice of quiet space for work and tests. Code tests to support processing of directions and details.

Support Schedule and Flexible Instructional Time (FIT) for Tabitha

	Monday	Tuesday	Wednesday	Thursday	Friday
10:00–11:00 FIT choices	Extended reading Work with teacher Yoga	Extended reading Work with teacher Yoga	Extended reading Work with teacher Yoga	Extended reading Work with teacher Yoga	Extended reading Work with teacher Yoga

Goals and Practices

Tabitha's Goals	Inclusive Practices
Tabitha will utilize extra time and quiet space to support need for increased processing time.	TM1. Plan for a variety of assessments, timed and untimed, to allow success for all students. TM3. For all graded assessments (e.g., tests, quizzes, classwork, online programs), give target student and other students the choice to remain at their desks, use the classroom quiet area, go to the library, or go to the alternative testing room. SR17. Provide a self-amplifier for student to self-talk or read aloud to support processing. (See Resources for Inclusion list in Appendix B.)
Tabitha will complete tests in parts.	TM6. Chunk tests/tasks into manageable parts. Chunk Tabitha's tests into manageable parts, with brief breaks in between.

Rapp, Arndt, and Hildenbrand

Victoria

lives her mother, Jiao, her father, Quianfan, her brother (age 10), and her sister (age 4). Victoria's mother stays home with the children, and her father is an engineer.

The family's first language is Mandarin. Victoria's father speaks English, but the rest of the family is learning ENL.

Victoria is curious and inquisitive. She likes to watch what others are doing. She uses gestures and sometimes draws pictures when she does not have the words to express herself in English. She is a very good artist and likes to draw mechanical things, buildings, and bridges. She often chooses to build with LEGOs during free time.

Age: 8;7 years/Grade 3

Fountas & Pinnell Reading Level: G

Math Level: At grade level

Disability Classification: None

Intervention/Notes: According to the ENL teacher, Victoria is considered a low intermediate or emerging ENL learner. She is making the transition from the early production stage to the speech emergence phase of ENL, with approximately 2000 receptive and active words used in one- to two-word phrases. Victoria has strong math and spatial skills. Her reading and writing in Mandarin is very advanced.

Ways to Support Victoria

Engagement	**Environment/Group Work** Label classroom in braille, Ukrainian, Russian, Spanish, Mandarin, and English. Create predictable, comfortable, and culturally responsive environment through the following choices: comprehensive input context clues, increased verbal interaction, active participation in all activities, predictable routines, consistent formats for work, and purposeful seating.	**Social Skills/Communication** Utilize think-write-pair-share.
Input	**Instructional Methods and Materials** Pair all information with visuals. Provide materials in Mandarin. Co-plan and co-teach with English as a new language (ENL) teacher. Explicitly teach/translate academic language, new concepts, and symbol systems (e.g., comma vs. decimal) through the following means: drawn time lines, charts, highlighting, use of Venn diagrams, think-alouds, and learning logs. Write legibly. Give purposeful step-by-step directions.	**Technology** Provide a translator. Provide manipulatives.
Output	**Self-Management/Executive Functions** No needs at this time	**Test Accommodations** Provide extended time. Provide authentic performance tasks.

Support Schedule and Flexible Instructional Time (FIT) for Victoria

	Monday	Tuesday	Wednesday	Thursday	Friday
8:00–9:00 During morning meeting and English language arts (ELA)	English as a new language (ENL) teacher in classroom	ENL teacher in classroom	ENL teacher in classroom	ENL teacher in classroom	ENL teacher in classroom
10:00–11:00 FIT choices	ENL	ENL	ENL	ENL	ENL

Goals and Practices

Victoria's Goals	Inclusive Practices
Victoria will increase fluency in spoken and written English.	CR1. Provide culturally responsive curricular materials, materials that reflect student interests, and resources other than textbooks. ES4. For all information that the teacher reviews orally, write the information clearly for all students and/or post it on the class web site—announcements, homework assignments, notes, agenda. ES7. Think aloud when writing, spelling, or punctuating on the board/during lessons. LAE1. Before group time, give target student a question that can be answered with a new or familiar icon or vocabulary word. LAR2. Embed one-step directions into whole-class morning routines, such as handing in homework, completing and handing in bell work, and following attendance procedures. LAR4. Allow students to work with a partner to take turns retelling details. R1. Provide charts of academic language and symbols. R6. Build peer reading buddies into daily literacy lesson activities. R8. Provide labels in classroom. Everything in the classroom is labeled with its name in multiple languages. Student's belongings have his or her photo on them. R9. Incorporate sight word work into station work, with individual lists of sight words available for all learners. R11. Create a variety of word study activities for whole-class use at different levels of understanding (e.g., portable word walls, guess the covered word, speed sorting, add an ending). R12. Create word wall in braille at child height for all to touch and read. Add braille words and words in multiple languages to all printed words throughout the classroom. MS2. Offer multiple ways for all students to practice counting, number facts, and so forth: sand tray for copying numbers, number magnets on cookie sheets, number line on the floor on which to step. MS4. Offer graphic organizers and templates to all students. Stock them in common areas of the classroom, stored neatly in bins with the student's name and a piece of the template glued to the front, and save them on the computers that students use for work. OS4. Provide seating options for the whole class. TM1. Plan for a variety of types of tests, timed and untimed, to allow success for all students. TM5. For all assessments, ensure that the reading level matches student's independent reading level. WS13. Use graphic organizers with the whole class, allowing for student choice. Scaffold the organizers to meet diverse learning needs (e.g., fewer items to fill in, some text provided, use of a word or sentence bank). Stock them in common areas of the classroom and save them on the computers that students use for work.

Rapp, Arndt, and Hildenbrand

SUPPLEMENTAL DOCUMENTATION

As previously noted, four students in this class—Ethan, Kacey, Odette, and Sebastian—have documented disabilities necessitating education plans. Ethan's 504 plan addressing his ADHD is provided in this section in Figure 3.1. Take a few minutes to review it to get a deeper sense of his strengths and challenges and the supports that help him succeed.

THIRD-GRADE READING LEVELS

Table 3.1 shows the typical Fountas & Pinnell reading levels for students entering third grade, the levels they typically reach as the school year progresses quarter by quarter, and the Lexile ranges for texts that are appropriate for students reading at that level.

Table 3.1. Reading-level goals for the year

Fountas & Pinnell	Lexile
Beginning of year: M/N	M: 551–650
	N: 651–730
First interval of year: N	N: 651–730
Second interval of year: O	O: 691–770
End of year: P	P: 731–770

Table 3.2 shows each student's Fountas & Pinnell reading level in the fall, along with the corresponding Lexile range for appropriate texts. Mr. Albert uses this information for some lesson activities involving reading—including the featured ELA lesson in this chapter—to group his students and to select or create related texts, differentiated by Lexile, that correspond to the reading level of students in each group.

Table 3.2. Third-grade reading levels: Fall

Student	Fountas & Pinnell Reading level— Fall of third grade	Lexile that aligns with the reading level
Antoine	M	M: 551–650
Bobby	M	M: 551–650
Chelsea	R	R: 771–830
Deirdre	K	K: 501–550
Ethan	M	M: 551–650
Fabian	N	N: 651–730
Gabrielle	P	P: 731–770
Heaven	O	O: 691–770
Ian	N	N: 651–730
Justice	S	S: 801–860
Kacey	I	I: 80–450
Latoya	L	L: 551–600
Maddox	L	L: 551–600
Nathaniel	E	E: 80–450
Odette	O	O: 691–770
Paige	O	O: 691–770
Randolph	P	P: 731–770
Sebastian	P	P: 731–770
Tabitha	N	N: 651–730
Victoria	G	G: 80–450

Panorama Valley Central School District

SECTION 504 ACCOMMODATION PLAN

STUDENT INFORMATION

Student: Ethan	Contacts: Andrea, Mother; Paul, Father	Review date: May of next year	Home school: Panorama
Date of birth: July 10		Plan start: September	Recommended school: Panorama
Gender: Male	Native language: English	Plan end: June	Special alerts: Prescription medication for attention-deficit/hyperactivity disorder (ADHD)
Age: 8.5 years	Interpreter required: No		
Grade: 3			

MEETING INFORMATION

Meeting date: May

Reason: Annual review

Participants: Second-grade teacher, mother, father, school psychologist, occupational therapist

Comments: Although Ethan is capable of grade level work in all academic areas, he has difficulty completing assignments, activities, and tests in a timely manner and correctly due to his lack of focus. His Fountas & Pinnell reading level is M. He requires extra time for tests and a quiet location free of distractions. Ethan takes prescription medication at home before school every day to address his ADHD. He often prefers interacting with his peers to working on assignments, and he can distract his peers from completing their work as well. Organization of materials and time is a challenge for Ethan, and he frequently has missing assignments.

INITIAL OR MOST RECENT EVALUATIONS/REPORTS

Date	Evaluation/report: The Attention-Deficit/Hyperactivity Disorder Test (ADHDT) rating scale was completed for Ethan 2 years ago. It indicated significant results in the areas of hyperactivity/impulsivity and inattention.
April, 2 years ago	The Behavior Rating Inventory of Executive Function (BRIEF) was also completed for Ethan. It indicated Ethan has difficulty in the areas of inhibitory control, shift (task to task), time and material management, goal setting and monitoring, task initiation, and completion.

STATE AND DISTRICTWIDE ASSESSMENTS

None

DETERMINATION

It has been determined that the student has a physical or mental impairment that substantially limits a major life activity.

Identify the physical or mental impairment:

ADHD

Identify the major life activity affected by this physical or mental impairment:

Attention, focus on task, executive functioning

Describe how this impairment substantially limits a major life activity:

Ethan's difficulty with attention, focus, and executive functioning tasks limits his ability to complete school work and attend to instruction needed to fully learn new knowledge and skills.

1

PROGRAM ACCOMMODATIONS, MODIFICATIONS, AND SUPPORTS

	Description	Frequency	Duration	Location	Start date
Related services					
None					
Supplementary aids and services/programs modifications/accommodations					
Choice of seating (device—chair, desk, table, beanbag, floor, Vidget; location—various "offices" in classroom)	Available in the classroom at all times; student chooses as needed	Ongoing/daily	Throughout the school day	Classroom	September
Fidgets	Available in the classroom at all times; student chooses as needed	Ongoing/daily	Throughout the school day	Classroom	September
Movement breaks	Available in the classroom at all times; student chooses as needed	Ongoing/daily	Throughout the school day	Classroom	September
Assistive technology devices or services					
Tablet applications for tracking assignments and homework	Available in the classroom at all times; student chooses as needed	Ongoing/daily	Throughout the school day	Classroom	September
Supports for school personnel on behalf of the student					
Occupational therapy	Consults with classroom teacher about limiting distraction in the classroom and incorporating movement	Four times a year	1 hour	Classroom	September
Technology specialist consult	Consults with classroom teacher about new software applications	Four times a year	1 hour	Classroom	September

TESTING ACCOMMODATIONS

Individual testing accommodations in the administration of districtwide assessments of student achievement and, in accordance with department policy, state assessments of student achievement.

Testing accommodation	Conditions*	Implementation recommendations**
Extended time	For all tests except when prohibited by state education department standards and regulations	May need extended time; to be reviewed and monitored
Location with minimal distractions (can be within the classroom setting)	For all tests	Flexible seating with minimal distractions
Alternative seating	For all tests	May choose to sit in device other than student chair

*Conditions—test characteristics: Describe the type, length, and purpose of the test on which the use of testing accommodations is conditioned, if applicable.
**Implementation recommendations: Identify the amount of extended time, type of setting, and so forth specific to the testing accommodations, if applicable.

SAFETY NET ELIGIBILITY

The student is eligible for the 55–64 Passing Score Safety Net and the Compensatory Option of the Safety Net.

2

Figure 3.1. Ethan's 504 plan addressing his attention-deficit/hyperactivity disorder.

THIRD-GRADE WEEKLY SCHEDULE

Figure 3.2 provides details about the daily and weekly third-grade class schedule for core subjects and specials as well as FIT. Noted in this schedule are days and times when some students see educational professionals who provide additional services they need (e.g., literacy specialist, psychologist). Review students' individual profiles for additional details about how this schedule meets students' support needs.

Weekly schedule: Third-grade related services professionals

	Monday	Tuesday	Wednesday	Thursday	Friday
8:00–8:30 Arrival/morning meeting	English as a new language (ENL) (Nathaniel, Victoria)	ENL (Nathaniel, Victoria)	ENL (Nathaniel, Victoria)	ENL (Nathaniel, Victoria)	ENL (Nathaniel, Victoria)
8:30–9:30 English language arts (ELA)	ENL (Nathaniel, Victoria) ; Leveled literacy intervention (LLI)–30 minutes (Deirdre)	ENL (Nathaniel, Victoria) ; LLI–30 minutes (Deirdre)	ENL (Nathaniel, Victoria) ; LLI–30 minutes (Deirdre)	ENL (Nathaniel, Victoria) ; LLI–30 minutes (Deirdre)	ENL (Nathaniel, Victoria) ; LLI–30 minutes (Deirdre)
9:30–10:00 Special	Art	Music	Art	Music	Art
10:00–11:00 Flexible instructional time (FIT)	See student profiles for individualized FIT support choices	See student profiles for individualized FIT support choices	See student profiles for individualized FIT support choices	See student profiles for individualized FIT support choices	See student profiles for individualized FIT support choices
11:00–11:30 Recess	Psychologist (Randolph)		Psychologist (Randolph)		Psychologist (Randolph)
11:30–12:00 Lunch	Counselor (Heaven, Ian, Sebastian)	Counselor (Antoine, Latoya, Maddox)	Counselor (Chelsea, Heaven, Ian, Sebastian)	Counselor (Antoine, Latoya, Maddox)	Counselor (Heaven, Ian, Sebastian)
12:00–12:30 Science					
12:30–1:00 Social studies					
1:00–1:30 Special	Physical education/adapted physical education is indirect (Kacey) ; Teacher of visually impaired (TVI)–indirect (Kacey)	Technology ; TVI–indirect (Kacey) ; Occupational therapy–indirect (Ethan)	Physical education ; TVI–indirect (Kacey)	Technology ; TVI–indirect (Kacey)	Physical education ; TVI–indirect (Kacey)
1:30–2:30 Math	Math specialist (Odette) ; TVI (Kacey)	TVI (Kacey)	Math specialist (Odette) ; TVI (Kacey)	TVI (Kacey)	Math specialist (Odette) ; TVI (Kacey)
2:30–3:00 Dismissal	Certified orientation and mobility specialist (COMS) (Kacey)	COMS (Kacey)	COMS (Kacey)	COMS (Kacey)	COMS (Kacey)

Figure 3.2. Weekly schedule: Third-grade related services professionals.

LESSON PLANS

Mr. Albert has been teaching third grade for 10 years. He has certification in elementary education with an annotation in urban education. Mr. Albert strives to become proficient with one new instructional technology each year. This year, he has worked to include multimedia in his lessons, using two new programs the district purchased for the elementary classrooms. He has also been working closely with several specialists and related services providers to be sure all of his students are supported.

Following are eight lessons that Mr. Albert and the specials teachers have chosen to highlight. Students in ELA read a news article, determine the main idea of the text, and find key details that support the main idea. The math lesson focuses on multiplication and the commutative property. Students are introduced to the concept that multiplying A × B means "A groups of B." The science lesson requires students to conduct an investigation by pushing and flicking balls to explore Newton's first law of motion—an object at rest tends to stay at rest, and an object in motion tends to stay in motion unless acted on by an outside, unbalanced force. The social studies lesson focuses on economics of communities and the concepts of scarcity and opportunity cost, and it addresses how to make decisions about purchasing goods and services.

In the art lesson, students create a monochromatic painting of an animal to teach drawing from observation, simplifying details, understanding color theory, mixing shades and tints, caring for brushes and choosing the appropriate size, and displaying craftsmanship. The physical education lesson focuses on the importance of warming up before stretching and physical activity to avoid muscle injury. The music lesson is about using musical instruments to tell a story. Finally, in the technology lesson, students practice using digital tools to find and organize information, and they talk about the importance of evaluating web sites for accuracy.

THIRD-GRADE LESSON: English Language Arts

Time allotted: 45 minutes

Standards used: The New York Next Generation Learning Standards were used for this lesson.

This lesson also addresses a related CCSS ELA standard for third grade, "Ask and answer questions to demonstrate understanding of a text, referring explicitly to the text as the basis for the answers" (CCSS.ELA-LITERACY.RI.3.1).

Context: Students in ELA have been learning strategies for how to read informational texts, such as articles and speeches. Asking and answering questions about a text is one strategy they have practiced. Today, students will read a news article, determine the main idea of the text, and find key details that support the main idea by asking and answering questions. Students will continue to work with the same texts in the next few lessons and analyze the text structure and the point of view. Because students in different reading groups will read different articles, the class will end this mini-unit by discussing ways the articles are alike and different (comparing texts).

This lesson includes students grouped by reading level so that each group of students is reading content at their instructional level. This requires differentiating the materials using Lexiles to match the reading assignment to students' abilities and having additional adults in the room to lead small groups. Students are in other large and small groups during other parts of the day; these groupings should not be the default for the rest of the school day. Table 3.3 shows the reading groups students will work with for this lesson, along with the Lexile ranges of the texts each group will read.

Table 3.3. Third-grade reading levels: Fall

Student	Reading level—Fall of third grade, divided into four reading groups	Lexile that aligns with the reading level
Group 1		
Nathaniel	L	E: 80–450
Victoria	G	G: 80–450
Kacey	I	I: 80–450
Group 2		
Deirdre	K	K: 501–550
Latoya	L	L: 551–600
Maddox	L	L: 551–600
Antoine	M	M: 551–650
Bobby	M	M: 551–650
Ethan	M	M: 551–650
Group 3		
Fabian	N	N: 651–730
Ian	N	N: 651–730
Tabitha	N	N: 651–730
Heaven	O	O: 691–770
Odette	O	O: 691–770
Paige	O	O: 691–770
Gabrielle	P	P: 731–770
Randolph	P	P: 731–770
Sebastian	P	P: 731–770
Group 4		
Chelsea	R	R: 771–830
Justice	S	S: 801–860

NEWS-ELA is a great resource that teachers can use to find informational texts with Lexile information available and can be found at http://newsela.com. Mr. Albert uses this resource to locate two similar news articles on related topics and download two versions of each article at different Lexile levels.

Four adults are utilized in this lesson. Three adults are present only for ELA and not for the whole school day; ELA receives particular attention in many elementary schools today. Reading interventionists, reading specialists, and other support providers often push in to classrooms using RTI as a framework to allow small-group support during ELA. Scheduling faculty and staff for ELA allows targeted interventions and progress monitoring with small groups of students. A general education teacher, a special education teacher, and a reading specialist are the three adults who often join Mr. Albert's class during ELA. Other adults who might push in might be an SLP or a teaching assistant; teacher preparation candidates or family members can be assigned to a small group with clear directions about how to move through the lesson.

Lesson Objectives

1. Develop and answer questions to locate relevant and specific details in a text to support an answer or inference. (3R1 [reading informational text: RI & reading literacy text: RL])

2. Determine a theme or central idea and explain how it is supported by key details; summarize portions of a text. (3R2 [RI & RL])

Before This Lesson

Advance Preparation

1. Ensure that three other adults are present to lead small groups during the guided reading portion—about 30 minutes.

2. Prepare a box—put a fidget in it, wrap the box as a present (for the anticipatory set).

3. Print the Informational Text Self-Assessment (see Figure 3.3). Laminate. Label in braille and all first languages.

4. Locate a brief (one paragraph) news article to use during the modeling portion of the lesson.

5. Use the NEWS-ELA web site or a similar resource to locate, download, and print two related readings for informational text (news articles) at two Lexile levels for each (four readings in total).

6. Reproduce the reading for Group 1 in braille, Ukrainian, and Mandarin. Post readings on web site. Review reading with Nathaniel and Victoria during ENL instruction.

Connections With Other Team Members

- Consult with TVI and ENL teacher.

- Plan for introduction of vocabulary during ENL instruction.

Desired Results

"I Can" Statements

- I can find the main idea.

- I can ask and answer questions to help me find the main idea.

- I can find key details.

- I can show that key details support the main idea.

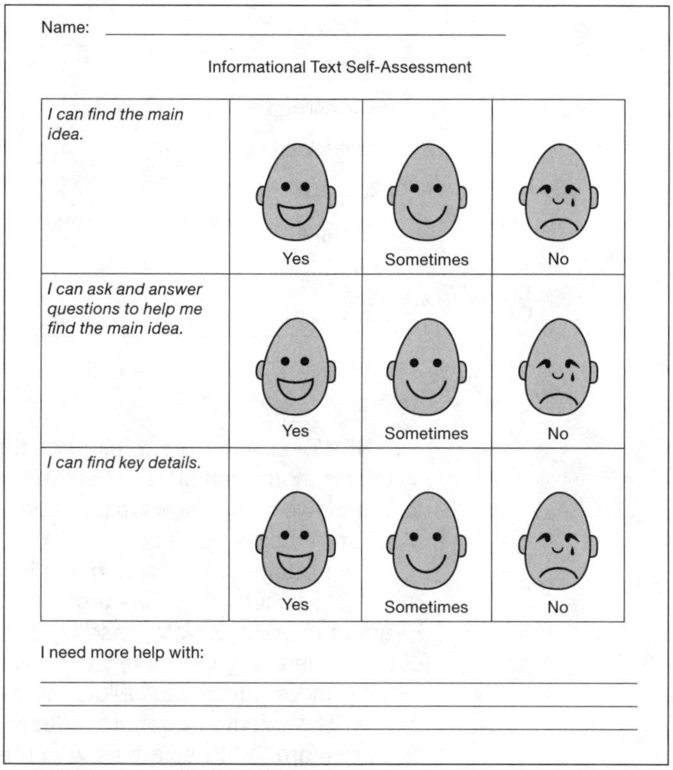

Figure 3.3. Informational Text Self-Assessment for third-grade English language arts (ELA) lesson.

INCLUSIVE PRACTICES

These apply to all students and should not be differentiated. Regardless of the supports individual students receive, they are all working toward these goals and understandings.

Assessment Evidence

Assessment evidence will consist of performance tasks, self-assessments, and other evidence that the students are mastering the identified goals and understandings. The following evidence will be used for this lesson:

- Students will share examples during class discussion.

- Students will respond to the teacher's questions during a demonstration.

- Students will complete the Informational Text Self-Assessment shown in Figure 3.3.

- The teacher will observe students responding to teacher questions during the demonstration.

- The teacher will observe students sharing examples during class discussion.

Classroom Arrangement

- Students will sit at their desks or on the floor in the front of the room with the teacher for the first part of the lesson.

- Students will move to one area of the room with an adult for small-group instruction. Once in their assigned space, students may choose how they prefer to work (e.g., sit, stand, lie down, use a range of seating options).

- Students will return to the front of the room for the closure.

INCLUSIVE PRACTICES

SR5. Provide all students a choice of seating in the classroom. This is a support for Ethan and Gabrielle.

Materials

- New fidget for the class, wrapped in a box like a present

- Teacher-created worksheets (in braille, multiple languages, loaded on laptops, posted on the class web site)

- Variety of writing tools (e.g., pencils, markers) with pencil grips

- Teacher-created desk map on the board to show which materials to gather and have on desk.

- Fidgets

- Self-amplifiers

- Brief (one paragraph) news article to use during the modeling portion of the lesson

- Brief (one paragraph) news articles at four reading levels (see the information about individual students' reading levels in Tables 3.2 and 3.3). Each article should have an explicitly stated main idea.

Reading groups are as follows:

1. Nathaniel, Victoria, Kacey

2. Deirdre, Latoya, Maddox, Antoine, Bobby, Ethan

3. Fabian, Ian, Tabitha, Heaven, Odette, Paige, Gabrielle, Randolph, Sebastian

4. Chelsea, Justice

INCLUSIVE PRACTICES

ES8. Provide all written materials in braille. This supports Kacey.

R8. Provide labels in classroom. Everything in the classroom is labeled with its name in multiple languages. Student's belongings have his or her photo on them. This supports Nathaniel and Victoria.

OS7. Tape a small drawing of the inside of the desk to the top of the desk, showing where books, notebooks, writing utensils, or other materials are stored. This is a support for Justice.

SR4. Ensure that all students are familiar with regulation scales, and many have them at their desks for self-checks. Some are for voice volume and emotional escalation; some for effective use of work time; some for interest or independence level for an activity. This supports Antoine, Chelsea, Heaven, Latoya, and Randolph.

SR8: Provide fidgets and mandalas to all students. This will particularly support Ethan and Latoya while watching videos and listening to instruction.

SR17. Provide a self-amplifier for student to self-talk or read aloud to support processing. This supports Tabitha. (See Resources for Inclusion List in Appendix B for specific examples.)

Learning Activities

Allow for breaks, walks, and use of the "calming corner" during the lesson.

Anticipatory Set

Time: 5 minutes

1. Reveal a beautifully wrapped shirt box, complete with ribbon and bow. Hand it to Kacey so she can explore it tactilely. Listen as students ask questions about the box. Jot down their questions without providing any answers. [Examples of questions students may ask: What is that? Who's it for? What's inside? Are you going to open it? Is it clothes?]

2. As the questions slow down, ask Kacey to join you, and begin unwrapping the box with her. Continue writing down every question asked. Show the box lid and move the box around, allowing students to hear its contents shifting inside.

3. Slowly lift the lid to reveal a new fidget with which students are unfamiliar. As more questions ensue, continue to log them into the growing list. [Examples of questions students may ask: What is it? Where did you get it? What does it do? Why do you think it will be a good fidget for us?]

4. Tell students that what they just did is similar to what people do when they read something new. Explain that the students were the readers, and the present was the text. The point is to show that they do ask questions about texts. Count the number of questions you jotted down and explain that readers comprehend text better when they are engaged.

5. Review the list of questions. Highlight the ones that were answered (e.g., What's inside? Are you going to open it?) and those still unanswered (e.g., What kind are they? Who made them? Did you buy them?) Remind students that sometimes a reader asks more questions than the text can answer, but the key is that they should be invested in the text enough to wonder about it.

INCLUSIVE PRACTICES

SR7. Provide a "calming corner" for all students, equipped with soft seating, carpet, sensory tools, and so forth. Students may go to corner as needed. This supports Antoine and Latoya.

ES7. Think aloud when writing, spelling, or punctuating on the board/during lessons. This supports Kacey.

ES16. Provide sensory bottles. This supports Kacey.

SR3. Allow all students breaks in or out of the classroom. This supports Antoine and Ethan.

SR2. Allow all students short walks down the hall. This supports Gabrielle.

Modeling

Time: 10 minutes

1. Say: *Now we are going to look at an article from today's news that has a picture, a caption, and a paragraph.* Project a brief article from the local news online.

2. Think aloud as you describe the picture and read the caption. Briefly predict what the article will be about based on the picture and caption.

3. Read the first paragraph of the article and discuss.

4. Show the "I Can" statements:

    • I can use specific details and refer to the text to ask and answer questions.

    • I can show how the main idea and key details are connected.

    • I can show that key details support the main idea.

5. End with a review of each "I can" statement, leading into these questions:

    • *What questions do you have after reading this paragraph?*

    • *What are one or two details from the text?*

    • *What is a main idea? What is a key detail? How are they connected?*

Guide students to these understandings: *The main idea of a text is the "big point" or most important idea the author wants you to understand from the reading. Key details are related to the main idea. They give supporting examples or information that helps you understand the main idea better.*

INCLUSIVE PRACTICES

ES7. Think aloud when writing, spelling, or punctuating on the board/during lessons. This supports Kacey, Nathaniel, Odette, and Victoria.

Guided Practice

Time: 25 minutes

1. Each adult has one small group. Students are grouped homogeneously for this lesson. The result is four groups of different sizes—a large group of nine, a group of six, a group of three, and a group of two.

   - Group 1: Nathaniel, Victoria, Kacey

   - Group 2: Deirdre, Latoya, Maddox, Antoine, Bobby, Ethan

   - Group 3: Fabian, Ian, Tabitha, Heaven, Odette, Paige, Gabrielle, Randolph, Sebastian

   - Group 4: Chelsea, Justice

2. Say: *Now we are going to separate into four reading groups. Each group will read a short article and use the text to ask and answer questions. Asking and answering questions about the text will help you to determine the main idea and the details in the text that support the main idea.*

3. Each adult meets with a group. In each group, the adult previews the self-assessment. The goal in this reading is for students to review the text and address each "I Can" statement. Adults may choose to read aloud while students listen, choral read, or "popcorn read" (students each taking a turn), depending on students' abilities and interests. Make predictions and ask questions about the content.

4. After reading the text as a group, identify the main idea and supporting details. Take notes on the main idea and supporting details throughout this process. To identify the main idea, consider using a process that includes step-by-step guidance from the adult leading the group. For example, say: *Now that we have finished reading, let's look at our "I Can" sentences:*

   - *I can find the main idea.*

   - *I can ask and answer questions to help me find the main idea.*

   - *I can find key details.*

   First, let's find the main idea. What do we think the main idea is? Hear ideas and lead the group toward shared understanding of the main idea. Discussion must meet the needs of the group. Some groups will need direct teaching, such as: *Here is the main idea; let's talk about why it is the main idea.* Other groups will generate main ideas and key details at the same time, and may benefit from the adult saying, *We have information from the reading that includes the main idea and key details. Let's make a list of all our ideas and separate them into the main idea and key details.* Some groups may need to be reminded that the author often states the main idea at the beginning or end of the first paragraph.

5. Review the second "I Can" statement after the whole group has confirmed the main idea. Check with students that they are able to ask and answer questions that helped them understand the main idea, including reviewing the conversation that just happened and pointing out the questions that led to distinguishing between a detail and the main idea.

6. Conduct a second reading as a group. Reconsider the main ideas; revise or add to these ideas as a group. Add key details.

7. Watch time and prepare for closure as a whole class.

LESSON PLANS

INCLUSIVE PRACTICES

ES7. Think aloud when writing, spelling, or punctuating on board/during lessons. This supports Kacey, Nathaniel, Odette and Victoria.

LAR4. Allow students to work with a partner to take turns retelling details. This supports Nathaniel and Victoria.

SR12. Provide vibrating wrist alarm to remind student to return to task. This supports Justice. (See Resources for Inclusion list in Appendix B.)

SR17. Provide a self-amplifier for student to self-talk or read aloud to support processing. This supports Tabitha. (See Resources for Inclusion list in Appendix B.)

Closure

Time: 5 minutes

1. Call groups back to the large group in front of class. Have an Informational Text Self-Assessment available for each person. Students self-assess.

2. After the self-assessment, ask students to turn to an elbow buddy and review what they learned and what they will continue to practice.

THIRD-GRADE LESSON: Mathematics

Time allotted: 45 minutes

Standards used: The Common Core State Standards for Mathematics

Context: The scope and sequence of the third-grade math curriculum begins by introducing multiplication concepts and the commutative property. Mr. Albert reviewed second-grade concepts at the beginning of the school year. Preceding this lesson on products of whole numbers, he anchored with a lesson on addition and gave examples of times students need to add larger numbers or lists of numbers when it might not make sense to use addition strategies such as counting on or number lines.

Today, students will be introduced to multiplication strategies. They will begin by watching a BrainPOP video in which Tim and Moby must determine how many units of food are needed to feed each group of animals (e.g., the total number of bananas in all if three monkeys get seven bananas each). The video introduces the terms *multiplication, factors,* and *product.* Students will then work in small groups with manipulatives to solve problems with Mr. Albert's guidance. Each student will complete a worksheet to provide collectible assessment of individual understanding. Finally, they will play beach ball math to review.

There are three adults in the room during this math class. The TVI pushes in to support Kacey, and the math specialist pushes in to support Odette. Several strategies used simultaneously support both of these students. For example, naming aloud each student who catches the beach ball allows Kacey to have the same access to the activity as others, and it also helps Odette match names with faces.

Lesson Objective

Interpret products of whole numbers (e.g., interpret 5×7 as the total number of objects in 5 groups of 7 objects each). *For example, describe a context in which a total number of objects can be expressed as 5×7* (CCSS.Math.Content.3.OA.A.1) (Common Core State Standards Initiative, n.d.).

Before This Lesson

Advance Preparation

1. Create labels for materials in braille and all first languages. (This will be done at the beginning of the school year for all materials stored in the room and subsequently as new materials are acquired.)

2. Create a Multiplication Worksheet (see Figure 3.4); reproduce in braille, Ukrainian, and Mandarin.

3. Create a desk map (see Figure 3.5) with items students need to gather for the guided practice portion of the lesson.

4. Have stoplight response cards available that students can use to show their level of understanding (green = working independently; yellow = working but have a question; red = stuck, need help). An example is shown in Figure 3.6; note that these can be used in multiple lessons across content areas.

Connections With Other Team Members

Consult with TVI and ENL teacher for accuracy of labels and worksheet content.

Name _____

Multiplication Worksheet

Directions: Work alone or with a partner to complete problems 1–4.

1. Antoine has 3 puzzles. Each puzzle has 8 pieces. How many puzzle pieces are there in all?

2. There are 6 horses at the stable where Dierdre rides. Each horse has 4 hooves. How many hooves are there in all?

3. Maddox takes 3 friends to see the new *Star Wars* movie. Each friend needs $5.00 for the ticket. How many dollars will it cost for everyone to see the movie?

4. Victoria builds 4 houses with her LEGOs. Each house has 5 windows. How many windows will she need?

Figure 3.4. Multiplication worksheet for third-grade math lesson.

Desk Map

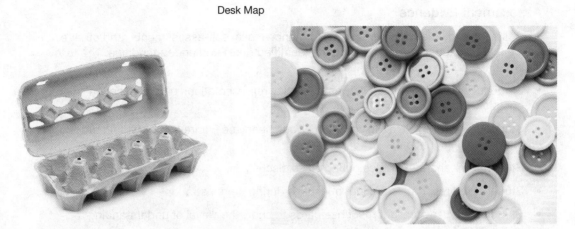

Figure 3.5.   Desk map with items students need to gather for guided practice in the third-grade math lesson.

Desired Results

"I Can" Statements

- I can interpret products of whole numbers.

- I can tell you that A x B = A groups of B objects each, and this applies to all products.

- I can tell you that multiplication helps us plan, make sure there is enough of something to go around, and add large amounts quickly.

- I can group numbers according to the equation and determine the product.

- I can describe contexts in which it is important to determine the exact number of objects by groups.

INCLUSIVE PRACTICES

These apply to all students and should not be differentiated. Regardless of the supports individual students receive, they are all working toward these goals and understandings.

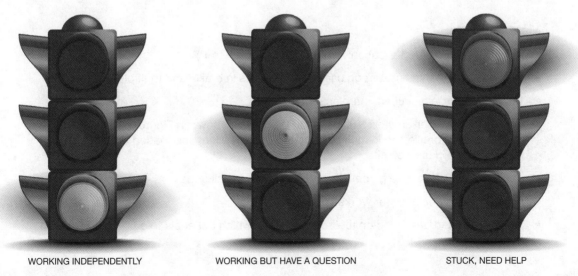

WORKING INDEPENDENTLY   WORKING BUT HAVE A QUESTION   STUCK, NEED HELP

Figure 3.6.   Stoplight response card to show level of understanding (green = working independently; yellow = working but have a question; red = stuck, need help).

Assessment Evidence

Assessment evidence will consist of performance tasks, self-assessments, and other evidence that the students are mastering the identified goals and understandings. The following evidence will be used for this lesson:

- Students will arrange manipulatives to display representations of multiplication equations.

- Students will complete a Multiplication Worksheet (see Figure 3.4) by writing products of multiplication equations.

- Students will share examples during class discussion.

- Students will respond to teacher questions during demonstration.

- Students will use stoplight response cards to show their level of understanding (see Figure 3.6)

- The teacher will observe students sharing examples during class discussion.

- The teacher will observe students responding to teacher questions during demonstration.

Classroom Arrangement

- Students sit at their desks, arranged in groups of three or four. Create heterogeneous groups based on skill development, and have them face the interactive whiteboard at the front of the classroom.

- Students may choose to sit on the floor or other seating (cushion).

 INCLUSIVE PRACTICES

SS1. Use peer groups to practice conversations about topics that are centered around the curriculum. This is a support for Ian, Nathaniel, and Sebastian.

SS9. Allow cooperative work to happen during all content areas with flexible grouping. This is a support for Antoine, Chelsea, Ethan, and Sebastian.

SR5. Provide all students a choice of seating in the classroom. This is a support for Ethan and Gabrielle.

Materials

- BrainPOP video ("Multiplication: Tim and Moby at the Zoo")

- Small dishes, muffin tins, or egg cartons with labels in braille and multiple languages

- Math counters (e.g., cubes, marbles, buttons)

- Copies of a teacher-created Multiplication Worksheet shown in Figure 3.4 (enough for all students, in braille and in multiple languages as needed, and loaded on laptops and posted on the class web site)

- Variety of writing tools (e.g., pencils, markers) with pencil grips

- Colored strips of plastic for worksheets

- Teacher-created desk map on the board to show which materials to gather and have on desk (see Figure 3.5)

LESSON PLANS

- Stoplight response cards (enough for all students)
- Fidgets
- Beach ball with numbers between 1 and 10 written on each colored section

 INCLUSIVE PRACTICES

MS6. Provide computer/tablet time to use math software and apps (e.g., Arthur's math games, Reader Rabbit math, Math Blaster, Kids Academy—123 Tracing, Number Monster, Wee Kids Math). This supports Bobby and Kacey.

ES8. Provide all written materials in braille. This supports Kacey.

R8. Provide labels in classroom. Everything in the classroom is labeled with its name in multiple languages. Student's belongings have his or her photo on them. This supports Nathaniel and Victoria.

MS5. Provide multiple sets of counters, plastic linking cubes, and fraction circles; have abacuses available so that all students can choose to use them. This supports Kacey and Odette.

OS7. Tape a small drawing of the inside of the desk to the top of the desk, showing where books, notebooks, writing utensils, or other materials are stored. This is a support for Justice.

SR4. Ensure that all students are familiar with regulation scales, and many have them at their desks for self-checks. Some are for voice volume and emotional escalation; some for effective use of work time; some for interest or independence level for an activity. This supports Antoine, Chelsea, Heaven, Latoya, and Randolph.

SR8. Provide fidgets and mandalas to all students. This will particularly support Ethan and Latoya while watching videos and listening to instruction.

ES17. Provide materials for target student to explore with hands when objects are described. This supports Kacey.

Learning Activities

Allow for breaks, walks, and use of the "calming corner" during the lesson.

Anticipatory Set

Time: 5 minutes

1. Show the BrainPOP video "Multiplication: Tim and Moby at the Zoo" to the class. (This video can be accessed at https://www.brainpop.com/math/numbersandoperations/multiplication/)

2. Ask: *How did Tim and Moby use multiplication to help them make sure each animal was fed the right amount of food?* Have the students "Think-Pair-Share" their responses and then ask the whole group to share. [Sample student responses: Tim and Moby made groups of food for each animal in the enclosure, then counted all the food in the groups; Tim and Moby used their multiplication table; Tim and Moby counted out the food, then counted for every animal.]

3. Say: *Yes, they made groups and then counted how many were in all of the groups together. That is what multiplication is. Tim practiced his multiplication a lot, so he knew what the product was without having to count all the individual servings of food. Today, we will practice making groups and counting the product, which is the first step in learning our multiplication facts.*

INCLUSIVE PRACTICES

SR3. Allow all students breaks in or out of the classroom. This supports Antoine and Ethan.

SR7. Provide a "calming corner" for all students, equipped with soft seating, carpet, sensory tools, and so forth. Students may go to corner as needed. This supports Antoine and Latoya.

SR2. Allow all students short walks down the hall. This supports Gabrielle.

Modeling

Time: 10 minutes

1. Transition into another example. Say: *Imagine you are handing out snack to 10 students. What if you would like each student to have two cookies? How can you figure out how many cookies you will need altogether?*

2. Think aloud as you set out 10 dishes to represent the 10 students and give each student two cookies (counters). Pause to write the equation on the board (10 students x 2 cookies). Skip count by 2s to arrive at 20. Emphasize that skip counting works for this example, but it will be harder to skip count as the numbers get larger, so knowing multiplication facts will become more important.

3. Do another example using the math counters to show how to set it up for multiplication. Ask: *What if you wanted each of the students to have three carrot sticks?* Be sure to think aloud as you write information or display objects.

INCLUSIVE PRACTICES

ES7. Think aloud when writing, spelling, or punctuating on board/during lessons. This supports Kacey, Nathaniel, Odette, and Victoria.

ES17. Provide materials for target student to explore with hands when objects are described. This supports Kacey.

Guided Practice

Time: 10 minutes

1. Post the desk map on the board to show that each student needs to gather several small dishes or egg cartons and a choice of math manipulatives.

2. Have students offer their own examples. Talk through each problem while students use their manipulatives. They may work together in their small groups or individually. Have them contribute to writing the equations on the interactive whiteboard each time, repeating the concept (3 x 4 = 3 groups of 4, or 3 rows of 4, or 3 stacks of 4). Pause at each step before giving the next one.

3. Say: *If each person in the class has two shoes on, then how many shoes are we wearing altogether?* Then offer a more challenging example: *You need a lunch ticket to get lunch each day in the school cafeteria, so each student needs five lunch tickets per week. How many lunch tickets does your family need each week? How many does our class need each week?*

4. Switch to writing equations and talking through the representations and solution. Think aloud as you write.

INCLUSIVE PRACTICES

ES7. Think aloud when writing, spelling, or punctuating on board/during lessons. This supports Kacey, Nathaniel, Odette, and Victoria.

CR1. Provide culturally responsive curricular materials, materials that reflect student interests, and resources other than textbooks. This supports Fabian, Maddox, Nathaniel, Paige, and Victoria.

Independent Practice

Time: 15 minutes

1. Provide each student with a copy of the Multiplication Worksheet (in multiple languages, braille, and posted on the class web site).

2. Circulate through the room while students work independently, assisting when they display their yellow or red stoplight response cards. Allow students to work with a partner or alone, but encourage each to complete his or her own worksheet.

3. Make sure Justice uses his wrist reminder.

 INCLUSIVE PRACTICES

LAR4. Allow students to work with a partner to take turns retelling details. This supports Nathaniel and Victoria.

SR12. Provide vibrating wrist alarm to remind student to return to task. This supports Justice. (See Resources for Inclusion list in Appendix B.)

Closure

Time: 5 minutes

1. Review one or two more examples with a kinesthetic activity (e.g., beach ball math).

2. Use a ball labeled with raised numbers placed on each color (i.e., each section is labeled with a number from 0 to 9) for the beach ball math activity. When the ball is thrown/rolled and a student catches it, the student states the two numbers on which his or her hands landed. Use the numbers to come up with an example of a multiplication problem and work through it.

3. Use the children as counters as you work through each problem. Group them around the room.

4. Describe the ball coming and going between students and name who receives it.

 INCLUSIVE PRACTICES

Movement games benefit Ethan, Gabrielle, and Randolph.

ES11. Model and teach the class about identifying self and locations in the room ("It's under the window on the top shelf" versus "It's over there by Paige"). This supports Kacey.

LESSON PLANS

THIRD-GRADE LESSON: Science

Time allotted: 45 minutes

Standards used: NGSS[1] were used for this lesson.

Context: The NGSS have a storyline for each grade. As second graders, students explored matter, ecosystems, biological evolution, Earth's place in the universe and Earth's systems, and engineering design. As third graders, they will revisit most of these topics and learn new content and strategies for exploring and making sense of the world around them. Today, students will explore Newton's first law of motion: An object at rest tends to stay at rest, and an object in motion tends to stay in motion, unless acted on by an outside, unbalanced force. They will measure how far balls move when pushed or flicked. In the process, students will practice conducting an investigation. As students progress with this science unit, they will explore Newton's second law of motion: The greater the force placed on an object, the greater the change in motion. The activities in this lesson lay the groundwork for students to learn both of these physics concepts.

Lesson Objectives

Motion and Stability: Forces and Interactions. Plan and conduct an investigation to provide evidence of the effects of balanced and unbalanced forces on the motion of an object (NGSS, 2013). (3-PS2-1)

The terms *engage, explore, explain, elaborate,* and *evaluate* are used because science lessons are often developed using the 5-E model.

CCSS connections are listed next.

ELA/Literacy

1. Conduct short research projects that build knowledge about a topic. (W.3.7) (3-PS2-1) (3-PS2-2)

2. Recall information from experiences or gather information from print and digital sources; take brief notes on sources and sort evidence into provided categories. (W.3.8) (3-PS2-1) (3-PS2-2)

Mathematics

1. Reason abstractly and quantitatively. (MP.2) (3-PS2-1)

2. Use appropriate tools strategically. (MP.5) (3-PS2-1)

Before This Lesson

Advance Preparation

1. Make copies of the Flicking and Forces Record Sheet (see Figure 3.7) and the Flicking and Forces Self-Assessment (see Figure 3.8).

2. Prepare "explain" questions for Ian.

3. Prepare vocabulary list: *variables, force, massive, mass, controlled*

4. Gather materials (see following).

Connections With Other Team Members

Give handouts to ENL teacher for translation for Nathaniel (Ukrainian) and Victoria (Mandarin).

Give handouts to the TVI for translation into braille for Kacey.

Get two balls with bells/noisemakers and a braille tape measure for Kacey from TVI or adapted physical education teacher.

---

[1]NGSS Lead States. (2013). *Next Generation Science Standards: For states, by states.* Washington, DC: National Academies Press.

NGSS is a registered trademark of Achieve. Neither Achieve nor the lead states and partners that developed the NGSS were involved in the production of this product and do not endorse it.

Names: _____

Flicking and Forces Record Sheet

Directions
1. For each type of ball, flick the ball three times with a soft flick and three times with a hard flick.
2. Try to flick the ball the same way every time: three soft flicks that are the same and three hard flicks that are the same.
3. After each flick, measure the distance the ball traveled and record it below.

Ball 1: What kind of ball is ball 1? _____

Trial	Soft flick: Distance traveled	Hard flick: Distance traveled
1		
2		
3		

What was the greatest distance traveled? _____

What kind of flick caused the greatest distance traveled? _____

Ball 2: What kind of ball is ball 2? _____

Trial	Soft flick: Distance traveled	Hard flick: Distance traveled
1		
2		
3		

What was the greatest distance traveled? _____

What kind of flick caused the greatest distance traveled? _____

Figure 3.7. Flicking and Forces Record Sheet for third-grade science lesson.

Name: _____

Flicking and Forces Self-Assessment

	I do not understand how to do this skill: I need help!	I can do this with some help: I am almost there!	I can do this: I got it!
I can tell you that force is anything that changes how an object rests or moves.			
I can plan and conduct an investigation with a friend and record data.			
I can use fair tests and control variables like how hard we flick a ball.			
I can tell you that each force acts on one particular object and force has strength and direction.			
I can recognize cause-and-effect relationships.			

Figure 3.8. Flicking and Forces Self-Assessment for third-grade science lesson.

Desired Results

"I Can" Statements

- I can explain that force is anything that tends to change the state of rest or motion of an object.

- I can plan and conduct an investigation.

- I can collect data and use fair tests in which variables are controlled and the number of trials considered.

- I can tell you that each force acts on one particular object and has both strength and direction. An object at rest typically has multiple forces acting on it, but the forces add up to zero net force on the object. Forces that do not sum to zero can cause changes in the object's speed or direction of motion. (3-PS2-1)

- I can recognize that cause-and-effect relationships are routinely identified. (3-PS2-1)

 INCLUSIVE PRACTICES

These apply to all students and should not be differentiated. Regardless of the supports individual students receive, they are all working toward these goals and understandings.

Assessment Evidence

Assessment evidence will consist of performance tasks, self-assessments, and other evidence that the students are mastering the identified goals and understandings. The following evidence will be used for this lesson:

- Students will complete the Flicking and Forces Record Sheet (see Figure 3.7).

- Students will complete the Flicking and Forces Self-Assessment (see Figure 3.8).

- Students will share examples during class discussion.

- Students will respond to teacher questions during demonstration.

- The teacher will observe students conducting an experiment.

Classroom Arrangement

- Students sit at their desks, arranged in groups of three or four.

- Create groups based on skill development, and have them face the interactive whiteboard at the front of the classroom.

- Students may choose to sit on the floor or other seating (cushion).

 INCLUSIVE PRACTICES

SS9. Allow cooperative work to happen during all content areas with flexible grouping. This is a support for Antoine, Chelsea, Ethan, and Sebastian.

SR5. Provide all students a choice of seating in the classroom. This is a support for Ethan and Gabrielle.

Materials

- Copies of Flicking and Forces Self-Assessment (enough for all students)
- Bin of different balls, some with bells or sounds, including at least one large ball (e.g., yoga ball)
- For each pair of students:
  - One ping pong ball
  - One golf ball
  - One tape measure
  - Flicking and Forces Record Sheet to record six trials for flicking ping pong ball and six trials for flicking golf ball (three soft flicks and three hard flicks for each ball)
- For Kacey and her partner:
  - Two different balls with bells/noisemakers
  - Braille tape measure

Learning Activities

Allow for breaks, walks, and use of the "calming corner" during the lesson.

Engage

Time: 10 minutes

1. Take out a large ball (e.g., yoga ball). Give Kacey the ball and ask her to place it in front of you, then keep a hand on it lightly to feel it move. Tell the class: *I am going to make this ball move!*

2. Use both hands to point at it as you say: *Move, yoga ball!* Ask: *Did the ball move?* [Student response: No.] Walk around the ball thoughtfully.

3. Say: *I will try again from the other side. Maybe it didn't move because I did not say please.*

4. Point again, saying: *Please move, yoga ball!* Then ask: *Did the ball move?* [Student response: No.]

5. Ask: *How can I make this ball move?* [Possible student responses: Push it, kick it, roll it, touch it.]

6. Push the ball. Ask: *What do we know about forces and how balls move and change direction?*

7. Review: *A force is a push or pull on an object. Most of what we know about forces was discovered by Sir Isaac Newton, a famous mathematician and scientist. He developed three laws involving forces and motion. In this activity, we will explore Newton's first law of motion: An object at rest tends to stay at rest, and an object in motion tends to stay in motion, unless acted on by an outside, unbalanced force. We will talk about the second law of motion in our next lesson.*

LESSON PLANS

 INCLUSIVE PRACTICES

SR3. Allow all students breaks in or out of the classroom. This supports Antoine and Ethan.

SR7. Provide a "calming corner" for all students, equipped with soft seating, carpet, sensory tools, and so forth. Students may go to the corner as needed. This supports Antoine and Latoya.

SR2. Allow all students short walks down the hall. This supports Gabrielle.

ES17. Provide materials for target student to explore with hands when objects are described. This supports Kacey.

Explore

Time: 15 minutes

1. Say: *You are going to explore forces in this lesson. You and a partner will have two or three balls, a tape measure, a recording sheet, a pencil, and a spot on the floor for a ball to roll. We will spread out so everyone has room to do this. Some people will be in the hall.*

2. Have students form pairs. Say: *Each pair will have two balls, a tape measure, and a record sheet. You will conduct the experiment. It is important that you keep things the same as much as you can when doing an experiment. The experiment is controlled when everything is kept the same. That means we're being careful about how we do the experiment so we can see the effect of changing one thing—our variable.*

3. Say: *When you push or flick the balls, try to do each kind of flick the same way—every soft flick is the same as other soft flicks. Every hard flick is the same as every other hard flick. Take turns flicking the balls, measuring how far the ball rolls each time and recording your observations.*

4. Send students in pairs to work areas. Circulate as students conduct the experiment.

5. Provide Ian with the "explain" prompts:
   - What do forces do?
   - Which moves more with the same push: a light ball or a heavy ball?
   - What steps did you do with your partner in this experiment?

 INCLUSIVE PRACTICES

ES7. Think aloud when writing, spelling, or punctuating on the board/during lessons. This supports Kacey, Nathaniel, Odette, and Victoria.

LAR4. Allow students to work with a partner to take turns retelling details. This supports Nathaniel and Victoria.

SR12. Provide vibrating wrist alarm to remind student to return to task. This supports Justice.

SS12. Strategically use prequestions before discussions. Provide two to three questions on index cards that will be asked during discussion so student can formulate answers in advance and be encouraged to volunteer during discussion. This supports Ian.

Explain

Time: 15 minutes

1. Call students back to the common area. Say: *Let's review what you learned. What is a force?* [Sample student response: Anything that tends to change the state of rest or motion of an object.] *What do forces do?* [Sample student response: Forces cause changes in the speed or direction of the motion of an object.] *What is Newton's first law*

of motion? [Student response: An object at rest tends to stay at rest, and an object in motion tends to stay in motion, unless acted on by an outside, unbalanced force.] *What did you observe today that showed Newton's first law in action?* [Student response: The balls did not move until we pushed or flicked them. Then the force made them move. Without force, they stayed at rest.] *Which moves more with the same push: a light ball or a heavy ball?* [Student response: a light ball] *That's right! What steps did you do with your partner in this experiment?*

2. Review the "I Can" statements with the class. Ask students to restate what they did. Following are the "I Can" statements with possible rephrasing students might use:

   • I did an investigation.

   • We collected data, and we kept everything the same—we controlled variables. The variables were how hard we flicked the ball and using the same ball every time.

   • I know that a force can make things move, like the balls. When a ball is not moving, the forces on it are all the same. When a ball is moving, that means that there is a force making it move.

INCLUSIVE PRACTICES

ES7. Think aloud when writing, spelling, or punctuating on board/during lessons. This supports Kacey, Nathaniel, Odette, and Victoria.

ES17. Provide target student with materials for exploration with hands when objects are described. This supports Kacey.

SS6. Encourage active listening by routinely asking students to restate or summarize what has been said by peers. This supports Heaven, Ian, and Randolph.

Evaluate

Time: 5 minutes

Say: *Please complete this self-evaluation and talk with a friend about what you learned and you still need help with.* Have students complete the Flicking and Forces Self-Assessment shown in Figure 3.8.

THIRD-GRADE LESSON: Social Studies

Time allotted: 45 minutes

Standards used: The Ohio State Social Studies Standards were used for this lesson (Ohio Department of Education, 2010).

Context: Students learn all about communities in third-grade social studies. They have learned about time lines, maps, and primary documents, such as photographs, as sources for understanding how communities change over time. They have learned to read physical and political maps and understand that the way people in a community live influences the environment. The students have learned about government structures and how laws are made to protect and regulate communities. They are now learning about the economics of communities and have completed lessons on reading line graphs that provide data on communities. They understand the concepts of goods versus services, income, and use of currency to acquire goods and services. Today, they are learning about scarcity, opportunity cost, and how to make decisions about purchasing goods and services.

Lesson Objective

Students will understand the following topic and content standard.

Theme: Communities: Past and Present, Near and Far

Strand: Economics

Topic: Scarcity

Content statement: 16. Individuals must make decisions because of the scarcity of resources. Making a decision involves an opportunity cost, the value of the next best alternative given up when an economic choice is made (Ohio Department of Education, 2010, p. 16).

Before This Lesson

Advance Preparation

1. Print colored photos of 10 goods and 10 services (see the "Materials" section). Laminate. Label in braille and all first languages. Review with Nathaniel and Victoria before school during ENL instruction.

2. Create an Opportunity Costs worksheet as an exit ticket for the lesson (see Figure 3.9). Reproduce in braille, Ukrainian, and Mandarin. Post on the class web site.

3. Have available stoplight response cards that students can use to show their level of understanding (green = working independently; yellow = working but have a question; red = stuck, need help).

Connections With Other Team Members

Consult with the TVI and ENL teacher. Plan for introduction of vocabulary during before-school ENL instruction.

Name: _____		
Opportunity Cost: Exit Ticket		
What are three essential goods or services?	What are three nonessential goods or services?	If you could not afford all six of these, which would you buy? Why?

Figure 3.9. Opportunity Cost worksheet third-grade social studies lesson.

Desired Results

"I Can" Statements

- I can determine which goods and services are needs and which are wants.

- I can analyze which goods and services to purchase.

- I can explore the impact, or opportunity cost, of my purchasing decisions.

- I can examine factors that make purchasing decisions more difficult for some people.

INCLUSIVE PRACTICES

These apply to all students and should not be differentiated. Regardless of the supports individual students receive, they are all working toward these goals and understandings.

Assessment Evidence

Assessment evidence will consist of performance tasks, self-assessments, and other evidence that the students are mastering the identified goals and understandings. The following evidence will be used for this lesson:

- Student lists goods and services that are necessary (needs) and goods and services that are not necessary but enjoyable (wants).

- Student plays role of consumer and decides how to spend his or her money.

- Student uses stoplight response cards to show level of understanding.

- Teacher observes students sharing examples during class discussion.

- Teacher observes students responding to teacher questions during demonstration.

INCLUSIVE PRACTICES

All students will engage in discussion and participate in the activity.

Classroom Arrangement

- Students sit at their desks, arranged in five groups of four. Create heterogeneous groups based on skill development, and have them face the interactive whiteboard at the front of the classroom.

- Students may choose to sit on the floor or other seating (cushion).

INCLUSIVE PRACTICES

SS1. Use peer groups to practice conversations about topics that are centered around the curriculum. This is a support for Ian, Nathaniel, and Sebastian.

SS9. Allow cooperative work to happen during all content areas with flexible grouping. This is a support for Antoine, Chelsea, Ethan, and Sebastian.

SR5. Provide all students a choice of seating in the classroom. This is a support for Ethan and Gabrielle.

Materials

- Pictures of 10 goods (food, water, clothes, house, medicine, car, cell phone, television, toys, books) and 10 services (hospital, dentist's office, school, police, sanitation removal, barber shop/hair salon, landscape services, amusement park, airline, radio broadcast), 20 copies each, labeled in multiple languages and braille. Arrange the pictures into 5 "kits," each with four copies of each picture.

- Icons of the same 10 goods and 10 services on the interactive whiteboard

- Five cards, each with a different number (3, 6, 9, 12, 15), labeled in braille

- Teacher-created exit tickets (in braille, multiple languages, loaded on laptops, posted on the class web site)

- Variety of writing tools (e.g., pencils, markers) with pencil grips

- Colored strips of plastic for worksheets

- Teacher-created desk map on the board to show which materials to gather and have on desk

- Stoplight response cards

- Fidgets

- Self-amplifiers

INCLUSIVE PRACTICES

ES8. Provide all written materials in braille. Provide all written materials in first languages.

This is a support for Kacey, Nathaniel, and Victoria.

R8. Provide labels in classroom. Everything in the classroom is labeled with its name in multiple languages. Student's belongings have his or her photo on them. This supports Nathaniel and Victoria.

OS7. Tape a small drawing of the inside of the desk to the top of the desk, showing where books, notebooks, writing utensils, or other materials are stored. This is a support for Justice.

SR4. Ensure that all students are familiar with regulation scales, and many have them at their desks for self-checks. Some are for voice volume and emotional escalation; some for effective use of work time; some for interest or independence level for an activity. This supports Antoine, Chelsea, Heaven, Latoya, and Randolph.

SR8: Provide fidgets and mandalas to all students. This will particularly support Ethan and Latoya while watching videos and listening to instruction.

SR17. Provide a self-amplifier for student to self-talk or read aloud to support processing.

This supports Tabitha.

WS1. Ensure that all students have access to computers and instructional technology for all writing tasks.

Learning Activities

Allow for breaks, walks, and use of the "calming corner" during the lesson. Share vocabulary on goods cards with Nathaniel and Victoria in advance.

Anticipatory Set

Time: 10 minutes

1. Display the 10 goods and 10 services on the interactive whiteboard alongside a *t*-chart labeled "Essential (Needs)" and "Nonessential (Wants)."

2. Say: *I have displayed several goods on top of the board here and several services on the bottom. I would like you to help me decide which are essential, or needs, and which are nonessential, or wants. Who can tell me what* essential *means?* [Sample student responses: Something you need to live; something you can't do without; something that you need to be healthy; something that is important instead of fun.]

3. Call on a student to determine if an item is essential or nonessential. There are a few items that may be trickier and require discussion (e.g., car, cell phone, sanitation removal). Provide explanations as needed. For example: *Cars and cell phones may be necessary to call or travel to essential services, such as the hospital, but they do not keep you healthy themselves, so they are not essential. Although sanitation removal does not provide you with essentials such as food, water, medicine, clothes or shelter, it is important for prevention of polluted water and spread of pests who carry disease, so it does keep you healthy.*

4. Say: *Now that we have determined which goods and services are essential and nonessential, I am going to give you a chance to purchase the goods and services you would prefer.*

INCLUSIVE PRACTICES

SR3. Allow all students breaks in or out of the classroom. This supports Antoine and Ethan.

SR7. Provide a "calming corner" for all students, equipped with soft seating, carpet, sensory tools, and so forth. Students may go to the corner as needed. This supports Antoine and Latoya.

SR2. Allow all students short walks down the hall. This supports Gabrielle.

LAE1. Before group time, give target student a question that can be answered with a new or familiar icon or vocabulary word. This supports Nathaniel and Victoria.

Modeling

Time: 5 minutes

Say: *Everyone in a community can make their own decisions about what goods and services to purchase, but they may be unable to afford everything that is available. In that case, they must think about which is the best purchase to make. If they purchase one thing, then they will have to go without something else. That is called* opportunity cost. *They don't have the opportunity to have everything, so they have to figure out what they can manage without. For example, if I had all of my essential goods and services, and I could afford one nonessential good or service, then I would have to choose the best one for me. I would choose books because reading is my favorite activity.*

INCLUSIVE PRACTICES

ES8. Provide all written materials in braille. Provide all written materials in first languages. This is a support for Kacey, Nathaniel, and Victoria.

Guided to Independent Practice

Time: 15 minutes

1. Have students form five groups with four students each. Distribute a kit of goods and services to the center of each small group. Explain that each person in the group can afford a total of 12 goods and services.

2. Give them 1–2 minutes to make their selections and lay the selected items on their desks. This will give them enough time to buy all of the essential items and then make decisions about which two nonessential items to buy. Have two to three students share what they chose.

3. Have students return their items to the center. Then tell them they now have fewer resources, so each person can only afford seven goods and services. Give them 1–2 minutes to make their selections.

4. Ask: *Was your decision easier or more difficult to make that time? Why?* [Students' opinions may vary. Some may say that it was easier because they knew they had to buy all essential items. Others may say it was more difficult to choose which essential items to do without.]

5. Say: *A scarcity, or lack, of resources for purchasing goods and services changes the decision you have to make.*

6. Place a numbered card at each group of desks and explain that the card tells them the number of items each person in the group can now afford. Give them 1–2 minutes to make their selections. Have one student from each table share how many items they were able to afford.

7. Ask: *Why would some people in a community be able to afford more than others?* [Student responses may include: because they make more money; because they save their money.]

 INCLUSIVE PRACTICES

ES8. Provide all written materials in braille. Provide all written materials in first languages. This is a support for Kacey, Nathaniel, and Victoria.

ES4. For all information that the teacher reviews orally, write the information clearly for all students and/or post it on the class web site—announcements, homework assignments, notes, agenda. This supports Nathaniel and Victoria.

ES7. Think aloud when writing, spelling, or punctuating on board/during lessons. This supports Kacey, Odette, Nathaniel, and Victoria.

R1. Provide charts of academic language and symbols. This supports Nathaniel and Victoria.

WS13. Use graphic organizers with the whole class, allowing for student choice. Scaffold the organizers to meet diverse learning needs (e.g., fewer items to fill in, some text provided, use of a word or sentence bank). Stock them in common areas of the classroom and save them on the computers that students use for work. This supports Sebastian, Nathaniel, and Victoria.

Critical Thinking Discussion

Time: 10 minutes

1. Ask: *What happens when some people in a community have more scarcity of resources than others and can't afford all of the essentials?* If needed, provide examples (e.g., what if they had to decide to do without a doctor or education). [Students' responses

might include: they might not be able to stay healthy or live well; they might not be able to go places or read books and get an education.]

2. Explain: *Their opportunity cost would be greater because their decision would be much harder to make.*

INCLUSIVE PRACTICES

SS12. Strategically use prequestions before discussions. Provide two to three questions on index cards that will be asked during discussion so student can formulate answers in advance and be encouraged to volunteer during discussion. This supports Ian.

SR17. Provide a self-amplifier for student to self-talk or read aloud to support processing. This supports Tabitha.

Closure

Time: 5 minutes

1. Have students engage in a 2-minute think-pair-share to discuss what they learned about scarcity and opportunity cost.

2. Distribute Opportunity Costs worksheet, with the following questions, as an exit ticket:
    *   What are three essential goods or services?
    *   What are three nonessential goods or services?
    *   If you cannot afford all six of these, then which would you buy? Why?

INCLUSIVE PRACTICES

R8. Provide labels in classroom. Everything in the classroom is labeled with its name in multiple languages. Student's belongings have his or her photo on them. This supports Nathaniel and Victoria.

ES8. Provide all written materials in braille. Provide all written materials in first languages. This is a support for Kacey, Nathaniel, and Victoria.

SS9. Allow cooperative work to happen during all content areas with flexible grouping. This benefits Antoine, Chelsea, Ethan, and Sebastian.

THIRD-GRADE LESSON: Art

Time allotted: 60 minutes (two art classes, based on 30-minute specials)

Standards used: The New York State Learning Standards for the Arts: Visual Arts Standards were used to identify standards, essential questions, and enduring understandings for this lesson.

Context: The arts curriculum covers several areas—creating; performing, presenting, and producing; responding; and connecting. Students in pre-K through sixth grade build their knowledge and skills in these areas over several years as they learn new techniques, present their original work in different ways, and delve deeper into the historical and cultural facets of art. In this lesson, students are creating original works of art while they investigate the concepts of monochromatic design, color theory, and simplified details in drawing. The high-contrast elements of this project are natural supports for Kacey.

The art instruction and activities presented in this lesson are credited to Lisa Jordan, Art Teacher, Brighton Central School District, New York.

As with other specials, art is taught by a specialist; in this case, a certified art teacher.

Lesson Objectives

1. Organize and develop artistic ideas and work. (New York State Visual Arts Anchor Standard 2)

2. Create artwork using a variety of artistic processes and materials. (VA: Cr2.1.3)

Before This Lesson

Advance Preparation

1. Print images of animals with simple, yet distinctive characteristics (e.g., birds, fish, insects).

2. Complete the art project multiple times in various stages for modeling.

Connections With Other Team Members

• Consult the TVI and ENL teacher for accurate translation.

• Check in with the art teacher a day or two before the scheduled art lesson to discuss supports students might need for specific activities, including materials for Kacey to explore with her hands and other supports for individual students, as described next.

Desired Results

"I Can" Statements

• I can draw from observation.

• I can simplify details of the subject I am drawing.

• I can tell you about color theory.

• I can mix shades and tints.

• I can demonstrate brush care and size choice.

• I can tell you about my craftsmanship.

INCLUSIVE PRACTICES

These apply to all students and should not be differentiated. Regardless of the supports individual students receive, they are all working toward these goals and understandings. All of the students will choose their own materials and create their own project.

Assessment Evidence

Assessment evidence will consist of performance tasks, self-assessments, and other evidence that the students are mastering the identified goals and understandings. The following evidence will be used for this lesson:

• Students will create a drawing of an animal of their choice, simplifying detail and focusing on distinctive characteristics (Day 1).

• Students will portion their drawings into sections, akin to a paint-by-number template (Day 1).

• Students will mix five to six different shades and tints of the same color (Day 2).

• Students will paint the sections of their drawing (Day 2).

- Students will use stoplight response cards to show level of understanding (green = working independently; yellow = working but have a question; red = stuck, need help).

- The teacher will observe students sharing examples during class discussion.

- The teacher will observe students responding to teacher questions during demonstration.

- The teacher will observe students' safe and appropriate use of materials and tools.

 INCLUSIVE PRACTICES

All students will create a project and reflect on their work.

Classroom Arrangement

- Students sit at art tables, on stools, arranged in groups of three.

- Create heterogeneous groups based on skill development, and have them face the interactive whiteboard at the front of the classroom.

- Students may choose to sit at an easel on a standard chair with or without a cushion.

 INCLUSIVE PRACTICES

SS1. Use peer groups to practice conversations about topics that are centered around the curriculum. This is a support for Ian, Nathaniel, and Sebastian.

SS9. Allow cooperative work to happen during all content areas with flexible grouping. This is a support for Antoine, Chelsea, Ethan, and Sebastian.

SR5. Provide all students a choice of seating in the classroom. This is a support for Ethan and Gabrielle.

Materials

- Several photos of birds, fish, and insects

- 16" x 20" sheet of watercolor paper for each student

- Bright-colored paints

- High-contrast paint trays

- Pencils

- Black marking pens with varying tip widths

- Paintbrushes of various sizes

- Pencil grips

- Wax craft sticks

- Stoplight response cards

- Fidgets

- Self-amplifiers

- Models of each stage of project (simple drawing, drawing with sections, painted drawing), each with raised outlines added for Kacey. See Figure 3.10, which shows stages 1, 2, 3, and 4 of the project.

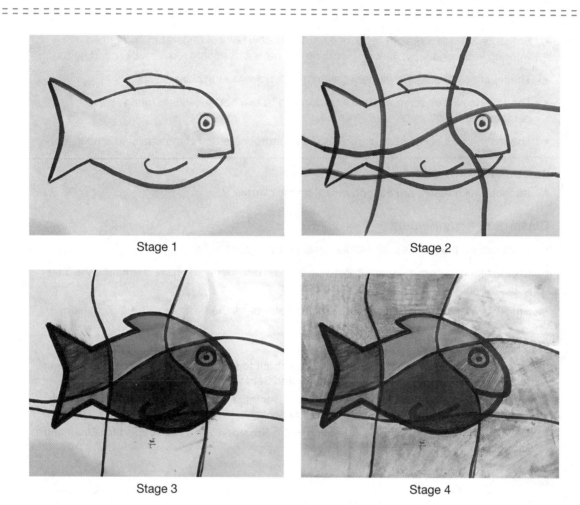

Figure 3.10. Stages 1–4 of a monochromatic watercolor painting for a third-grade art lesson.

 INCLUSIVE PRACTICES

ES17. Provide materials for target student to explore with hands when objects are described. This supports Kacey.

OS10. Create a coded classroom. Have all items and storage units in classroom labeled in first languages and braille, with photos. This supports Kacey, Nathaniel, and Victoria.

R8. Provide labels in classroom. Everything in the classroom is labeled with its name in multiple languages. Student's belongings have his or her photo on them. This supports Nathaniel and Victoria.

SR4. Ensure that all students are familiar with regulation scales, and many have them at their desks for self-checks. Some are for voice volume and emotional escalation; some for effective use of work time; some for interest or independence level for an activity. This supports Antoine, Chelsea, Heaven, Latoya, and Randolph.

SR8. Provide fidgets and mandalas to all students. This will particularly support Ethan and Latoya while watching videos and listening to instruction.

SR17. Provide a self-amplifier for student to self-talk or read aloud to support processing. This supports Tabitha.

Learning Activities

Allow for breaks and walks during the lesson.

Anticipatory Set (Day 1)

Time: 5 minutes

1. Display photos of animals in hard copy or on the interactive whiteboard. Ask: *Which features stand out when you study these animals?* [Student responses may include: birds' wings, feathers, beaks, feet; fishes' gills, fins lips, eyes; insects' legs wings, body sections.]

2. Say: *Yes, you are analyzing their most distinctive characteristics. The project we are going to complete over the next 2 days will focus on these characteristics. We are going to highlight them using simple drawings and monochromatic colors. If I told you that* mono *means single or one, and* chromo *means color, what would you say* monochromatic *means?* [Student responses may include: one color; single color; only one color].

3. Hold up your finished project (see the example in Figure 3.10) and point out how simple details and one color can highlight the main features of the subject.

INCLUSIVE PRACTICES

SR3. Allow all students breaks in or out of the classroom. This supports Antoine and Ethan.

SR2. Allow all students short walks down the hall. This supports Gabrielle.

Modeling

Time: 5 minutes

1. Say: *You may choose any animal you like for this project. I chose a fish because I like the gracefulness in their lines and the simplicity of their defining characteristics—the fins and eyes. This project has four steps. We will work on the first two today and finish next time.*

2. Hold up the model of the first step of your project (the simple drawing; see Stage 1 in Figure 3.10). Provide one with raised lines for Kacey to explore. Say: *The first step is to create a simple drawing of the animal. Which characteristics did I include in my drawing?* [Student responses: fins, eyes, tail.] *Which details did I leave out?* [Student responses: scales, lips, gills.]

3. Say: *Yes, right. You do not need every detail to represent the image of a fish. I focused on the main details. Now let's get you started on your drawings.*

INCLUSIVE PRACTICES

ES17. Provide target student with materials for exploration with hands when objects are described. This supports Kacey.

LESSON PLANS

Guided to Independent Practice

Time: 15 minutes

1. Distribute the following to each work area (or have one student from each area collect each supply):
   - Watercolor paper for each student
   - Pencils
   - Black marking pens

2. Circulate and guide students as they choose the subject and begin their drawings. You may need to redirect students to focus on two or three main details at the most and not try to recreate every detail.

3. When students have completed their simple drawings, hold up your model of the second step (the sectioned drawing; see Stage 2 in Figure 3.10), providing one with raised lines for Kacey to explore. Demonstrate how you drew lines across the page and through your drawing to section the whole page into parts that will be painted. Say: *You may choose to draw straight lines or curvy lines. I chose curvy lines to represent water around my fish. You may also draw lines up and down or diagonally across the page. You only want a few lines in each direction so your sections are not too small. We will be painting each section next time. Once my lines were drawn with pencil, I retraced the lines and my drawing with black marking pen to emphasize each section.*

INCLUSIVE PRACTICES

ES8. Provide all written materials in braille. Provide all written materials in first languages. This applies to labels on material bins/shelves to benefit Kacey, Nathaniel, and Victoria.

R8. Provide labels in classroom. Everything in the classroom is labeled with its name in multiple languages. Student's belongings have his or her photo on them. This supports Nathaniel and Victoria.

ES11. Model and teach the class about identifying self and locations in the room ("It's under the window on the top shelf" versus "It's over there by Paige"). This benefits Kacey and Odette.

ES17. Provide target student with materials for exploration with hands when objects are described. This supports Kacey.

Closure (Day 1)

Time: 5 minutes

Say: *As we wrap up for today, who would like to share their drawing?* As two to three students share, ask which features they chose to highlight and how they chose to section the page. This facilitates reflection on their artwork and presentation to an audience.

Anticipatory Set (Day 2)

Time: 2 minutes

When students enter, have their drawings out for them to quickly pick up from the previous class and maximize painting time. Say: *I've put your developing artwork on your workspaces. Who thinks they know the next step?* [Student response: Painting!]

Guided to Independent Practice

Time: 20 minutes

1. Hold up your model of the painted monochromatic fish (see Stage 3 in Figure 3.10), providing one with raised lines for Kacey to explore. Say: *Remember what we said* monochromatic *means? Think about the separate word parts* mono *and* chromo. [Student response: One color.] *As you can see, it doesn't mean painting the whole page the same shade of the same color; rather, painting each section a different shade of the color. I chose green.* As you think aloud, demonstrate how you placed some green paint in each of the six wells of your paint tray, then added varying amounts of white paint to create five to six different shades. Then show how you numbered each section of your drawing, thinking about which sections to paint which color.

2. Have students think for 2 minutes about their project and the color they would like to use. Have students gather the following materials:

   - Three colors of paint—black, white, and a color of their choice

   - Paint tray

   - Paintbrushes, with pencil grips if they choose

   - Smock or apron

3. Purposefully talk through each step of mixing shades of paint.

4. Have them number the sections of their drawings, making sure there are different shades in adjacent sections.

5. Circulate as students paint.

INCLUSIVE PRACTICES

ES7. Think aloud when writing, spelling, or punctuating on board/during lessons.

SR17. Provide a self-amplifier for student to self-talk or read aloud to support processing. This supports Tabitha.

SR12. Provide vibrating wrist alarm to remind student to return to task. This supports Justice.

Closure

Time: 8 minutes

When paintings are complete, have students clean up supplies and ask about their experiences with choosing which features to highlight, mixing paint to create different shades, and mapping out their drawings before painting the sections.

INCLUSIVE PRACTICES

ES8. Provide all written materials in braille. Provide all written materials in first languages. This supports Kacey, Nathaniel, and Victoria.

ES17. Provide target student with materials for exploration with hands when objects are described. This supports Kacey.

SR17. Provide a self-amplifier for student to self-talk or read aloud to support processing. This supports Tabitha.

THIRD-GRADE LESSON: Physical Education

Time allotted: 30 minutes

Standards used: The SHAPE America's National Standards & Grade-Level Outcomes for K–12 Physical Education were used for this lesson.

Context: The physical education curriculum focuses on the areas of motor skills; knowledge of movement and performance in various games and sports; maintaining physical fitness; and safety, responsibility, self-expressions, and social aspects of physical fitness. Students in kindergarten through sixth grade build on their knowledge and skills across all areas. Today, the students are learning about the importance and benefits of warming up and cooling down when exercising to remain healthy and avoid injury.

As with other specials, physical education is taught by a specialist; in this case, a certified physical education teacher.

Lesson Objectives

1. The physically literate individual demonstrates the knowledge and skills to maintain a health-enhancing level of physical activity and fitness. (SHAPE Standard 3)

2. [The physically literate individual] recognizes the importance of warm-up and cool-down relative to vigorous physical exercise (SHAPE America, 2013, p. 16). (S3.E4.3)

Before This Lesson

Advance preparation

1. Learn supports for Kacey.

2. Translate academic language for Nathaniel and Victoria.

Connections With Other Team Members

• Consult with the TVI and COMS regarding supports for Kacey in demonstrating performance of skills.

• Consult with ENL teacher.

• Check in with the physical education teacher a day or two before the scheduled physical education lesson to discuss supports students might need for specific activities, as described next.

Desired Results

"I Can" Statements

• I can recognize the importance of warm up and cool down.

• I can tell you that safety and knowledge of the body is important in exercise and fitness.

• I can recognize that unsafe exercise can result in injury.

 INCLUSIVE PRACTICES

These apply to all students and should not be differentiated. Regardless of the supports individual students receive, they are all working toward these goals and understandings.

Assessment Evidence

Assessment evidence will consist of performance tasks, self-assessments, and other evidence that the students are mastering the identified goals and understandings. The following evidence will be used for this lesson:

- Students will perform safe and effective warm-up exercises.

- Students will explain why warming up before stretching and exercising is important.

- Students will demonstrate favorite stretches that are effective for warming up.

- The teacher will observe students sharing examples during class discussion.

- The teacher will observe students responding to teacher questions during demonstration.

INCLUSIVE PRACTICES

All of the students will perform the activities. All of the students will answer questions about safe exercise and the impact of warming up.

Classroom Arrangement

- Students are positioned on the mat, spaced evenly.

INCLUSIVE PRACTICES

SR5. Provide all students with a choice of seating in the classroom. This is a support for Ethan and Gabrielle.

Materials

- Regulation scales

INCLUSIVE PRACTICES

SR4. Ensure that all students are familiar with regulation scales, and many have them at their desks for self-checks. Some are for voice volume and emotional escalation; some for effective use of work time; some for interest or independence level for an activity. This supports Antoine, Chelsea, Heaven, Latoya, and Randolph.

Learning Activities

Allow for breaks and walks during the lesson.

Anticipatory Set

Time: 10 minutes

1. Have students gently and slowly attempt a V-sit and reach stretch. Have students mentally record how tight they feel and the difficulty of the tasks.

2. Have the students walk or jog around the gym for a few minutes.

3. Ask: *How do you feel? Is your heart rate increased or decreased? Are you sweating? Are you warmer or colder?* [Students' responses will vary.] Allow a few moments for them to discuss their physical sensations and any changes they notice. Say: *Try the V-sit and reach stretch again. How does it feel now?*

4. Explain that warmed-up muscles stretch and work better. Slow and steady is important. A muscle might tear if it is not warmed up or is stretched too hard too fast.

INCLUSIVE PRACTICES

SR3. Allow all students breaks in or out of the classroom. This supports Antoine and Ethan.

SR2. Allow all students short walks down the hall. This supports Gabrielle.

R1. Provide charts of academic language and symbols. This supports Nathaniel and Victoria.

Modeling and Guided Practice

Time: 15 minutes

1. Introduce safe and effective warm-up activities. Think aloud as you do each one to model safe, purposeful movements. To introduce dancing, say: *This activity is one of my favorites because I can do any movements I like as I listen to the music. I like to start out slowly and swing my arms while I move my feet a little, then go a bit faster and swivel in place too. I like that it gently warms up my arms, legs, and torso.*

   To introduce high knees, say: *I am going to walk clockwise around the room, being careful to give my friends lots of space. While I walk, I lift my knees high in the air. I can feel my legs warming up and my heart working more. After a bit, sometimes I hold my arms up and touch the opposite knee as I raise it. That takes a little practice, but I like the challenge.*

2. Continue to think aloud in this way for the rest of the movements:

   • Lunges: Step forward with one leg and lower so the knee is at a 90-degree angle and the back leg is stretched out long. Alternate legs.

   • Arm circles: Hold arms outstretched from shoulders and turn in small circles, then increase the size of the circles.

   • Jumping jacks: When you are ready to add some more intensity to your warm-up exercises, incorporate jumping jacks—they involve both arms and legs and add impact to your routine.

   • Hopping: With feet together, jump from one side of an imaginary line to the other. Or hop on one foot and switch back and forth.

   • Sidewinder: Walk or jog sideways, crossing one foot in front of the other in an alternating pattern, or shuffle sideways without crossing feet.

INCLUSIVE PRACTICES

ES7. Think aloud when writing, spelling, or punctuating on board/during lessons. This benefits Kacey, Odette, Nathaniel, and Victoria.

LESSON PLANS

Closure

Time: 5 minutes

1. Have students volunteer to demonstrate their favorite warm-up exercises. They can choose to do this with a partner.

2. Ask: *Why do we warm up before stretching?* [Student responses may include: So we don't get hurt; so it is easier to stretch.] *What happens to our muscles when they become warmer?* [Student response: They loosen up so they can stretch easier.] *What could happen to our muscles if we stretch them when they are not warmed up?* [Student response: They might get hurt; they might get a strain.]

INCLUSIVE PRACTICES

SS1. Use peer groups to practice conversations about topics that are centered around the curriculum. This is a support for Ian, Nathaniel, and Sebastian.

SS9. Allow cooperative work to happen during all content areas with flexible grouping. This is a support for Antoine, Chelsea, Ethan, and Sebastian.

THIRD-GRADE LESSON: Music

Time allotted: 30 minutes

Standards used: NAFME 2014 General Music standards are used.

Context: Third-grade students copy and create music and become familiar with a range of instruments, and schools often use recorders or ukuleles as students begin third grade. Second-grade students are introduced to two-part songs and harmony and practice singing in tune and on pitch. Students also learn about musical symbols such as the treble clef, bar line, and measure. Students have recently explored different instruments such as shakers, maracas, rain sticks, wood blocks, and finger cymbals. Today, students will listen to a story (e.g., *Three Little Pigs*) and use instruments to express elements of the story.

As with other specials, music is taught by a specialist; in this case, a certified music teacher.

Lesson Objectives

1. Improvise rhythmic and melodic ideas and describe connection to specific purpose and context (such as, personal and social). (MU:Cr1.1.3a)

2. Generate musical ideas (such as rhythms and melodies) within a given tonality and/or meter. (MU:Cr1.1.3b)

INCLUSIVE PRACTICES

These apply to all students and should not be differentiated. Regardless of the supports individual students receive, they are all working toward these goals and understandings.

Before This Lesson

Advance Preparation

1. Select the song you will use in the lesson.

2. Plan to have audio or video available to play the song during the lesson.

3. Make copies of accompanying song lyrics (in multiple languages, braille, and posted on the class web site).

Connections With Other Team Members

- Consult with the TVI and ENL teacher. Plan for introduction of vocabulary during before-school ENL instruction.

- Check in with the music teacher a day or two before the scheduled music lesson to discuss supports students might need for specific activities, as described next.

Desired Results

"I Can" Statements

- I can retell a story.

- I can make a rhythm or melody to share an idea.

- I can use an instrument to share an idea.

Assessment Evidence

Assessment evidence will consist of performance tasks, self-assessments, and other evidence that the students are mastering the identified goals and understandings. The following evidence will be used for this lesson:

- Students will be assessed based on objectives. Encourage the students to be creative in coming up with their instruments and rhythms.

- Students will respond thoughtfully when asked why they chose the instrument they did.

- The teacher will observe students sharing examples during class discussion.

- The teacher will observe students responding to teacher questions during demonstration.

Classroom Arrangement

- Students are arranged in groups of six.

- Students may choose to sit on the floor or other seating (cushion).

 INCLUSIVE PRACTICES

SS1. Use peer groups to practice conversations about topics that are centered around the curriculum. This is a support for Ian, Nathaniel, and Sebastian.

SS9. Allow cooperative work to happen during all content areas with flexible grouping. This is a support for Antoine, Chelsea, Ethan, and Sebastian.

SR5. Provide all students with a choice of seating in the classroom. This is a support for Ethan and Gabrielle.

Materials

- Rhythm instruments (e.g., shakers, maracas, rain stick, wood block, finger cymbals)

- Video or audio recording of a song that tells a story

- Copies of accompanying song lyrics (in multiple languages, braille, and posted on the class web site).

INCLUSIVE PRACTICES

ES8. Provide all written materials in braille. Provide all written materials in first languages. This is a support for Kacey.

R8. Provide labels in classroom. Everything in the classroom is labeled with its name in multiple languages. Student's belongings have his or her photo on them. This is a support for Nathaniel and Victoria.

SR4. Ensure that all students are familiar with regulation scales, and many have them at their desks for self-checks. Some are for voice volume and emotional escalation; some for effective use of work time; some for interest or independence level for an activity. This supports Antoine, Chelsea, Heaven, Latoya, and Randolph.

SR8: Provide fidgets and mandalas to all students. This will particularly support Ethan and Latoya while watching videos and listening to instruction.

Learning Activities

Allow for breaks, walks, and use of the "calming corner" during the lesson.

Anticipatory Set

Time: 5 minutes

1. Tell students they will listen to a song and select an instrument that will represent an action that happens in the story.

2. Play a song that includes a story. There are many examples online! *Three Little Pigs* is used as an example in this lesson. (A quick Internet search will yield multiple sung versions.) Play it straight through one time. Ask students to retell the story to a peer.

3. Say: *Now that we have heard and talked about the story, we are going to retell it using our instruments! I will show you what I mean.*

INCLUSIVE PRACTICES

ES8. Provide all written materials in braille. Provide all written materials in first languages. This is a support for Kacey, Nathaniel, and Victoria.

SR3. Allow all students breaks in or out of the classroom. This supports Antoine and Ethan.

SR2. Allow all students short walks down the hall. This supports Gabrielle.

Modeling

Time: 5 minutes

1. Say: *To show you what I mean by telling a story with instruments, we are going to hear the story again. This time, I am going to add an instrument each time the wolf comes to the door. I will use the shaker to stand for the wolf coming up to the door.*

2. Play the song again, stopping it each time the wolf comes to the door and demonstrating using the shaker softly, then louder for each time the wolf approaches.

INCLUSIVE PRACTICES

ES17. Provide target student with materials for exploration with hands when objects are described. This supports Kacey.

Guided Practice

Time: 5 minutes

1. Say: *Now that we have a song with a story, we are going to add in all the instruments. Here are our instruments.* Show a range of instruments, including shakers, maracas, rain sticks, wood blocks, finger cymbals, or other rhythm instruments.

2. *Let's pick a part of the story to use the instrument.* As a class, decide what each instrument will stand for. Examples of places to add instruments for the *Three Little Pigs* include the pigs running and hiding (in the straw house, wood house, and brick house), the wolf calling to the pigs ("Let me in!"), the pigs replying ("Not by the hair of my chinny-chin-chin!"), the wolf trying to blow each house down, and the pigs escaping to the wooden/brick house.

Independent Practice

Time: 10 minutes

1. Say: *Now we will have stations for each instrument, and you will rotate to each station to try each instrument. Try each one and think about how you would represent the part of the story with that instrument.*

2. Put instruments around the room in small groupings and divide the class into groups of three to four. Provide each student with the lyrics (in multiple languages, braille, and posted on the class web site).

3. Say: *I will tell you when it is time to move to the next station.* Give students 1–2 minutes at each station, then cue students to rotate.

4. With 1–2 minutes left, say: *Now that you have tried the instruments, it is time to pick the instrument you want to use as we finish by hearing the whole story with instruments. Please choose your instrument and come back to the front of the room.*

INCLUSIVE PRACTICES

LAR4. Allow students to work with a partner to take turns retelling details. This supports Nathaniel and Victoria.

Closure: Whole-Group Performance

Time: 5 minutes

1. Say: *Now that you have practiced all instruments for parts of the story, we will hear the story with all the instruments.*

2. Play the story with the whole class using their instruments for parts of the story.

3. After the song, have students return instruments and line up to leave class.

THIRD-GRADE LESSON: Technology

Time allotted: 30 minutes

Standards used: ISTE 3 Knowledge Constructor standards were used for this lesson.

Note: Technology lessons can be connected to other content areas. The technology skills in this lesson are connected to ELA. This lesson is designed for third or fourth grades. Technology standards from several states, including Missouri, California, and Michigan, were reviewed. The overlap in what is taught at various grade levels for technology was targeted for this lesson.

Context: Students have been learning strategies for research and information literacy. In this unit, they will practice using digital tools to find and organize information. They will talk about the importance of evaluating web sites and how some web sites may have information that is incorrect. In subsequent units, students will explore how to create content using technology (e.g., making computer art, using animation, coding) and how to communicate with technology (e.g., using blogs, wikis, or good apps).

Lesson Objectives

1. Students critically curate a variety of resources using digital tools to construct knowledge, produce creative artifacts, and make meaningful learning experiences for themselves and others (ISTE, 2017). (ISTE 3: Knowledge Constructor)

2. Students plan and employ effective research strategies to locate information and other resources for their intellectual or creative pursuits (ISTE, 2017). (ISTE 3a: Knowledge Constructor)

Before This Lesson

Advance Preparation

1. Make sure the voice output for Kacey's device or laptop is working.

2. Reserve devices or computer lab so that each student or pair of students has a device.

3. Ensure that devices are networked to a printer.

4. Ensure that filters recommended by the district are in place.

5. Ensure access to the Internet for the search.

6. Have stoplight response cards available for students to use to show level of understanding (green = working independently; yellow = working but have a question; red = stuck, need help).

7. Review the Scavenger Learning Hunt list (see Figure 3.11). Adjust it for your location. (In this example, words on the list were taken from third-grade spelling lists: short *a, e* words; short *i, o, u* words; long *a, e* words; long *i, o* words; words with the blends *st/str, kn/wr;* academic vocabulary.)

8. Create Internet Scavenger Hunt Self-Assessment; include the standard alignment (see Figure 3.12).

Name: _____

Scavenger Learning Hunt

Directions

1. Search for items 1–10. Copy and paste the address of the web site you found for each item.

2. Circle the items you found.

3. If you have time, continue your scavenger hunt with items 11–20.

I found these items:

1. Dress
2. Butterfly
3. Country
4. Plant
5. Lunch
6. Pond
7. Yard
8. School
9. Grade
10. Highway

If you have time:

11. Ocean
12. City
13. Earth
14. Stone
15. Wave
16. Stream
17. Milk
18. Knot
19. Wrist
20. Knee

Figure 3.11. Scavenger Learning Hunt list for third-grade technology lesson.

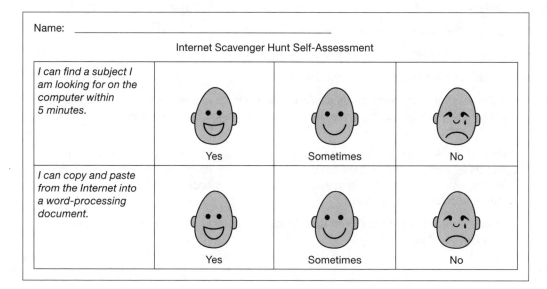

Figure 3.12. Internet Scavenger Hunt Self-Assessment for third-grade technology lesson.

Connections With Other Team Members

- Give scavenger hunt list and "I Can" statements to ENL teacher for translation for Nathaniel (Russian) and Victoria (Mandarin).

- Give scavenger hunt list and "I Can" statements to the TVI for translation into braille for Kacey.

- Check in with the school media specialist a day or two before the scheduled technology lesson to discuss other supports students might need for specific activities, as described next.

Desired Results

"I Can" Statements

- I can find a subject I am looking for on the computer within 5 minutes.

- I can copy and paste from the Internet into a word-processing document.

INCLUSIVE PRACTICES

These apply to all students and should not be differentiated. Regardless of the supports individual students receive, they are all working toward these goals and understandings.

Assessment Evidence

Assessment evidence will consist of performance tasks, self-assessments, and other evidence that the students are mastering the identified goals and understandings. The following evidence will be used for this lesson:

- For each item on the Scavenger Learning Hunt list, students will find a related web site with an image of the item and copy and paste the image into the list.

- Students will use stoplight response cards to show level of understanding.

- Students will complete the Internet Scavenger Hunt Self-Assessment.

- The teacher will conduct a review of students' self-assessment and materials to make a determination about reteaching or moving on to next lesson.

Classroom Arrangement

- Students sit at computers in computer lab.

INCLUSIVE PRACTICES

SS1. Use peer groups to practice conversations about topics that are centered around the curriculum. This is a support for Ian, Nathaniel, and Sebastian.

SS9. Allow cooperative work to happen during all content areas with flexible grouping. This is a support for Antoine, Chelsea, Ethan, and Sebastian.

SR5. Provide all students with a choice of seating in the classroom. This is a support for Ethan and Gabrielle.

Materials

- Projection of your computer screen to the class
- Access to the Internet, with appropriate filters as determined by the district
- Devices—enough for each child or each pair of children
- Devices networked to a printer
- Scavenger Learning Hunt worksheet (see Figure 3.11), provided in braille and in multiple languages, loaded on laptops, and posted on the class web site
- Internet Scavenger Hunt Self-Assessment (see Figure 3.12), provided in braille and in multiple languages, loaded on laptops, and posted on the class web site
- Stoplight response cards
- Fidgets
- Self-amplifiers

INCLUSIVE PRACTICES

ES8. Provide all written materials in braille. Provide all written materials in first languages. This is a support for Kacey, Nathaniel, and Victoria.

R8. Provide labels in classroom. Everything in the classroom is labeled with its name in multiple languages. Student's belongings have his or her photo on them. This is a support for Nathaniel and Victoria.

SR8: Provide fidgets and mandalas to all students. This will particularly support Ethan and Latoya while watching videos and listening to instruction.

SR17. Provide a self-amplifier for student to self-talk or read aloud to support processing. This supports Tabitha.

Learning Activities

Allow for breaks, walks, and use of the "calming corner" during the lesson.

Anticipatory Set

Time: 5 minutes

1. Say: *Today we are going to go on a scavenger hunt! Has anyone gone on one before? What do you do?* [Review scavenger hunts: Given a list of items, try to find them all.]

2. Continue: *In today's hunt, we are not going to walk around looking for things. We are going to use the Internet to find web sites with information about certain things. We are going to use the computers to search, and then we are going to copy and paste the web site addresses onto our document.*

INCLUSIVE PRACTICES

ES7. Think aloud when writing, spelling, or punctuating on the board/during lessons. This supports Kacey.

SR3. Allow all students breaks in or out of the classroom. This supports Antoine and Ethan.

SR7. Provide a "calming corner" for all students, equipped with soft seating, carpet, sensory tools, and so forth. Students may go to the corner as needed. This supports Antoine and Latoya.

SR2. Allow all students short walks down the hall. This supports Gabrielle.

Modeling

Time: 10 minutes

1. Tell students to put their name and date at the top of the page. Say: *Next, open a word-processing document on your screen and number from 1 to 20 in the program.*

2. Explain how to cut and paste, demonstrating each step as you narrate: *First, highlight the material you want from the Internet, then hold down the CTRL key and press the letter c at the same time. Next, go to your Word document and hold down the CTRL key and press the letter v at the same time. This will put the information from the Internet into a word-processing document.* (2–3 minutes)

3. Explain how the hunt will be done. Everyone will be given a list of items to find on the Internet using whichever search engine the student prefers. (If the class is not familiar with computers, then you might want to limit students to one search engine.) Say: *For each item on your list, you will need find a web site that tells about the item, and copy and paste the web address (located in the address bar) into your word-processing document.* (2 minutes)

4. Say: *Write the information on the Scavenger Learning Hunt.* If possible, go to a computer station that projects for all students to see. Say: *I will do the first word now. The first word is dress. I type d-r-e-s-s into the search bar at the top of my page.* Do so as you explain, and display the search results. Say: *See how many sites come up. The first one looks like a picture of a dress. That's what I need! Now I will go to that site.* Follow the link. Once at the site, say *Now I will decide if this fits. Do you think this site works for the word* dress? Check for questions. *If the site works, now I paste the web address to my document.* Demonstrate how to copy and paste. *Now that I have done the first word on the list, let's look at the "I Can" sentences.*

5. Show the "I Can" statements on the Internet Scavenger Hunt Self-Assessment:

    *   I can find a subject I am looking for on the computer within 5 minutes.

    *   I can copy and paste from the Internet into a word-processing document.

6. Say: *The subjects you are looking for are on the list of words. You saw me use copy and paste. Now it is your turn to find subjects using the list of words. As you work, I will move around the room to help you if you need it. You may begin your work.*

INCLUSIVE PRACTICES

ES7. Think aloud when writing, spelling, or punctuating on board/during lessons. This supports Kacey, Nathaniel, Odette, and Victoria.

Guided Practice

Time: 10 minutes

1. Have students open a word-processing program and document on the computer and then open their Internet browser to a search engine (2–3 minutes). Each student will have 10–15 minutes to find as many items on the list as they can.

2. Remind students that they can use their stoplight response cards.

3. Pass out the Scavenger Learning Hunt list, and tell the students to begin.

4. Walk around the room and monitor students' progress, helping the students if they need it.

5. Have students copy and paste each web site address into their word-processing document and then print the entire list when they are finished.

6. Announce a 5-minute warning when 5 minutes remain for independent work.

INCLUSIVE PRACTICES

ES7. Think aloud when writing, spelling, or punctuating on the board/during lessons. This supports Kacey, Nathaniel, Odette, and Victoria.

LAR4. Allow students to work with a partner to take turns retelling details. This supports Nathaniel and Victoria.

SR12. Provide vibrating wrist alarm to remind student to return to task. This supports Justice.

SR17. Provide a self-amplifier for student to self-talk or read aloud to support processing. This supports Tabitha.

Closure

Time: 5 minutes

Say: *It is time to stop your hunt! Please print your list. Then, complete the Internet Scavenger Hunt Self-Assessment.*

INCLUSIVE PRACTICES

LAR2. Embed one-step directions into whole-class morning routines, such as handing in homework, completing and handing in bell work, and following attendance procedures. This supports Nathaniel and Victoria.

Ms. Lee's Fifth-Grade Class

Ms. Lee's classroom has 20 students and is culturally and linguistically diverse. For example, Nigel lives in a multigenerational household with his mother and grandmother since his father's passing 2 years ago. Lucy is bilingual in English and Spanish. Paulette's family are Jehovah's Witnesses, which is uncommon in this school district, so teachers have sought ways to be sure their teaching is culturally responsive to this family. One student, John, has a 504 plan addressing needs for executive functioning difficulties, and three students—Grace, Mercedes, and Brian—have IEPs addressing their needs related to intellectual disability, cerebral palsy, and SLD dyslexia.

Grace has an intellectual disability. The SLP works with Grace each day to strengthen both receptive and expressive language skills during FIT. The literacy specialist pushes in to the ELA classroom every day to support Grace and Ms. Lee. Grace also has a one-to-one aide who supports her at all times.

Mercedes has cerebral palsy, uses a wheelchair, and receives occupational and physical therapy on alternate days in both specials and during FIT time. Mercedes attends physical education with the class with the support of the adaptive physical education teacher. The SLP pushes in every day during ELA to support Mercedes. Ms. Lee thinks about mobility and physical access for Mercedes on a day-to-day basis and manages a classroom with several professionals present.

Brian has dyslexia and works with Ms. Lee daily during FIT time for extra reading support. He also enjoys the sensory room and yoga. The literacy specialist who pushes in during ELA for Grace also works with Brian during this time.

Several students benefit from social skill support and have access to the Social Skill Manual as an inclusive practice. All students have an opportunity to contribute to or consult the Social Skill Manual, which the class created with the help of the counselor, who helped them come up with possible social scenarios and who facilitates the contribution of good social skill advice. Review the student profiles as you read these fifth-grade lesson plans for information about each child in the class.

STUDENT PROFILES AND
SUMMARY OF INCLUSIVE SUPPORTS

Alison

is outgoing and cheerful. She is willing to try new things and is not afraid to make mistakes. She loves cooking and baking, and her older brother is in culinary school. She lives with her parents, Sara and Paul, and three older siblings. Sara is a teacher's aide, and Paul works construction.

Alison loves art and writes many short stories. She benefits from a classroom that allows creative expression and choices in work time. She sometimes resists working with students other than her two best friends, and this caused some stress in fourth grade. Providing Alison with many opportunities to work with a range of peers in small groups will support her ability to work in groups.

Age: 11;0 years/Grade 5

Fountas & Pinnell Reading Level: T (grade level)

Math Level: Below grade

Disability Classification: None

Intervention/Notes: Alison has said that her parents will get her a math tutor. She receives math support in the classroom three times a week. Alison struggles with a schedule that is too rigid; it is helpful to give her plenty of time to make the transition from one activity or subject to the next. A block schedule would support her because limiting transitions is best for her.

Ways to Support Alison		
Engagement	**Environment/Group Work** Encourage making mistakes and talking about process, particularly in math. Assign small groups regularly, mixing groups weekly to support all students' getting to know each other.	**Social Skills/Communication** No needs at this time
Input	**Instructional Methods and Materials** No needs at this time	**Technology** No needs at this time
Output	**Self-Management/Executive Functions** Post schedule daily with times. Give 5- and 1-minute warnings at the end of each period to allow time for clean-up and transition.	**Test Accommodations** No needs at this time

Support Schedule and Flexible Instructional Time (FIT) for Alison

	Monday	Tuesday	Wednesday	Thursday	Friday
9:00–10:00 FIT choices	Social skill group Work with teacher Math support Yoga	Math support	Social skill group Work with teacher Math support Yoga	Math support	Social skill group Work with teacher Math support Yoga
10:00–10:45 During math	Math specialist in classroom		Math specialist in classroom		Math specialist in classroom

Goals and Practices

Alison's Goals	Inclusive Practices
Alison will increase her circle of friends and peers for group interactions.	SS9. Allow cooperative work to happen during all content areas with flexible grouping. SS10. Build in time each day for small-group work with peers, assigning individual roles within the group, to scaffold the interactions. SS11. Provide choices in working in pairs or small groups.
Alison will develop grade-level math skills.	MS5. Provide multiple sets of counters, plastic linking cubes, and fraction circles; have abacuses available so that all students can choose to use them. MS8. Provide a calculator for operations.
Alison will improve self-management skills.	ES5. Timer on interactive whiteboard that chimes and changes color to signal transitions to next task.

Brian

lives with his mothers, Katherine and Julie, and his younger brother. Katherine is a social worker, and Julie is an engineer. Brian is energetic and loves to talk about sports. He has a dog, two cats, and a fish tank at home, and he plans to be a vet.

Brian loves going to hockey and baseball games and reading about sports. His favorite baseball team is the Minnesota Twins. Brian benefits from regular breaks for movement, and he loved taking part in the Go Noodle classroom movement program in fourth grade.

Age: 10;4 years/Grade 5

Fountas & Pinnell Reading Level: P (typical for a third grader)

Math Level: At grade level

Disability Classification: IEP, dyslexia (SLD)

Intervention/Notes: Brian reads 120 words per minute, a typical rate for a beginning fourth grader. He has had an IEP since first grade for his dyslexia.

STUDENT SNAPSHOTS

Ways to Support Brian

Engagement	**Environment/Group Work** Provide a "move and learn" area of the room for all students where they can walk back and forth, jump, or jump rope.	**Social Skills/Communication** No needs at this time
Input	**Instructional Methods and Materials** Provide materials that reflect Brian's interests. When writing text on board or chart paper, alternate colors line by line to aid tracking. Build peer reading buddies into daily literacy lesson activities.	**Technology** Use Go Noodle and other apps to encourage movement. Use books on CD.
Output	**Self-Management/Executive Functions** Provide reminder questions for self-checking that his shoes are tied, chair is in, backpack is in cubby, and so forth.	**Test Accommodations** Do not time his math fact practice sheets.

Support Schedule and Flexible Instructional Time (FIT) for Brian

	Monday	Tuesday	Wednesday	Thursday	Friday
9:00–10:00 FIT choices	Reading support Work with teacher Sensory room Yoga	Reading support Work with teacher Sensory room Yoga	Reading support Work with teacher Sensory room Yoga	Reading support Work with teacher Sensory room Yoga	Reading support Work with teacher Sensory room Yoga
1:00–1:30 During English language arts (ELA)	Literacy specialist (leveled literacy intervention [LLI]) in classroom	Literacy specialist (LLI) in classroom	Literacy specialist (LLI) in classroom	Literacy specialist (LLI) in classroom	Literacy specialist (LLI) in classroom

Goals and Practices

Brian's Goals	Inclusive Practices
Brian will read texts at his independent and instructional level.	CR1. Provide culturally responsive curricular materials, materials that reflect student interest, and resources other than textbooks.
Brian will read to first-grade students regularly.	R6. Build peer reading buddies into daily literacy lesson activities.
Brian will increase his reading speed to 180 words per minute by the end of fifth grade.	R5. Provide several different eye-tracking supports, such as index cards, colored strips of plastic, and so forth. R6. Build peer reading buddies into daily literacy lesson activities.
Brian will regulate his movement in the classroom.	ES12. Provide a "move and learn" area of the room for all students where they can walk back and forth, jump, or jump rope. OS8. Post reminder questions in key locations, prompting students to self-check materials, work, and so forth (Rapp, 2014).

176

Rapp, Arndt, and Hildenbrand

Chloe

is caring and responsible. She is always on the lookout for how to help her peers and has a wide circle of friends. She lives with her mom, Meghan, her stepdad, Mark, her younger brother, Malcolm, and several stepsiblings in one household. Her dad, Drew, and an older half-brother live in a second household. Chloe and Malcolm make the transition between homes together. She is protective of Malcolm and sometimes goes to his classroom to read to his class.

Chloe loves to read, draw, and create. She is gifted and is sometimes a perfectionist.

Age: 10;8 years/Grade 5

Fountas & Pinnell Reading Level: Z (seventh- or eighth-grade level)

Math Level: Above grade

Disability Classification: None

Intervention/Notes: Chloe receives accelerated instruction for gifted and talented students twice a week. She benefits from a gentle style because she is sensitive and can be easily overwhelmed with harsh critique. She struggles to turn in work if she feels she made any mistakes.

Ways to Support Chloe

Engagement	**Environment/Group Work** No needs at this time	**Social Skills/Communication** No needs at this time
Input	**Instructional Methods and Materials** No needs at this time	**Technology** No needs at this time
Output	**Self-Management/Executive Functions** Provide response scale for quality of work. Chloe's scale has five choices because she tends to avoid making mistakes: 1—This work is not ready to turn in. I will work on it some more. 2—I have started this work. It is not complete. I will work on it some more. 3—I did some good work on this. I could turn it in now or work on it some more. 4—I worked hard on this. I am ready for feedback. I will turn it in. 5—This is my best work. I am ready for feedback. I will turn it in.	**Test Accommodations** No needs at this time

Support Schedule and Flexible Instructional Time (FIT) for Chloe

	Monday	Tuesday	Wednesday	Thursday	Friday
9:00–10:00 FIT choices	Accelerated instruction	Extended reading Social skill group Work with teacher Yoga	Accelerated instruction	Extended reading Social skill group Work with teacher Yoga	Accelerated instruction

Goals and Practices

Chloe's Goals	Inclusive Practices
Chloe will recognize her need for perfection in her work. Chloe will identify and utilize coping strategies to self-calm.	SR4. Ensure that all students are familiar with regulation scales, and many have them at their desks for self-checks. Chloe's will support her anxiety over making mistakes.
Chloe will engage in conversations and activities with peers.	SS9. Allow cooperative work to happen during all content areas with flexible grouping.

David

is quiet and funny. He is kind and generous and a good friend. He gravitates toward other boys and tends to ignore girls.

David lives with his mom, dad, and older sister. His mom, Alex, is an administrative assistant. His dad, Peter, is a building and grounds worker for the local school district. David loves fishing and camping and has done several weeklong hikes with his family.

Age: 10;5 years/Grade 5

Fountas & Pinnell Reading Level: N (third grade)

Math Level: At grade level

Disability Classification: None

Intervention/Notes: David is a reluctant reader and is embarrassed about reading below grade level. He benefits from opportunities to read aloud in a small group or with a teacher. His other academic skills are on grade level, as is his social-emotional development.

Ways to Support David

Engagement	**Environment/Group Work** Providing opportunities to lead a small group or presenting to others would benefit David.	**Social Skills/Communication** Assign partners, which will sometimes support David to get to know all his peers, including the girls. Be explicit that everyone reads at a different level, which will help David feel less embarrassed about his reading.
Input	**Instructional Methods and Materials** Talk about the outdoors and the environment to engage David. Encourage David to use a line guide for reading. He can be embarrassed if he sees that he is the only one using one. He would benefit if guides are offered to everyone.	**Technology** Providing opportunities to use iPads, tablets, or computers typically engages him.
Output	**Self-Management/Executive Functions** Encourage David to self-monitor his fluency; provide frequent feedback.	**Test Accommodations** No needs at this time

Support Schedule and Flexible Instructional Time (FIT) for David

	Monday	Tuesday	Wednesday	Thursday	Friday
9:00–10:00 FIT choices	Reading support Work with teacher Sensory room Yoga	Reading support Work with teacher Sensory room Yoga	Reading support Work with teacher Sensory room Yoga	Reading support Work with teacher Sensory room Yoga	Reading support Work with teacher Sensory room Yoga
1:00–1:30 During English language arts (ELA)	Literacy specialist (leveled literacy intervention [LLI]) in classroom	Literacy specialist (LLI) in classroom	Literacy specialist (LLI) in classroom	Literacy specialist (LLI) in classroom	Literacy specialist (LLI) in classroom

Goals and Practices

David's Goals	Inclusive Practices
David will increase fluency to fifth-grade standards.	R5. Provide several different eye-tracking supports, such as index cards, colored strips of plastic, and so forth. R6. Build peer reading buddies into daily literacy lesson activities.
David will increase ability to retell stories.	LAR4. Allow students to work with a partner to take turns retelling details.
David will improve sight word vocabulary.	R13. Ensure that abcmouse.com and Brainzy online reading games are among the apps and software programs installed on all computers and tablets in the classroom.

Ellie

is outgoing and assertive. She is colorful literally and figuratively; her hair color changed four times in fourth grade. She lives with her parents, older brother, and younger sister. Her mother, Susan, was a pilot in the Air Force and retired after Ellie's sister was born, and her dad, Grant, is still a pilot in the Air Force. Her family chose to buy a house and settle down when her sister was born to be close to extended family. Her brother is a Marine and is deployed.

Her interests are building structures in sandbox video games, creating art, and playing with her little sister. Her strengths include her loyalty to her friends and her artistic expression—she won the fourth-grade art competition for watercolors.

Age: 10;9 years/Grade 5

Fountas & Pinnell Reading Level: U (grade level)

Math Level: At grade level

Disability Classification: None

Intervention/Notes: Ellie can get easily distracted and sometimes has difficulty completing assignments on time. She benefits from clear and direct instructions. Her academic and social-emotional development are typically at or slightly below grade level.

Ways to Support Ellie

Engagement	**Environment/Group Work** Give options for seating—Ellie sometimes works best by herself; at other times, she likes to be with a small group.	**Social Skills and Communication** Be sure Ellie is paying attention when giving directions to the class by standing near her or making eye contact with her.
Input	**Instructional Methods and Materials** No needs at this time	**Technology** No needs at this time
Output	**Self-Management/Executive Functions** Post directions on the board.	**Test Accommodations** No needs at this time

Support Schedule and Flexible Instructional Time (FIT) for Ellie

	Monday	Tuesday	Wednesday	Thursday	Friday
9:00–10:00 FIT choices	Extended reading Social skill group Work with teacher Yoga	Extended reading Social skill group Work with teacher Yoga	Extended reading Social skill group Work with teacher Yoga	Extended reading Social skill group Work with teacher Yoga	Extended reading Social skill group Work with teacher Yoga

Goals and Practices

Ellie's Goals	Inclusive Practices
Ellie will improve transitions to maximize effective use of time.	ES5. Use an interactive whiteboard with a timer that chimes and changes color to signal transitions to next task. OS5. Ensure that students are at small groups of desks for most of instructional time. Provide extra tables and desks that any student can move to if he or she chooses.
Ellie will recognize the need for, and select, a seat that is most productive and comfortable for her, with decreasing teacher support.	SR5. Provide all students a choice of seating in the classroom.

Fred

lives with his mom, dad, older sister, and younger brother; all three children attend this school, and teachers know the family well. His mom, Carol, is a librarian, and his dad, Hans, is a musician. Hans often travels for performances.

Fred loves to play baseball. He is funny and silly, and he drums on flat surfaces all the time. He loves to roughhouse and play active games. He benefits from many opportunities to move and have time to socialize with friends.

Age: 10;7 years/Grade 5

Fountas & Pinnell Reading Level: Z (seventh- or eighth-grade level)

Math Level: Above grade

Disability Classification: None

Intervention/Notes: Fred gets his work done quickly and well. He is beyond grade level in math and reading and is a strong writer. He benefits from opportunities to extend his learning beyond grade-level expectations.

Ways to Support Fred

Engagement	**Environment/Group Work** Pair Fred with a range of students—sometimes with those above grade level, as he is, and at other times with those who struggle. Make connections to baseball when possible.	**Social Skills/Communication** No needs at this time
Input	**Instructional Methods and Materials** Challenge Fred with materials that match his abilities, particularly in math. Consider accelerating him in math with sixth- or seventh-grade material, perhaps by sending him to the math class that meets his needs.	**Technology** Provide tablets and iPads.
Output	**Self-Management/Executive Functions** Provide places and times for drumming, and provide options for using fidgets when drumming would be distracting to others.	**Test Accommodations** Allow Fred to move to other work when he has completed assessments (do not force him to sit with nothing to do while others finish).

Support Schedule and Flexible Instructional Time (FIT) for Fred

	Monday	Tuesday	Wednesday	Thursday	Friday
9:00–10:00 FIT choices	Accelerated instruction	Accelerated education Social skill group Work with teacher Sensory room Yoga	Accelerated instruction	Accelerated education Social skill group Work with teacher Sensory room Yoga	Accelerated instruction

Goals and Practices

Fred's Goals	Inclusive Practices
Fred will be aware of when and where to drum or use a fidget.	SR4. Ensure that all students are familiar with regulation scales, and many have them at their desks for self-checks. Fred's will support his awareness of his need to move or fidget. ES12. Provide a "move and learn" area of the room for all students where they can walk back and forth, jump, or jump rope. SR8. Provide fidgets and mandalas to all students.

Grace

generally knows what she wants. She is most interested in playing with other girls and acting out stories; she loves dolls—in particular, a brand representing characters from classic fairy tales—and princesses. She lives with her mom, Jennifer, her dad, David, and two younger brothers. Jennifer is a lab tech, and David is a minister. Grace's younger brothers attend the same school, and all three children like seeing each other in the halls.

Grace is cheerful most of the time. When she is frustrated she shows it, sometimes by throwing things or screaming loudly. She benefits from adults who are able to gently joke with or cajole her when she is frustrated.

Grace's IEP team emphasizes presuming competence and treating her as a fifth grader.

Age: 11;3 years/Grade 5

Fountas & Pinnell Reading Level: Beginning reader (not yet reading)

Math Level: Below grade

Disability Classification: IEP (intellectual and developmental disability)

Intervention/Notes: Grace is learning to read and is a reluctant reader, preferring to tell stories rather than read them. Her IEP team wants her to gain access to grade-level content and standards. Grace has been in a range of classroom settings, and her IEP team has decided that a mix of general education fifth-grade instruction and access to a resource room would best serve her needs this year. She will use the resource room for regrouping as needed when she is frustrated. An aide is assigned to her and will be in fifth grade all year with her. Grace's IEP addresses her needs pertaining to her intellectual and developmental disability.

Ways to Support Grace

Engagement	**Environment/Group Work** Presume competence. Give Grace a limited number of choices for group work. Typically, two options are manageable for her. For example, "Do you want to work with [name a student] or work by yourself? Offer Grace a cycle of brief direct instruction, time to work independently, review of her work, and a brief break. Break options that work well include leaving the room for a quick walk. For example, taking mail or messages to the office, visiting the cafeteria to say hello to the staff, and visiting the nurse to say hello.	**Social Skills/Communication** Grace benefits from hearing appropriate ways to talk to peers. Modeling how to make requests, engage in conversational exchanges, and ask others about themselves is helpful. Give Grace space to interact with peers without hovering. She is aware that she has more adult attention than her peers, and she does not like it. Adults supporting Grace can support surrounding peers while staying available to her as needed.
Input	**Instructional Methods and Materials** Grace likes to do the same work as everyone else, but she is easily frustrated with her inability to read. Giving her the same class materials along with supplemental materials has been very successful. For example, her class is reading *The Phantom Tollbooth* (Juster, 1961). She has the book and the audiobook on a tablet. She also has the movie, which she watches with a headset, alternating listening and summarizing with watching the film.	**Technology** Grace uses a tablet that is preloaded with apps that support her learning. She leaves it on a charger at the end of the school day.
Output	**Self-Management/Executive Functions** Grace benefits from reminders to "Listen to your body" and ask herself "What are you feeling?" to help her be aware of times when she is getting frustrated or irritated.	**Test Accommodations** Grace does not take traditional tests or complete traditional assignments. She is expected to complete end-of-unit assessments that align with grade-level standards and evaluate what she has been learning. Grace completes alternate assessments based on alternate achievement standards.

Support Schedule and Flexible Instructional Time (FIT) for Grace

	Monday	Tuesday	Wednesday	Thursday	Friday
One-to-one para-professional	6.5 hours	6.5 hours	6.5 hours	6.5 hours	6.5 hours
9:00–10:00 FIT choices	Speech-language therapy	Speech-language therapy	Speech-language therapy	Speech-language therapy	Speech-language therapy
1:00–1:30 During English language arts (ELA)	Literacy specialist (leveled literacy intervention [LLI]) in classroom	Literacy specialist (LLI) in classroom	Literacy specialist (LLI) in classroom	Literacy specialist (LLI) in classroom	Literacy specialist (LLI) in classroom

Goals and Practices

Grace's Goals	Inclusive Practices
Grace will meet alternate assessment literacy goals.	R4. Ensure that student studies the same-grade curricular units. Adapt materials to provide reworded prompts and prewritten answers to be matched or cloze sentences to be completed. Have student sit with a peer group for all content lessons. R9. Incorporate sight word work into station work, with individual lists of sight words available for all learners.
Grace will meet alternate assessment math goals.	MS1. Incorporate counting into daily routines for the whole class, using small groups for review of basic counting principles with scaffolding.
Grace will increase self-awareness of her frustration level and use of calming strategies.	SR2. Allow all students short walks down the hall. SR3. Allow all students breaks in or out of the classroom. SR4. Ensure that all students are familiar with regulation scales, and many have them at their desks for self-checks. Grace's will support her level of frustration. SR7. Provide a "calming corner" for all students, equipped with soft seating, carpet, sensory tools, and so forth. Students may go to the corner as needed.

Harry

loves making lists. Statistics and numbers are fascinating to him, and he tracks major league baseball players intently. He completes all work at grade level, often rushing and making errors in the process. He lives with his mom, Harriet, his dad, Giovanni, his twin sister, Iris (also in this class), and their younger sister. Harriet is an office clerk, and Giovanni is a customer service representative. Iris and Harry are in the same class this year after several years of being in separate classes—the fourth-grade team recommended it, and Harry and Iris are doing well together in class.

Harry is serious and sometimes has hurt feelings when he is not part of others' games. He does not always read social cues well, not understanding why everyone does not share his intense interest in baseball statistics.

Age: 11;1 years/Grade 5

Fountas & Pinnell Reading Level: T (grade level)

Math Level: At grade level

Disability Classification: None

Intervention/Notes: Harry meets or exceeds grade-level expectations academically, and his social-emotional development is typical. He can be careless with his work and benefits from reminders to complete his work carefully. He has a lisp and receives speech-language therapy twice a week for it outside of school.

He had an IEP for 2 years for speech and was declassified last year. The SLP greeted him when she was in the room, and he enjoyed seeing her.

Ways to Support Harry

Engagement	**Environment/Group Work** Pair Harry and Iris intentionally several times a week—they enjoy working together and challenge each other in a healthy way. Make connections to baseball when possible.	**Social Skills/Communication** Support Harry in developing social and communication skills, including active listening. Help Harry restate what others say.
Input	**Instructional Methods and Materials** No needs at this time	**Technology** No needs at this time
Output	**Self-Management/Executive Functions** Provide checklist for reviewing work before submitting it.	**Test Accommodations** No needs at this time

Support Schedule and Flexible Instructional Time (FIT) for Harry

	Monday	**Tuesday**	**Wednesday**	**Thursday**	**Friday**
9:00–10:00 FIT choices	Social skill group Work with teacher	Social skill group Work with teacher	Social skill group Work with teacher	Social skill group Work with teacher	Social skill group Work with teacher

Goals and Practices

Harry's Goals	**Inclusive Practices**
Harry will recognize when peers are avoiding his company because he does not want to talk about anything but baseball, and he will utilize social skills to better collaborate with peers during play time.	SS3. Facilitate a peer lunch group. During lunch, there is one table for students to gather and play games that entail conversation and turn-taking. Some students have reserved spots. Any additional students may sign up to reserve remaining seats each day. SS5. Ensure that all students have an opportunity to contribute to or consult the Social Skill Manual for advice. SS6. Encourage active listening by routinely asking students to restate or summarize what has been said by peers. SS10. Build in time each day for small-group work with peers, assigning individual roles within the group, to scaffold the interactions. SR10. Teach strategy of self-monitoring: identify behavior, design self-monitoring strategy, teach strategy (Menzies, Lane, & Lee, 2009). The strategy for Harry is PEER – Pause, Evaluate peer's response, Empathize with their point of view or interests, Respond. SR11. Provide checklist for reviewing assignments before submitting.

Iris

is the twin sister of Harry, another student in this class. The twins live with their younger sister; their mother, Harriet, who works as an office clerk; and their dad, Giovanni, who works as a customer service representative. The twins are in the same class again for the

first time in several years based on the recommendation of the fourth-grade team. The arrangement is working out well for both.

Iris is serious and hard working. She can be silly with her friends, but generally she is a thoughtful, reserved student. She loves anime and watches anime and films with her dad, particularly works by Japanese artists.

Age: 11;1 years/Grade 5

Fountas & Pinnell Reading Level: U (grade level)

Math Level: Above grade level

Disability Classification: None

Intervention/Notes: Iris benefits from time to work independently and time to draw. She completes all of her work during class and has strong work habits. Iris meets or exceeds grade-level expectations academically, and her social-emotional development is typical.

Ways to Support Iris

Engagement	**Environment/Group Work** Pair Iris and Harry intentionally several times a week—they enjoy working together and challenge each other in a healthy way. They like being able to work together sometimes.	**Social Skills/Communication** No needs at this time
Input	**Instructional Methods and Materials** No needs at this time	**Technology** Allow the use of video as part of assignments whenever possible.
Output	**Self-Management/Executive Functions** No needs at this time	**Test Accommodations** No needs at this time

Support Schedule and Flexible Instructional Time (FIT) for Iris

	Monday	**Tuesday**	**Wednesday**	**Thursday**	**Friday**
9:00–10:00 FIT choices	Extended reading Work with teacher Yoga	Extended reading Work with teacher Yoga	Extended reading Work with teacher Yoga	Extended reading Work with teacher Yoga	Extended reading Work with teacher Yoga

Goals and Practices

Iris' Goals	**Inclusive Practices**
Iris will utilize drawing in her work.	SR1. Allow all students to draw or doodle during lessons.

John

lives with his mom, Sally, his dad, Al, and three younger siblings. His little brother is in third grade, and his twin sisters are in first grade.

John is a quiet student. He loves building structures in his favorite sandbox video game, and he has a weekly livestream that he and his dad do together. He is most interested in science and math. He likes drawing and puzzles, and he often draws during any free time at school.

Age: 10;10 years/Grade 5

Fountas & Pinnell Reading Level: T (grade level)

Math Level: At grade level

Disability Classification: 504 plan, executive function disorder

Intervention/Notes: John benefits from support for organizing materials and his thoughts. He has difficulty storing information in his memory, such as information obtained from reading to himself. He also has difficulty organizing his thoughts, which makes writing a paper challenging. His 504 plan includes provisions for organization supports with materials and provisions for supporting his writing; see Figure 4.1 in the section titled "Supplemental Documentation" for details.

Ways to Support John

Engagement	**Environment/Group Work** Labeled bins for school work, bell work, notes home, and so forth.	**Social Skills/Communication** No needs at this time
Input	**Instructional Methods and Materials** John uses a planner and needs support to accurately record homework.	**Technology** Provide device (John's phone or tablet) to take a picture of daily schedule and homework. Keep teacher web site up to date with assignments and deadlines. This will be a significant help to John at home.
Output	**Self-Management/Executive Functions** Labeled bins for school work, bell work, notes home, and so forth. Provide extra pencils and have paper available in the classroom. Provide extra set of books at home.	**Test Accommodations** Repeat directions. Use amplification system for verbal directions or listening passages. Provide written directions for all assessments.

Support Schedule and Flexible Instructional Time (FIT) for John

	Monday	Tuesday	Wednesday	Thursday	Friday
9:00–10:00 FIT choices	Extended reading Work with teacher Sensory room Yoga	Extended reading Work with teacher Sensory room Yoga	Extended reading Work with teacher Sensory room Yoga	Extended reading Work with teacher Sensory room Yoga	Extended reading Work with teacher Sensory room Yoga

Goals and Practices

John's Goals	Inclusive Practices
With support, John will manage materials and assignments effectively.	OS1. Support the use of a planner of each student's design/choosing customized for his or her subject areas and materials.
	OS2. Many students, including the target student, have luggage tags on their backpacks listing items to go home/come back to school.
	OS3. Set up a bulletin board in the classroom that lists longer assignments and supports working backward from due dates, chunking parts of major assignments and providing sub-due dates, available to all for reference.
	OS7. Tape a small drawing of the inside of the desk to the top of the desk, showing where books, notebooks, writing utensils, or other materials are stored.
	TM2. For all assessments with verbal directions or listening passages, use amplification system, repeat content as necessary, and supply written versions as allowed by test parameters.

Kiana

lives with her dad, Dave, her stepmom, Melanie, and her stepsister, who is also in fifth grade in this school in another class. Kiana's mom, Cheryl, appreciates notifications about school events being sent to her house as well as to Kiana's dad's house.

Kiana is social and outgoing. She went to cheerleading camp last summer and loved it. She loves history, particularly women's history.

Age: 11;2 years/Grade 5

Fountas & Pinnell Reading Level: T (grade level)

Math Level: At grade level

Disability Classification: None

Intervention/Notes: Kiana is a strong writer. She benefits from clear directions and opportunities to work in groups.

Ways to Support Kiana

Engagement	**Environment/Group Work** Provide opportunities to work in groups.	**Social Skills/Communication** No needs at this time
Input	**Instructional Methods and Materials** No needs at this time	**Technology** No needs at this time
Output	**Self-Management/Executive Functions** Provide visual reminders of multistep directions. Post agenda for the day on the board.	**Test Accommodations** No needs at this time

Rapp, Arndt, and Hildenbrand

STUDENT SNAPSHOTS

Support Schedule and Flexible Instructional Time (FIT) for Kiana

	Monday	Tuesday	Wednesday	Thursday	Friday
9:00–10:00 FIT choices	Extended reading Social skill group Work with teacher Yoga	Extended reading Social skill group Work with teacher Yoga	Extended reading Social skill group Work with teacher Yoga	Extended reading Social skill group Work with teacher Yoga	Extended reading Social skill group Work with teacher Yoga

Goals and Practices

Kiana's Goals	Inclusive Practices
Kiana will work in small groups.	SS11. Provide choices in working in pairs or small groups.
Kiana will complete assignments with visual reminders.	OS11. For multipart assignments/processes, write each step/part on an index card, so students can see the parts. They have a visual of how much is left to do as they work through each step.
Kiana will complete assignments with visual reminders.	ES4. For all information that the teacher reviews orally, write the information clearly for all students and/or post it on the class web site—announcements, homework assignments, notes, agenda.

Lucy

lives with her mom, Angie, who stays at home, and her dad, Chris, who is an attorney. Lucy is an only child, and her family is bilingual, speaking both Spanish and English. Lucy loves animals and taking care of her pet rabbit. She takes horseback riding lesson.

Lucy is warm and friendly. She is often the student who will greet visitors, welcome new students, and sit with children who are alone. She loves being around people and nurturing others.

Age: 11;1 years/Grade 5

Fountas & Pinnell Reading Level: R (slightly below grade level)

Math Level: At grade level

Disability Classification: None

Intervention/Notes: Lucy typically completes work at grade level. She can be easily distracted by peers and is often more interested in talking with others than working alone. She benefits from reminders to complete her own work before helping others. She receives support from the ENL teacher and is in the transitioning stage of language development.

Ways to Support Lucy

Engagement	**Environment/Group Work** Provide a seat that is relatively separate for Lucy to use when she is distracted by peers.	**Social Skills/Communication** Provide regular times for talking with peers throughout the day. Incorporate group work regularly.
Input	**Instructional Methods and Materials** No needs at this time	**Technology** No needs at this time
Output	**Self-Management/Executive Functions** Help Lucy complete her work by using a checklist for completion of a task before talking with others. At times, give Lucy the chance to talk with friends before starting work.	**Test Accommodations** No needs at this time

Support Schedule and Flexible Instructional Time (FIT) for Lucy

	Monday	Tuesday	Wednesday	Thursday	Friday
9:00–10:00 FIT choices	English as a new language (ENL)	ENL	ENL	ENL	ENL

Goals and Practices

Lucy's Goals	Inclusive Practices
Lucy will complete work on time.	SR5. Provide all students a choice of seating in the classroom. SR11. Provide checklist for reviewing assignments before submitting.
Lucy will continue her language development from transitioning stage to expanding stage.	CR1. Provide culturally responsive curricular materials, materials that reflect student interests, and resources other than textbooks. CR2. Provide opportunities (e.g., morning meetings) for discussions about perspectives, events, diversity, culture, and interests and opportunities to problem-solve with students. CR8. Incorporate meaningful sharing of background experiences and perspectives into lessons. ES7. Think aloud when writing, spelling, or punctuating on the board/during lessons. ES8. Provide all written materials in first languages. LAR4. Allow students to work with a partner to take turns retelling details. R8. Provide labels in classroom. Everything in the classroom is labeled with its name in multiple languages. Student's belongings have his or her photo on them. R9. Incorporate sight word work into station work, with individual lists of sight words available for all learners. MS4. Offer graphic organizers and templates to all students. Stock them in common areas of the classroom, stored neatly in bins with the student's name and a piece of the template glued to the front, and save them on the computers that students use for work. TM5. For all assessments, ensure that the reading level matches student's independent reading level. WS13. Use graphic organizers with the whole class, allowing for student choice. Scaffold the organizers to meet diverse learning needs (e.g., fewer items to fill in, some text provided, use of a word or sentence bank). Stock them in common areas of the classroom and save them on the computers that students use for work.

Mercedes lives with her mom, Barb, her dad, Steve, her older brother, and her older sister. Her mom is an accountant for a local hospital, and her dad is a mechanic—he owns his own shop.

Mercedes is outgoing and funny. She loves going to live music performances, and she attends several area jazz fests with her family in the summer.

Mercedes is on grade level academically and shows great persistence with all academics. All adults should presume competence with her.

Age: 10;3 years/Grade 5

Fountas & Pinnell Reading Level: T (grade level)

Math Level: At grade level

Disability Classification: IEP, cerebral palsy

Intervention/Notes: Mercedes gets her work done with the support of her one-to-one aide, Carol, who knows her from fourth grade. Mercedes got a power wheelchair last year and uses it independently. Carol has had training to move Mercedes safely, and Mercedes uses a stander in the classroom twice daily.

Mercedes uses a communication device to express herself and uses it fluently. She benefits from frequent vocabulary updates to her AAC device for expressive communication; the SLP makes these updates. Mercedes' device travels with her from home to school. Mercedes has strong receptive communication skills. Her IEP addresses her needs pertaining to her cerebral palsy.

Ways to Support Mercedes

Engagement	**Environment/Group Work** Mercedes needs regular position changes, and her stander is in the classroom. She needs to be standing for 30–60 minutes in the morning and 30–60 minutes in the afternoon. Carol knows how to lift and position her in the stander, and Carol can move Mercedes without help from a second adult because she is relatively small for her age.	**Social Skills/Communication** Train Mercedes' classmates in use of the text-to-speech device so they can support her in small-group work.
Input	**Instructional Methods and Materials** No needs at this time	**Technology** Provide augmentative and alternative communication device, programmed by the speech-language pathologist.
Output	**Self-Management/Executive Functions** No needs at this time	**Test Accommodations** Extended time to complete testing. Support from one-to-one aide.

Support Schedule and Flexible Instructional Time (FIT) for Mercedes

	Monday	**Tuesday**	**Wednesday**	**Thursday**	**Friday**
One-to-one para-professional	6.5 hours	6.5 hours	6.5 hours	6.5 hours	6.5 hours
8:30–9:00 During special	Physical therapist in classroom with teacher for consultation	Occupational therapist in classroom with teacher for consultation	Physical therapist in classroom with teacher for consultation	Occupational therapist in classroom with teacher for consultation	Physical therapist in classroom with teacher for consultation

(continued)

Support Schedule and Flexible Instructional Time (FIT) for Mercedes *(continued)*					
	Monday	**Tuesday**	**Wednesday**	**Thursday**	**Friday**
9:00–10:00 FIT choices	Physical therapy	Occupational therapy	Physical therapy	Occupational therapy	Physical therapy
12:30–1:00 During special	Adapted physical education teacher in physical education		Adapted physical education teacher in physical education		
1:00–1:30 During English language arts (ELA)	Speech-language pathologist (SLP) in classroom	SLP in classroom	SLP in classroom	SLP in classroom	SLP in classroom

Goals and Practices

Mercedes' Goals	**Inclusive Practices**
Mercedes will maintain range of motion and strength in her upper and lower body.	MD1. In class, use games that support crossing the midline of the body. For example: • Popping bubbles with one hand (students will reach across the body to pop bubbles on that side). • Sand table play—have students scoop sand from one side and put in a bucket on the other side. • Have students use manipulatives for counting/categorizing items in piles. MD2. Bear weight using stander. In class, create space for stander with a work tray so student can work while supported safely. MD3. In class, provide opportunities for reaching forward, back, and to the side by teaching movement sequences and activities. For example: • Teach stretching sequences such as reach up/reach down/swing your arms/all around. • Use brief movement apps and videos to provide movement breaks. Choose breaks that include arm swinging and stretching.
Mercedes will meet grade-level expectations.	Train Mercedes's classmates in use of the text-to-speech device so they can support her in small-group work. Provide augmentative and alternative communication device, programmed by the speech-language pathologist.

Rapp, Arndt, and Hildenbrand

Nigel

lives with his mom, Bianca, his grandmother, Patricia, and his older brother. Bianca is a nurse and often works the second shift. His dad passed away unexpectedly 2 years ago, and his grandmother has lived with them since.

Nigel is kind and perceptive. He can be shy and fearful in new situations. He is small for his age, and he is generally one of the youngest students in the class because of his early September birthday.

He loves doing things with his brother, who is in eighth grade. They like to play a sandbox video game where they use blocks to build elaborate structures.

Age: 10;3 years/Grade 5

Fountas & Pinnell Reading Level: S (slightly below grade level)

Math Level: At grade level

Disability Classification: None

Intervention/Notes: Nigel benefits from a nurturing, supportive environment. He meets grade-level expectations in academic and social-emotional areas.

Ways to Support Nigel

Engagement	**Environment/Group Work** Help new groups conduct introductions and icebreakers to help Nigel work with peers and to help him overcome his shyness.	**Social Skills/Communication** Provide structured opportunities for talking with peers (at lunch or other typically unstructured times).
Input	**Instructional Methods and Materials** No needs at this time	**Technology** No needs at this time
Output	**Self-Management/Executive Functions** No needs at this time	**Test Accommodations** No needs at this time

Support Schedule and Flexible Instructional Time (FIT) for Nigel

	Monday	**Tuesday**	**Wednesday**	**Thursday**	**Friday**
9:00–10:00 FIT choices	Social skill group	Extended reading Social skill group Work with teacher Yoga	Social skill group	Extended reading Social skill group Work with teacher Yoga	Social skill group

Goals and Practices

Nigel's Goals	**Inclusive Practices**
Nigel will increase his ability to talk with other students and socialize.	SS3. Facilitate a peer lunch group. During lunch, there is one table for students to gather and play games that entail conversation and turn-taking. Some students have reserved spots. Any additional students may sign up to reserve remaining seats each day.
	SS5. Ensure that all students have an opportunity to contribute to or consult the Social Skill Manual for advice.
	(The counselor helped the class come up with possible social scenarios and facilitated the contribution of good social skill advice to the manual.)

Oliver

lives with his mom, dad, older sister, and younger brother. His mom, Charity, is a teacher. After having had an accident at work, his dad, Charles, stays at home on disability.

Oliver is creative and imaginative. He is easygoing and cheerful, with a sunny personality. He loves playing outside and cooking and plans to be a chef. He watches cooking shows with his parents and helps plan the weekly menus at home.

Age: 10;6 years/Grade 5

Fountas & Pinnell Reading Level: T (grade level)

Math Level: At grade level

Disability Classification: None

Intervention/Notes: Oliver benefits from clear expectations and structure and likes to see the agenda for the day posted on the board. He is on grade level academically and gets along with everyone.

Ways to Support Oliver

Engagement	**Environment/Group Work** No needs at this time	**Social Skills/Communication** Post the schedule prominently, and provide a small schedule for him at his desk; be clear about deadlines.
Input	**Instructional Methods and Materials** No needs at this time	**Technology** No needs at this time
Output	**Self-Management/Executive Functions** Post the schedule prominently, and provide a small schedule for him at his desk; be clear about deadlines. Give Oliver time to talk through upcoming deadlines and update his planner at the end of each day.	**Test Accommodations** No needs at this time

Support Schedule and Flexible Instructional Time (FIT) for Oliver

	Monday	Tuesday	Wednesday	Thursday	Friday
9:00–10:00 FIT choices	Extended reading Social skill group Work with teacher Sensory room Yoga	Extended reading Social skill group Work with teacher Sensory room Yoga	Extended reading Social skill group Work with teacher Sensory room Yoga	Extended reading Social skill group Work with teacher Sensory room Yoga	Extended reading Social skill group Work with teacher Sensory room Yoga

Goals and Practices

Oliver's Goals	Inclusive Practices
Oliver will complete assignments and submit work on time with the help of a planner.	OS1. Support the use of a planner of each student's design/choosing customized for his or her subject areas and materials. OS3. Set up a bulletin board in the classroom that lists longer assignments and supports working backward from due dates, chunking parts of major assignments and providing sub-due dates, available to all for reference.

Paulette

is an only child and lives with her mom and dad. Her mom, Alys, stays at home, and her dad, William, is an accountant.

Paulette is sweet and very quiet. She has several very close girlfriends in class and likes to sit with them. Her family are Jehovah's Witnesses, and Paulette is excused to the library during celebrations that conflict with her family's belief system.

Age: 10;10 years/Grade 5

Fountas & Pinnell Reading Level: V (slightly above grade level)

Math Level: Slightly below grade

Disability Classification: None

Intervention/Notes: Paulette meets grade-level expectations in literacy and loves reading. She benefits from a daily schedule and a small timer on her desk—she likes knowing what is coming and how long activities last. Using a calculator for math operations supports her understanding. Paulette continues to develop automaticity in math facts and works on math with the resource teacher in a small group twice a week.

Ways to Support Paulette

Engagement	**Environment/Group Work** Post the daily schedule in front of the room clearly and refer to it regularly to help Paulette know what is coming.	**Social Skills/Communication** No needs at this time
Input	**Instructional Methods and Materials** No needs at this time	**Technology** Load math applications on class tablets or laptops that have materials that match Paulette's needs.
Output	**Self-Management/Executive Functions** Provide a small countdown timer for Paulette to keep at her desk.	**Test Accommodations** No needs at this time

Support Schedule and Flexible Instructional Time (FIT) for Paulette

	Monday	**Tuesday**	**Wednesday**	**Thursday**	**Friday**
9:00–10:00 FIT choices	Social skill group Work with teacher Math support Yoga	Math support	Social skill group Work with teacher Math support Yoga	Math support	Social skill group Work with teacher Math support Yoga
10:00–10:45 During math	Math specialist in classroom		Math specialist in classroom		Math specialist in classroom

Goals and Practices

Paulette's Goals	**Inclusive Practices**
Paulette will complete tasks and transition activities with class and personal timers.	ES5. Use an interactive whiteboard with a timer that chimes and changes color to signal transitions to next task. OS9. Provide a small 1-hour countdown timer for student's personal use.
Paulette will meet grade-level standards in math.	MS2. Offer multiple ways for all students to practice counting, facts, and so forth: sand tray for copying numbers, number magnets on cookie sheets, number line on the floor on which to step. MS8. Provide a calculator for operations.

Quentin

lives with his mom, Sue, and his dad, Bruce; he is an only child. Sue is a nurse's aide, and Bruce is a truck driver. Bruce is often away for several days at a time, and he and Quentin stay in touch with video chats when he is gone. Sue works a day shift so that she can be with Quentin in the afternoon and evening.

Quentin is curious, outgoing, and friendly. He is happiest when surrounded by friends, organizing and directing activity. He loves acting and gaming, and he participates in the local children's theater.

Age: 10;3 years/Grade 5

Fountas & Pinnell Reading Level: R (slightly below grade level)

Math Level: Slightly below grade

Disability Classification: None

Intervention/Notes: Quentin benefits from activities that include presentations and creating plays. He struggles at times to share the "stage"—he enjoys being the center of attention.

Ways to Support Quentin

Engagement	**Environment/Group Work** No needs at this time	**Social Skills/Communication** Encourage Quentin to be a good listener by asking him to restate or summarize others' comments. Learning to listen is a great skill for him as an actor.
Input	**Instructional Methods and Materials** Use a range of paired activities in English language arts (ELA) for word study because Quentin works well in small groups.	**Technology** Provide YouTube videos that allow Quentin to see movies of books read in class.
Output	**Self-Management/Executive Functions** Teach Quentin to monitor how often he talks and how often others talk. Encourage a good balance between the two. Encourage Quentin to make comments mindfully when his thoughts will be strong additions to the conversation.	**Test Accommodations** No needs at this time

Support Schedule and Flexible Instructional Time (FIT) for Quentin

	Monday	Tuesday	Wednesday	Thursday	Friday
9:00–10:00 FIT choices	Reading support	Math support	Reading support	Math support	Reading support

Goals and Practices

Quentin's Goals	Inclusive Practices
Quentin will meet grade-level standards in math.	MS5. Provide multiple sets of counters, plastic linking cubes, and fraction circles; have abacuses available so that all students can choose to use them. MS6. Provide computer/tablet time to use math software and apps (e.g., Arthur's math games, Reader Rabbit math, Math Blaster, Kids Academy–123 Tracing, Number Monster, Wee Kids Math).

(continued)

Goals and Practices (continued)

Quentin's Goals	Inclusive Practices
Quentin will meet grade-level standards in English language arts (ELA).	R11. Create a variety of word study activities for whole-class use at different levels of understanding (e.g., portable word walls, guess the covered word, speed sorting, add an ending).
Quentin will use self-monitoring to support listening to others.	SS6. Encourage active listening by routinely asking students to restate or summarize what has been said by peers. SR10. Teach strategy of self-monitoring: identify behavior, design self-monitoring strategy, teach strategy (Menzies et al., 2009).

STUDENT SNAPSHOTS

Sam

lives with his mom, Gretchen, his dad Tom, and three older siblings. Gretchen is a stay-at-home mom, and Tom is a mechanic. Sam loves taking things apart and putting them back together, and he plans to work with his dad when he is out of high school.

Sam is on the local swim team and swims all year. He takes advantage of his role as the youngest child in the family sometimes, pretending he cannot do things that he can do. Sam is creative.

Age: 10;11 years/Grade 5

Fountas & Pinnell Reading Level: Q (fourth-grade level)

Math Level: Above grade

Disability Classification: None

Intervention/Notes: Sam benefits from strategies to support his fluency and comprehension.

Ways to Support Sam

Engagement	Environment/Group Work No needs at this time	Social Skills/Communication No needs at this time
Input	**Instructional Methods and Materials** Provide math work that challenges Sam. Consider how he can gain access to challenging math content, which may mean creating a small accelerated group that attends sixth-grade math.	**Technology** No needs at this time
Output	**Self-Management/Executive Functions** Provide prompts and work that allows Sam to select from lists of options rather than generate the responses independently.	**Test Accommodations** Be sure that tests are evaluating the content rather than the reading. Sam needs to be tested with materials that match his reading level.

Support Schedule and Flexible Instructional Time (FIT) for Sam

	Monday	Tuesday	Wednesday	Thursday	Friday
9:00–10:00 FIT choices	Extended reading Work with teacher Sensory room Yoga	Extended reading Work with teacher Sensory room Yoga	Extended reading Work with teacher Sensory room Yoga	Extended reading Work with teacher Sensory room Yoga	Extended reading Work with teacher Sensory room Yoga
1:00–1:30 During English language arts (ELA)		Literacy specialist (leveled literacy intervention [LLI]) in classroom		Literacy specialist (LLI)	

Goals and Practices

Sam's Goals	Inclusive Practices
Sam will meet grade-level expectations in literacy.	WS13. Use graphic organizers with the whole class, allowing for student choice. Scaffold the organizers to meet diverse learning needs (e.g., fewer items to fill in, some text provided, use of a word or sentence bank). Stock them in common areas of the classroom and save them on the computers that students use for work. TM5. For all assessments, ensure that the reading level matches student's independent reading level.

Tyler

is an only child who lives with his dad, also named Tyler, who is a computer programmer. He loves hunting with his dad and playing video games.

Tyler is good at math and loves to play basketball. He had a growth spurt over the summer and is the tallest student in class. He is sometimes treated as though he were older because he looks mature for his age.

Age: 10;9 years/Grade 5

Fountas & Pinnell Reading Level: S (grade level)

Math Level: At grade level

Disability Classification: None

Intervention/Notes: Tyler's academic and social-emotional development are at grade level. He benefits from opportunities to move during the day and short breaks between activities. He also benefits from pairing visual and auditory information and having a consistent way to record assignments.

Rapp, Arndt, and Hildenbrand

Ways to Support Tyler

Engagement	**Environment/Group Work** Provide adult-size desk and chair due to his growth spurt.	**Social Skills/Communication** No needs at this time
Input	**Instructional Methods and Materials** Draw attention to any posted information about assignments, rubrics, or checklists.	**Technology** Give Tyler opportunities to suggest ways to add technology to lecture. Incorporating technology through the use of brief videos supports his engagement.
Output	**Self-Management/Executive Functions** Teach Tyler to review posted information and visit the class web site regularly. Teach Tyler about using his planner to record homework. Review assignment details in a small group, which supports his completing tasks on time.	**Test Accommodations** No needs at this time

Support Schedule and Flexible Instructional Time (FIT) for Tyler

	Monday	Tuesday	Wednesday	Thursday	Friday
9:00–10:00 FIT choices	Extended reading Social skill group Work with teacher Sensory room Yoga	Work with teacher	Extended reading Social skill group Work with teacher Sensory room Yoga	Work with teacher	Extended reading Social skill group Work with teacher Sensory room Yoga

Goals and Practices

Tyler's Goals	Inclusive Practices
Tyler will meet fifth-grade expectations for completing work.	ES4. For all information that the teacher reviews orally, write the information clearly for all students and/or post it on the class web site—announcements, homework assignments, notes, agenda. OS1. Support the use of a planner of each student's design/choosing customized for his or her subject areas and materials. OS3. Set up a bulletin board in the classroom that lists longer assignments and supports working backward from due dates, chunking parts of major assignments, and providing sub-due dates, available to all for reference. SR2. Allow all students short walks down the hall. SR3. Allow all students breaks in or out of the classroom.

Vivian

lives with her mom, Sarah, her dad, Andy, her older sister, and her younger sister. Her mom is a doctor, and her dad is a teacher's aide in an area high school.

Vivian is a great runner and biker. She has many friends and learns best in cooperative groups.

Age: 10;6 years/Grade 5

Fountas & Pinnell Reading Level: T (grade level)

Math Level: Slightly above grade level

Disability Classification: None

Intervention/Notes: Vivian benefits from help finding books that are at her reading level and are interesting to her. Once she finds a series she likes, she prefers to keep reading the same author.

Her academic and social-emotional skills are at or slightly above grade level.

Ways to Support Vivian

Engagement	**Environment/Group Work** Provide many opportunities for group work.	**Social Skills/Communication** Support conflict resolution skills for all students. Teach strategies for talking and listening respectfully.
Input	**Instructional Methods and Materials** Provide a range of reading materials (e.g., narrative, fiction, nonfiction) at and above grade level. Encourage Vivian to explore genres and authors widely.	**Technology** No needs at this time
Output	**Self-Management/Executive Functions** No needs at this time	**Test Accommodations** No needs at this time

Support Schedule and Flexible Instructional Time (FIT) for Vivian

	Monday	Tuesday	Wednesday	Thursday	Friday
9:00–10:00 FIT choices	Extended reading Work with teacher Yoga	Extended reading Work with teacher Yoga	Extended reading Work with teacher Yoga	Extended reading Work with teacher Yoga	Extended reading Work with teacher Yoga

Goals and Practices

Vivian's Goals	Inclusive Practices
Vivian will continue to improve in all content areas.	SS9. Allow cooperative work to happen during all content areas with flexible grouping.

SUPPLEMENTAL DOCUMENTATION

As previously noted, four students in this class—Brian, Grace, John, and Mercedes—have documented disabilities necessitating education plans. John's 504 plan addressing his executive functioning needs is provided in this section in Figure 4.1 as an example. Take a few minutes to review it to get a deeper sense of his strengths and challenges and the supports that help him succeed.

Rapp, Arndt, and Hildenbrand

Panorama Valley Central School District

SECTION 504 ACCOMMODATION PLAN

STUDENT INFORMATION

Student: John	Contacts:	Review date: May of next year	Home school: Panorama Valley
Date of birth: August 8	Sally, mother	Plan start: September	Recommended school: Panorama Valley
Gender: Male	-Al, father	Plan end: June	Special alerts: Wears hearing aids in both ears (must stay dry)
Age: 10:10	Native language: English		
Grade: 5	Interpreter required: No		

MEETING INFORMATION

Meeting date: April of this year
Reason: Annual review
Participants: Fifth-grade teacher, John, John's parents Sally and Al, school psychologist
Comments: John has executive function disorder and benefits from support for organization and writing.

INITIAL OR MOST RECENT EVALUATIONS/REPORTS

Date	Evaluation/report
March of this year	John's parents and teachers completed the Behavior Rating Inventory of Executive Functions-2 (BRIEF2) in fourth grade and found that John showed weaknesses in two Cognitive Regulation Index areas: Plan/Organize and Organization of Materials.

He has executive dysfunction disorder and benefits from support for organizing materials and organizing his thoughts. He has difficulty storing information in his memory, such as information from reading to himself. He also has difficulty organizing his thoughts, which makes writing a paper challenging. His 504 plan includes provisions for organization supports with materials and supporting his writing. His reading level with Fountas & Pinnell is T (grade level).

John lives with his mom, Sally, dad, Al, and three younger siblings. His little brother is in third grade, and his twin sisters are in first grade.

John is a quiet student. He loves playing sandbox video games and has a weekly livestream that he and his dad do together. He is most interested in science and math and is on grade level in math. He likes drawing and puzzles and often draws during any free time at school.

STATE AND DISTRICTWIDE ASSESSMENTS

None

DETERMINATION

It has been determined that the student has a physical or mental impairment that substantially limits a major life activity.
Identify the physical or mental impairment:
Executive function disorder
Identify the major life activity affected by this physical or mental impairment:
John's executive function disorder affects his ability to learn.
Describe how this impairment substantially limits a major life activity:
John's executive function disorder limits his ability to organize his assignments and tasks. Because he has difficulty with organization, he frequently misses assignment deadlines, turns in incomplete work, or turns in work that has not been completed correctly.

1

PROGRAM ACCOMMODATIONS, MODIFICATIONS, AND SUPPORTS

	Description	Frequency	Duration	Location	Start date
Related services					
No related services needed					
Supplementary aids and services/programs modifications/accommodations					
Use of a planner customized for his or her subject areas and materials	Provide flexible seating near the teacher and away from sources of noise and distraction.	Ongoing/daily	Throughout the school day	Classroom	September
Pair visual information with auditory information	Use visual reinforcements for everything in content work.	Ongoing/daily	Throughout the school day	Classroom	September
Visual supports for organization	A small drawing of the inside of the desk is taped to the top of the desk showing where books, notebooks, writing utensils, or other materials are stored.	Ongoing/daily	Throughout the school day	Classroom	September
	Provide luggage tags on backpack that list items to go home/come back to school.	Ongoing/daily	Throughout the school day	Classroom	September
	Set up a bulletin board in the classroom that lists longer assignments and works backward from due dates, chunks them into subdue dates, and is available to all for reference.				
Assistive technology devices or services					
Digital amplifier	The digital amplifier is for use by teachers and peers in all settings to assist with spoken language.	Daily	Throughout the school say	School	September
Amplification system is used for all assessments with verbal directions or listening passages, they are repeated as necessary, and written versions are supplied as allowed by test parameters.					
Supports for school personnel on behalf of the student					
Executive function disorder in-service	Professional development about executive function disorder and strategies to support organization in fifth and sixth grades is provided before the start of the school year.	Once a year	3 hours	School	September

TESTING ACCOMMODATIONS

Individual testing accommodations in the administration of districtwide assessments of student achievement and, in accordance with department policy, state assessments of student achievement.

Testing accommodation	Conditions*	Implementation recommendations**
Test given over multiple administrations	All tests	Flexible setting with minimal distractions; may be in the classroom

*Conditions—test characteristics: Describe the type, length, and purpose of the test on which the use of testing accommodations is conditioned, if applicable.
**Implementation recommendations: Identify the amount of extended time, type of setting, and so forth specific to the testing accommodations, if applicable.

SAFETY NET ELIGIBILITY

The student is eligible for the 55–64 Passing Score Safety New and the Compensatory Option of the Safety Net.

2

Figure 4.1. John's 504 plan addressing his executive function disorder.

FIFTH-GRADE READING LEVELS

Table 4.1 shows the typical Fountas & Pinnell reading levels for students entering fifth grade, the levels they typically reach as the school year progresses quarter by quarter, and the Lexile ranges for texts that are appropriate for students reading at that level.

Table 4.2 shows each student's Fountas & Pinnell reading level in the fall, along with the corresponding Lexile range for appropriate texts. For some lesson activities involving reading—including the featured ELA lesson in this chapter—Ms. Lee uses this information to group her students and select or create related texts, differentiated by Lexile, that correspond to the reading level of students in each group.

Table 4.1. Reading-level goals for the year

Fountas & Pinnell	Lexile
Beginning of year: S	S: 691–770
First interval of year: T	T: 731–770
Second interval of year: U	U: 771–800
End of year: V	V: 771–830

Table 4.2. Fifth-grade reading levels: Fall

Student	Reading level–Fall of fifth grade, divided into five reading groups	Lexile that aligns with the Fountas & Pinnell reading level
Alison	T	731–770
Brian	P	601–650
Chloe	Z	891–980
David	N	551–650
Ellie	U	771–800
Fred	Z	891–980
Grace	Beginning reader (BR)	BR
Harry	T	731–770
Iris	U	771–800
John	T	731–770
Kiana	T	731–770
Lucy (English as a new language)	R	651–730
Mercedes	T	731–770
Nigel	S	691–770
Oliver	T	731–770
Paulette	V	771–830
Quentin	R	651–730
Sam	Q	651–690
Tyler	S	691–770
Vivian	T	731–770

FIFTH-GRADE WEEKLY SCHEDULE

Figure 4.2 provides details about the daily and weekly fifth-grade class schedule for core subjects and specials as well as FIT. Days and times when some students see educational professionals who provide additional services they need (e.g., math specialist, LLI) are noted in this schedule. Review students' individual profiles for additional details about how this schedule meets students' support needs.

	Monday		Tuesday		Wednesday		Thursday		Friday	
8:00–8:30 Arrival/ morning meeting										
8:30–9:00 Special	Art for students Physical therapy— indirect with teacher		Music for students Occupational therapy—indirect with teacher		Art for students Physical therapy— indirect with teacher		Music for students Occupational therapy—indirect with teacher		Art for students	
9:00–10:00 Flexible instructional time (FIT)	See student profiles for individualized FIT support choices		See student profiles for individualized FIT support choices		See student profiles for individualized FIT support choices		See student profiles for individualized FIT support choices		See student profiles for individualized FIT support choices	
10:00–10:45 Math	Math specialist (Alison, Paulette)				Math specialist (Alison, Paulette)				Math specialist (Alison, Paulette)	
10:45–11:30 Science										
11:30–12:00 Recess										
12:00–12:30 Lunch										
12:30–1:00 Special	Physical education Adapted physical education (Mercedes)		Technology		Physical education Adapted physical education (Mercedes)		Technology		Physical education	
1:00–2:30 English language arts (ELA)/social studies	Leveled literacy intervention (LLI) (Brian, David, Grace)	Speech-language (Mercedes)	LLI (Brian, David, Grace, Sam)	Speech-language (Mercedes)	LLI (Brian, David, Grace)	Speech-language (Mercedes)	LLI (Brian, David, Grace, Sam)	Speech-language (Mercedes)	LLI (Brian, David, Grace)	Speech-language (Mercedes)
2:30–3:00 Dismissal										

Two one-to-one aides are present in the classroom for Grace and Mercedes.

Figure 4.2. Weekly schedule: Fifth-grade related services professionals.

LESSON PLANS

Ms. Lee has been teaching fifth grade for 3 years and has certification in elementary and special education. She has just completed her first year of graduate school in a Teachers of Speakers of Other Languages (TESOL) program. This year, Ms. Lee's goals are to learn more about culturally responsive teaching, effective community building with preteens in diverse classrooms, and facilitating self-management skills in students who will soon be making the transition to middle school. Ms. Lee is working with a mentor in her graduate program who has recommended several readings and webinars in these areas. She has also been working closely with several specialists and related services providers to be sure all of her students are supported.

Following are eight lessons that Ms. Lee and the specials teachers have chosen to highlight. The ELA lesson focuses on reading informational text, determining the main idea, and drawing inferences from details. The math lesson requires students to use their analytical skills to determine if various geometric shapes can be classified as certain polygons. In the science lesson, students investigate whether substances dissolve in liquid to form new substances, with particles too small to be seen. The social studies lesson compares and contrasts democracies, dictatorships, and monarchies. In the art lesson, students create a blind contour drawing to teach the concept of abstract portraiture. In the physical education lesson, students work in teams and use physical and problem-solving skills to transport every team member from one location to another without walking. The music lesson is a drumming lesson; students are hearing and copying beats and creating their own. Finally, the technology lesson requires students to role-play technology consultants who are asked to review several student-run active citizenship projects. Their task is to analyze the projects and make recommendations on how to incorporate information communication technology to better the project's operation.

FIFTH-GRADE LESSON: English Language Arts

Time allotted: 45 minutes

Standards used: New York State Next Generation English Language Arts Learning Standards (New York State Education Department, 2017) were used in this lesson. The New York State Alternate Performance Indicators (New York State Education Department, 2018) were used for Grace.

Fifth-grade students read informational and literary text in ELA. In literature, students have been working on determining a theme and comparing and contrasting characters, settings, and events. In writing, students have been writing arguments and supporting claims with reason and evidence. In weekly lessons, students are exposed to complex text with a shared reading, which is the case for part of the lesson here.

This lesson includes students reading the same text as a whole class and then working in small reading groups organized by reading level, which requires additional adults in the room to lead small groups. Students are in other large and small groups during other parts of the day; these groupings should not be the default for the rest of the school day. Table 4.3 shows the reading groups students will work with for this lesson, along with the Lexile ranges of the texts each group will read.

Prior to the lesson, Ms. Lee consults with the literacy specialist, paraprofessional, SLP, and ENL teacher. During the lesson, the literacy specialist pushes in to support Brian, David, and Grace. The SLP pushes in to support Mercedes. Grace's and Mercedes' one-to-one aides are also present for support.

Table 4.3.   Reading and lexile levels

Student	Reading level—Fall of fifth grade, divided into five reading groups	Lexile that aligns with the Fountas & Pinnell reading level
Group 1		
Grace	Beginning reader (BR)	BR
David	N	551–650
Brian	P	601–650
Group 2		
Sam	Q	651–690
Quentin	R	651–730
Lucy (English as a new language)	R	651–730
Nigel	S	691–770
Tyler	S	691–770
Group 3		
Vivian	T	731–770
Oliver	T	731–770
Mercedes	T	731–770
John	T	731–770
Kiana	T	731–770
Harry	T	731–770
Alison	T	731–770
Iris	U	771–800
Ellie	U	771–800
Group 4		
Paulette	V	771–830
Chloe	Z	891–980
Fred	Z	891–980

Lesson Objective

Locate and refer to relevant details and evidence when explaining what a text says explicitly/implicitly and make logical inferences (New York State Education Department, 2017, p. 65). (5R1) (RI & RL)

Before This Lesson

Advance Preparation

1.   Ensure that three adults are present to lead small groups during the guided reading portion (about 30 minutes).

2.   Select the model text and the texts for each reading group. Prepare reading material for Grace.

3.   Prepare the steps of the small-group activity for Kiana.

4. Make copies of graphic organizers for main idea and supporting details. These are optional for students' use during the lesson (see Figures 4.3 and 4.4).

5. Make copies of the Informational Text Self-Assessment/Reading Rubric (see Figure 4.5).

6. Have stoplight response cards available (see Figure 4.6).

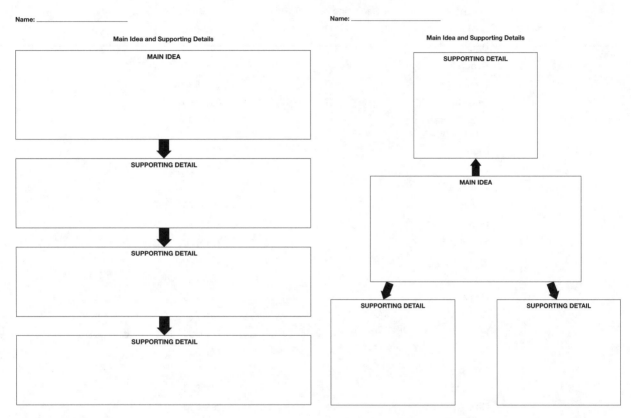

Figure 4.3. Sample Main Idea and Supporting Details graphic organizer for fifth-grade ELA lesson.

Figure 4.4. Alternate Main Idea and Supporting Details graphic organizer for fifth-grade English language arts (ELA) lesson.

Name: _____

Informational Text Self-Assessment/Reading Rubric

	Developing	Almost there	Just right
I can identify the main idea of a text.	Main idea may be incorrect or is not found.	The main idea is correct and stated in general terms.	The main idea is correct and stated in clear terms.
I can find relevant details and evidence in the text to explain what a text says.	Details or evidence are not stated or are not relevant	A relevant detail or piece of evidence is stated.	Several relevant details or evidence are stated.
I can make logical inferences about what a text means.	Does not make an inference, or inference is illogical.	Makes inferences that are logical and general. Inferences are not supported by main idea or details.	Inferences are logical and specific. Details support inferences.

Standard

Reading: Literary and Informational Text, Key Ideas and Details. Locate and refer to relevant details and evidence when explaining what a text says explicitly/implicitly and make logical inferences (New York State Education Department, 2017, p. 51). (5R1) (RI & RL)

Key: RI = reading informational text; RL= reading literary text

Figure 4.5. "I Can" Informational Text Self-Assessment for fifth-grade English language arts (ELA) lesson.

Connections With Other Team Members

Consult with the following team members: literacy specialist (joins Grace and David's group; sometimes supports Sam); paraprofessional; SLP (supports Mercedes); ENL teacher.

Desired Results

"I Can" Statements

- I can find relevant details and evidence in the text to explain what a text says.

- I can make logical inferences about what a text means.

INCLUSIVE PRACTICES

These apply to all students and should not be differentiated. Regardless of the supports individual students receive, they are all working toward these goals and understandings. All students will ask and answer questions that refer directly to the text.

Alternate standard/key idea for Grace:

- *Standard 1—Language for Information and Understanding.* Students will read, write, listen, and speak for information and understanding (New York State Education Department, n.d.a.).

- *Alternate Level—Listening and Reading.* Listening and reading to acquire information and understanding involves collecting data, facts, and ideas; discovering relationships, concepts, and generalizations; and using knowledge from oral, written, and electronic sources (New York State Education Department, n.d.a.).

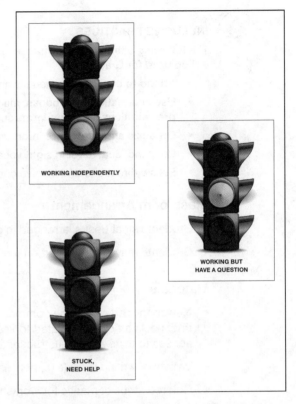

Figure 4.6. Stoplight response cards.

Assessment Evidence

Assessment evidence will consist of performance tasks, self-assessments, and other evidence that the students are mastering the identified goals and understandings. The following evidence will be used for this lesson:

- Students will share examples during class discussion.

- Students will respond to teacher questions.

- Students will use stoplight response cards to show level of understanding (green = working independently; yellow = working but have a question; red = stuck, need help).

- Students will complete the Informational Text Self-Assessment/Reading Rubric shown in Figure 4.5. (For this assessment tool, the student initially assesses his or her own performance on the criteria listed; then the teacher uses the rubric to assess the student's performance on the same criteria. The teacher and student discuss both sets of ratings, including any discrepancies.)

INCLUSIVE PRACTICES

The following alternate performance indicators (New York State Education Department, n.d.a.) will be used for Grace:

- Attend to the speaker, visually and/or auditorily, or task.
- Use information from books, magazines, newspapers, textbooks, and audio and media presentations and from forms such as basic charts, graphs, maps, and diagrams.
- Organize and categorize information/materials.
- Use functional reading sight vocabulary.
- Follow directions that involve one or two steps.

Classroom Arrangement

- Students sit at desks, arranged in groups of three or four.
- Students may choose to sit on the floor or other seating (cushion).

Materials

- Newspaper articles—one common text the class will read together, and four additional brief news articles on related topics. Ensure that students in all reading groups have access to texts at their instructional reading level.
- Variety of writing tools (e.g., pencils, markers) with pencil grips
- Colored strips of plastic for worksheets
- Teacher-created desk map on the board to show which materials to gather and have on desk
- Stoplight response cards
- Fidgets
- Self-amplifiers

Learning Activities

Allow for breaks, walks, and use of the "calming corner" during the lesson.

Anticipatory Set

Time: 5 minutes
Say: *Today we are going to work as detectives—finding evidence from a text to explain it. First, we will read a news article together. Next, we will identify the main idea and relevant supporting details. Then, we will make inferences about what the text says. We will look at one article together as a class, and then you will work with your reading group to read another article, identify the main idea and supporting details, and make inferences.*

INCLUSIVE PRACTICES

SR7. Provide a "calming corner" for all students, equipped with soft seating, carpet, sensory tools, and so forth. Students may go to the corner as needed.

OS5. Ensure that students are at small groups of desks for most of instructional time. Provide extra tables and desks that any student can move to if he or she chooses. This supports Ellie.

Modeling

Time: 15 minutes

1. Modeling consists of large-group review of a common text—"Why the Teacher Walkout Movement Won't Reach Every State" from the May 16, 2018, edition of the *New York Times*. Say: *Here is what we are working on today* as you show the "I Can" statements for the Informational Text Self-Assessment/Reading Rubric:

   - I can identify the main idea of the text.

   - I can find relevant details and evidence in the text to explain what a text says.

   - I can make logical inferences about what a text means.

2. Say: *We are going to read this article from today's news.*

3. Read the first three paragraph(s) of the article about teacher walkouts and discuss with students. Identify the main idea and several supporting details. Model how to make inferences about what will come next (additional discussion of the role of state governments in educational funding and policy and how the degree of state government involvement differs from state to state). The main idea is that states where teachers are walking out have state governments that have a strong role in education. Some supporting details are teachers want higher pay and more money for education, and the states where teachers have walked out are different in some ways, such as the strength of the economy or how much funding schools get.

 INCLUSIVE PRACTICES

SR1. Allow all students to draw or doodle during lessons. This supports Iris.

SR5. Provide all students a choice of seating in the classroom. This supports Ellie and Lucy.

Guided Practice

Time: 20 minutes

1. Each adult in the room works with one small group during this portion of the lesson. Students are grouped homogeneously for this lesson. The result is four groups of different sizes—two groups of three students, a group of five, and a large group of nine students. (Students' reading levels and the groupings based on these levels are listed in Table 4.3.)

   - Group 1: Grace, David, Brian

   - Group 2: Sam, Quentin, Lucy, Nigel, Tyler

   - Group 3: Vivian, Oliver, Mercedes, John, Kiana, Harry, Alison, Iris, Ellie

   - Group 4: Paulette, Chloe, Fred

2. Say: *Now we are going to separate into four reading groups. Each group will read a short article and use the text to ask and answer questions.*

3. Provide texts to each reading group written at students' instructional level.

4. The adult assigned to each group should work with students to review the reading together and find the main idea of the text.

5. In the course of discussion, the adult working with each group should underline or highlight the main idea. Next, the adult should work with students to identify supporting details. Provide options of graphic organizers for each group to use. For example, an organizer with a large box on the top half of the paper with three smaller boxes below with the words *main ideas* and *supporting details* is common (see Figure 4.3). A second

graphic is a large rectangle in the center for the main idea with three labeled smaller boxes for supporting details (see Figure 4.4).

6. The adult assigned to each group should discuss logical inferences, giving examples of logical and illogical inferences based on the assigned article and showing how to support inferences with information from the reading.

 INCLUSIVE PRACTICES

LAR4. Groups 1 and 2: Allow students to work with a partner to take turns retelling details. This supports David and Lucy.

SS10. Group 3: Build in time each day for small-group work with peers, assigning individual roles within the group, to scaffold the interactions. This supports Alison.

OS11. For multi-part assignments and processes, write each step/part on an index card, so students can see the parts. They have a visual of how much is left to do as they work through each step. This supports Kiana.

R4. Ensure that student studies the same-grade curricular units. Adapt materials to provide reworded prompts and prewritten answers to be matched or cloze sentences to be completed. Have student sit with a peer group for all content lessons. This supports Grace.

R5. Provide several different eye-tracking supports, such as index cards, colored strips of plastic, and so forth. This supports Brian and David.

WS13. Use graphic organizers with the whole class, allowing for student choice. Scaffold the organizers to meet diverse learning needs (e.g., fewer items to fill in, some text provided, use of a word or sentence bank). Stock them in common areas of the classroom and save them on the computers that students use for work. This supports Sam and Lucy.

Closure

Time: 5 minutes

1. Call the groups together and reconvene the large group. Spend 1–2 minutes reviewing the articles, the main idea each group identified for its assigned article and details that support the main idea, and the inferences students made based on the article, along with information from the reading that makes these inferences reasonable.

2. Say: *To close our reading session, here is the Informational Text Self-Assessment/Reading Rubric for today. When you have completed it, please turn it in to me.* Review the rubric statements with students as needed:

    • I can identify the main idea of the text.

    • I can find relevant details and evidence in the text to explain what a text says.

    • I can make logical inferences about what a text means.

Students should assess themselves on these skills (developing, almost there, just right); the adult who led each group will complete the rubric by assessing how students in that group did. Follow-up one-to-one discussion will address both sets of ratings and any discrepancies between them.

FIFTH-GRADE LESSON: Mathematics

Time allotted: 45 minutes

Standards used: The Common Core Learning Standards for Mathematics (Common Core State Standards Initiative, n.d.) were used for this lesson. The New York State Alternate Performance Indicators (New York State Education Department, n.d.b.) were used for Grace.

LESSON PLANS

So far this year in math, the fifth-graders have become proficient with numerical expressions; patterns and relationships; operations in base 10; place value; decimals; multiplying and dividing fractions; measurement conversions; interpreting data; finding area, perimeter, and volume; and graphing to solve problems. One of the last units of the year focuses on categories and properties of two-dimensional geometric figures. The students have been introduced to all of the geometric figures, their individual properties, and the hierarchy of quadrilaterals. Today, the students will reinforce this knowledge by analyzing more figures and their properties to determine whether the different figures qualify as certain types of polygons (e.g., Is a square a rectangle?). They will start out by watching a video by MashUp Math (2015) that uses an analogy to describe how every Oreo is a cookie but not every cookie is an Oreo. An Oreo is a special kind of cookie. Then, the video applies the same mathematical reasoning, along with a review of characteristics of rectangles, to determine that every square is a rectangle, but not every rectangle is a square. A square is a special kind of rectangle.

After viewing the video, the teacher will guide students through an investigative exercise of reviewing the definitions and characteristics of various polygons to determine which figures qualify as which polygons. Then, the students will work in pairs to investigate on their own. The lesson ends with a discussion about other contexts that might call for this type of categorizing or subcategorizing.

There are four adults in the room during this math class. In addition to Ms. Lee, the math specialist pushes in to support Alison and Paulette. Both students benefit from clear instructions, opportunities for repeated practice with concepts, and visuals. Grace's and Mercedes' one-to-one aides are also present for support.

Lesson Objective

Understand that attributes belonging to a category of two-dimensional figures also belong to all subcategories of that category. For example, all rectangles have four right angles and squares are rectangles, so all squares have four right angles (Common Core State Standards Initiative, n.d.). (CCSS.Math.Content.5.G.B.3)

Before This Lesson

Advance Preparation

1. Create a poster for each concept, alternating text color. Laminate. (See Figures 4.7a–4. 7c.)

2. Prepare half-sheets with assessment questions, one per student (see examples in Figure 4.8); modify for Grace (see Figure 4.9). Use the questions in Figure 4.10 to prepare the half-worksheets. Provide Spanish translations as indicated in Figure 4.10.

Connections With Other Team Members

No special connections with other team members are needed for this lesson.

Desired Results

"I Can" Statements for Objective

- I can tell you that categories of figures can be further subcategorized by attributes.

- I can recognize that categories tell us more detailed information for problem solving.

- I can recognize that categorizing can be used in other areas (e.g., science).

- I can categorize figures by attributes.

- I can compose my own question/subcategorization problem to solve.

Polygon	Polígono
❏ A plane shape ❏ At least 3 straight sides ❏ At least 3 angles	❏ Una forma plana ❏ Por lo menos 3 lados rectos ❏ Al menos 3 ángulos

Quadrilateral	Cuadrilátero
❏ 4 straight sides ❏ 4 angles ❏ All of the interior angles add up to 360°	❏ 4 lados rectos ❏ 4 ángulos ❏ Todos los ángulos interiores se suman a 360°

Triangle	Triángulo
❏ 3 straight sides ❏ 3 angles ❏ All of the angles add up to 180°	❏ 3 lados rectos ❏ 3 ángulos ❏ Todos los ángulos suman hasta 180°

Circle	Círculo
❏ Enclosed curved line ❏ All points on the curved line are equidistant from the center point	❏ Línea curva cerrada ❏ Todos los puntos de la línea curva son equidistantes del punto central

Figure 4.7a. Polygon posters for fifth-grade math lesson (polygon, quadrilateral, triangle, circle).

Square	Plaza
❏ 4 straight sides ❏ 4 angles ❏ Each angle is 90° (right angle) ❏ All sides are equal in length ❏ Opposite sides are parallel	❏ 4 lados rectos ❏ 4 ángulos ❏ Cada ángulo es 90° (ángulo recto) ❏ Todos los lados son iguales en longitud ❏ Lados opuestos son paralelos

Rectangle	Rectángulo
❏ 4 straight sides ❏ 4 angles ❏ Each angle is 90° (right angle) ❏ Opposite sides are equal in length ❏ Opposite sides are parallel	❏ 4 lados rectos ❏ 4 ángulos ❏ Cada ángulo es 90° (ángulo recto) ❏ Lados opuestos son iguales en longitud ❏ Lados opuestos son paralelos

Rhombus	Rombo
❏ 4 straight sides ❏ 4 angles ❏ All sides are equal in length ❏ Opposite sides are parallel ❏ Opposite angles are equal ❏ Angles are not 90° (right angles) ❏ Looks like a diamond	❏ 4 lados rectos ❏ 4 ángulos ❏ todos los lados son iguales en ❏ lados opuestos de la longitud son paralelos ❏ Ángulos opuestos son iguales ❏ Los ángulos no son 90° (ángulos rectos) ❏ Parece un diamante

Figure 4.7b. Polygon posters for fifth-grade math lesson (square, rectangle, rhombus).

LESSON PLANS

Parallelogram
❏ 4 straight sides
❏ 4 angles
❏ Opposite sides are equal in length
❏ Opposite sides are parallel
❏ Opposite angles are equal

Paralelogramo
❏ 4 lados rectos
❏ 4 ángulos
❏ Lados opuestos son iguales en longitud
❏ Lados opuestos son paralelos
❏ Ángulos opuestos son iguales

Trapezoid
❏ 4 straight sides
❏ 4 angles
❏ 1 pair of opposite sides are parallel
❏ The other pair of opposite sides may or may not be parallel

Trapezoide
❏ 4 lados rectos
❏ 4 ángulos
❏ 1 par de lados opuestos son paralelos
❏ El otro par de lados opuestos puede o no ser paralelo

Kite
❏ 4 straight sides
❏ 4 angles
❏ 2 sets of equal sides
❏ Equal sides are adjacent to each other

Cometa
❏ 4 lados rectos
❏ 4 ángulos
❏ 2 juegos de lados iguales
❏ Lados iguales son adyacentes el uno al otro

Figure 4.7c. Polygon posters for fifth-grade math lesson (parallelogram, trapezoid, kite).

Names: _____	Nombres: _____
Is a square a rectangle?	¿Es un cuadrado un rectángulo?
This is how I know. . .	Así es como sé. . .

Figure 4.8. Sample half-sheet for fifth-grade math lesson.

INCLUSIVE PRACTICES

These apply to all students and should not be differentiated. Regardless of the supports individual students receive, they are all working toward these goals and understandings.

Alternate standard/key idea for Grace:

- *Standard 1—Analysis, Inquiry, and Design.* Students will use mathematical analysis, scientific inquiry, and engineering design, as appropriate, to pose questions, seek answers, and develop solutions (New York State Education Department, n.d.b.).

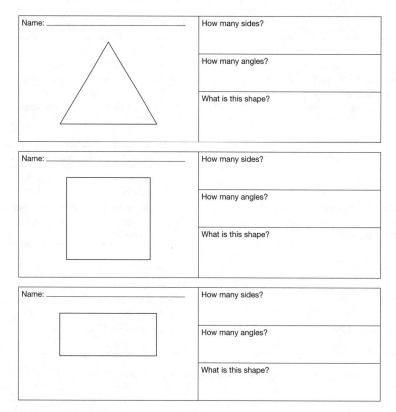

Figure 4.9. Sample half-sheets for Grace for fifth-grade math lesson.

Half-Sheet Question	Spanish Translation
1. Is a rectangle a square?	1. ¿Es un rectángulo un cuadrado?
2. Is a triangle a polygon?	2. ¿Es un triángulo un polígono?
3. Is a triangle a quadrilateral?	3. ¿Es un triángulo un cuadrilátero?
4. Is a circle a polygon?	4. ¿Es un círculo un polígono?
5. Is a rhombus a quadrilateral?	5. ¿Es un rombo un cuadrilátero?
6. Is a rhombus a parallelogram?	6. ¿Es un rombo un paralelogramo?
7. Is a parallelogram a quadrilateral?	7. ¿Es un paralelogramo un cuadrilátero?
8. Is a parallelogram a rhombus?	8. ¿Es un paralelogramo un rombo?
9. Is a trapezoid a quadrilateral?	9. ¿Es un trapecio un cuadrilátero?
10. Is a trapezoid a parallelogram?	10. ¿Es un trapecio un paralelogramo?
11. Is a parallelogram a trapezoid?	11. ¿Es un paralelogramo un trapezoide?
12. Is a kite a quadrilateral?	12, ¿Es una cometa un cuadrilátero?
13. Is a kite a parallelogram?	13. ¿Es una cometa un paralelogramo?
14. Is a square a kite?	14. ¿Es una cuadrado una cometa?
15. Is a rhombus a kite?	15. ¿Es una rombo una cometa?

Figure 4.10. Worksheet questions with translations for fifth-grade math lesson.

- *Alternate Level–Mathematical Analysis.* Symbolic representation is used to communicate mathematically (New York State Education Department, n.d.b.).

Assessment Evidence

Assessment evidence will consist of performance tasks, self-assessments, and other evidence that the students are mastering the identified goals and understandings. The following evidence will be used for this lesson:

- Students will write answers to questions regarding figures after consulting attribute checklists.

- Students will compose a problem to solve that involves subcategorizing by attributes.

- Students will provide a rationale for their answer after consulting checklists and answering questions.

- The teacher will observe the students using checklists.

- The teacher will observe the students' collaboration.

- The teacher will conduct questioning about the importance of generalization of this skill.

INCLUSIVE PRACTICES

R5. Provide several different eye-tracking supports, such as index cards, colored strips of plastic, and so forth. This supports Brian and David.

The following alternate performance indicators will be used for Grace:

- Use mathematics and symbolism to communicate in mathematics.

- Compare and describe quantities.

- Demonstrate knowledge of mathematical relationships.

- Relate mathematics to their immediate environment (New York State Education Department, n.d.b.).

Classroom Arrangement

- Posters are spaced evenly around classroom walls.

- Students work in pairs (pair Harry with Iris).

- Students move around the classroom, and they may choose to do written work at desks, at tables, or on the floor.

- The "calming corner" and "move to learn" area support students as indicated in Inclusive Practices.

INCLUSIVE PRACTICES

R4. Ensure that student studies the same-grade curricular units. Adapt materials to provide reworded prompts and prewritten answers to be matched or cloze sentences to be completed. Have student sit with a peer group for all content lessons. This supports Grace.

OS5. Ensure that students are at small groups of desks for most of instructional time. Provide extra tables and desks that any student can move to if he or she chooses. This supports Ellie.

SR5. Provide all students a choice of seating in the classroom. This supports Ellie and Lucy.

SR7. Provide a "calming corner" for all students, equipped with soft seating, carpet, sensory tools, and so forth. Students may go to the corner as needed. This supports Grace.

SS9. Allow cooperative work to happen during all content areas with flexible grouping. This supports Alison, Chloe, and Grace.

ES12. Provide a "move and learn" area of the room for all students where they can walk back and forth, jump, or jump rope. This supports Brian and Fred.

Materials

- Laminated posters with checklists of attributes for the following polygons: polygon, quadrilateral, rectangle, square, triangle, circle, rhombus, and parallelogram. Each checklist should use alternating colors (see Figures 4. 7a-4.7c). If students get the concept quickly and are ready for a greater challenge, then use additional polygon posters for the following shapes with more sides: pentagon, hexagon, and octagon.

- Whiteboard markers and erasers (one of each, placed at each poster)

- Half-sheets of papers with questions (see example in Figure 4.8); modified for Grace (see Figure 4.9)

- Pencils or other preferred writing utensils

- Interactive whiteboard displaying table with shapes and labels (see Figure 4.11)

- Line guides for reading

Polygons/Polígonos	Quadrilaterals/Cuadriláteros	Triangles/Triángulos
Squares/Plazas	Rectangles/Rectángulos	Circles/Círculos
Rhombuses/Rombos	Parallelograms/Paralelogramos	Trapezoids/Trapezoides

Figure 4.11. Interactive whiteboard for fifth-grade math lesson.

- Fidgets
- Regulation scales for Chloe and Fred

INCLUSIVE PRACTICES

R5. Provide several different eye-tracking supports, such as index cards, colored strips of plastic, and so forth. This supports Brian and David.

SR4. Ensure that all students are familiar with regulation scales, and many have them at their desks for self-checks. Some are for voice volume and emotional escalation; some for effective use of work time; some for interest or independence level for an activity. This supports Chloe and Fred.

SR8. Provide fidgets and mandalas to all students. This supports Fred.

Learning Activities

Allow for breaks, walks, and use of the "calming corner" during the lesson.

Anticipatory Set

Time: 5 minutes

1. Display examples of a square shape and a rectangle shape, or draw these on the board. Say: *I am wondering if a square is also a rectangle and if a rectangle is also a square. They are two different shapes, but I am thinking about how I can find out the answers to these questions mathematically. Let's watch this video and see what it shows us.*

2. Show the MashUp Math (2015) video "Is a Square a Rectangle? Yes or No?"

3. Ask: *What did you find out?*

INCLUSIVE PRACTICES

SR2. Allow all students short walks down the hall. This supports Brian, Grace, and Tyler.

SR3. Allow all students breaks in or out of the classroom. This supports Grace and Tyler.

SR7. Provide a "calming corner" for all students, equipped with soft seating, carpet, sensory tools, and so forth. Students may go to the corner as needed. This supports Grace.

ES12. Provide a "move and learn" area of the room for all students where they can walk back and forth, jump, or jump rope. This supports Fred.

Modeling

Time: 5 minutes

1. Model an activity to further use mathematical reasoning to subcategorize figures. First, pair students and explain that each pair will receive a half-worksheet with one problem to solve (see Figure 4.8).

2. Demonstrate what to do for the half-worksheet.

3. Think aloud as you consult the rectangle poster to answer the question (see Figure 4.7b). Point out that all boxes in the rectangle poster must be checked for you to answer "yes" on the half-worksheet (Figure 4.8).

4. Think aloud as you write notes about why a square is a rectangle. For example, say: *As I look over the checklist of characteristics that all rectangles must have, I see that each characteristic applies to squares too. A square has four straight sides and four angles, and each angle is a 90-degree or right angle. Each pair of opposite sides is parallel, and*

the opposite sides are equal in length in each pair. A square has all of the characteristics required to classify a shape as a rectangle. Really, a square is just a special type of rectangle—a rectangle in which all sides are the same length.

5. Move a square shape to the rectangle box on the interactive whiteboard.

 INCLUSIVE PRACTICES

ES7. Think aloud when writing, spelling, or punctuating on the board/during lessons. This supports David and Lucy.

Guided Practice

Time: 10 minutes

1. Do one more problem together from Figure 4.8.

2. Ask students questions about squares to determine if a rectangle qualifies. Be sure to purposefully count sides and angles.

3. Write the answer ("no") and explanation. Draw attention to the fact that you will not move the shape on the interactive whiteboard.

 INCLUSIVE PRACTICES

MS1. Incorporate counting into daily routines for the whole class, using small groups for review of basic counting principles with scaffolding. This supports Grace.

Independent Practice

Time: 15 minutes

1. Distribute half-worksheets to each pair. Once a student pair finishes their half-worksheet, they can swap with other partners to provide a second mathematical opinion on the back of the sheet.

2. Have Grace count sides and angles for each shape and identify the shape.

3. Circulate to observe and facilitate analysis when needed. (Although some resources classify squares as rhombuses, rhombuses excludes squares for the purpose of this lesson; see worksheet criteria.)

 INCLUSIVE PRACTICES

MS1. Incorporate counting into daily routines for the whole class, using small groups for review of basic counting principles with scaffolding. This supports Grace.

ES5. Use an interactive whiteboard with a timer that chimes and changes color to signal transitions to next task. This supports Alison, Ellie, and Paulette.

LAR4. Allow students to work with a partner to take turns retelling details. This supports Lucy.

Closure

Time: 10 minutes

1. Review shapes on interactive whiteboard for accuracy. The subcategories included within each category are listed next:

    •   Polygons include the following subcategories: quadrilaterals, triangles, squares, rectangles, rhombuses, parallelograms, and trapezoids.

    •   Quadrilaterals include the following subcategories: squares, rectangles, rhombuses, parallelograms, and trapezoids.

- Rectangles include the following subcategory: squares.

- Parallelograms include the following subcategories: squares, rectangles, and rhombuses. In addition, some trapezoids are parallelograms.

- Rhombuses include some trapezoids and parallelograms.

- Kites include squares and rhombuses.

2. Ask, *Why is it important to do that? When else would you use subcategorization skills like that?* [Students' responses will vary. Possible responses include medical symptoms and nutritional choices.]

3. Use 5- and 1-minute warnings on interactive whiteboard timer to indicate transition to next subject.

FIFTH-GRADE LESSON: Science

Time allotted: 45 minutes

Standards used: NGSS[1] are used for this lesson. New York State Alternate Performance Indicators (New York State Education Department, n.d.b.) were used for Grace.

Context: The expectation for fifth-grade science in the NGSS is that students will answer questions about matter, such as whether the weight of matter changes if matter changes. Students consider things such as where water is found on Earth and how to create substances. They consider how day and night change and how the appearance of stars is affected throughout the seasons (NGSS, 2013).

This year, students have explored geology, rocks, and minerals. They learned general science vocabulary, including *investigation* and *variables,* throughout the year. They spent time learning about the planets, primarily the differences between Earth and Mars. They visited the Rochester Museum & Science Center and completed a mission to Mars through the Challenger Learning Center. Following this unit, students will have a weeklong eco-camp to consider what variables affect the environment. They will use 2-liter bottles to create terrariums. Students have been introduced to vocabulary specifically related to matter, including *mixture* and *solution.* They mixed materials in a previous lesson to explore how weight and matter are related. They dissolved food dye in water, then observed what happened when the water evaporated.

Today, students will work with a partner to mix water with three different materials— sand, salt, and sugar. They will determine whether each combination is a mixture or a solution. They will review how to control variables such as stirring speed and number of stirs and the amount of time provided for the material to dissolve. Students will repeat the experiment twice more this week to practice conducting an experiment and making observations.

The lesson ends with a whole-class discussion about how conducting an experiment has specific steps and procedures and how a systematic process can be used in writing, math, and reading.

Grace's and Mercedes' one-to-one aides are present during the lesson. Ms. Lee is aware of supporting Alison and Paulette with clear instructions, opportunities for repeated practice with concepts, and visuals. Ms. Lee decides to have students work in pairs, with a strong student in each pair, and place the pairs close to each other so that she can monitor the groups.

This lesson was developed with Mark Denecke and Sue Liquori of East Rochester Elementary School in East Rochester, New York.

---

[1]NGSS Lead States. (2013). *Next Generation Science Standards: For states, by states.* Washington, DC: National Academies Press.

NGSS is a registered trademark of Achieve. Neither Achieve nor the lead states and partners that developed the NGSS were involved in the production of this product and do not endorse it.

Lesson Objective

Matter and Its Interactions. Conduct an investigation to determine whether mixing two or more substances results in new substances (NGSS, 2013). (5-PS1-4)

Because science lessons are often developed using the 5-E model, those terms are added to this plan. The terms *engage, explore, explain, elaborate*, and *evaluate* are used.

CCSS Connections are listed next.

ELA/Literacy

1. Conduct short research projects that use several sources to build knowledge through investigation of different aspects of a topic (Common Core State Standards Initiative, n.d.). (W.5.7) (5-PS1-2), (5-PS1-3), (5-PS1-4)

Math

1. Use appropriate tools strategically (Common Core State Standards Initiative, n.d.). (5-PS1-2), (5-PS1-3) (MP.5)

Before This Lesson

Advance Preparation

1. Copy the following handouts:

   • Physical Changes, Mixtures, and Solutions handout (see Figure 4.12)

Physical Changes, Mixtures, and Solutions

(1)

Physical change

A physical change is a change in which no new substances form.

It does not change the type of matter an object is made of.

You change the shape, size, or more physical properties.

Many changes can be easily reversed.

Examples of physical change:
• Folding paper in half—changes the shape
• Taking an ice cube out of the freezer—changes from solid to liquid
• Chopping a log in half—changes the shape, size, and number of pieces

(2)

A mixture

A mixture is a combination of two or more substances.

Each substance keeps its own properties.

You can separate mixtures.

Examples of mixtures:
• Fruit salad
• Cereal with milk

(3)

A solution

A solution is a mixture in which one substance dissolves into another.

When a substance dissolves, it mixes evenly into another substance and seems to disappear.

Examples of solutions:
• Sugar and water
• Gatorade powder and water

Figure 4.12. Physical Changes, Mixtures, and Solutions for fifth-grade science lesson.

Group members: _____

Lab Worksheet

Directions

1. Pour 1 cup of water into the measuring cup. Pour the water into the large cup.
2. Measure 1 cup of a substance.
3. Get your stopwatch and stirrer ready. When you are ready to start the timer, add the substance to the cup of water and start the timer.
4. Conduct one trial for each substance. If you have time, conduct a repeat trial for each.

TRIALS:

Trial 1: Substance: Sugar   Time to dissolve: _____

Trial 2: Substance: Salt   Time to dissolve: _____

Trial 3: Substance: Sand   Time to dissolve: _____

If you have time:

REPEATED TRIALS:

Trial 4: Substance: Sugar   Time to dissolve: _____

Trial 5: Substance: Salt   Time to dissolve: _____

Trial 6: Substance: Sand   Time to dissolve: _____

Figure 4.13. Lab Worksheet for fifth-grade science lesson.

- Lab Worksheet (see Figure 4.13)
- Matter and Its Interactions: Self-Assessment (see Figure 4.14)

2. Gather materials: Clear cup, drink mix for Engage portion of the lesson; 10 sets of the items listed in the Materials section of the lesson.

3. Write steps on index card for Kiana.

Connections With Other Team Members

No special connections with other team members are needed for this lesson.

Desired Results

"I Can" Statements

- I can demonstrate safe practices during investigations.
- I can use tools to collect and record information in an experiment.
- I can use the scientific method to test a hypothesis through an experiment.
- I can classify matter by its physical state.

INCLUSIVE PRACTICES

These apply to all students and should not be differentiated. Regardless of the supports individual students receive, they are all working toward these goals and understandings.

Name: _____

Matter and Its Interactions: Self-Assessment

	I do not understand how to do this: I need help!	I can do this with some help: I am almost there!	I can do this: I got it!
I can demonstrate safe practices during investigations.			
I can use tools to collect and record information in an experiment.			
I can use the scientific method to test a hypothesis through an experiment.			
I can classify matter by its physical state.			

Standard

Physical Science, Matter and Its Interactions, Structure and Properties of Matter. Conduct an investigation to determine whether the mixing of two or more substances results in new substances (Next Generation Science Standards. 2013). (5-PS1-4)

Figure 4.14. Matter and Its Interactions Self-Assessment for fifth-grade science lesson.

Alternate standard/key idea for Grace:

- *Standard 4—Science.* Students will understand and apply scientific concepts, principles, and theories pertaining to the physical setting and living environment and recognize the historical development of ideas in science (New York State Education Department, n.d.b.).

- *Alternate Level for Physical Setting: Key Idea.* Matter is made up of particles whose properties determine the observable characteristics of matter and its reactivity (New York State Education Department, n.d.b.).

Assessment Evidence

Assessment evidence will consist of performance tasks, self-assessments, and other evidence that the students are mastering the identified goals and understandings. The following evidence will be used for this lesson:

- Students will complete a lab worksheet.

- Students will complete a self-assessment.

- Students will share examples during class discussion.

- The teacher will observe students during the lab activity.

The 5-E alignment for this assessment evidence is *evaluate*.

INCLUSIVE PRACTICES

The following alternate performance indicators will be used for Grace:

- Observe and describe properties of materials, using appropriate tools.

- Observe chemical and physical changes, including changes in states of matter (New York State Education Department, n.d.b.).

Classroom Arrangement

- Students sit at desks, arranged in groups of three or four.

- Create heterogeneous groups based on skill development; students sit facing interactive whiteboard at front of the classroom.

- Students may choose to sit on the floor or other seating (cushion).

INCLUSIVE PRACTICES

SR5. Provide all students with a choice of seating in the classroom. This is a support for Ethan and Gabrielle.

Pair students mindfully to support engagement in an activity-based lesson.

Materials

- Physical Changes, Mixtures, and Solutions handout

- Lab Worksheet

- Matter and Its Interactions: Self-Assessment

- For each pair of students (10 sets):

  - Plastic beakers (2-cup capacity or more)

  - Paper towels

- Half-gallon of water

- 1/2 cup each of sand, salt, and sugar

- Measuring cups: 1/2 cup for dry ingredients, 1 cup for liquid

- Stirrers (long popsicle sticks, spoons)

- Stopwatch or timer

- Variety of writing tools (e.g., pencils, markers) with pencil grips

- Colored strips of plastic for worksheets

- Teacher-created desk map on the board to show which materials to gather and have on desk

- Stoplight response cards

- Fidgets

- Self-amplifiers

Learning Activities

Allow for breaks, walks, and use of the "calming corner" during the lesson.

Engage

Time: 5 minutes

1. Say: *Why do we mix drink powder and water?* [Record a few responses, such as to make it taste better, to add vitamins or electrolytes.]

2. Show: Demonstrate adding a scoop of drink powder to a cup of water.

3. Ask: *What happened?* [Possible responses: it melted into it; it dissolved; it made a sports drink.]

4. Ask: *Why did the water and powder mix so well? What makes a solid such as drink powder dissolve in water? Those are the questions that you get to consider today in your science experiment. Remember that a mixture is one or more elements combined physically.*

5. Explain: *A solution is a liquid mixture. Mixing two liquid substances together can make a solution, such as mixing chocolate syrup with milk to make chocolate milk. Mixing a liquid and a solid together can also make a solution, such as dissolving drink powder into water to make a sport drink. A mixture that is homogeneous is a solution: think of lemonade. Sometimes two things do not mix together—they stay separate and are heterogeneous: think of trail mix. Today you are going to mix three different items—sugar, salt, and sand—with water and see what happens to each one.*

 INCLUSIVE PRACTICES

OS5. Ensure that students are at small groups of desks for most of instructional time. Provide extra tables and desks that any student can move to if he or she chooses. This supports Ellie.

SR5. Provide all students with a choice of seating in the classroom. This supports Ellie and Lucy.

Explore

Time: 20 minutes

1. Divide students into pairs. Say: *Test whether each substance—salt, sugar, or sand—dissolves in water to make a solution. If it does dissolve, then how long does it take.*

2. Distribute the Lab Worksheet shown in Figure 4.13 and explain that they will use it to record their data.

3. Provide tips on how to perform the steps accurately and consistently with each substance. Remind students: *Be careful not to spill when you are measuring and pouring. Remember that a variable is something you can change. Think about the variables in this experiment [pause]. When you stir the solid in the water, stir the same way each time; count the number of stirs and stir at the same speed. That is controlling the variables. The variables I see are how much water and salt, sand, or sugar you put in each cup, how many times you stir, how fast you stir, and how long you watch each cup.*

4. Prompt students: *On your lab worksheet, record the time it takes for the solid to dissolve, or stop recording at 5 minutes and record 5 minutes.*

5. Monitor students as they work; circulate to provide guidance or assistance as needed.

LESSON PLANS

INCLUSIVE PRACTICES

SS11. Provide choices in working in pairs or small groups. This supports Alison and Kiana.

LAR4. Allow students to work with a partner to take turns retelling details. This supports David and Lucy.

MS1. Incorporate counting into daily routines for the whole class, using small groups for review of basic counting principles with scaffolding. This supports Grace.

R4. Ensure that student studies the same-grade curricular units. Adapt materials to provide reworded prompts and prewritten answers to be matched or cloze sentences to be completed. Have student sit with a peer group for all content lessons. This supports Grace.

OS11. For multipart assignments or processes, write each step/part on an index card so that students can see the parts. They have a visual of how much is left to do as they work through each step. This supports Kiana.

Explain

Time: 10 minutes

1. Call the groups back together. Say: *Now that you have had time to see if salt, sugar, and sand dissolve in water and how long it took, let's talk about what happened. First, let's review the steps you took. Turn to your elbow partner and talk about what you did.* Allow time for brief discussion.

2. Say: *Let's gather information about what we saw. First, did sugar dissolve in water?* Record notes. Discuss how long it took.

3. Ask: *Did salt dissolve in water?* Repeat recording and discussion.

4. Ask: *Did sand dissolve in water?* Repeat recording and discussion.

5. Say: *We should see that sugar and salt dissolved in water and sand did not. Sugar and salt can mix into water and make a solution. Sand and water are a mixture because the sand and water kept their own properties.*

6. Say: *Talk with your partner about what happened in your experiment. If the salt and sugar did not dissolve, or did not dissolve completely, then talk about why that happened.*

7. Conclude with a review of the main ideas from the Physical Changes, Mixtures, and Solutions handout (see Figure 4.12).

Elaborate

Time: 5 minutes

1. To begin discussion, say: *Why is using specific steps and procedures important?* Discuss the scientific process, the importance of consistent steps, and how variables can affect the results.

2. Ask: *How can we use a systematic process in writing, math, and reading?* Discuss setting up an essay with a format, using steps to solve math problems.

Evaluate

Time: 5 minutes

1. Say: *Please complete the Matter and Its Interactions: Self-Assessment.*

2. Hand out the self-assessment (see Figure 4.14) and circulate.

FIFTH-GRADE LESSON: Social Studies

Time allotted: 45 minutes

Standards used: The Ohio State Social Studies Standards (Ohio Department of Education, 2010) were used for this lesson.

Context: Students in fifth-grade social studies learn all about regions and people of the Western Hemisphere. So far, they have learned about multitier time lines; the governments, social structures, technologies, religions, and agricultural practices of early Indian civilizations; the effects of European exploration and colonization; globes, geographic tools, and cartographers; longitude and latitude; physical geography and impact on way of life; and interpreting political data from multiple sources. Today's lesson builds on the fourth-grade curriculum about United States government and democracy. The students are comparing and contrasting democracies, dictatorships, and monarchies. They will also be discussing the power of the citizens versus those in authority.

The students have spent a lot of time this year with jigsaw learning, the structure used in today's lesson. They are familiar with the process of forming a small group, being assigned an expert role or subtopic, researching their subtopic with all other group members who were assigned that subtopic, and returning to their original small group and reporting on their expertise subtopic.

There are five adults in the room during this social studies class. In addition to Ms. Lee, the literacy specialist pushes in to support Brian, David, and Grace. The SLP pushes in to support Mercedes. Grace's and Mercedes' one-to-one aides are also present for support.

Lesson Objective

Students will understand the following topic and content standard.

- *Theme:* Regions and people of the Western Hemisphere

- *Strand:* Government

- *Topic:* Roles and systems of government. The purpose of government in the United States is to establish order, protect the rights of individuals, and promote the common good. Governments may be organized in different ways and have limited or unlimited powers.

- *Content Statement: 12.* Democracies, dictatorships, and monarchies are categories for understanding the relationship between those in power or authority and citizens (Ohio Department of Education, 2010, p. 20).

Before This Lesson

Advance Preparation

1. Prepare graphic organizers in English and Spanish for the concepts of democracy (see Figure 4.15), monarchy (see Figure 4.16), and dictatorship (see Figure 4.17). (The teacher will complete the democracy organizer as an example; each student will need a copy of the monarchy or dictatorship organizer, per the student groupings listed next.)

2. Prepare modified monarchy organizer for Grace (see Figure 4.18).

3. Prepare Exit Ticket: Systems of Government (see Figure 4.19).

4. Determine groups of four and the research roles for each group member. The groups for jigsaw cooperative learning should be heterogeneous by gender, race, ethnicity, and ability. There are four components to research for each type of government (i.e., definition,

Name: _____

Jigsaw Research Template: Democracy

Definition	Definición	Examples	Ejemplos

Democracy
Democracia

Authority figures	Figuras de autoridad	Power of citizens	Poder de los ciudadanos

Figure 4.15. Blank democracy graphic organizer for fifth-grade social studies lesson.

Name: _____

Jigsaw Research Template: Monarchy

Definition	Definición	Examples	Ejemplos

Monarchy
Monarquía

Authority figures	Figuras de autoridad	Power of citizens	Poder de los ciudadanos

Figure 4.16. Blank monarchy graphic organizer for fifth-grade social studies lesson.

examples, authority figure, power of citizens), so each group has four students. Two groups will research monarchies, and three groups will research dictatorships. Each government group and each research role group should be diverse and have an assigned discussion leader whose job is to make sure everyone has a chance to share so no one student dominates the conversation. The groups and research roles for this class are as follows:

- Monarchy group 1: Oliver (leader/researching definition), Mercedes (researching examples), Ellie (researching authority figure), and Sam (researching power of citizens)

- Monarchy group 2: Tyler (researching definition), Fred (researching examples), Grace (researching authority figure), and Lucy (leader/researching power of citizens)

Name: _____

Jigsaw Research Template: Dictatorship

Definition	Definición	Examples	Ejemplos

Dictatorship
Dictadura

Authority figures	Figuras de autoridad	Power of citizens	Poder de los ciudadanos

Figure 4.17. Blank dictatorship graphic organizer for fifth-grade social studies lesson.

Name: _____

Jigsaw Research Template: Monarchy

What is it?	Where is it?

Monarchy

Who is the leader?	The people follow the king or queen's rules.

Figure 4.18. Blank monarchy graphic organizer for fifth-grade social studies lesson, adapted for Grace.

Name: _____

Exit Ticket: Systems of Government

Democracy Democracia	Dictatorship Dictadura	Monarchy Monarquía

Figure 4.19. Exit Ticket: Systems of Government for fifth-grade social studies lesson.

- Dictatorship group 1: Paulette (researching definition), Iris (leader/researching examples), Harry (researching authority figure), and Brian (researching power of citizens)

- Dictatorship group 2: David (researching definition), Vivian (researching examples), John (leader/researching authority figure), and Kiana (researching power of citizens)

- Dictatorship group 3: Chloe (leader/researching definition), Nigel (researching examples), Quentin (researching authority figure), and Alison (researching power of citizens)

Connections With Other Team Members

- Connect with the SLP who will push in during lesson to support Mercedes.

- Connect with literacy interventionist who will push in during lesson to support Brian, David, and Grace.

Desired Results

"I Can" Statements

- I can compare and contrast democracies, dictatorships, and monarchies.

- I can list examples of each of these types of government.

- I can discuss the power of citizens in each of these types of government.

- I can work with peers to research information and report back to small and large groups.

 INCLUSIVE PRACTICES

These apply to all students and should not be differentiated. Regardless of the supports individual students receive, they are all working toward these goals and understandings.

Alternate standards/key ideas for Grace

- Identify central authority figures at school, state, or national levels (e.g., teacher, principal, governor, president). (GVT.35.5c)

- Match the job responsibility to an authority figure (e.g., principal runs the school, mayor runs the town) (Ohio's Academic Content Standards–Extended Social Studies). (GVT.35.6c)

Assessment Evidence

Assessment evidence will consist of performance tasks, self-assessments, and other evidence that the students are mastering the identified goals and understandings. The following evidence will be used for this lesson:

- Students will work in jigsaw cooperative learning groups to research components of dictatorships or monarchies.

- Students will use technology and the Internet to gather information.

- Students will complete graphic organizers on two types of government—democracy and dictatorship or monarchy.

- Students will participate in a large-group discussion about the power of citizens in each of the three types of government.

 INCLUSIVE PRACTICES

WS13. Use graphic organizers with the whole class, allowing for student choice. Scaffold the organizers to meet diverse learning needs (e.g., fewer items to fill in, some text provided,

use of a word or sentence bank). Stock them in common areas of the classroom and save them on the computers that students use for work. This supports Lucy and Sam.

R4. Ensure that student studies the same-grade curricular units. Adapt materials to provide reworded prompts and prewritten answers to be matched or cloze sentences to be completed. Have student sit with a peer group for all content lessons. This supports Grace.

OS5. Ensure that students are at small groups of desks for most of instructional time. Provide extra tables and desks that any student can move to if he or she chooses. This supports Ellie.

SS9. Allow cooperative work to happen during all content areas with flexible grouping. This supports Alison, Chloe, and Vivian.

Classroom Arrangement

- The classroom arrangement includes a "calming corner" and "move and learn" area that students may use as needed.

- Students sit at desks in small groups of four, facing board in front of classroom.

- Students have the option to move to tables or floor.

INCLUSIVE PRACTICES

SR7. Provide a "calming corner" for all students, equipped with soft seating, carpet, sensory tools, and so forth. Students may go to the corner as needed. This supports Grace.

ES12. Provide a "move and learn" area of the room for all students where they can walk back and forth, jump, or jump rope. This supports Brian and Fred.

R4. Ensure that student studies the same-grade curricular units. Adapt materials to provide reworded prompts and prewritten answers to be matched or cloze sentences to be completed. Have student sit with a peer group for all content lessons. This supports Grace.

OS5. Ensure that students are at small groups of desks for most of instructional time. Provide extra tables and desks that any student can move to if he or she chooses. This supports Ellie.

SS9. Allow cooperative work to happen during all content areas with flexible grouping. This supports Alison, Chloe, and Vivian.

SR5. Provide all students with a choice of seating in the classroom. This supports Ellie and Lucy.

Materials

- Jigsaw research templates (see Figures 4.15–4.17), in English and Spanish, with adaptation of monarchy template for Grace (see Figure 4.18)

- Pens, pencils, pencil grips

- Tablets, laptops

- Exit Ticket: Systems of Government in English and Spanish (see Figure 4.19)

- Fidgets

- Self-regulation scales for Chloe and Fred

- Line guides for reading

- Mercedes' stander and text-to-speech device

LESSON PLANS

INCLUSIVE PRACTICES

ES8. Provide all written materials in first languages. This supports Lucy.

R4. Ensure that student studies the same-grade curricular units. Adapt materials to provide reworded prompts and prewritten answers to be matched or cloze sentences to be completed. Have student sit with a peer group for all content lessons. This supports Grace.

R5. Provide several different eye-tracking supports, such as index cards, colored strips of plastic, and so forth. This supports Brian and David.

WS13. Use graphic organizers with the whole class, allowing for student choice. Scaffold the organizers to meet diverse learning needs (e.g., fewer items to fill in, some text provided, use of a word or sentence bank). Stock them in common areas of the classroom and save them on the computers that students use for work. This supports Lucy and Sam.

SR8. Provide fidgets and mandalas to all students. This supports Fred.

SR4. Ensure that all students are familiar with regulation scales, and many have them at their desks for self-checks. Some are for voice volume and emotional escalation; some for effective use of work time; some for interest or independence level for an activity. This supports Chloe and Fred.

R11. Create a variety of word study activities for whole-class use at different levels of understanding (e.g., portable word walls, guess the covered word, speed sorting, add an ending). This supports Quentin.

Learning Activities

Allow for breaks, walks, use of the "calming corner," and use of the "move and learn" area during the lesson.

Anticipatory Set

Time: 5 minutes

1. Open the lesson by asking: *What type of government do we have in the United States?* [Student response: Democracy.] *What are some things you can tell me about the United States government?* [Possible responses: There is a president and Congress; we vote; there are laws to follow; we have a Constitution and Bill of Rights.]

2. Ask: *Do all nations or countries have a democracy? What if the leader of the country was not elected? What if someone fought the current government, took over, and made him- or herself the leader? What would that be like? What if that leader had good ideas and made sure everyone had what they needed? What if that leader was really mean and made the people suffer?*

3. Say: *Today we are going to research two different types of governments and see what they are like compared with a democracy. One is called a* dictatorship *and the other is called a* monarchy.

INCLUSIVE PRACTICES

SR2. Allow all students short walks down the hall. This supports Brian, Grace, and Tyler.

SR3. Allow all students breaks in or out of the classroom. This supports Grace and Tyler.

SR7. Provide a "calming corner" for all students, equipped with soft seating, carpet, sensory tools, and so forth. Students may go to the corner as needed. This supports Grace.

ES12. Provide a "move and learn" area of the room for all students where they can walk back and forth, jump, or jump rope. This supports Fred.

R4. Ensure that student studies the same-grade curricular units. Adapt materials to provide reworded prompts and prewritten answers to be matched or cloze sentences to be completed. Have student sit with a peer group for all content lessons. This supports Grace.

R5. Provide several different eye-tracking supports, such as index cards, colored strips of plastic, and so forth. This supports Brian and David.

Modeling/Guided Practice

Time: 10 minutes

1. Distribute graphic organizers for democracy. Say: *Think back to what we have discussed about democracies. As we review, I am going to fill in this research template; you can take notes in yours as well. In a little while, you will work in your jigsaw groups to complete research templates on dictatorships and monarchies.*

2. Review each section of the graphic organizer/template on democracy—the definition, examples of nations that have democracies, who is the authority figure or leader in a democracy, and the power citizens have in a democracy. Include important facts in each section as your own ideas if students do not mention them. See an example of a completed template in Figure 4.20.

INCLUSIVE PRACTICES

WS13. Use graphic organizers with the whole class, allowing for student choice. Scaffold the organizers to meet diverse learning needs (e.g., fewer items to fill in, some text provided, use of a word or sentence bank). Stock them in common areas of the classroom and save them on the computers that students use for work. This supports Lucy and Sam.

ES4. For all information that the teacher reviews orally, write the information clearly for all students and/or post it on the class web site—announcements, homework assignments, notes, agenda. This supports Kiana.

SR1. Allow all students to draw or doodle during lessons. This supports Iris.

ES7. Think aloud when writing, spelling, or punctuating on the board/during lessons. This supports David and Lucy.

Independent Practice

Time: 20 minutes

1. Once complete, have students get into their jigsaw cooperative learning groups and assign each member his or her role/subtopic.

2. Have each student get a laptop or tablet from the cart, along with his or her research template (dictatorship or monarchy), and group with other experts. For example, the two students researching the definition of *monarchies* will work together; the three students researching examples of dictatorships will work together.

3. Give students 15 minutes to research their expert roles and 5 minutes to share their findings with their small groups.

Name: _____

Jigsaw Research Template: Democracy

Definition Definición	Examples Ejemplos
A government ruled by the people. Leaders are chosen by the people in free elections.	United States, India, Canada, Germany, Finland, Sweden, Spain, Australia, Denmark, Ireland, Iceland, United Kingdom

Democracy
Democracia

Authority figures Figuras de autoridad	Power of citizens Poder de los ciudadanos
President or Prime Minister Congress or Parliament Justice Department	Citizens can vote and run for office. Their rights are protected by a constitution. All citizens are equal under the law.

Figure 4.20. Completed democracy graphic organizer for fifth-grade social studies lesson.

4. Distribute dictatorship templates and have three small groups provide information for each section as you act as scribe on the interactive whiteboard. Have students complete their own templates.

5. Repeat for the monarchy template. See sample completed templates for monarchy and dictatorship in Figures 4.21 and 4.22; Grace's completed template is shown in Figure 4.23.

INCLUSIVE PRACTICES

LAR4. Allow students to work with a partner to take turns retelling details. This supports David and Lucy.

R4. Ensure that student studies the same-grade curricular units. Adapt materials to provide reworded prompts and prewritten answers to be matched or cloze sentences to be completed. Have student sit with a peer group for all content lessons. This supports Grace.

R6. Build peer reading buddies into daily literacy lesson activities. This supports Brian and David.

ES5. Use an interactive whiteboard with a timer that chimes and changes color to signal transitions to next task. This supports Alison, Ellie, and Paulette.

Closure

Time: 10 minutes

1. Say: *Wow. We have found out a lot of information today about three different types of government. Let's talk about the power of the citizens and the authority figure or leader in each type. In which type of government do people have the most power?* [Student response: Democracy.] *The least?* [Student response: Dictatorship.] *When might people want to have a monarch or a dictator make all the decisions for the people?* [Possible responses: emergencies; when the people need a boss; to stop crime; when they want to help all the people.]

2. Distribute exit ticket and have students complete it with what they now know about each type of government.

Name: _____

Jigsaw Research Template: Monarchy

Definition Definición	Examples Ejemplos
A government ruled by a monarch (king or queen). There may also be an elected body.	Constitutional: United Kingdom, Cambodia, Malaysia, Australia, Japan, Vietnam Absolute: Saudi Arabia, Qatar, Monaco, Kuwait

Monarchy / Monarquía

Authority figures Figuras de autoridad	Power of citizens Poder de los ciudadanos
Monarch (King or Queen)	Citizens in a constitutional monarchy have the rights that the constitution protects. Citizens in an absolute monarchy have only the rights the monarch gives them.

Figure 4.21. Completed monarchy graphic organizer for fifth-grade social studies lesson.

Name: _____

Jigsaw Research Template: Dictatorship

Definition Definición	Examples Ejemplos
A government with one person in absolute power, often taken by force. Authoritarian government with no elections.	Belarus, Cameroon, Chad, China, Cuba, Egypt, Ethiopia, Iran, Libya, Madagascar, Myanmar, North Korea, Rwanda, Sudan, Syria

Dictatorship / Dictadura

Authority figures Figuras de autoridad	Power of citizens Poder de los ciudadanos
Dictator	Citizens have very few if any rights. Every aspect of public and private behavior is controlled by the dictator.

Figure 4.22. Completed dictatorship graphic organizer for fifth-grade social studies lesson.

Name: _____

Jigsaw Research Template: Monarchy

What is it?	Where is it?
	Spain has a king. United Kingdom has a queen.

Monarchy

Who is the leader?	The people follow the king or queen's rules.
KING QUEEN	

Figure 4.23. Completed monarchy graphic organizer for fifth-grade social studies lesson, adapted for Grace.

INCLUSIVE PRACTICES

ES4. For all information that the teacher reviews orally, write the information clearly for all students and/or post it on the class web site—announcements, homework assignments, notes, agenda. This supports Kiana.

R5. Provide several different eye-tracking supports, such as index cards, colored strips of plastic, and so forth. This supports Brian and David.

FIFTH-GRADE LESSON: Art

Time allotted: 30 minutes

Standards used: The National Core Art Standards (2014) for Visual Arts were used to identify standards, essential questions, and enduring understandings for this lesson.

The New York State Alternate Performance Indicators (New York State Education Department, n.d.c.) were used for Grace.

Context: The arts curriculum covers five areas: creating; performing, presenting, and producing; responding; and connecting. Students in pre-K through sixth grade build their knowledge and skills in these areas over several years as they learn new techniques, present their original work in different ways, and delve deeper into the historical and cultural facets of art. In this lesson, students are creating original works of art while they investigate blind contour drawing, color theory of warm versus cool colors, and abstract versus realistic representations of a person's face or hands.

The art instruction and activities presented in this lesson are credited to Lisa Jordan, art teacher, Brighton Central School District, New York.

As with other specials, art is taught by a specialist; in this case, a certified art teacher.

Lesson Objectives

1. Organize and develop artistic ideas and work. (National Core Art Standards for Visual Arts, Anchor Standard 2)

2. Experiment and develop skills in multiple art-making techniques and approaches through practice. (VA: Cr2.1.5)

Before This Lesson

Advance Preparation

1. Complete the art project multiple times in various stages for modeling (see Figures 4.24–4.25).

2. Pair students so they do not have to choose someone, purposefully planning for their abilities and personalities in working together. These are the pairings for this class: Alison and Brian; Chloe and Ellie; David and Harry; Fred and Kiana; Grace and Lucy; Iris and Paulette; John and Nigel; Mercedes and Vivian; Oliver and Quentin; Sam and Tyler.

3. Create written list of steps, with photos of each step, alternating text color step by step (see Figure 4.26). Reproduce in Spanish.

Figure 4.24. Model for blind contour drawing (Step 1) for fifth-grade art lesson.

LESSON PLANS

Connections With Other Team Members

Check in with the art teacher a day or two before the scheduled art lesson to discuss what supports students might need for specific activities. For this lesson, the art teacher will create a written list of steps for John and Kiana, reproducing it in Spanish for Lucy. Chloe may need reminders that a blind contour drawing need not look perfect; this lesson is about process as much as product. Grace should be supported in meeting the alternate performance indicators listed next.

Desired Results

"I Can" Statements

- I can tell you about abstract art versus realism.

- I can create a blind contour drawing.

- I can reflect on my artwork and choice of color.

- I can write a statement about my artwork.

Figure 4.25. Finished, watercolor-painted model of contour drawing (Step 2) for fifth-grade art lesson.

Name: _____

Blind Contour Drawing

Step 1: Look directly at your subject.

Using a permanent marker and draw what you see on the paper.

Look at your subject the whole time you draw.

Do not lift your marker from the paper or look at the paper until you finish.

Step 2: Review warm and cool color palettes.

Decide which fits your drawing best, warm or cool.

Paint your drawing with watercolors in the palette you chose.

Figure 4.26. Written steps with photos for fifth-grade art lesson.

LESSON PLANS

INCLUSIVE PRACTICES

These apply to all students and should not be differentiated. Regardless of the supports individual students receive, they are all working toward these goals and understandings. Alternate standards/key ideas for Grace:

- *Standard 1—Creating, Performing, and Participating in the Arts.* Students will actively engage in the processes that constitute creation and performance in the arts (dance, music, theatre, and visual arts) and participate in various roles in the arts (New York State Education Department, n.d.c.).

- *Alternate Level for Visual Arts: Key Ideas.* Students will make works of art that explore different kinds of subject matter, topics, themes, and metaphors. Students will understand and use sensory elements, organizational principles, and expressive images to communicate their own ideas in works of art. Students will use a variety of art materials, processes, mediums, and techniques and use appropriate technologies for creating and exhibiting visual art works (New York State Education Department, n.d.c.).

Assessment Evidence

Assessment evidence will consist of performance tasks, self-assessments, and other evidence that the students are mastering the identified goals and understandings. The following evidence will be used for this lesson:

- Students will create a blind contour drawing of a partner's face or hands.

- Students will watercolor the drawing using cool or warm colors.

- Students will compose/write a statement regarding the work, using art vocabulary.

- Students will answer self-reflection questions on choices made in artwork.

- The teacher will observe students creating contour drawings.

- Teacher and students will engage in questioning about artwork and art vocabulary.

INCLUSIVE PRACTICES

Alternate performance indicators for Grace:

- Demonstrate the basic skills in using a marker and paintbrush.

- Create works of art based on what they see, as well as their imagination.

- Learn to name visual elements (e.g., shapes, textures, colors) through multisensory experiences.

- Make works of art that incorporate selected visual elements.

- Guide students to reflect on what their artwork looks like and how they used the medium (e.g., paint, crayon).

Classroom Arrangement

- Students sit at art tables, on stools, with no more than three students at a table. Create heterogeneous groups based on skill development; have students face demonstration area at front of the classroom.

- Students may choose to sit at an easel on a standard chair with or without a cushion.

- Allow breaks and short walks down the hall.

INCLUSIVE PRACTICES

SR5. Provide all students with a choice of seating in the classroom. This supports Ellie and Lucy.

SR2. Allow all students short walks down the hall.

SR3. Allow all students breaks in or out of the classroom. These support Brian, Grace, and Tyler.

Materials

- Models of artwork for each step (e.g., contour drawing, finished painted product)
- 9″ x 12″ watercolor art paper
- Permanent markers
- Paintbrushes
- Pencil grips
- Watercolor paints
- Index cards
- List of steps for creating drawing—with photos and alternating color line by line
- Timer on interactive whiteboard
- Self-regulation scales for Chloe, Fred, and Grace
- Mercedes' stander and text-to-speech device

INCLUSIVE PRACTICES

ES4. For all information that the teacher reviews orally, write the information clearly for all students and/or post it on the class web site—announcements, homework assignments, notes, agenda. This supports Tyler and Kiana.

R4. Ensure that student studies the same-grade curricular units. Adapt materials to provide reworded prompts and prewritten answers to be matched or cloze sentences to be completed. Have student sit with a peer group for all content lessons. This supports Grace.

R5. Provide several different eye-tracking supports, such as index cards, colored strips of plastic, and so forth. This supports Brian and David.

SR4. Ensure that all students are familiar with regulation scales, and many have them at their desks for self-checks. Some are for voice volume and emotional escalation; some for effective use of work time; some for interest or independence level for an activity. This supports Chloe and Fred.

Learning Activities

Allow for breaks and walks during the lesson.

Make sure Chloe, Fred, and Grace have their self-regulation scales before proceeding with the anticipatory set.

Anticipatory Set

Time: 5 minutes

1. Hold up your finished model (see Figure 4.25). Ask: *What can you tell me about the subject of this watercolor drawing?* [Sample responses may include: It's a person/man/woman; it's sloppy/messy; it looks like a person but not really.]

2. Say: *You are right. It is a person, but it is difficult to tell exactly who it is. It is also a little messy, but that is the nature of this type of abstract artwork, called a* blind contour drawing. *It is called* blind *not because the artist cannot see, but because the artist does not look at the paper while drawing, only the subject! Today, each of you is going to create a blind contour drawing of a classmate. This is an example of what it will look like when it is complete.* Display. *Now let's look at the first step.*

INCLUSIVE PRACTICES

SR2. Allow all students short walks down the hall.

SR3. Allow all students breaks in or out of the classroom. These support Brian, Grace, and Tyler.

SR4. Ensure that all students are familiar with regulation scales, and many have them at their desks for self-checks. Some are for voice volume and emotional escalation; some for effective use of work time; some for interest or independence level for an activity.

Modeling

Time: 5 minutes

1. Post your model of the blind contour drawing (before it was painted) on the board, captioned with the first step's instructions (see Figure 4.24). Say: *This is what my project looked like after the first step. Watch while I demonstrate.*

2. Call one student to the front of the room to pose as the subject. Sit the student with his or her back to the board, setting up your easel so you are facing the student and the class can see what you are drawing on the easel.

3. Think aloud as you create a contour drawing of the student's face. *I am going to create a contour drawing of my subject's face. You may choose to do your partner's hands if that feels more comfortable* (staring at someone's face may be too intimidating for some students). *I am using a permanent marker to honor the lines I draw the first time. The purpose is to record your first attempt of what you see. It is okay that it is not neat and perfect and doesn't look exactly like a person because that makes it abstract art. Okay, here I go. I am only looking at my subject, not my paper, and I am not lifting my pen! I am starting with the eyebrows, then the ear, then the hair. Now the other ear and the face shape, onto the mouth, nose, and ending with the eyes. See how fast I did it. It might take you a little longer, but this is a quick drawing. We just want to get it done!*

INCLUSIVE PRACTICES

ES4. For all information that the teacher reviews orally, write the information clearly for all students and/or post it on the class web site—announcements, homework assignments, notes, agenda. This supports Tyler and Kiana.

ES8. Provide all written materials in first languages. This supports Lucy.

R4. Ensure that student studies the same-grade curricular units. Adapt materials to provide reworded prompts and prewritten answers to be matched or cloze sentences to be completed. Have student sit with a peer group for all content lessons. This supports Grace.

R5. Provide several different eye-tracking supports, such as index cards, colored strips of plastic, and so forth. This supports Brian and David.

ES7. Think aloud when writing, spelling, or punctuating on the board/during lessons. This supports David and Lucy.

Guided/Independent Practice

Time: 15 minutes

1. Pair students up and supply each pair with watercolor art paper and permanent markers. Have each pair decide who will draw first.

2. Say: *The first artist should have his or her paper ready. Remember to look only at your subject, not your paper! Now, put your markers on your starting point, don't lift your pens, and go!*

3. Repeat for second artist. While students are drawing, circulate and model constructive comments on their work.

4. Give students 2 minutes to share their projects with others. Remind them that this is abstract art, so their comments on each other's work should focus on choices the artist made (e.g., face versus hands, where they began), not perfection or realistic representation of the subject. They will look a little silly, but that is the style.

5. Say: *Now, let's talk about colorizing our drawings.* Post your finished product. Say: *Notice that I used all warm watercolors. Who can use the reference chart on the wall and remind us of the warm color palette? And the cool palette? Choose the warm or cool palette, but not both, for this project. Then you can color it anyway you like.*

6. Have students hang paintings to dry.

 INCLUSIVE PRACTICES

ES8. Provide all written materials in first languages. This supports Lucy.

ES5. Use an interactive whiteboard with a timer that chimes and changes color to signal transitions to next task. This supports Alison, Ellie, and Paulette.

Closure

Time: 5 minutes

1. Say: *Look around at the drying work. What comments do you have about this process? Who would like to share which palette they chose and why?*

2. Supply each student with an index card to create a label for their work. Post a large version of yours on the board. Instruct them to include their name, a title for their work, the style and type of work (e.g., abstract, blind contour drawing), and one sentence about their palette choice.

 INCLUSIVE PRACTICES

CR8. Incorporate meaningful sharing of background experiences and perspectives into lessons. This supports Lucy.

LAR4. Allow students to work with a partner to take turns retelling details. This supports David and Lucy.

SS11. Provide choices in working in pairs or small groups. This supports Alison and Kiana.

FIFTH-GRADE LESSON: Physical Education

Time allotted: 30 minutes

Standards used: The SHAPE America National Standards & Grade-Level Outcomes for K-12 Physical Education (2013) were used for this lesson.

New York State Alternate Performance Indicators (New York State Department of Education, n.d.d.) were used for Grace.

Context: The physical education curriculum focuses on the areas of motor skills, knowledge of movement and performance in various games and sports, maintaining physical fitness, safety, responsibility, self-expressions, and social aspects of physical fitness. Students in kindergarten through sixth grade build on their knowledge and skills across all areas. Today, the students are learning about the value of physical activity for social interaction. They will do this by role playing a rescue scenario in which teams of students must work together to problem-solve and, using certain equipment, transport each team member from one location to a second location without walking.

As with other specials, physical education is taught by a specialist; in this case, a certified physical education teacher.

Lesson Objectives

1. The physically literate individual recognizes the value of physical activity for health, enjoyment, challenge, self-expression, and/or social interaction. (SHAPE Standard 5)

2. [The physically literate individual] describes the social benefits gained from participating in physical activity (e.g., recess, youth sport). (S5.E4.5)

Before This Lesson

Advance Preparation

1. Create a poster of a deserted island scenario, with text briefly describing the scenario (see Figure 4.27). Use alternating text color. Provide the poster in English and Spanish (see Figure 4.28).

2. In each corner area of the gym, place two parallel lines of marking tape on the floor, approximately 10 feet long, 15–20 feet apart, as space allows. (The area between the lines is the water.)

3. Share skills needed with physical therapist and occupational therapist for preskill work during morning physical and occupational therapy sessions.

Connections With Other Team Members

• Consult with physical therapist and occupational therapist.

• Check in with the physical education teacher a day or two before the scheduled physical education lesson to discuss what supports students might need for specific activities. For this lesson, written materials explaining the game will need to be provided in English and Spanish; these support Tyler, Kiana, and Lucy.

• Grace should be supported in meeting the alternate performance indicators listed next.

• Mercedes will need to have her stander and text-to-speech device easily accessible throughout the activity.

Desired Results

"I Can" Statements

• I can tell you that engaging in physical activity can increase opportunities for social interaction.

LESSON PLANS

Scenario: Rescue from Deserted Island

You and your friends decide to go skydiving. After much training, you are ready for your first jump.

Just as you all open your chutes safely, the wind changes, and you land on a deserted island instead.

You need to figure out how to get your whole group off of the deserted island and back to the mainland.

You have one rope

and one boat.

You may not touch the water.

Everyone must be rescued.

Be sure to use each person's best skills!

Figure 4.27. "Desert Island" poster for fifth-grade physical education lesson.

Situación: Rescate de la Isla Desierta

Tú y tus amigos decidieron hacer paracaidismo. Después de mucho entrenamiento, usted está listo para su primer salto.

Así como todos ustedes abren sus paracaídas con seguridad, el viento cambia, y aterrizas en una isla desierta en lugar.

Tienes que averiguar cómo conseguir que todo el grupo fuera de la isla desierta y volver a la península.

Tienes una cuerda

y un bote.

Usted no puede tocar el agua.

Todos deben ser rescatados.

¡Asegúrese de utilizar las mejores habilidades de cada persona!

Figure 4.28. "Desert Island" poster for fifth-grade physical education lesson, Spanish version.

- I can tell you that teamwork in physical activity improves social and communication skills.

- I can communicate ideas for "rescuing" peers.

- I can scoot on a floor scooter.

- I can throw and pull rope.

- I can communicate/list ways teams worked together; issues that were solved.

- I can communicate/discuss how teams (sports, games) work together.

- I can list other social benefits of physical activity.

 INCLUSIVE PRACTICES

These apply to all students and should not be differentiated. Regardless of the supports individual students receive, they are all working toward these goals and understandings. Alternate standard/key idea for Grace:

- *Standard 2—A Safe and Healthy Environment.* Students will acquire the knowledge and ability necessary to create and maintain a safe and healthy environment (New York State Education Department, n.d.d.).

- *Alternate Level for Physical Education: Key Ideas.* Students will demonstrate responsible personal and social behavior while engaged in physical activity. They will understand that physical activity provides the opportunity for enjoyment, challenge, self-expression, and communication. Students will be able to identify safety hazards and react effectively to ensure a safe and positive experience for all participants (New York State Education Department, n.d.d.).

Assessment Evidence

Assessment evidence will consist of performance tasks, self-assessments, and other evidence that the students are mastering the identified goals and understandings. The following evidence will be used for this lesson:

- Students will work in small groups and create and execute a plan to move all participants from one area (deserted island) to another area (home) of the gym.

- Students will communicate a list of teamwork skills and social benefits of physical activity.

- Students will conduct analyses of their own group's solution and compare/contrast it to solutions of other small groups.

- The teacher will observe communication skills and problem solving in small groups.

 INCLUSIVE PRACTICES

Alternate performance indicators for Grace:

- Contribute to a safe and healthy environment by observing safe conditions for games, recreation, and outdoor activities.

- Learn and practice appropriate participation and spectator behaviors to produce a safe and positive environment.

- Work constructively with others to accomplish a variety of tasks.

- Demonstrate how injuries from physical activity can be prevented.

- Demonstrate care, consideration, and respect of self and others during physical activity.

Classroom Arrangement

- For this lesson, four areas of the gym are marked with designated deserted islands, water, and mainland.

- Students are in groups of four or five.

- Allow for breaks/walks.

INCLUSIVE PRACTICES

SS9. Allow cooperative work to happen during all content areas with flexible grouping. This supports Alison, Chloe, and Vivian.

SR2. Allow all students short walks down the hall.

SR3. Allow all students breaks in or out of the classroom. These support Brian, Grace, and Tyler.

Materials

- Four areas taped off

- Four ropes

- Four floor scooters (boats)

- Large-group mat (for gathering for discussion)

- Poster of deserted island scenario (see Figure 4.27 and Spanish translation in Figure 4.28)

- Easel with chart paper and markers or interactive whiteboard

- Self-regulation scales for Chloe and Fred

- Mercedes' stander and text-to-speech device

INCLUSIVE PRACTICES

SR4. Ensure that all students are familiar with regulation scales, and many have them at their desks for self-checks. Some are for voice volume and emotional escalation; some for effective use of work time; some for interest or independence level for an activity.

Learning Activities

Allow for breaks or walks down the hall during the lesson.

Anticipatory Set

Time: 5 minutes

1. With large group gathered on mat, ask:

    - *What do you like about physical education class, sports, and playing outdoor games with friends?*

    - *What do you like about group work in class?*

2. Explain: *We are going to combine all those things—having fun, working together, and learning from each other—by solving a problem that requires physical activity.*

3. Read aloud the scenario from the poster about getting stuck on a deserted island while displaying text with visuals.

INCLUSIVE PRACTICES

SR2. Allow all students short walks down the hall.

SR3. Allow all students breaks in or out of the classroom. These support Brian, Grace, and Tyler.

ES8. Provide all written materials in first languages. This supports Lucy.

ES4. For all information that the teacher reviews orally, write the information clearly for all students and/or post it on the class web site—announcements, homework assignments, notes, agenda. This supports Tyler and Kiana.

R4. Ensure that student studies the same-grade curricular units. Adapt materials to provide reworded prompts and prewritten answers to be matched or cloze sentences to be completed. Have student sit with a peer group for all content lessons. This supports Grace.

Modeling

Time: 5 minutes

Describe the end goal of the activity and the rules while displaying text with visuals:

- Everyone has to be rescued.

- No touching the water.

- Think about everyone's skills.

 INCLUSIVE PRACTICES

ES4. For all information that the teacher reviews orally, write the information clearly for all students and/or post it on the class web site—announcements, homework assignments, notes, agenda. This supports Tyler and Kiana.

R4. Ensure that student studies the same-grade curricular units. Adapt materials to provide reworded prompts and prewritten answers to be matched or cloze sentences to be completed. Have student sit with a peer group for all content lessons. This supports Grace.

Guided/Independent Practice

Time: 15 minutes

1. Have students form teams of five students each. Place teams in four corner areas of the gym so they are spread apart and also have plenty of room to complete the activity.

2. Supply each team with one rope and one floor scooter. Reinstruct each team to start behind one line of tape. Remind them that the space between the two lines of tape is the dangerous water that cannot be touched, and they must rescue all team members to the area beyond the second line of tape.

3. Circulate while teams problem solve and create their plans to rescue everyone. Facilitate safe decisions and use of everyone's skills. Comment on teamwork and communication skills being used effectively.

4. Once everyone has been rescued, have each team talk for 2 minutes about what went well and what could have been improved.

 INCLUSIVE PRACTICES

LAR4. Allow students to work with a partner to take turns retelling details. This supports David and Lucy.

SS11. Provide choices in working in pairs or small groups. This supports Alison and Kiana.

Closure

Time: 5 minutes

1. Gather the students back on the large mat. Ask:

   - *What skills did you use to rescue everyone?* [Sample responses may include: pushing the scooter, tying the rope to the scooter and pulling it; sending one person across then sending the scooter back.]

   - *What was it like to work together to do a physical task?* [Sample responses may include: fun, frustrating, hard, had to try different things; had to listen to everyone's ideas; sometimes we had to start over.]

   - *How do other teams work together?* [Sample responses may include: they work together to play a sport and win the game, they solve problems together.]

   - *How do teammates help each other?* [Sample responses may include: they encourage each other; they make sure they come to practice; they play safely.]

   - *What are the social benefits of playing, exercising together?* [Sample responses may include: getting to know people better; solve problems together; have fun together.]

2. As students respond, list responses on board with visuals and alternating colors.

 INCLUSIVE PRACTICES

R4. Ensure that student studies the same-grade curricular units. Adapt materials to provide reworded prompts and prewritten answers to be matched or cloze sentences to be completed. Have student sit with a peer group for all content lessons. This supports Grace.

R5. Provide several different eye-tracking supports, such as index cards, colored strips of plastic, and so forth. This supports Brian.

FIFTH-GRADE LESSON: Music

Time allotted: 30 minutes

Standards used: Music standards are the NAFME 2014 General Music standards. (The NAFME standards were used to identify standards, key ideas, and conceptual understandings for this lesson. State music curricula from several states were reviewed in the process of lesson development; Virginia, Missouri, and California state guidelines for music education were reviewed in depth.)
New York State Alternate Performance Indicators were used for Grace.

Context: Students in third and fourth grade build on their knowledge and skills across all areas. The music curriculum in third grade typically includes building skills in singing, playing instruments, listening and composing, and understanding rhythm and movement. Some schools use recorders in third or fourth grades, whereas others use ukuleles as students begin to explore using instruments. Students learn to sing in an octave range in the treble clef, sing rounds about music from all parts of the world. Today, the students are in small groups practicing copying, creating, and performing rhythms using a range of notes and rests.

This lesson was developed with the support of music teachers Mykel Sapienza and Katie Rupert from East Rochester Elementary School in East Rochester, New York.

As with other specials, music is taught by a specialist; in this case, a certified music teacher.

Lesson Objectives

1. Improvise rhythmic, melodic, and harmonic ideas and explain connection to specific purpose and context (e.g., social, cultural, historical). (MU:Cr1.1.5a)

2. Generate musical ideas (e.g., rhythms, melodies, accompaniment patterns) within specific related tonalities, meters, and simple chord changes. (MU:Cr1.1.5b)

Before This Lesson

Advance Preparation

1. Prepare a song to use with students during the anticipatory set. Identify the song's rhythm using whole, half, quarter, and eighth notes and rests and be prepared to discuss it with students.

2. Prepare a 16-beat rhythm to model, and prepare it as a handout (see Figure 4.29).

3. Prepare copies of the Rhythm Pattern Worksheet (one for each group) (see Figure 4.30).

4. Prepare copies of the Rhythms: Self-Assessment exit ticket (see Figure 4.31).

5. Prepare large colored squares: whole note/rest; half note/rest; quarter note/rest.

6. Note that the guided practice portion of the lesson includes an option to have students follow printed musical notation to practice a 16-beat rhythm. If you plan to have students do this, then provide copies of the music you wish them to use.

7. Prep vocabulary list for review with Grace:

    *   Whole note, whole rest

    *   Half note, half rest

    *   Quarter note, quarter rest

8. Create written list of steps, with photos of each step, alternating text color step by step. Reproduce in Spanish.

Connections With Other Team Members

*   Get terms to SLP for Mercedes' AAC device:

    *   Whole note, whole rest

    *   Half note, half rest

    *   Quarter note, quarter rest

*   Check in with the music teacher a day or two before the scheduled music lesson to discuss what supports students might need for specific activities as described throughout the lesson steps.

*   Grace should be supported in meeting the alternate performance indicators listed next.

Figure 4.29. Sample 16-beat rhythm for fifth-grade music lesson.

Group members: _____

Rhythm Pattern Worksheet

Figure 4.30. Rhythm Pattern Worksheet for fifth-grade music lesson.

Name: _____

Rhythms: Self-Assessment

	I do not understand how to do this: I need help!	I can do this with some help: I am almost there!	I can do this: I got it!
I can create a rhythm with whole, half, and quarter notes and rests.			
I can clap, stomp, or make the rhythm accurately in a small group.			
I can listen to a rhythm and recreate it.			

Standards

1. Improvise rhythmic, melodic, and harmonic ideas and explain connection to specific purpose and context (e.g., social, cultural, historical). (MU:Cr1.1.5a)
2. Generate musical ideas (e.g., rhythms, melodies, accompaniment patterns) within specific related tonalities, meters, and simple chord changes. (MU:Cr1.1.5b)

Figure 4.31. Rhythms: Self-Assessment exit ticket for fifth-grade music lesson.

LESSON PLANS

Desired Results

"I Can" Statements

- I can create a rhythm with whole, half, and quarter notes and rests.
- I can clap, stomp, or make the rhythm accurately in a small group.
- I can listen to a rhythm and recreate it.
- I can define vocabulary words:
    - Whole note, whole rest
    - Half note, half rest
    - Quarter note, quarter rest

 INCLUSIVE PRACTICES

These apply to all students and should not be differentiated. Regardless of the supports individual students receive, they are all working toward these goals and understandings.

Alternate standards/key ideas for Grace:

- *Standard 1—Creating, Performing, and Participating in the Arts.* Students will actively engage in the processes that constitute creation and performance in the arts (dance, music, theatre, and visual arts) and participate in various roles in the arts (New York State Education Department, n.d.c.).
- *Key Idea:* Students will explore and perform music in formal and informal contexts and will improvise, create, and perform music based on their own ideas (New York State Education Department, n.d.c.).

Assessment Evidence

Assessment evidence will consist of performance tasks, self-assessments, and other evidence that the students are mastering the identified goals and understandings. The following evidence will be used for this lesson:

- Students will work in small groups of two to three to create and practice a rhythm with four measures (16 beats) using whole, half, and quarter notes and rests. (Alternatively, students will practice a printed rhythm with 16 beats.)
- The teacher will observe students' participation.
- Students will complete an exit ticket.

 INCLUSIVE PRACTICES

Alternate performance indicators for Grace:

- Explore musical elements.
- Create short musical pieces consisting of sounds from a variety of traditional (e.g., tambourine, recorder, piano, voice), electronic (e.g., keyboard), and nontraditional sound sources (e.g., water-filled glasses).
- Sing songs and play instruments maintaining pitch, rhythm, tone, and tempo.
- Sing or play simple repeated rhythm patterns with familiar songs and rounds.

Classroom Arrangement

- Have students sit in chairs in rows facing the teacher for anticipatory set and modeling.

- Students work in small groups of two to three, scattered around the room, for guided practice.

- Students return chairs to rows for closure.

INCLUSIVE PRACTICES

SR5. Provide all students with a choice of seating in the classroom. This supports Ellie and Lucy.

SR2. Allow all students short walks down the hall.

SR3. Allow all students breaks in or out of the classroom. These support Brian, Grace, and Tyler.

Materials

- Large colored squares: whole note/rest; half note/rest; quarter note/rest

- Handout showing notation for a model 16-beat rhythm (see Figure 4.29)

- Rhythm Pattern Worksheet (one for each group) (see Figure 4.30)

- Rhythms: Self-Assessment exit ticket (see Figure 4.31)

INCLUSIVE PRACTICES

WS13. Use graphic organizers with the whole class, allowing for student choice. Scaffold the organizers to meet diverse learning needs (e.g., fewer items to fill in, some text provided, use of a word or sentence bank). Stock them in common areas of the classroom and save them on the computers that students use for work. This supports Lucy and Sam.

Learning Activities

Anticipatory Set

Time: 5 minutes

1. Say: *Today we are going to use rhythms! We will practice making rhythms as a whole group, and then you will create your own rhythm in small groups to share with the class.*

2. Teacher asks: *What do you know about using rhythm from your own experiences?*

3. Prepare to play the musical segment (four measures, 16 beats) you identified prior to the lesson (see Figure 4.30). Direct students: *Now, listen for the rhythm in this piece of a song. Hear the rhythm in your head.* Play part of a song with easily identifiable rhythms two times.

4. *Here is the rhythm I heard*: [Say the rhythm aloud]. *Now say it with me.*

5. *Now let's tap the rhythm on our bodies.* Model tapping rhythm on body, repeating it once or twice].

6. *Finally, let's clap the rhythm.*

LESSON PLANS

INCLUSIVE PRACTICES

CR8. Incorporate meaningful sharing of background experiences and perspectives into lessons. This supports Lucy.

SR5. Provide all students with a choice of seating in the classroom. This supports Ellie and Lucy.

Modeling

Time: 5 minutes

1. Show the "I Can" statements:

   - I can create a rhythm with whole, half, quarter, and eighth notes and rests.

   - I can clap, stomp, or make the rhythm accurately in a small group.

   - I can listen to a rhythm and recreate it.

2. Say: *Today we will copy, create, and perform rhythms in small groups. We already heard a rhythm of 16 beats. Now I will share one that I made up myself. I will clap it two times with the notes, and you will copy it.*

3. Clap the rhythm two times so students can see and hear it.

4. Ask students to think the rhythm, then say it to themselves, then tap it on their bodies.

5. End with students clapping the rhythm with you. Say: *You practiced hearing and copying a rhythm! Now you will have a chance to make your own 16-beat rhythms.*

INCLUSIVE PRACTICES

MS1. Incorporate counting into daily routines for the whole class, using small groups for review of basic counting principles with scaffolding. This supports Grace.

ES12. Provide a "move and learn" area of the room for all students where they can walk back and forth, jump, or jump rope. This supports Brian and Fred.

ES4. For all information that the teacher reviews orally, write the information clearly for all students and/or post it on the class web site—announcements, homework assignments, notes, agenda. This supports Kiana.

SR1. Allow all students to draw or doodle during lessons. This supports Iris.

Guided Practice

Time: 15 minutes (small-group work followed by whole-class performance and copying)

1. Say: *Today you are going to work in your small group to create rhythms of 16 beats in four measures, or practice a rhythm with 16 beats. You will work in different parts of the room, and I will call everyone together when it is time to share.*

2. Students will work in small groups of two to three to create and practice a rhythm with four measures (16 beats) using whole, half, quarter notes and rests. Alternatively, have students practice a printed rhythm with 16 beats. That can be the rhythm you modeled or a different rhythm, depending on students' ability and how much they benefit from repeated practice.

3. Explain: *I will give each group a worksheet to use. If you are creating a rhythm, then you will record it. If you are practicing one, then you will follow what I give you.*

4. Give each group a worksheet to create a rhythm or practice a prepared rhythm.

5. Send each group to a different area of the room to work together.

6. Circulate to each group as they work to create a rhythm. Provide support as needed.

7. After 7–8 minutes, ask students to practice their rhythm as a small group and prepare to return to the center of the room with chairs to share their rhythm and copy others' rhythms.

8. Ask each group to share their rhythm, then ask the rest of the class to think, say, tap, and clap/stomp the rhythm.

INCLUSIVE PRACTICES

LAR4. Groups 1 and 2: Allow students to work with a partner to take turns retelling details. This supports David and Lucy.

SS9. Allow cooperative work to happen during all content areas with flexible grouping. This supports Alison, Chloe, and Vivian.

OS11. For multipart assignments or processes, write each step/part on an index card so that students can see the parts. They have a visual of how much is left to do as they work through each step. This supports Kiana.

R4. Ensure that student studies the same-grade curricular units. Adapt materials to provide reworded prompts and prewritten answers to be matched or cloze sentences to be completed. Have student sit with a peer group for all content lessons. This supports Grace.

R5. Provide several different eye-tracking supports, such as index cards, colored strips of plastic, and so forth. This supports Brian and David.

SR3. Allow all students breaks in or out of the classroom. This supports Grace and Tyler.

ES5. Use an interactive whiteboard with a timer that chimes and changes color to signal transitions to next task. This supports Alison, Ellie, and Paulette.

Closure

Time: 5 minutes

1. Say: *Today you practiced creating and recreating rhythms! What notes and rests did we use?* [Student response: whole notes/rests, half notes/rests, quarter notes/rests.]

2. Say: *Now class is almost over and it is time to reflect. Please put your name on this self-assessment and use it as your exit ticket today.*

3. Give students the Rhythms: Self-Assessment with rating scale and ask students to complete it and turn it in on their way out the door.

INCLUSIVE PRACTICES

ES8. Provide all written materials in first languages. This supports Lucy.

FIFTH-GRADE LESSON: Technology

Time allotted: 30 minutes

Standards used: ISTE standards for students were used.
New York State Alternate Performance Indicators were used for Grace.

Context: Technology lessons can be connected to any content area. In this lesson, technology skills are connected to a lesson on active citizenship. Students have been learning about the concept of active citizenship since first grade, and it has been addressed in fifth-grade social studies as well. They are familiar with the use of various online media, including social media, to communicate—web sites, blogs, e-mail, social networks, text messages, and so forth. Most students use one or more of these communication formats in and out of school.

This lesson is the first of a three- to five-part lesson, adapted with permission of Teaching Tolerance, a project of the Southern Poverty Law Center (Teaching Tolerance, n.d.).

As is typical in many school districts, technology is taught by a specialist; in this case, a certified school media specialist.

Lesson Objectives

1. Students use a variety of technologies within a design process to identify and solve problems by creating new, useful, or imaginative solutions (ISTE, 2017). (ISTE 4: Innovative Designer)

2. Students will be able to

   - Understand the use of digital tools in active citizenship

   - Evaluate the strengths and weaknesses of digital remedies in active citizenship (Teaching Tolerance, n.d.).

Before This Lesson

Advance Preparation

1. Make copies of the following Teaching Tolerance handouts in English and Spanish:

   - Improving the Active Citizenship Project Through Information Communication Technology (see Figure 4.32)

   - Assessing Active Citizenship Projects and Making Recommendations (see Figure 4.33)

2. Adapt the Assessing Active Citizenship Projects and Making Recommendations handout for Grace: Create a handout with four pictures of people doing things—two that are helpful to the community and two that are harmful. When reviewing the activity with her, ask her to show which actions help and which actions hurt (see Figure 4.34).

3. Choose one example from the Examples of Active Citizenship Projects handout (see Figure 4.35) to discuss with students during the guided practice portion of today's lesson. (Students will work with the remaining examples on this handout in subsequent lessons.)

4. If you plan to use the optional vocabulary handout (see Figure 4.36), then prepare copies for students.

Connections With Other Team Members

Check in with the school media specialist a day or two before the scheduled technology lesson to discuss what supports students might need for specific activities as described throughout the lesson steps. Grace should be supported in meeting the alternate performance indicators listed next; provide the school media specialist with the modified active citizenship worksheet shown in Figure 4.34.

Desired Results

"I Can" Statements

- I can explain active citizenship.

- I can explain how digital tools can be used in active citizenship.

- I can evaluate strengths and weaknesses of digital tools in active citizenship.

Improving the Active Citizenship Project Through Information Communication Technology

Introduction

Many students in schools across the country are involved in active citizenship projects because they feel a need to contribute to the community they live in. These projects range from food drives to teaching senior citizens how to use digital technology, and they are often organized and sponsored by schools.

Building an Active Citizenship Project

Having a desire and an idea to help are the first step to building a successful active citizenship project. The second is learning how to organize a project and utilize effective tools and methods. All projects require the following basic planning steps:

➲ Describe the project.
What is the problem and why is it important? Reach out to the community to see if they agree that 1) this is a problem and 2) there is a need for a solution. Let their feedback inform your project. This information is important as you begin to organize, and funders and volunteers will want it as well.

➲ Bring awareness to the project.
It is important that other people know what the problem is, why it's important and how your actions will help. People who experience these problems will need to know you are out there with an idea on how to help.

➲ Develop a plan of action for the project.
Answer the how. How will you execute the project? How will your actions make a difference?

➲ Communicate with people helping or contributing to the project.
All projects need help—people to work directly on the project and funds to support it. You need to get your message out to people who can do either or both. In the digital age, this means implementing the right information communication (ICT) tools.

➲ Evaluate the project.
You need to understand how effective the project is as it progresses. How can you measure how successful the project has been? What data supports the need for the project and how well the actions taken successfully address the problem?

ICT Tools

A basic understanding of which information communication technology tools best suit a project can be the difference between failure and success.

➲ Blogs: An abbreviated term for weblog, a blog is a web site that features information that can be shared by individuals involved in a project or the general public. Blogs allow users to access information, comment on it and share it.

➲ Web sites: The basic definition for a web site is a collection of webpages containing information—text, images or video—for the purposes of communicating an idea on the web. For active citizenship projects, a webpage is mission control. All aspects of the project are housed here—purpose statement, goals, management, operations, participation, funding info and successes.

➲ Text messaging: Text communication on a digital device, most often a mobile phone. Active citizenship organizations use text messaging for internal communication and to get the word out about events and actions taken.

➲ Social networks: Social networks are dedicated web sites that enable users to communicate with each other by posting information, making comments and sending messages, images and video. A social network differs from a web site in that it does more than just present information. It allows users to contribute new information and comment on information provided.

Figure 4.32. Improving the Active Citizenship Project Through Information Communication Technology handout for fifth-grade technology lesson.

These statements relate to the essential question: What role does digital technology play in active citizenship?

INCLUSIVE PRACTICES

These apply to all students and should not be differentiated. Regardless of the supports individual students receive, they are all working toward these goals and understandings.

Assessing Active Citizenship Projects And Making Recommendations

Instructions The active citizenship projects you will be examining were all successful to greater or lesser degrees. Your task is to review the project description and determine if incorporating appropriate information communication technology (ICT) tools would have improved their operation and increased their chances for success.

As you review the active citizenship project you've been assigned, think about the project's organizational needs and what type of ICT tools could have been applied to improve its operation. Write your recommendations and an explanation of your thought process in the chart below.

Example Name of Project: Homeless in Our Town, raising awareness of the plight of people without homes. Organizational Need Addressed: Bringing awareness; Type of ICT Tools: Social media page and texting; Why? Establishing networks with friends and interested parties would help spread word about the problem.

Name of project, brief description, and social problem addressed	
What does the project need to increase its chances for success?	
What type of ict would you implement into this project?	
Why? How would your recommendation help the project?	
Summarize your recommendations (incorporate all information above. Use extra paper if necessary.)	

Figure 4.33. Assessing Active Citizenship Projects and Making Recommendations handout for fifth-grade technology lesson.

Alternate standards/key ideas for Grace:

- *Alternate Level–Computer Technology: Key Ideas.* Computers, as tools for design, modeling, information processing, communication, and system control, have greatly increased human productivity and knowledge.

- *Alternate Level–Information Systems: Key Ideas.* Information technology is used to retrieve, process, and communicate information and as a tool to enhance learning (New York State Education Department, n.d.b.).

Assessment Evidence

Assessment evidence will consist of performance tasks, self-assessments, and other evidence that the students are mastering the identified goals and understandings. The following evidence will be used for this lesson:

1. Students will use stoplight response cards to show level of understanding (green = working independently; yellow = working but have a question; red = stuck, need help)

2. The teacher will review each group's assessments and recommendations.

INCLUSIVE PRACTICES

Alternate performance indicators for Grace (New York State Education Department, n.d.b.):

Name: _____

Circle whether the picture shows someone helping or harming his or her community.

Figure 4.34. Active Citizenship Projects handout for fifth-grade technology lesson, adapted for Grace.

Performance indicators–students:

- Use the computer as a tool.

Sample tasks:
  For example, this is evident when students

- Use a computer to communicate their ideas/thoughts.

- Use a computer-operated voice command to move a wheelchair or turn the lights on and off.

Performance indicators–students:

- Use a variety of equipment and software packages to enter, process, display, and communicate information in different forms using text, pictures, and sound.

- Access needed information from media, electronic databases, and community resources.

- Use familiar communication systems to satisfy personal needs.

LESSON PLANS

Examples of Active Citizenship Projects

"Souper Bowl" of Caring
A high school participated in the "Souper Bowl" of Caring active citizenship project. In the week before the Super Bowl game, students held a canned food and money drive and donated their collections to a local food bank. They took the donations there on the Saturday before the game and spent the morning working there to sort all of the food. February is an important time of year for food banks to receive donations because, after a big push for giving during the holiday season, they receive very few donations early in the year.

Active Citizenship Fair
Students at a middle school sponsored an all-day, school-wide active citizenship fair. Students invited community organizations and nonprofit groups to set up booths to inform students about volunteer opportunities. More than 1,000 students visited the fair, and 20 organizations participated, including Black Lives Matter, Anti-war Movement, Honoring Veterans and the Alliance for Climate Protection. Ninety-eight percent of students surveyed at the fair said they had a previous interest in many of the topics represented but needed more information.

Hitting the Books for Charity
High school students sponsored a read-a-thon benefit for juvenile diabetes. This school-wide fund-raising activity encouraged students to read, raised money to help researchers and provided an opportunity for students to earn active citizenship hours of credit.

Students collected pledges, read in the library for two hours after school and later returned to collect the donations. The event was open to all students. The local chapter of the Juvenile Diabetes Research Foundation presented the school with an award in recognition of the $1,100 raised through the event.

Operation Sandbox/Shoebox
Students and student organizations organized a district-wide project called Operation Shoebox to gather items requested by deployed soldiers and aviators from the National Guard. The shoeboxes were filled with items such as lip balm, small bottles of glass cleaner, sunscreen, beef jerky, nuts and flavor packets. For service members' downtime, students also included video games, books and board games in the boxes. By the end of the project, students had collected and delivered approximately 480 shoeboxes full of items.

Bundles of Love
Students from a high school's student council held a blanket drive and made 35 blankets for Bundles of Love, a nonprofit organization that provides clothing, bedding and other necessities for infants. The local chapter gives out 25 baby blankets each month and regularly helps more than 60 clinics, agencies and hospitals. The local Wal-Mart donated the fabric for the blankets, which students made out of two pieces of overlapping fleece with the edges cut into strips and tied into knots.

Reducing Racial Stereotypes
Several students at a local high school organized an effort to reduce racial stereotyping and profiling of people of Middle Eastern descent. Their awareness campaign alerted students and the community to the problem. Organizers wrote a position paper to declare their concerns and goals. They then printed fliers summarizing the issue and possible remedies with a call for volunteers who felt the same way. They didn't get much response and are looking for better ways to get the word out.

Figure 4.35.   Examples of Active Citizenship Projects handout for fifth-grade technology lesson.

Classroom Arrangement

- All students have access to a "calming corner" and a "move to learn" area at any time, as needed.

- Students sit at their desks in small groups of three to four, facing the board in the front of the classroom.

- Students have the option to move to tables or floor.

Vocabulary: Active Citizenship Project

active citizenship [**ak**-tiv **sit**-uh-zuh n-ship OR **ak**-tiv **sit**-uh-suh n-ship] (*noun*) one's involvement in their local community and democracy, from the municipal to the national level; for example, a campaign to clean up streets or to educate young people about democratic values, skills, and participation

information communication technology [in-fer-**mey**-shuh n kuh-myoo-ni-**key**-shuh n tek-**nol**-uh-jee] (*noun*) a collection of communication technologies composed of messages, photos, and videos sent instantly with the potential to reach massive audiences through social media networks

blog [blawg] (*noun*) short for "web log," a web page containing written entries of a writer's or group of writers' experiences, observations, opinions, and so forth, updated frequently

web site [**web**-sahyt] (*noun*) a connected group of pages on the web devoted to a single topic or several closely related topics

text message [tekst **mes**-ij] (*noun*) an electronic message sent over a cellular network from one mobile phone to another

social network [**soh**-shuh l **net**-wurk] (*noun*) an online community of people with a common interest who use a web site or other technologies to communicate with each other and share information, resources, and so forth.

Sources: dictionarv.com. techterms.com. freethesaurus.com

Figure 4.36. Optional vocabulary handout for fifth-grade technology lesson.

 INCLUSIVE PRACTICES

SR7. Provide a "calming corner" for all students, equipped with soft seating, carpet, sensory tools, and so forth. Students may go to the corner as needed. This supports Grace.

ES12. Provide a "move and learn" area of the room for all students where they can walk back and forth, jump, or jump rope. This supports Brian and Fred.

R4. Ensure that student studies the same-grade curricular units. Adapt materials to provide reworded prompts and prewritten answers to be matched or cloze sentences to be completed. Have student sit with a peer group for all content lessons. This supports Grace.

OS5. Ensure that students are at small groups of desks for most of instructional time. Provide extra tables and desks that any student can move to if he or she chooses. This supports Ellie.

SS9. Allow cooperative work to happen during all content areas with flexible grouping. This supports Alison, Chloe, and Vivian.

SR5. Provide all students with a choice of seating in the classroom. This supports Ellie and Lucy.

Materials

- Handout: Improving the Active Citizenship Project Through Information Communication Technology (see Figure 4.32)

- Handout: Assessing Active Citizenship Projects and Making Recommendations (see Figure 4.33 and Grace's adapted handout in Figure 4.34)

LESSON PLANS

- Handout: Examples of Active Citizenship Projects (see Figure 4.35)
- Vocabulary handout (optional) if you want to use it as a resource (see Figure 4.36)

INCLUSIVE PRACTICES

ES8. Provide all written materials in first languages. This supports Lucy.

R4. Ensure that student studies the same-grade curricular units. Adapt materials to provide reworded prompts and prewritten answers to be matched or cloze sentences to be completed. Have student sit with a peer group for all content lessons. This supports Grace.

R5. Provide several different eye-tracking supports, such as index cards, colored strips of plastic, and so forth. This supports Brian and David.

WS13. Use graphic organizers with the whole class, allowing for student choice. Scaffold the organizers to meet diverse learning needs (e.g., fewer items to fill in, some text provided, use of a word or sentence bank). Stock them in common areas of the classroom and save them on the computers that students use for work. This supports Lucy and Sam.

SR8. Provide fidgets and mandalas to all students. This supports Fred.

SR4. Ensure that all students are familiar with regulation scales, and many have them at their desks for self-checks. Some are for voice volume and emotional escalation; some for effective use of work time; some for interest or independence level for an activity. This supports Chloe and Fred.

R11. Create a variety of word study activities for whole-class use at different levels of understanding (e.g., portable word walls, guess the covered word, speed sorting, add an ending). This supports Quentin.

Learning Activities

Allow for breaks, walks, and use of the "calming corner" during the lesson.

Anticipatory Set

Time: 5 minutes

1. Tell students that people have started integrating digital technology into social activism since the mid-2000s. Social and political movements and organizations have been successful by incorporating digital technologies into their operations. Examples include the Arab Spring, Occupy Wall Street, Black Lives Matter, MoveOn.org, and the Tea Party. (As needed, provide students with concise background information about these movements' stated concerns and goals.)

2. Explain that information communication technology—messages, photos, and videos that can reach massive audiences through social media networks—can be used to distribute messages, conduct operations, communicate within the organization, and achieve goals. Encourage students to share examples of ways they use technology to communicate with others (e.g., sending text messages, posting photos on a class web site or blog). Point out that they are knowledgeable about different information communication technologies, some of which did not even exist 15–20 years ago.

3. Explain to students that social activism is not only for adults; many kids their age have also participated in or even run projects to advance social causes, raise money for charities, or otherwise improve their world. Encourage students to share examples of times they have participated in social activism of some kind (e.g., bringing in canned goods for a food drive).

4. Tell students that they will be role-playing technology consultants who are asked to review several student-run active citizenship projects. Their task is to analyze the projects and make recommendations on how to incorporate information communication technology to better the project's operation.

 INCLUSIVE PRACTICES

SR2. Allow all students short walks down the hall. This supports Brian, Grace, and Tyler.

SR3. Allow all students breaks in or out of the classroom. This supports Grace and Tyler.

SR7. Provide a "calming corner" for all students, equipped with soft seating, carpet, sensory tools, and so forth. Students may go to the corner as needed. This supports Grace.

ES12. Provide a "move and learn" area of the room for all students where they can walk back and forth, jump, or jump rope. This supports Fred.

R4. Ensure that student studies the same-grade curricular units. Adapt materials to provide reworded prompts and prewritten answers to be matched or cloze sentences to be completed. Have student sit with a peer group for all content lessons. This supports Grace.

R5. Provide several different eye-tracking supports, such as index cards, colored strips of plastic, and so forth. This supports Brian and David.

Guided Practice

Time: 20 minutes

1. Divide the class into small groups of three to four students. Distribute the Improving the Active Citizenship Project Through Information Communication Technology handout to all groups.

2. Review the introduction with students and then conduct a shared reading activity on the Building an Active Citizenship Project and Information Communication Technology Tools sections. In this review, you might have a class discussion that sounds like this: *Let's talk about active citizenship. What are ways that we see people contributing to the community around us?* [Students: The high schoolers doing a food drive, the fire station having blood pressure checks for free, the recreation center doing a park clean-up.] *Right, these examples are ways that people are working together for the community. More examples are from our school—remember when we did the book drive last year? Or when the high school kids went on a service trip to help after the flooding?* The discussion moves to a review of the sample you have chosen.

3. Distribute the Assessing Active Citizenship Projects and Making Recommendations handout along with a sample student active citizenship project chosen from the Examples of Active Citizenship Projects.

4. Review the instructions with students and go over the example. Say: *Let's review the directions. There are five tasks: describe your project, bring awareness to the project (i.e., getting information from people outside this class), make a plan of action, communicate about the project, and evaluate it when it is done. We are going to look at this example and find each step. First, what is the description of the project?* Continue the review of the sample, discussing each task.

5. Allow students time to begin making assessments and recommendations.

 INCLUSIVE PRACTICES

WS13. Use graphic organizers with the whole class, allowing for student choice. Scaffold the organizers to meet diverse learning needs (e.g., fewer items to fill in, some text provided,

use of a word or sentence bank). Stock them in common areas of the classroom and save them on the computers that students use for work. This supports Lucy and Sam.

ES4. For all information that the teacher reviews orally, write the information clearly for all students and/or post it on the class web site—announcements, homework assignments, notes, agenda. This supports Kiana.

SR1. Allow all students to draw or doodle during lessons. This supports Iris.

ES7. Think aloud when writing, spelling, or punctuating on the board/during lessons. This supports David and Lucy.

Independent Practice and Closure

Time: 5 minutes

1. There is no independent work in this first lesson; the class is divided into groups for continued work on this project in the next lesson.

2. Close with a review that digital technology can be used to identify and solve problems as students act as innovative designers.

INCLUSIVE PRACTICES

SS9. Allow cooperative work to happen during all content areas with flexible grouping. This supports Alison, Chloe, and Vivian.

Revisiting Inclusive Practice

Diversity is infinite. The three classrooms featured in this book comprise a great deal of diversity and individualized student needs, but what we covered is far from representing all there is in classrooms today. We created classrooms based on the diversity and needs that we see directly in working in schools, without focusing on a single existing classroom case study, to show that lessons can be planned to meet the needs of any class. First, we developed the student profiles based on children we know—children we have met in our more than 60 combined years as educators. Then, we developed the goals for the students to meet. We did not consider separate, segregated goals for students with complex learning needs. We presumed that all have the competence to reach the essential understanding of the end goals. The "I Can" statements in the lesson plans apply to all. Finally, we developed the lesson plans so the learning activities that lead to the goals are made to support the needs of the students. It can be done! And it is our job as teachers to create the environments where it is done.

In his 2017 book, *Wait, What?: And Life's Other Essential Questions*, Dr. James Ryan, Dean of the Harvard Graduate School of Education, asks five questions that are particularly pertinent to the content of our book. The question "Wait, what?" makes one pause to ask for clarification and essential understanding before drawing conclusions or making decisions. Educators must slow down to ask for clarifications about students' interests, strengths, needs, and backgrounds. Seeking information about parents' hopes, concerns, suggestions, and goals supports culturally responsive teaching for all students (Nieto, 1996). Another question starter from Ryan's book, "I wonder why . . . ," is at the basis of all curiosity. As a teacher, it keeps you wondering about students in the classrooms and the reasons behind behavior, academic success or difficulty, social relationships, and level of engagement. The alternate form of this question, "I wonder if . . . ," gets you thinking about new strategies or instructional methods that might lead to improved outcomes. "Couldn't we at least . . ." enables you to get started when you are stuck and move past dissenting points of view to focus on an outcome everyone can agree on—success of students. Asking "How can I help?" puts you in a position to lend a hand to others while avoiding the savior complex. It recognizes that others are the experts in their lives, not you. Students are experts in their own lives. You are the expert in the classroom. Your job is not to fix them or their lives. Your job is to fix the classroom so it is a place where they belong and where their needs are met so they can succeed. Last, asking "What truly matters?" gets to the heart of what is the most important—that success.

We often hear that full inclusion will not work and students with complex needs cannot be included in the general education classroom all of the time for all of the curriculum. When we dig deeper, we often find out that the previous questions have not been asked and new ideas have not been explored or tried. The reaction of some teachers, administrators, and families in the face of problems is often to assume that inclusion does not work—when in fact, inclusion was not even happening. True inclusive practice involves

- High expectations, presumed competence, and making the least dangerous assumption about all students' abilities

- Full class membership and participation in all activities of the school day

- Quality augmentative and alternative communication (AAC)

- Curriculum and instruction designed to accommodate the full range of student diversity

- Social, behavioral, and academic supports

- Ongoing assessment and evaluation of learning through authentic, performance-based assessments

- Meaningful, equitable family–school partnerships

- A valuing of school and community partnerships and resources

- Team collaboration

- Rich friendships and social relationships with diverse peers

- Quality planning for transition to adult life

- Opportunities for self-determination

- Schoolwide improvement

- Ongoing professional development (Jorgensen et al., 2012)

If these elements are not in place, then you are not doing inclusion, so you do not know if it works.

Widening your view of what a successful, productive class looks like and widening your view of acceptable school behavior and classroom activity is perhaps the most essential part of inclusive practice, even when all the elements are in place. What does a classroom look and sound like when inclusion is working? If you believe it looks like all students doing the same thing the same way at the same time, then you will not succeed in creating an inclusive classroom because this is an attitudinal barrier to inclusion. When inclusion is really working, and when it is really inclusion of all students with diverse interests, abilities, and needs, the classroom will look and sound like students meeting goals and being productive in a social context, with feelings of belonging and self-efficacy, while they do differentiated things in differentiated ways.

In Chapter 1, we talked about providing supports for students in their zones of proximal development, rather than "dumbing down" the work. This is also necessary for schools and teachers. Support for inclusive practice must be given to schools and teachers in their zones of proximal development (Vygotsky, 1978). They must be ready to meet new challenges that are not too small or too large for effective change. They must have the guidance of a more knowledgeable individual, and it must occur in a social context where it is okay to keep trying, learning, and growing in differentiated ways.

ELEMENTS OF INCLUSIVE PRAXIS

We set out to examine the praxis of inclusive teaching by providing a strong theoretical knowledge base about good teaching and noting that teachers need a strong ability to put theory into practice in the inclusive classroom. We addressed specific elements of the learning environment to help teachers. The elements we identified as effective and essential are a manageable class size, a manageable number of shared transitions, the presence of highly trained professionals as well as paraprofessionals, and collaboration with families (see specific examples from Chapters 2–4).

Manageable Class Size

Reviews of research on class sizes generally agree that class sizes of 13–20 students per teacher result in greater achievement for students (Center for Public Education, n.d.; Mathis, 2016). We decided to create class sizes of 20 students with a full-time teacher and a full-time paraprofessional in the classroom, which is a student–adult ratio of 10:1, below that recommended in the reviews. We wanted to create classroom sizes that follow research-based recommendations and also represent the reality for many schools. All of the students' needs can be met with two teaching professionals in the classroom at all times, plus in-class, co-teaching support from related services professionals.

Each class we described includes two to three students with IEPs and one to two students with 504 plans, for a total of four students in each class (20%) who have a documented need for special educational supports. This is actually slightly overrepresentative of the general population of students. According to the most recent data available from the U.S. Department of Education, 13% of all school-age children in 2015–2016 received services under IDEA (National Center for Educational Statistics, 2018), and 1.8% of all school-age children in 2013–2014 received services under Section 504 of the Rehabilitation Act (U.S. Department of Education, 2018). If all classrooms in a school district are inclusive (no greater concentration of students with disabilities in any one classroom), then it can be expected that about 15% of the students will have IEPs and 504 plans. We have shown how classrooms with up to 20% of students with IEPs and 504s can be fully supported in an inclusive classroom.

Some readers may still consider this unrealistic, that the percentage is actually much higher. Consider what happens sometimes in a school that has multiple classrooms per grade level: if not all general education classrooms have students with disabilities present, then the percentage of students with documented special needs will be much higher than 15% or 20%, and therefore the education of these students will be more difficult to manage effectively. Our suggested class size and composition represents effective classroom and schoolwide practice.

Manageable, Shared Transitions

Jorgensen et al. (2012) identified transition of all students, with and without disabilities, alongside each other as a key indicator of general education class membership and full participation. Students in each of the three inclusive classrooms we depicted remain together as classmates transition as a group throughout the school day. There are multiple transitions as students arrive in the morning; travel to and from specials, FIT, and lunch; and leave after dismissal at the end of the day. Students with disabilities, however, experience fewer transitions than they would if they were leaving to go to pull-out services or special education classes throughout the day. All students make the same number of transitions and, more important, they transition together.

Every student goes to FIT at the same time each day. Some students receive their related services or accelerated instruction, whereas others receive Tier 2 RTI supports that they may currently need in reading or math. Still others have a choice of academic or behavioral support activities that meet their needs at the time. For example, first-grader Bridget receives her 60 minutes of daily speech-language therapy; third-grader Odette always receives math support twice each week but chooses from several options the other 3 days of the week; and fifth-grader Iris may choose from a few different activities each day. Although students may be located in different parts of the school during this time, no one is missing instruction or social opportunities in the classroom.

Instruction From Highly/Specially Trained Professionals

Not all of the teachers in the classrooms we described are dually certified in general and special education or initially prepared with an inclusive education focus. They all are committed to inclusion of all students, however, and engage in ongoing, meaningful collaboration with related services professionals and specials teachers. All related services professionals and specials teachers have met national professional preparation standards in their respective fields. The daily schedules are designed to support consultation between teachers and other professionals. The school and district provide ongoing professional development opportunities for all staff.

We chose to depict teachers who represent the variety of preparation backgrounds we see in classrooms today. At the same time, we believe there should be a shift in the field of teacher education toward preparing all teacher candidates with an inclusive education focus, one that is fundamentally different than dual- or double-major preparation of general education plus special education, which risks portraying two separate populations of students who are essentially different.

Fisher, Frey, and Thousand (2003) referenced several areas of knowledge, skills, and dispositions needed by teachers for successful inclusive education, including content knowledge, outcomes-based education, multicultural education, constructivist learning, interdisciplinary curriculum, authentic ways of assessing student learning, multiage grouping, instructional technology, cooperative learning, development of positive social skills and schoolwide behavior management approaches, collaboration with families and colleagues, meeting professional performance standards for pedagogy and ethical practice, and seeing themselves as lifelong learners.

Educators need to be able to instruct and assess students with and without disabilities, lead paraprofessionals, coordinate related services, and encourage natural peer supports and friendships. We feel that separating this list into separate areas of preparation for general education and special educators would perpetuate the partitioned teaching of students. As Fisher et al. noted, "None of these abilities or dispositions is disability-specific, nor do they rely on etiology to be realized. Instead, they are common factors that transcend the restrictions of labels and categories" (2003, pp. 45–46).

Inclusive classrooms are more than and different from general education classrooms with mainstreamed students with special needs. With school populations consisting of students with and without disabilities and students from different racial, linguistic, and socioeconomic backgrounds, teacher education must encompass responsive preparation at the preservice and in-service levels for inclusion to be successful (Forlin, 2012).

Assistance From Paraprofessionals

As mentioned earlier, each classroom we described has a full-time paraprofessional to support instruction and management. The fifth-grade classroom also has two one-to-one paraprofessionals, one who works with Grace and one who works with Mercedes. It is important to note that the main focus of the one-to-one paraprofessionals should be the student to whom they are assigned to work. The paraprofessionals in our hypothetical fifth-grade classroom, however, are also able to support others who are working in small groups with Grace or Mercedes, thus benefiting many students in the classroom while facilitating meaningful peer relationships for Grace and Mercedes.

Family Collaboration

The families of the students are valuable members of the education team and the school community. Family members are an integral part of every case management meeting and often attend grade-level planning meetings. Ongoing, open communication is established at the beginning of the year. Preferred communication methods and manageable communication times and schedules are planned. Families help complete the student profiles in the beginning of the year and help keep them up to date, and they are revisited during quarterly conferences. The goals, hopes, and concerns that families have for their students are respected and considered in all planning and goal setting.

REVISITING THEORETICAL FOUNDATIONS

The following sections review the theoretical foundations for inclusion introduced in Chapter 1—the social model of disability, the least dangerous assumption and presumption of competence, and the meaning of full citizenship—with examples of how these are the basis of the classrooms described in Chapters 2–4.

Revisiting the Social Model of Disability

Because views on disability are socially constructed, an essential component to the inclusive classrooms in this book is that all teachers and professionals model the perspective that disability is a challenge, an opportunity for problem solving, and a difference, not an inability. Morning meetings are held every day in the three classrooms we described to build a strong classroom community. Students have the opportunity to get to know each other's strengths, interests, and needs during these meetings. Teachers model this by sharing their own strengths, interests, and needs. Students are taught directly, and observe indirectly, that strategies and supports benefit many different students, and everyone needs support with something sometime. For example, first-grader Taylor uses pencil grips to support her dysgraphia, but a basket of different pencil grips is available for anyone to use. Taylor benefits a great deal from this assistive device and uses it all the time. Another student may benefit slightly and use it sometimes. Another student may not find it useful and never use a pencil grip. It is the availability to all and the option that facilitates the social model of disability. If the pencil grip was given only to Taylor, then her disability would set her apart from her peers. Instead, access to, and optional use of, the pencil grip is something she shares with everyone in the classroom community.

Revisiting the Least Dangerous Assumption and Presumption of Competence

The foundational belief underlying this book is that every student can and will learn and be successful. In designing the classrooms described in Chapters 2–4, we have gotten to know each of these hypothetical students very well and have researched many inclusive practices to meet their abilities, interests, and needs. It would be impossible for us to think of every possible practice that will support them. It is also impossible to know if everything will work every time. But we choose to make the least dangerous assumption. We choose to teach and teach well, even if we are not sure of exactly what works best yet in every learning situation. We collect data, assess the result, and improve the practice for next time.

What Full Citizenship Means

The four components of full citizenship that Kliewer (1998) described are present in these classrooms:

1. A belief in one's ability to think

2. A belief in one's individuality

3. A belief in reciprocity of the relationship

4. A shared location.

First, we believe in everyone's ability to think and achieve high academic standards. Fifth-grader Grace is included in all cooperative learning activities because she is able to learn knowledge and skills through the same grade-level content and curriculum as her peers. Grace is placed in a jigsaw group during the fifth-grade social studies lesson that is researching the definition, leadership, examples, and citizen rights of monarchies. Grace's alternate standard indicates she should be identifying the central authority figure at the school, state, or national level. Grace's research role in the jigsaw group is to identify the leader of the monarchy. She is accomplishing the same thing with her materials and support as all of the other students with that research role in the other jigsaw groups. Third-graders Nathaniel and Victoria are learning ENL. They are challenged with grade-level academic language with ENL supports because they are capable of learning the same concepts and vocabulary and responding to higher level questions as their peers.

Second, each student is an individual. All students with IEPs are not the same. All students with the same disability label are not the same. Students with different needs are supported by the same support. For example, third-grader Kacey has a visual impairment, and third-grader Odette has dysgraphia. Kacey is unable to recognize her classmates by sight, and Odette has difficulty connecting names with faces. They both are supported by the practice of calling on students by name each and every time and teaching students to identify themselves by name to their peers. Likewise, some students with similar characteristics need different supports. First-graders Kody and Natalie are both very quiet. Kody needs social skill supports and counseling, whereas Natalie does not.

Third, the relationships in the classroom are reciprocal. All of the students in the class are believed to be intelligent and an integral part of the community. The classroom is different when someone is absent, and that person is missed. Everyone misses out when someone is unable to contribute to a discussion or activity. A climate is created where friendships among all students are supported and benefit everyone.

Finally, it is a shared space. The classroom belongs to everyone. The classroom landscape was designed with everyone's needs in mind. The displays showcase everyone's work. The materials depict the diversity of everyone in the class. Instruction occurs with everyone present. If some students leave the room for services, then it is during FIT time when all students leave the room, never when new instruction is to occur.

REVISITING CLASSROOM APPLICATIONS

We now review four ideas that inform our praxis of inclusion—universal design for learning, response to intervention with multiple tiers of supports, embedded instruction, and clustering—with examples of how these apply to the classrooms described in Chapters 2–4.

Universal Design for Learning

Several aspects of the classrooms we designed reflect UDL, which is based on three primary principles: 1) provide multiple means of engagement, 2) provide multiple means of representation, and 3) provide multiple means of action and expression (National Center on Universal Design for Learning, 2011; Rose & Meyer, 2002).

Multiple means of engagement are incorporated in the student profiles, which include each student's strengths, interests, needs, and inclusive practices. In addition, each classroom arrangement includes a "move and learn" area, a "calming corner," and a choice of work areas. There are several options in first grade to recruit students' interests, sustain their effort and persistence, and support their self-regulation, including opportunities to work in small groups, choice of seating options, books about students' favorite subjects (e.g., animals for Leela), and fidgets available for everyone. In third grade, the "calming corner" is available for everyone, breaks for movement or calming activities (e.g., coloring for Latoya) are worked in throughout the day, roles are assigned during group work, there is soft lighting in areas of the classroom, there is a consistent routine, and several books on students' specific interests (e.g., mythical creatures for Paige) are available. In fifth grade, the "move and learn" area is used regularly; there are opportunities to lead groups and work with different peers; various seating options, including Mercedes' standers, are available; and several icebreaker activities help students get to know each other.

Multiple means of representation are available for all. Students' perception, language, mathematical expressions and symbols, and comprehension are supported in many ways. In first grade, visual information is paired with audio information; manipulatives are used during math (Evan likes the linking cubes in particular); tactile ways to practice math facts, such as sand trays, are used; graphic organizers, opportunities to play games with a partner, hands-on materials, and leveled reading books, particularly with higher levels for Padma, are available. In third grade, multiplication charts, computer reading programs, kinesthetic math games, graphic novel versions of texts, and chunked assignments are implemented. Language is accessed in multiple ways, including braille for Kacey, Ukrainian for Nathaniel, and Mandarin for Victoria. In fifth grade, there are adapted materials, photos of notes on the board, math computer programs, multimedia lessons, multilevel math materials, and a vast array of books to choose.

Multiple means of action and expression are provided so students can demonstrate their progress in various ways. Students' physical actions, expression, communication, and executive functioning are supported. In first grade, the daily schedule is posted and there is a variety of materials to use, including large-print paper for Taylor and art supplies for Rebecca. There is a "Common Feelings" poster on the wall to support articulation of emotions, as well as wrist timers for those who need or would like to use them, desk maps, and planning sheets. In third grade, several students use response scales, including Chelsea. There are also sentence starters, self-check questions, and a visual schedule. In fifth grade, a chime can often be heard for 1- and 5- minute warnings. There are alternative spaces for students to use so they can work quietly or not disturb others while fidgeting. Checklists and planners are used regularly. Alternate assessments and a variety of formats on assessments are provided in all grades. Most important, students have choice. Choosing among these options and learning about supports that work best for them as individuals is an essential skill.

The environment, instruction, materials, activities, and assessments are designed to connect to the ways the students learn. They match them where they are and are responsive to their natural ways of learning. Students are not expected to change who they are as learners.

Multi-Tiered Systems of Support and Response to Intervention

The lessons in each grade level are part of an MTSS, the system used in the RTI model. Recall that this model typically provides three tiers of intervention:

1. Tier 1 supports, provided to all students

2. Tier 2 supports, in the form of more intensive instruction, provided to students not making adequate progress in the regular classroom in Tier 1

3. Tier 3 supports, consisting of individualized, intensive interventions that target a student's particular areas of need and may include special education services

Many strategies and materials are proactive, preventative academic and behavioral supports. For example, a basket of fidgets, choice of seating, choice of work area, and graphic organizers are all Tier 1 supports any student may utilize to sustain engagement in a lesson or task. Self-regulation scales and many FIT activities are Tier 2 supports that support more complex student needs. Related services such as physical and occupational therapy, counseling, and primary project are more specialized Tier 3 supports for students who need them.

Embedded Instruction

The implementation of IEP goals, accommodations, and related services occurs within the context of the general education setting and curriculum at all times. All students are engaged in each content area together, including specials. For example, Grace's IEP goals for counting and identifying shapes are embedded in the fifth-grade math lesson. Grace is engaged in the same activity with a partner, as are all the students in the class. While Grace's partner is reading and analyzing the characteristics of polygons and quadrilaterals, Grace is counting sides and angles and identifying shapes. The students all have half-worksheets to complete; Grace's are modified to fit her assignment. They are all reading, writing, and analyzing mathematical concepts. They are working together in the context of grade-level curriculum and meaningful cooperative groups.

It is essential to return to the concept of zone of proximal development here. It is a misconception to think that Grace must be completing the exact same work (half-worksheets) as everyone else. That is not fair. Fair is not everyone gets the same. Fair is everyone gets what they need. If students are not challenged enough or challenged too much, then they are out of their zone of proximal development, frustrated, left out of quality instruction, and alienated.

Clustering

We have utilized clustering in the ELA lessons. Students are working toward the same standards with the same learning activities, but they are grouped according to their reading levels in Grades 3 and 5. If students receive literacy instruction with peers who have similar instructional reading levels, then the group can be challenged toward reading and writing gains. If this is all happening during a station teaching model, then all students in the classroom are engaged in the same content area at the same time, clustered into patterns by reading level.

FINAL THOUGHTS

Our hope is that you will use this text, its examples, its resources, and especially the Inclusive Practices Bank in Appendix A to plan even better lessons. Add to the bank all of the things you are already doing to connect with your students, respond to their individual needs, support their academic and behavioral needs, and provide them with meaningful social interactions in a rich learning environment. Begin with knowing your students. Find out everything you can about them. Complete their student profiles in collaboration with students and families. Perhaps you will use our template; perhaps you will add a section that is particularly informative for you. Add inclusive practices from the bank we provide and from your own practice and other resources. Then, arrange a classroom that is universally designed to belong to all students. From the second each student enters the classroom, he or she should feel like a member and that the room is made for him or her. Next, know your standards and set goals for your students. Plan according to these questions, in this order: What is the essential understanding that all students should leave with? How will they show you that they are reaching that understanding? Which learning activities will get them there? What are the multiple means that need to be incorporated so they all can gain access to new learning and express their questions, knowledge, and skills? How can I better inform my practice and continue to improve?

What can I tackle next?

Inclusive Practices Bank

This appendix provides lists of specific inclusive practices within 12 categories. For easy reference, each practice is described briefly, and cross-references are included noting which students are directly supported by the practice in the first-, third-, and fifth-grade classrooms described in Chapters 2–4.

Where applicable for certain practices, we have included references documenting the evidence base supporting teachers' use of the practice. Practices for which a specific source is not cited are based on the general principles and recommendations for inclusive education discussed in Chapters 1 and 5. The 12 categories of inclusive practices listed are as follows:

1. Cultural Responsiveness

2. Environmental Supports

3. Language—Expressive Supports

4. Language—Receptive Supports

5. Math Supports

6. Motor Development Supports

7. Organizational Supports

8. Reading Supports

9. Self-Regulation Supports

10. Social Skills Supports

11. Testing Modifications Supports

12. Writing Supports

Picture Inclusion! by Whitney H. Rapp, Katrina L. Arndt, and Susan M. Hildenbrand.
Copyright © 2019 by Paul H. Brookes Publishing Co. All rights reserved.

CULTURAL RESPONSIVENESS

Content/Goal area	Inclusive Practice	Student
CR1. Cultural responsiveness—materials	Provide culturally responsive curricular materials, materials that reflect student interests, and resources other than textbooks.	Megan, first grade Oscar, first grade Padma, first grade Fabian, third grade Maddox, third grade Nathaniel, third grade Victoria, third grade Brian, fifth grade Lucy, fifth grade
CR2. Cultural responsiveness—discussions	Provide opportunities (e.g., morning meetings) for discussions about perspectives, events, diversity, culture, and interests and opportunities to problem-solve with students.	Padma, first grade Fabian, third grade Nathaniel, third grade Victoria, third grade Lucy, fifth grade
CR3. Cultural responsiveness—grouping	Allow for flexible grouping, to move in and out of cooperative learning (New York University, 2008a).	Oscar, first grade
CR4. Cultural responsiveness—assessment	Provide multiple ways to assess (multi-option homework assignments, portfolios, observations, skills checklists, oral and written reports, demonstrations, performances, role-playing, work samples, models, taped responses, drawings, graphs, posters, tests) (New York University, 2008a).	
CR5. Cultural responsiveness—use of time	Use time flexibly (block scheduling, stations, team teaching) (New York University, 2008a).	
CR6. Cultural responsiveness—interest-based learning choices	Provide interest-based learning choices (stations, literature circles/book groups, student-generated project topics) (New York University, 2008a).	
CR7. Cultural responsiveness—families	Seek parents' hopes, concerns, suggestions, goals (Nieto, 1996).	
CR8. Cultural responsiveness—backgrounds	Incorporate meaningful sharing of background experiences and perspectives into lessons (Brown University, 2017).	Oscar, first grade Lucy, fifth grade
CR9. Cultural responsiveness—community resources	Research and utilize resources from students and communities (Brown University, 2017).	

ENVIRONMENTAL SUPPORTS

Content/Goal area	Inclusive Practice	Student
ES1. Environmental—digital amplification system, teachers	All teachers wear the amplifier during any direct instruction or giving of directions.	Charlie, first grade
ES2. Environmental—digital amplification system, all adults	Substitute teachers, special teachers, and guest speakers are directed to receive instruction on use of the amplification technology.	Charlie, first grade
ES3. Environmental—digital amplification system, peers	During small-group activities, give amplifier to student to position in the group's discussion space.	Charlie, first grade

Content/Goal area	Inclusive Practice	Student
ES4. Environmental—pair visual information with auditory information	For all information that the teacher reviews orally, write the information clearly for all students and/or post it on the class web site—announcements, homework assignments, notes, agenda.	Charlie, first grade Nathaniel, third grade Victoria, third grade Tyler, fifth grade Kiana, fifth grade
ES5. Environmental—pair visual information with auditory information	Use a timer on the interactive white board that chimes and changes color to signal transitions to next task.	Ellie, fifth grade Paulette, fifth grade Alison, fifth grade
ES6. Environmental—pair visual information with auditory information	Check that the school bell, telephone, and alarms are loud enough for student to hear unaided.	Charlie, first grade
ES7. Environmental—pair auditory information with visual information	Think aloud when writing, spelling, or punctuating on the board/during lessons.	Oscar, first grade Kacey, third grade Odette, third grade Nathaniel, third grade Victoria, third grade David, fifth grade Lucy, fifth grade
ES8. Environmental—pair visual information with tactile information and first language	Provide all written materials in braille. Provide all written materials in first languages.	Oscar, first grade Kacey, third grade Nathaniel, third grade Victoria, third grade Lucy, fifth grade
ES9. Environmental—pair visual information with tactile information	Provide tabs marking sections of reference books (with braille labels).	Kacey, third grade
ES10. Environmental—mobility	Think aloud when walking in the hallways, making turns, staying to the right, making the transition through doorways, and so forth.	Kacey, third grade Odette, third grade
ES11. Environmental—mobility	Model and teach the class about identifying self and locations in the room ("It's under the window on the top shelf" versus "It's over there by Paige").	Kacey, third grade Odette, third grade
ES12. Environmental—movement	Provide a "move and learn" area of the room for all students where they can walk back and forth, jump, or jump rope.	Bridget, first grade Brian, fifth grade Fred, fifth grade
ES13. Environmental—furniture	Provide choices for seating and workstations (e.g., Vidget chairs, yoga balls, chair bands, standing desks, bean bags). See the examples shown in Figures A.1, A.2, and A.3.	Greg, first grade
ES14. Environmental—arrangement	Provide portable desk and room dividers to rearrange space. *Note:* Balance this with need for mobility.	
ES15. Environmental—lighting	Provide colored light covers, soft lighting, and natural spectrum lighting.	
ES16. Environmental—sensory	Provide sensory bottles. Sensory bottles are clear plastic bottles filled with mineral oil, objects, glitter, and/or food coloring to create a slow-flowing, soothing visual experience. See the examples shown in Figure A.4.	
ES17. Environmental—tactile access	Provide materials for target student to explore with hands when objects are described.	Kacey, third grade

Figure A.1. Example of flexible seating option: yoga balls. (Environmental Supports, practice ES.13)

Figure A.2. Example of flexible seating option: student may sit or stand. (Environmental Supports, practice ES.13)

Figure A.3. Example of flexible seating option: sitting on the floor with pillows. (Environmental Supports, practice ES.13)

Figure A.4. Example of sensory bottles. (Environmental Supports, practice ES.16)

LANGUAGE—EXPRESSIVE SUPPORTS

Content/goal area	Inclusive practice	Student
LAE1. Language—expressive: large-group participation	Before group time, give target student a question that can be answered with a new or familiar icon or vocabulary word.	Bridget, first grade Nathaniel, third grade Victoria, third grade
LAE2. Language—expressive	Provide time to rehearse responses, ideas.	
LAE3. Language—expressive	Provide picture symbol systems.	
LAE4. Language—expressive	Color code sets of words.	
LAE5. Language—expressive	Use prompts and sentence starters.	Bridget, first grade

LANGUAGE—RECEPTIVE SUPPORTS

Content/goal area	Inclusive practice	Student
LAR1. Language—receptive	Reduce background noise.	
LAR2. Language—receptive: directions	Embed one-step directions into whole-class morning routines, such as handing in homework, completing and handing in bell work, and following attendance procedures.	Nathaniel, third grade Victoria, third grade
LAR3. Language—receptive: check for understanding	Repeat information and peer comments when necessary to ensure all students have same access to auditory information.	
LAR4. Language—receptive/expressive: retelling details	Allow students to work with a partner to take turns retelling details.	Bridget, first grade Nathaniel, third grade Victoria, third grade David, fifth grade Lucy, fifth grade
LAR5. Language—receptive	Chunk verbal information; use cue words such as *first*, *then*, and *last*.	
LAR6. Language—receptive/expressive	Provide visual cues, signs, rhymes, word play, and vocabulary lists to help students with word finding.	Bridget, first grade

MATH SUPPORTS

Content/goal area	Inclusive practice	Student
MS1. Math—counting	Incorporate counting into daily routines for the whole class, using small groups for review of basic counting principles with scaffolding.	Isaiah, first grade Grace, fifth grade
MS2. Math—multisensory approach	Offer multiple ways for all students to practice counting, facts, and so forth: sand tray for copying numbers, number magnets on cookie sheets, number line on the floor on which to step.	Haley, first grade Kacey, third grade Nathaniel, third grade Victoria, third grade Paulette, fifth grade
MS3. Math—money	Ensure that real money as well as representations (e.g., tokens) are available in one of the math manipulative bins. (This creates a continuum of abstractness.)	
MS4. Math—problem solving	Offer graphic organizers and templates to all students. Stock them in common areas of the classroom, stored neatly in bins with the student's name and a piece of the template glued to the front, and save them on the computers that students use for work (New York University, 2008b).	Isaiah, first grade Oscar, first grade Nathaniel, third grade Victoria, third grade Lucy, fifth grade
MS5. Math—manipulatives	Provide multiple sets of counters, plastic linking cubes, and fraction circles; have abacuses available so that all students can choose to use them.	Avery, first grade Evan, first grade Haley, first grade Oscar, first grade Odette, third grade Alison, fifth grade Quentin, fifth grade
MS6. Math—technology	Provide computer/tablet time to use math software and apps (e.g., Arthur's math games, Reader Rabbit math, Math Blaster, Kids Academy—123 Tracing, Number Monster, Wee Kids Math). See the Resources for Inclusion list in Appendix B for more about these helpful programs and apps.	Oscar, first grade Bobby, third grade Kacey, third grade Quentin, fifth grade
MS7. Math—technology	Provide digital/talking clocks, talking calculators, and so forth.	Bobby, third grade Kacey, third grade Odette, third grade
MS8. Math—technology	Provide a calculator for operations.	Avery, first grade Alison, fifth grade Paulette, fifth grade

MOTOR DEVELOPMENT SUPPORTS

Content/goal area	Inclusive practice	Student
MD1. Crossing midline	In class, use games that support crossing the midline of the body. For example: • Popping bubbles with one hand (students will reach across the body to pop bubbles on that side). • Sand table play—have students scoop sand from one side and put in a bucket on the other side. • Have students use manipulatives for counting/categorizing items in piles.	Mercedes, fifth grade
MD2. Bear weight using stander	In class, create space for stander with a work tray so student can work while supported safely.	Mercedes, fifth grade
MD3. Use full range of motion with arms	In class, provide opportunities for reaching forward, back, and to the side by teaching movement sequences and activities. For example: • Teach stretching sequences such as reach up/reach down/swing your arms/all around. • Use brief movement apps and videos to provide movement breaks. Choose breaks that include arm swinging and stretching.	Mercedes, fifth grade

ORGANIZATIONAL SUPPORTS

Content/goal area	Inclusive practice	Student
OS1. Organization—planning	Support the use of a planner of each student's design/choosing customized for his or her subject areas and materials. See the example shown in Figure A.5.	Ethan, third grade John, fifth grade Tyler, fifth grade Oliver, fifth grade
OS2. Organization—planning	Many students, including the target student, have luggage tags on their backpacks listing items to go home/come back to school. See the example shown in Figure A.6.	Megan, first grade Justice, third grade John, fifth grade
OS3. Organization—planning/projects	Set up a bulletin board in the classroom that lists longer assignments and supports working backward from due dates, chunking parts of major assignments and providing sub-due dates, available to all for reference. See the sample calendar shown in Figure A.7.	John, fifth grade Tyler, fifth grade Oliver, fifth grade
OS4. Organization—preferential seating	Provide seating options for the whole class.	Nathaniel, third grade Victoria, third grade
OS5. Organization—workspace	Ensure that students are at small groups of desks for most of instructional time. Provide extra tables and desks that any student can move to if he or she chooses.	Ellie, fifth grade
OS6. Organization—stations	Ensure that all computer stations are equipped with adapter cords for hearing aids so student can choose to sit at any station.	
OS7. Organization—desk management	Tape a small drawing of the inside of the desk to the top of the desk, showing where books, notebooks, writing utensils, or other materials are stored. See the example shown in Figure A.8.	Megan, first grade Justice, third grade John, fifth grade

Content/goal area	Inclusive practice	Student
OS8. Organization—reminders	Post reminder questions in key locations, prompting students to self-check materials, work, and so forth (Rapp, 2014). See the example shown in Figure A.9.	Bobby, third grade Justice, third grade Brian, fifth grade
OS9. Organization—time management	Provide a small 1-hour countdown timer for student's personal use.	Jack, first grade Alison, fifth grade Paulette, fifth grade
OS10. Organization—materials	Create a coded classroom. Have all items and storage units in classroom labeled in first languages and braille, with photos. (Rapp, 2014)	Megan, first grade Justice, third grade
OS11. Organization—assignments	For multipart assignments or processes, write each step/part on an index card so that students can see the parts. They have a visual of how much is left to do as they work through each step.	Kiana, fifth grade
OS12. Organization—assignments	Provide visual or pie chart rubrics (Rapp, 2014). See the example shown in Figure A.10.	
OS13. Organization—space	Mark traffic patterns on the floor with feet.	
OS14. Organization—space	Mark spots for lining up by the door.	
OS15. Organization—schedule	Cue transition times with sounds, songs, movements, and/or signs.	
OS16. Organization—schedule	Post agenda with picture cues, braille, and multiple languages.	

Figure A.5. Example of individualized planner. (Organizational Supports, practice OS.1)

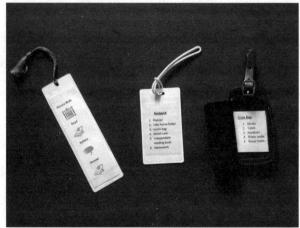

Figure A.6. Example of student's personalized bookmark and luggage tags for belongings. (Organizational Supports, practice OS.2)

March Homework Grid						
Sunday	Monday	Tuesday	Wednesday	Thursday	Friday	Saturday
1	2 Choose topic for social studies poster Read 20 minutes	3 Part 1 of math packet Read 20 minutes	4 Read 20 minutes	5 Read 20 minutes	6 Part 2 of math packet Read 20 minutes	7
8	9 Complete list of five resources for social studies poster Read 20 minutes	10 Part 3 of math packet Read 20 minutes	11 Read 20 minutes	12 Read 20 minutes	13 **Math packet due!** Read 20 minutes	14
15	16 Research complete for social studies poster Read 20 minutes	17 Part 1 of math packet Read 20 minutes	18 Read 20 minutes	19 Read 20 minutes	20 Part 2 of math packet Read 20 minutes	21
22	23 Rough draft of social studies poster done Read 20 minutes	24 Part 3 of math packet Read 20 minutes	25 Read 20 minutes	26 Read 20 minutes	27 **Math packet due!** Read 20 minutes	28
29	30 **Social studies poster due!** Read 20 minutes	31				

Figure A.7. Example of a monthly calendar for assignments, with extended assignments and projects chunked into manageable steps. (Organizational Supports, practice OS.3)

Figure A.8. Example of a student's desk map. (Organizational Supports, practice OS.7)

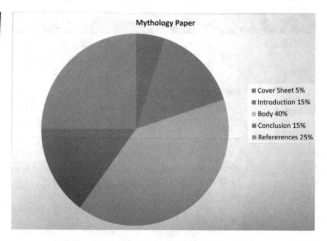

Figure A.9. Example of reminder questions on a sticky note. (Organizational Supports, practice OS.8)

Figure A.10. Example of a pie chart rubric. (Organizational Supports, practice OS.12; this doubles as an example of Writing Supports, practice WS.8.)

READING SUPPORTS

Content/goal area	Inclusive practice	Student
R1. Reading—comprehension	Provide charts of academic language and symbols.	Nathaniel, third grade Victoria, third grade
R2. Reading—comprehension/"Wh" questions	Have students use picture cue cards, individually or with a partner (Vicker, 2004).	Greg, first grade
R3. Reading—comprehension	Have as many books as possible available on CD. Record yourself reading them if necessary.	Leela, first grade Oscar, first grade Taylor, first grade Deirdre, third grade Maddox, third grade Brian, fifth grade
R4. Reading—access to content	Ensure that student studies the same-grade curricular units. Adapt materials to provide reworded prompts and prewritten answers to be matched or cloze sentences to be completed. Have student sit with a peer group for all content lessons.	Grace, fifth grade
R5. Reading—fluency	Provide several different eye-tracking supports, such as index cards, colored strips of plastic, and so forth.	Brian, fifth grade David, fifth grade

Content/goal area	Inclusive practice	Student
R6. Reading—fluency	Build peer reading buddies into daily literacy lesson activities.	Leela, first grade Oscar, first grade Taylor, first grade Deirdre, third grade Maddox, third grade Nathaniel, third grade Victoria, third grade Brian, fifth grade David, fifth grade
R7. Reading—short and long vowel sounds	Use partner activities or games to increase a student's understanding of long and short vowel sounds.	Sebastian, third grade
R8. Reading—sight words	Provide labels in classroom. Everything in the classroom is labeled with its name in multiple languages. Student's belongings have his or her photo on them. See the example shown in Figure A.11.	Oscar, first grade Nathaniel, third grade Victoria, third grade Lucy, fifth grade
R9. Reading—sight words	Incorporate sight word work into station work, with individual lists of sight words available for all learners.	Leela, first grade Oscar, first grade Taylor, first grade Nathaniel, third grade Victoria, third grade Grace, fifth grade Lucy, fifth grade
R10. Reading—vocabulary	Provide the speech-language pathologist with lists of reading and vocabulary words each week.	Charlie, first grade
R11. Reading—word study	Create a variety of word study activities for whole-class use at different levels of understanding (e.g., portable word walls, guess the covered word, speed sorting, add an ending).	Greg, first grade Leela, first grade Oscar, first grade Padma, first grade Taylor, first grade Sebastian, third grade Nathaniel, third grade Victoria, third grade Quentin, fifth grade
R12. Reading—word study	Create word wall in braille and first languages at child height for all to touch and read. Add braille words and words in multiple languages to all printed words throughout the classroom.	Kacey, third grade Nathaniel, third grade Victoria, third grade
R13. Reading in content areas—sight words	Ensure that abcmouse.com and Brainzy online reading games are among the apps and software programs installed on all computers and tablets in the classroom.	Leela, first grade Oscar, first grade Taylor, first grade Deirdre, third grade Maddox, third grade Sebastian, third grade David, fifth grade

Figure A.11. Example of labels on belongings with student's name and/or photo. (Reading, practice R.8)

SELF-REGULATION SUPPORTS

Content/goal area	Inclusive practice	Student
SR1. Self-regulation—focus strategies	Allow all students to draw or doodle during lessons.	Steven, first grade Iris, fifth grade
SR2. Self-regulation—movement	Allow all students short walks down the hall.	Greg, first grade Steven, first grade Gabrielle, third grade Brian, fifth grade Grace, fifth grade Tyler, fifth grade
SR3. Self-regulation—breaks	Allow all students breaks in or out of the classroom.	Greg, first grade Steven, first grade Antoine, third grade Ethan, third grade Latoya, third grade Grace, fifth grade Tyler, fifth grade
SR4. Self-regulation—emotional regulation	Ensure that all students are familiar with regulation scales, and many have them at their desks for self-checks. Some are for voice volume and emotional escalation; some for effective use of work time; some for interest or independence level for an activity. See the examples shown in Figures A.12 and A13.	Avery, first grade Padma, first grade Steven, first grade Antoine, third grade Chelsea, third grade Heaven, third grade Latoya, third grade Randolph, third grade Chloe, fifth grade Fred, fifth grade Grace, fifth grade

Content/goal area	Inclusive practice	Student
SR5. Self-regulation—seating	Provide all students a choice of seating in the classroom.	Steven, first grade Ethan, third grade Gabrielle, third grade Ellie, fifth grade Lucy, fifth grade
SR6. Self-regulation—mindfulness	Teach yoga/mindfulness exercises to the whole class.	Avery, first grade Steven, first grade Antoine, third grade Gabrielle, third grade Latoya, third grade
SR7. Self-regulation—personal space	Provide a "calming corner" for all students, equipped with soft seating, carpet, sensory tools, and so forth. Students may go to the corner as needed. See the example shown in Figure A.14.	Steven, first grade Antoine, third grade Latoya, third grade Grace, fifth grade
SR8. Self-regulation—sensory/stimulation	Provide fidgets and mandalas to all students.	Steven, first grade Ethan, third grade Latoya, third grade Fred, fifth grade
SR9. Self-regulation—materials	Provide chunked or coded materials to all students.	Ethan, third grade
SR10. Self-regulation—self-talk	Teach strategy of self-monitoring: identify behavior, design self-monitoring strategy, teach strategy (Menzies et al., 2009).	Heaven, third grade Randolph, third grade Chloe, fifth grade Quentin, fifth grade Harry, fifth grade
SR11. Self-regulation—checking work	Provide checklist for reviewing assignments before submitting. See the example shown in Figure A.15.	Harry, fifth grade Lucy, fifth grade
SR12. Self-regulation—reminders	Provide vibrating wrist alarm to remind student to return to task. See Resources for Inclusion list in Appendix B.	Jack, first grade Justice, third grade
SR13. Self-regulation—planning time	Provide planning sheet for choice time—student writes name or number or places sticker on planning sheet to indicate which activities to do during choice time. See the example shown in Figure A.16.	Oscar, first grade
SR14. Self-regulation—routines	Teach a song to sing that lists all steps in a routine—customize it to student's interest.	Megan, first grade
SR15. Self-regulation—schedule	Teach first-then strategy to help students complete less preferred tasks before choosing a preferred activity.	Jack, first grade
SR16. Self-regulation—awareness of feelings	Support self-awareness of feelings using poster with 20–30 of the most common feelings. See the example shown in Figure A.17.	Francis, first grade
SR17. Self-regulation—metacognitive processing	Provide a self-amplifier for student to self-talk or read aloud to support processing. See Resources for Inclusion List in Appendix B. See the examples shown in Figures A.18 and A.19.	Tabitha, third grade

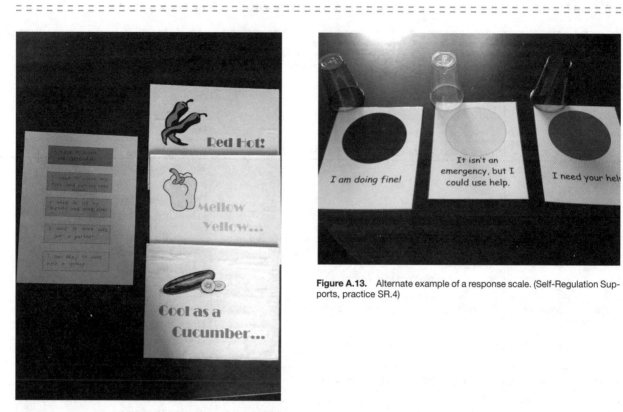

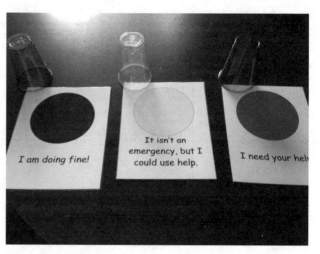

Figure A.13. Alternate example of a response scale. (Self-Regulation Supports, practice SR.4)

Figure A.12. Example of a response scale. (Self-Regulation Supports, practice SR.4)

Figure A.14. Example of a "calming corner." (Self-Regulation Supports, practice SR.7)

Social Studies Poster

The topic of my poster is: _____

RESOURCES
- ☐ I have at least five current resources.
- ☐ I made a bibliography page in MLA format.

MAP
- ☐ My map is in color.
- ☐ I have a legend to accompany my map.
- ☐ I have labeled the capital and major cities.
- ☐ I have labeled all bodies of water.

CONTENT
- ☐ My poster includes information on industry.
- ☐ My poster includes information on recreation.
- ☐ My poster includes information on government.

Figure A.15. Example of a checklist for an assignment. (Self-Regulation Supports, practice SR.11)

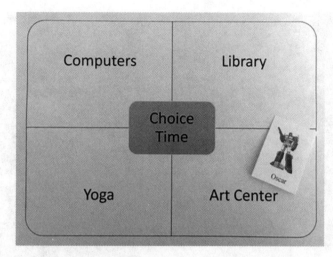

Figure A.16. Example of a planning sheet for choice time. (Self-Regulation Supports, practice SR.13)

FEELINGS

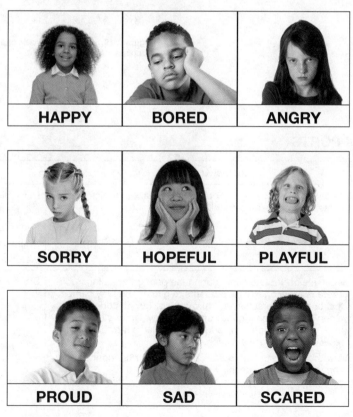

Figure A.17. Example of a feelings poster. (Self-Regulation Supports, practice SR.16)

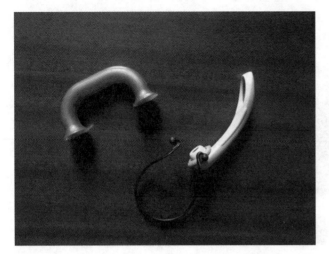

Figure A.18.   Example of a self-amplifier. (Self-Regulation Supports, practice SR.17)

Figure A.19.   Alternate example of a self-amplifier. (Self-Regulation Supports, practice SR.17)

SOCIAL SKILLS SUPPORTS

Content/goal area	Inclusive practice	Student
SS1. Social skills— conversation skills	Use peer groups to practice conversations about topics that are centered around the curriculum.	Devin, first grade Ian, third grade Sebastian, third grade Nathaniel, third grade Victoria, third grade
SS2. Social skills— conflict resolution	Model use of "I" statements during the peer group at lunch. There is a lunch table for students to gather and play games that entail conversation and turn-taking. Target student is reserved a spot on Monday and Thursday. Other students have reserved spots. Any additional students may sign up to reserve remaining seats each day. Allow the target student to draw or write his or her concerns and the solution he or she would like to see.	Steven, first grade

Content/goal area	Inclusive practice	Student
SS3. Social skills—peer interaction	Facilitate a peer lunch group. During lunch, there is one table for students to gather and play games that entails conversation and turn-taking. Some students have reserved spots. Any additional students may sign up to reserve remaining seats each day.	Kody, first grade Padma, first grade Steven, first grade Antoine, third grade Chelsea, third grade Heaven, third grade Ian, third grade Latoya, third grade Maddox, third grade Nigel, fifth grade Harry, fifth grade
SS4. Social skills—peer interaction	Strategically use games at recess. The psychologist goes to recess every day with the fourth and fifth grades and organizes a few playground games to facilitate friendly competition skills.	Randolph, third grade
SS5. Social skills—peer interaction	Ensure that all students have an opportunity to contribute to or consult the Social Skill Manual for advice. For both classes, the counselor helped the class come up with possible social scenarios and facilitated the contribution of good social skill advice to the manual.	Heaven, third grade Nigel, fifth grade Harry, fifth grade
SS6. Social skills—listening	Encourage active listening by routinely asking students to restate or summarize what has been said by peers.	Greg, first grade Heaven, third grade Ian, third grade Randolph, third grade Harry, fifth grade Quentin, fifth grade
SS7. Social skills—self-advocacy	Provide sentence starters for students to use when approaching teachers. Most students have key rings or bookmarks with reminders on them. Some students list advocacy sentence starters (e.g., "I need. . ." "I do better when. . .") See the example shown in Figure A.20.	Oscar, first grade Steven, first grade Heaven, third grade Ian, third grade
SS8. Social skills—self-advocacy	Ensure that all students have the option of creating personalized Social Stories. They can be kept at the desk for reference and they can read through them with the counselor or psychologist at least weekly.	
SS9. Social skills—working in small groups	Allow cooperative work to happen during all content areas with flexible grouping.	Avery, first grade Devin, first grade Natalie, first grade Antoine, third grade Chelsea, third grade Ethan, third grade Sebastian, third grade Alison, fifth grade Chloe, fifth grade Vivian, fifth grade

Content/goal area	Inclusive practice	Student
SS10. Social skills—Working in small groups	Build in time each day for small group work with peers, assigning individual roles within the group, to scaffold the interactions.	Avery, first grade Devin, first grade Oscar, first grade Padma, first grade Heaven, third grade Ian, third grade Randolph, third grade Alison, fifth grade Harry, fifth grade
SS11. Social skills—working in small groups	Provide choices in working in pairs or small groups.	Avery, first grade Kody, first grade Alison, fifth grade Kiana, fifth grade
SS12. Social skills—contribute to discussion	Strategically use prequestions before discussions. Provide two to three questions on index cards that will be asked during discussion so that student can formulate answers in advance and be encouraged to volunteer during discussion.	Ian, third grade
SS13. Social skills—cues	Use verbal or nonverbal cues to cue the student to use response scale or adjust behavior.	Padma, first grade
SS14. Social skills—tutoring	Provide opportunities for students to help/tutor others in their areas of strength.	Kody, first grade
SS15. Social skills—turn-taking	Provide instructional games (board, card, video) that require at least two students.	Kody, first grade

Figure A.20. Example of sentence starters on a key ring. (Social Skills Supports, practice SS.7)

TESTING MODIFICATIONS SUPPORTS

Content/goal area	Inclusive practice	Student
TM1. Testing modifications—variety of formats	Plan for a variety of types of tests, timed and untimed, to allow success for all students.	Ethan, third grade Tabitha, third grade Nathaniel, third grade Victoria, third grade
TM2. Testing modifications—method of presentation	For all assessments with verbal directions or listening passages, use amplification system, repeat content as necessary, and supply written versions as allowed by test parameters.	John, fifth grade
TM3. Testing modifications—flexibility in location	For all graded assessments (e.g., tests, quizzes, classwork, online programs), give target student and other students the choice to remain at their desks, use the classroom quiet area, go to the library, or go to the alternative testing room.	Tabitha, third grade
TM4. Testing modifications—flexibility in breaks	For all assessments, give students the option of movement breaks at two to three points during the assessment.	Brian, fifth grade
TM5. Testing modifications—reading level	For all assessments, ensure that the reading level matches student's independent reading level.	Leela, first grade Oscar, first grade Padma, first grade Taylor, first grade Nathaniel, third grade Victoria, third grade Lucy, fifth grade Samson, fifth grade
TM6. Testing modifications—test format	Chunk tests/tasks into manageable parts.	Tabitha, third grade

WRITING SUPPORTS

Content/goal area	Inclusive practice	Student
WS1. Writing—production	Ensure that all students have access to computers and instructional technology for all writing tasks.	Taylor, first grade
WS2. Writing—handwriting	Allow for use of paper with raised or wide lines or unlined paper. Stock supplies of each in common areas in the classroom.	Taylor, first grade
WS3. Writing—handwriting	Allow for use of pencil grips; provide many choices in a basket in the classroom.	Taylor, first grade
WS4. Writing—handwriting	Stock preheaded papers, with templates saved on computers.	Taylor, first grade
WS5. Writing—handwriting	Provide notes (hard copy and electronic) before lessons to all.	
WS6. Writing—handwriting	Allow for a choice of many different writing implements (e.g., pencils, pens, markers, chalk, gel pens).	Taylor, first grade

Content/goal area	Inclusive practice	Student
WS7. Writing—handwriting	Provide access to tracing apps. See the Resources for Inclusion list in Appendix B.	Taylor, first grade
WS8. Writing—process	Ensure that pie chart rubrics of expectations on writing assignments are available to all students. See the example shown in Figure A.10.	
WS9. Writing—process	Teach Fitzell's clustering strategy for writing assignments to all students (Fitzell, 2016).	
WS10. Writing—process	Ensure that student has a photo album full of pictures of him- or herself engaged in activities or with various friends and adults. The photos are labeled with names and other sight words. Student keeps the photo album in his or her desk and uses it to prompt verbal stories about him- or herself. He or she also uses it sometimes to prompt writing, when everyone gets out their "Book O'Writing Ideas."	
WS11. Writing—process	Ensure that all technological writing tools will be available to meet individual student writing needs.	
WS12. Writing—process	Provide a ring of topic transition sentence starters for the whole group to use, and have classmates model topic transitions.	
WS13. Writing—process	Use graphic organizers with the whole class, allowing for student choice. Scaffold the organizers to meet diverse learning needs (e.g., fewer items to fill in, some text provided, use of a word or sentence bank). Stock them in common areas of the classroom and save them on the computers that students use for work.	Oscar, first grade Sebastian, third grade Nathaniel, third grade Victoria, third grade Lucy, fifth grade Samson, fifth grade

Resources for Inclusion

This appendix lists organizations, classroom supplies, web sites, software programs, and other resources that can help teachers create more inclusive classrooms.

American Speech-Language-Hearing Association. This organization is a resource for information about augmentative and alternative communication. For more information, visit http://www.asha.org/public/speech/disorders/AAC/

Amplifiers. These are devices students use while reading or working out loud to amplify their own voices without disturbing others. Two specific products are available at the links below:

- Toobaloo: https://mayer-johnson.com/products/toobaloo
- Whisperphone: https://www.whisperphone.com/

Blogs and blog posts written by nonspeaking people with autism spectrum disorder. This resource supports the value of alternative communication and first-hand narrative. Emma's Hope Book provides a list at https://emmashopebook.com/resources/

Center on Response to Intervention. The Center on RTI is a national leader in supporting the successful implementation and scale-up of MTSS/RTI and its components. For more information, visit https://rti4success.org/

English Learner Toolkit. The tool kit is designed to help state and local education agencies in meeting their legal obligations to ELs and in providing all ELs with the support needed to attain English language proficiency while meeting college- and career-readiness standards. The EL Tool Kit is intended primarily for state, district, and school administrators, as well as teachers, but may also inform other stakeholders concerned with the education of ELs. The tool kit can be accessed at https://www2.ed.gov/about/offices/list/oela/english-learner-toolkit/index.html

Go Noodle. Go Noodle provides online movement and mindfulness games for kids. For more information, visit https://www.gonoodle.com/

Graphic organizers. These templates provide visual supports for students to help them organize and process content. There are several online sources for graphic organizers at the links below:

- Teacher Vision: https://www.teachervision.com/lesson-planning/graphic-organizer
- Education Place: https://www.eduplace.com/graphicorganizer/
- edHelper: https://worksheets.edhelper.com/teachers/graphic_organizers.htm

Picture Inclusion! by Whitney H. Rapp, Katrina L. Arndt, and Susan M. Hildenbrand.
Copyright © 2019 by Paul H. Brookes Publishing Co. All rights reserved.

Here are two resources about the use of graphic organizers:

- Cult of Pedagogy blog: https://www.cultofpedagogy.com/blog/

- Edutopia: https://www.edutopia.org/blog/using-graphic-organizers-correctly-rebecca-alber

Inclusion Lab blog. This blog created by Paul H. Brookes Publishing Co., Inc., provides information and resources on inclusion from preschool through Grade 12. For more information, visit http://blog.brookespublishing.com/

Intervention Central. Intervention Central provides teachers, schools and districts with free resources to help struggling learners and implement response to intervention and attain the Common Core State Standards. For more information, visit http://www.interventioncentral.org

Leveled Literacy Intervention (LLI). The *Fountas & Pinnell Leveled Literacy Intervention* is a powerful, short-term intervention that provides daily, intensive, small-group instruction, which supplements classroom literacy teaching. For more information, visit http://www.fountasandpinnell.com/lli/

Math manipulatives. There are many different objects that students can manipulate as they solve math problems. Many can be collected by the teacher—buttons, golf balls, coins. Here are a few examples of products available for purchase:

- Unifix Cubes from Didax, Inc. at http://www.didax.com/home/unifix-cubes.html?

- Teddy bear counters from Lakeshore Learning at https://www.lakeshorelearning.com/products/el/s/LC1657

- Two-color counters from EAI Education at https://www.eaieducation.com/Product/531067/Two-Color_Counters_Red_Yellow_-_Set_of_1000.aspx

- Fraction tiles from Hand2Mind at: https://www.hand2mind.com/item/rainbow-fraction-tiles-set-of-51/3234

Math software. There are several reading software applications or online games to support mathematical development. Specific examples include:

- Arthur's Math Games: http://www.ign.com/games/arthurs-math-games

- Reader Rabbit Math: http://www.reader-rabbit.com/

- Math Blaster: http://www.mathblaster.com/

- Kids Academy—123 Tracing: https://www.kidsacademy.mobi/playground/123tracing/

- Number Monster: http://www.coolmath.com/games/number-monster/addition

- The Wee Kids Math app: https://itunes.apple.com/us/app/wee-kids-math/id638457112?mt=8

Military Child Education Coalition. This is a resource for professionals for teaching students of military families. For more information, visit http://www.militarychild.org/

National Child Traumatic Stress Network. This resource provides information to help people working with traumatized children and their families. For more information, visit http://www.nctsn.org/

New York State Technical and Educational Assistance Center for Homeless Students (NYSTEACHS). This organization provides information to help people working with homeless students in the state of New York State. For more information, visit http://www.nysteachs.org/

Positive Behavioral Interventions and Supports (PBIS). Funded by the U.S. Department of Education's Office of Special Education Programs (OSEP), the Technical Assistance Center on PBIS supports schools, districts, and states to build systems capacity for implementing a multitiered approach to social, emotional, and behavior support. The broad purpose of PBIS is to improve the effectiveness, efficiency, and equity of schools and other agencies. PBIS improves social, emotional, and academic outcomes for all students, including students with disabilities and students from underrepresented groups. For more information, visit https://www.pbis.org/

Reading software. There are several reading software applications or online games to support literacy development. Specific examples include:

- Abcmouse: https://www.abcmouse.com/abt/homepage?8a08850bc2=T842102673.1530461785.0471

- Brainzy by education.com: https://www.education.com/games/info/

Renzulli Center for Creativity, Gifted Education, and Talent Development. The University of Connecticut is home to the Renzulli Center for Creativity, Gifted Education, and Talent Development. Studies focusing on meeting the needs of gifted and talented youth have received national and international attention for over 40 years. The earliest research emphasized studies related to creativity, assessment, identification, programming, and evaluation. For more information, visit https://gifted.uconn.edu/

Responsive Classroom. Responsive Classroom is an evidence-based approach to education that focuses on the strong relationship between academic success and social-emotional learning (SEL). The Responsive Classroom approach empowers educators to create safe, joyful, and engaging learning communities where all students have a sense of belonging and feel significant. For more information, visit https://www.responsiveclassroom.org

Rethinking Schools. This is a resource for culturally responsive, social justice education. For more information, visit https://rethinkingschools.org/

SWIFT. SWIFT is a national technical assistance center that builds whole system—state, district, school, and community—capacity to provide academic and behavioral support to improve outcomes for all students. For more information, visit http://www.swiftschools.org/

The Inclusive Class. This is a web site and blog of inclusive strategies, modifications, and accommodations to support inclusive classrooms, created by Nicole Eredics. For more information, visit http://www.theinclusiveclass.com/

The Incredible 5-Point Scale self-regulatory tool by Kari Dunn Burton. The 5-Point scale was developed to teach social and emotional concepts to individuals on the autism spectrum. For more information, visit https://www.5pointscale.com/

Trauma and Learning Policy Initiative (TLPI). The Trauma and Learning Policy Initiative's mission is to ensure that children traumatized by exposure to family violence and other adverse childhood experiences succeed in school. For more information, visit https://traumasensitiveschools.org/

Vidget 3-in-1 Flexible Seating System™. One can transform this system from an active seat into a supported stool or flat desk surface by simply turning it over. It provides many opportunities for collaboration by allowing children & teachers to create flexible learning spaces based on individual and group needs. Designing your own space supports the benefit of adaptable environments. For more information, visit https://www.viggikids.com/

Watchminder. This is a vibrating wristwatch that privately cues the wearer. For more information, visit http://www.watchminder.com/

Writing Supports are available through Kids Academy – 123 Tracing. For more information, visit https://www.kidsacademy.mobi/playground/123tracing/

References

Barnes, C., Oliver, M., & Barton, L. (Eds.). (2002). *Disability studies today.* Oxford, UK: Polity Press.

Bennetts, L. (1993, September). Letter from Las Vegas: Jerry vs. the kids. *Vanity Fair,* 82–98.

Bogdan, R., & Biklen, D. (1977, March/April). Handicapism. *Social Policy,* 14–19.

Brigance, A. H. (1999). *Brigance diagnostic inventory of basic skills (3rd ed).* Woburn, MA: Curriculum Associates.

Brown University. (2017). *Culturally responsive teaching.* Retrieved from https://www.brown.edu/academics/education-alliance/teaching-diverse-learners/strategies-0/culturally-responsive-teaching-0

Causton-Theoharis, J. (2009). *The paraprofessional's handbook for effective support in inclusive classrooms.* Baltimore, MD: Paul H. Brookes Publishing Co.

Center for Public Education. (n.d.). *Class size and student achievement research review.* Retrieved from http://www.centerforpubliceducation.org/Main-Menu/Organizing-a-school/Class-size-and-student-achievement-At-a-glance/Class-size-and-student-achievement-Research-review.htm

Center on Response to Intervention at American Institutes for Research. (n.d.a). *MTSS and RTI are often used interchangeably. What is it that separates them?* Retrieved from https://www.rti4success.org/video/mtss-and-rti-are-often-used-interchangeably-what-it-separates-them

Center on Response to Intervention at American Institutes for Research. (n.d.b). *Multi-level prevention system.* Retrieved from https://www.rti4success.org/essential-components-rti/multi-level-prevention-system

Charlton, J. I. (1998). *Nothing about us without us.* Berkeley, CA: University of California Press.

Cole, C. M., Waldron, N., & Majd, M. (2004). Academic progress of students across inclusive and traditional settings. *Mental Retardation, 42*(2), 136–144.

Common Core State Standards Initiative. (n.d.). *Preparing America's students for success.* Retrieved from http://www.corestandards.org

Cort, R. H. [2009]. *The state of special education 2009.* Retrieved from http://www.p12.nysed.gov/specialed/techassist/Statewide-Oct09/Oct09statewide.ppt

Cosier, M., Causton-Theoharis, J., & Theoharis, G. (2013). Does access matter? Time in general education and achievement for students with disabilities. *Remedial and Special Education, 34*(6), 323–332.

Davis, L. J. (1995). Constructing normalcy. In L. J. Davis (Ed.), *The disability studies reader* (pp. 9–28). New York: Routledge.

DeCoste, D. (2004). *DeCoste Writing Protocol.* Volo, IL: Don Johnston Inc.

Dessemontet, R. S., Bless, G., & Morin, D. (2012). Effects of inclusion on the academic achievement and adaptive behaviour of children with intellectual disabilities. *Journal of Intellectual Disability Research, 56*(6), 579–587.

Donnellan, A. (1984). The criterion of the least dangerous assumption. *Behavioral Disorders, 9*(2), 141–150.

Dunn, L. M., & Dunn, D. M. (2007). *Peabody Picture Vocabulary Test–4.* Pearson Education, Inc. Retrieved from: https://www.pearsonclinical.com/language/products/100000501/peabody-picture-vocabulary-test-fourth-edition-ppvt-4.html#tab-details

EngageNY. (n.d.). *New York State English as a second language achievement test (NYSESLAT) resources: Performance level descriptions.* Retrieved from https://www.engageny.org/resource/new-york-state-english-a-second-language-achievement-test-nyseslat-performance-level

Fisher, D., Frey, N., & Thousand, J. (2003). What do special educators need to know and be prepared to do for inclusive schooling to work? *Teacher Education and Special Education, 26*(1), 42–50.

Fitzell, S. (2016). *Overcome writer's block with this productive strategy.* Retrieved from http://susanfitzell.com/overcome-writers-block-with-this-productivity-strategy

Forlin, C. (2012). Responding to the need for inclusive education: Rhetoric or reality? In C. Forlin (Ed). *Future directions for inclusive teacher education: An international perspective* (pp. 3–12). London, England: Routledge.

Gay, G. (2000). *Culturally responsive teaching: Theory, research, & practice.* New York, NY: Teachers College Press.

Giangreco, M. F. (2017). Expanding opportunities for students with intellectual disability. *Educational Leadership, 74*(7), 52–57.

Gioia, G. A., Isquith, P. K., Guy, S. C., Kenworthy, L. (2015). BRIEF2: Behavior Rating Inventory of Executive Function, Second Edition. Lutz, FL: Psychological Assessment Resources.

Grant, M. C., & Jones-Goods, K. (2016). Identifying and correcting barriers to successful inclusive practices: A literature review. *Journal of the American Academy of Special Education Professionals,* (Winter 2016), 64–71.

Hammill, D. D., Wiederholt, J. L., & Allen, E. A. (2014). *Test of Silence Contextual Reading Fluency-2.* PRO-ED, 8700 Shoal Creek Blvd., Austin, TX, 78757-689, info@proedinc.com, http://www.proedinc.com

Hammond, Z. (2014). *Culturally responsive teaching and the brain: Promoting authentic engagement and rigor among culturally and linguistically diverse students.* Thousand Oaks, CA: Corwin.

Helmstetter, E., Curry, C. A., Brennan, M., & Sampson-Saul, M. (1998). Comparison of general and special education classrooms of students with severe disabilities. *Education and Training in Mental Retardation and Developmental Disabilities, 33,* 216–227.

Horn, E., Lieber, J., Li, S., Sandall, S., & Schwartz, I. (2000). Supporting young children's IEP goals in inclusive setting through embedded learning opportunities. *Topics in Early Childhood Special Education, 20*(4), 208–223.

Hunt, P., & Farron-Davis, F. (1992). A preliminary investigation of IEP quality and content associated with placement in general education versus special education. *Journal of The Association for Persons with Severe Handicaps, 17*(4), 247–253.

Hunt, P., Farron-Davis, F., Beckstead, S., Curtis, D., & Goetz, L. (1994). Evaluating the effects of placement of students with severe disabilities in general education versus special classes. *Journal of The Association for Persons with Severe Handipcaps, 19*(3), 200–214.

Hunt, P., Hirose-Hatae, A., Doering, K., Karasoff, P., & Goetz, L. (2000). Community is what I think everyone is talking about. *Remedial and Special Education, 21*(5), 305–317.

Individuals with Disabilities Education Act Amendments (IDEA) of 1997, PL 105-17, 20 U.S.C. §§ 1400 *et seq.*

Individuals with Disabilities Education Improvement Act of 2004, PL 108-446, 20 U.S.C. §§ 1400 *et seq.*

International Society for Technology in Education (ISTE). (2017). ISTE standards for students. Retrieved from: https://www.iste.org/standards/standards/for-students

Jorgensen, C. (2005). The least dangerous assumption: A challenge to create a new paradigm. *Disability Solutions, 6*(3), 1, 5–9, 15.

Jorgenseon, C. M., McSheehan, M., & Sonnenmeier, R. M. (2010). *The beyond access model: Promoting membership, participation, and learning for students with disabilities in the general education classroom.* Baltimore, MD: Paul H. Brookes Publishing Co.

Jorgensen, C. M., McSheehan, M., Schuh, M., & Sonnenmeier, R. M. (2012). *Essential best practices in inclusive schools.* Durham, NH: National Center on Inclusive Education.

Juster, N. (1961). *The phantom tollbooth.* New York, NY: Random House.

Kedar, I. (2014). *A challenge to autism professionals: Ido in autismland.* Retrieved from http://idoinautismland.blogspot.ca/2014/02/a-challenge-to-autism-professionals.html

Kedar, I. (2012). *Ido in Autismland: Climbing out of autism's silent prison.* (n.p.): Sharon Kedar.

Kleinart, H. L., & Kearns, J. F. (2001). *Alternate assessment: Measuring outcomes and supports for students with disabilities.* Baltimore, MD: Paul H. Brookes Publishing Co.

Kliewer, C. (1998). *Schooling children with Down syndrome.* New York, NY: Teachers College Press.

Linton, S. (1998). *Claiming disability.* New York, NY: New York University Press.

MashUp Math. (2015). *Is every square a rectangle? Yes or no?* Retrieved from: https://www.youtube.com/watch?v=TnKYox8wr8g

Mathis, W. J. (2016). *The effectiveness of class size reduction.* Retrieved from http://nepc.colorado.edu/files/publications/Mathis%20RBOPM-9%20Class%20Size.pdf

McDonnell, J., Thorson, N., & McQuivey, C. (2000). Comparison of the instructional contexts of students with severe disabilities and their peers in general education classes. *Journal of The Association for Persons with Severe Handicaps, 25,* 54–58.

McGregor, G., & Vogelsberg, R. T. (1998). *Inclusive schooling practices: Pedagogical and research foundations. A synthesis of the literature that informs best practices about inclusive schooling.* Missoula, MT: University of Montana, Rural Institute on Disabilities.

Menzies, H. M., Lane, K. L., & Lee, J. M. (2009). Self-monitoring strategies for use in the classroom: A promising practice to support productive behavior for students with emotional or behavioral disorders. *Beyond Behavior, 18*(2), 27–35.

Moore-Harris, B. (2005). *Strategies for teaching mathematics to English language learners.* Retrieved from http://www.tsusmell.org/downloads/Conferences/2005/Moore-Harris_2005.pdf

Murawski, W. W., & Dieker, L. (2008). 50 ways to keep your co-teacher. *Teaching Exceptional Children, 40*(4), 40–48.

National Center for Educational Statistics. (2018). *Children and youth with disabilities.* Retrieved from https://nces.ed.gov/programs/coe/indicator_cgg.asp

National Center for Learning Disabilities. (n.d.). *What is RTI?* Retrieved from http://www.rtinetwork.org/learn/what/whatisrti

National Center on Educational Outcomes. (2016a). *Alternate assessments based on alternate academic achievement standards.* Retrieved https://nceo.info/Resources/publications/TopicAreas/Alternate-Assessments/aa_aas.htm

National Center on Educational Outcomes. (2016b). *Alternate assessments based on grade-level academic achievement standards.* Retrieved from https://nceo.info/Resources/publications/TopicAreas/AlternateAssessments/aa_glas.htm

National Center on Educational Outcomes (2016c). *Alternate assessments based on modified academic achievement standards.* Retrieved from https://nceo.info/Resources/publications/TopicAreas/AlternateAssessments/aa_mas.htm

National Center on Educational Outcomes. (2016d). *Alternate assessments for students with disabilities.* Retrieved from https://nceo.info/Resources/publications/TopicAreas/AlternateAssessments/altAssessTopic.htm)

National Center on Educational Outcomes. (2017). *Alternate assessments.* Retrieved from: https://nceo.info/Assessments/alternate_assessments

National Center on Universal Design for Learning at CAST. (2012). *About universal design for learning.* Retrieved from http://www.udlcenter.org/aboutudl/whatisudl

National Center on Universal Design for Learning. (2011). *The three principles of UDL.* Retrieved from http://www.udlcenter.org/aboutudl/whatisudl/3principles

National Core Art Standards. (2014). *Visual arts at a glance.* Retrieved from: https://www.nationalartsstandards.org/sites/default/files/Visual%20Arts%20at%20a%20Glance%20-%20new%20copyright%20info.pdf

National Education Association. (2015). *Who are paraeducators?* Retrieved from http://www.nea.org/home/67057.htm

Nelson, T. (n.d.) *Locomotor license.* Retrieved from https://rm005.k12.sd.us/tracy%20nelson/activities%20for%20lessons.htm#Locomotor License

Neukrug, E., Brace-Thompson, J., Maurer, C., & Harman, C. (2015). *The SAGE encyclopedia of theory in counseling and psychotherapy.* Thousand Oaks, CA: SAGE Publications.

New York State Education Department. (2010). Guidelines for physical therapy practice in New York State. Retrieved from: http://www.op.nysed.gov/prof/pt/pt-guidelines-2010.pdf

New York State Education Department. (n.d.a.). *Alternate performance indicators: English/language arts. Retrieved from:* http://www.p12.nysed.gov/specialed/publications/learnstand/lrnstd2.htm

New York State Education Department. (n.d.b.). *Alternate performance indicators: Mathematics, science and technology.* Retrieved from: http://www.p12.nysed.gov/specialed/publications/learnstand/lrnstd4.htm

New York State Education Department. (n.d.c.). *Alternate performance indicators: The arts.* Retrieved from: http://www.p12.nysed.gov/specialed/publications/learnstand/lrnstd7.htm

New York State Education Department. (n.d.d.). *Alternate performance indicators: Health, physical education, and family and consumer sciences.* Retrieved from: http://www.p12.nysed.gov/specialed/publications/learnstand/lrnstd3.htm

New York State Education Department. (2014). *New York State bilingual common core initiative.* Retrieved from https://www.engageny.org/resource/new-york-state-bilingual-common-core-initiative

New York State Next Generation English Language Arts Learning Standards. (2015–2018). Revised Learning Standards Documents. Retrieved from: http://www.nysed.gov/common/nysed/files/programs/curriculum-instruction/nys-next-generation-ela-standards.pdf

New York University. (2008a). *Culturally responsive differentiated instructional strategies.* Retrieved from http://steinhardt.nyu.edu/scmsAdmin/uploads/005/120/Culturally%20Responsive%20Differentiated%20Instruction.pdf

New York University. (2008b). *ELLs and mathematics.* Retrieved from http://steinhardt.nyu.edu/scmsAdmin/uploads/004/738/NYU_PTE_Math_Module_For_ELLS_Oct_8_2009.pdf

Next Generation Science Standards Lead States. (2013). *Next Generation Science Standards: For states, by states.* Washington, DC: National Academies Press.

Nieto, S. (1996). *Affirming diversity: The sociopolitical context of multicultural education* (2nd ed.). New York, NY: Longman.

Nottingham, A. E., & Dearde, J. (2013). The effect of using 'full' language when working with a child with autism: Adopting the 'least dangerous assumption.' *Child Language Teaching and Therapy, 29*(2), 233–244.

Ohio Department of Education. (2010). *Ohio's new learning standards: Social studies standards.* Columbus, OH: Author.

Ohio Department of Education. (2012.) *Ohio's academic content standards: Extended social studies.* Columbus, OH: Author.

Peck, C. A., Staub, D., Gallucci, C., & Schwartz, B. (2004). Parent perception of the impacts of inclusion on their nondisabled child. *Research and Practice for Persons With Severe Disabilities, 29*(2), 135–143.

Pierce, R. L., Cassady, J. C., Adams, C. M., Neumeister, K. L. S., Dixon, F. A., & Cross, T. L. (2011, Summer). The effects of clustering and curriculum on the development of gifted learners' math achievement. *Journal for the Education of the Gifted, 34,* 569–594, 698, 700.

Positive Behavioral Interventions & Supports. (2017). *Multi-tiered system of support & PBIS.* Retrieved from https://www.pbis.org/school/rti

Public Law 107–110. 107th Congress. 115 STAT. 1425. Retrieved from: https://www.gpo.gov/fdsys/pkg/PLAW-107publ110/pdf/PLAW-107publ110.pdf

Rapp, W. H. (2014). *Universal design for learning in action: 100 ways to teach all learners.* Baltimore, MD: Paul H. Brookes Publishing Co.

Rapp, W. H. & Arndt, K. L. (2012). *Teaching everyone: An introduction to inclusive education.* Baltimore, MD: Paul H. Brookes Publishing Co.

Rehabilitation Act of 1973, PL 93-112, 29 U.S.C. §§ 701 *et seq.*

Robertson, K. (2017). *Math instruction for ELLs.* Retrieved from http://www.colorincolorado.org/teaching-ells/content-instruction-ells/math-instruction-ells

Rose, D. H. & Meyer, A. (2002). *Teaching every student in the digital age: Universal design for learning.* Alexandria, VA: Association for Supervision and Curriculum Development.

RTI Action Network. (n.d.). *What is RTI?* Retrieved from http://www.rtinetwork.org/learn/what/whatisrti

Rubin, S. M. (2014). *About me.* Retrieved from http://sue-rubin.org/about-me

Ryan, J. (2017). *Wait, what? And life's other essential questions.* New York, NY: Harper Collins.

Sailor, W., Doolittle, J., Bradley, R., & Danielson, L. C. (2009). Response to intervention and positive behavior support. In W. Sailor, G. Dunlap, G. Sugai, & R. Horner (Eds.), *Handbook of positive behavior support* (pp. 729–753). New York: NY: Springer.

Sailor, W. S., & McCart, A. B. (2014). Stars in alignment. *Research and Practice for Persons With Severe Disabilities, 39*(1), 55–64.

Sandomierski, T., Kincaid, D., & Algozzine, B. (2007). *Response to intervention and positive behavior support: Brothers from different mothers or sisters with different misters?* Retrieved from https://www.pbis.org/common/cms/files/Newsletter/Volume4%20Issue2.pdf

Semel, E., Wiig, E. H., & Secord, W. A. (2003). *Clinical Evaluation of Language Fundamentals–Fourth Edition (CELF-4).* London, England: Pearson.

SHAPE America. (2013). *Grade level outcomes for K–12 physical education.* Reston, VA: Author.

Shapiro, J. R., & Williams, A. M. (2012). The role of stereotype threats in undermining girls' and women's performance and interest in STEM fields. *Sex Roles, 66,* 175–183.

Silver, L. (2017). *Executive function disorder, explained!* Retrieved from https://www.additudemag.com/executive-function-disorder-adhd-explained

TASH. (2014). *Why assessment matters for students with significant cognitive disabilities.* Retrieved from https://tash.org/wp-content/uploads/2015/03/Alternate-Assessment-Report-Final-2.pdf

Teaching Tolerance. (n.d.). Digital tools as a mechanism for active citizenship. Retrieved from: *https://www.tolerance.org/classroom-resources/tolerance-lessons/digital-tools-as-a-mechanism-for-active-citizenship*

Tomlinson, C. A., & McTighe, J. (2006). *Integrating differentiated instruction and understanding by design.* Alexandria, VA: Association for Supervision and Curriculum Development.

U. S. Department of Education. (2018). *Civil rights data collection (CRDC) 2013–2104 state and national estimations.* Retrieved from https://ocrdata.ed.gov/StateNationalEstimations/Estimations_2013_14

Vicker, B. (2004). Using a visual support to enhance WH question comprehension. *The Reporter 9*(3), 9–10.

Virginia Department of Education. (2004). *Mathematics: Strategies for teaching LEP students.* Retrieved from http://www.doe.virginia.gov/instruction/esl/resources/strategies_teach_math.pdf

Vygotsky, L. (1978). *Mind in society: The formation of higher psychological processes.* Cambridge, MA: Harvard University Press.

Wagner, M., Newman, L., Cameto, R., & Levine, P. (2006). The academic achievement and functional performance of youth with disabilities: A report from the National Longitudinal Transition Study–2. Menlo Park, CA: SRI International.

Waldron, N., Cole, C., & Majd, M. (2001). *The academic progress of students across inclusive and traditional settings: A two year study Indiana inclusion study.* Bloomington, IN: Indiana Institute on Disability & Community.

Watchtower Bible and Tract Society of Pennsylvania. (2002). *Jehovah's Witnesses and education.* Retrieved from https://wol.jw.org/en/wol/d/r1/lp-e/1200273078

Wechsler, D. (2009). *Wechsler Individual Achievement Test (3rd ed.).* London: Pearson.

Wechsler, D. (2014). *Wechsler intelligence scale for children, (5th ed.).* Bloomington, MN: Pearson. Winter, J. A. (2003). The development of the disability rights movement as a social problem solver. *Disability Studies Quarterly, 23*(1), 33–61.

Woodcock, R. N. (2011). *Woodcock Reading Mastery Tests (3rd ed.).* Circle Pines, MN: American Guidance Service.

Woodcock, R. W., McGrew, K. S., Mather, N., & Schrank, F. A. (2001). *Woodcock-Johnson III–Tests of Achievement.* Houghton Mifflin Harcourt, One Pierce Place Suite 900, Itasca, IL, 60143, USA, AssessmentsCS@hmhco.com, www.hmhco.com/HMHAssessment.

Woodcock, R. W., McGrew, K. S., Mather, N., & Schrank, F. A. (2003). *Woodcock-Johnson III–Tests of Cognitive Ability.* Houghton Mifflin Harcourt, One Pierce Place Suite 900, Itasca, IL, 60143, USA, AssessmentsCS@hmhco.com, www.hmhco.com/HMHAssessment

Wurzburg, G. (Producer), & Rubin, S. (Writer). (2005). *Autism is a world* [motion picture]. Washington, DC: State of the Art.

Zachary, A., & Wistrom, E. (2012). *Education techniques to help children with cerebral palsy in the classroom.* Retrieved from http://www.brighthubeducation.com/special-ed-inclusion-strategies/43536-inclusive-teaching-strategies-for-students-with-cerebral-palsy

Zurcher-Long, E. (n.d.). *Blogs & blog posts written by non-speaking autistics.* Retrieved from https://emmashopebook.com/resources

Index

Note: Page numbers followed by *f* indicate figures and by *t* indicate tables.